'Straightforward, honest, and uncompromising in describing the socio-[...] political options. There is not a policymaker on this planet who should [...] what they're talking about and their editors know who they're talking to [...] political choices facing food and agriculture policymakers that has been [...]
Pat Mooney, Executive Director of the ETC Group

'This is a timely and valuable book about the most important "industry" of all, dominated by giant multinationals and governments of rich countries, who make the global rules. This concise overview is both authoritative and accessible for non-specialists – highly recommended to all who are concerned about food, health, and survival.'
Felix R. FitzRoy, Professor of Economics, University of St Andrews and Research Fellow, IZA, Bonn

'This book is an excellent resource for those mapping the increasing control of our food chain by international players. The agreements that impact on the ability of nations to be food-sovereign and food-secure are described in lucid detail. This is useful information for scholars and policymakers.'
Suman Sahai, Director, Gene Campaign, India

'In this volume, globally recognized legal and policy experts provide a comprehensive and outstanding analysis of the inter-relationships between intellectual property rights and systems for maintaining food quality, biosafety and plant biodiversity. These are demanding technical issues but have fundamental importance for the future of global agriculture. The book should be read by all concerned with how institutional and policy reforms in these critical areas will affect the livelihoods of poor farmers and the nutrition of societies worldwide.'
Keith E. Maskus, Professor of Economics and Associate Dean for Social Sciences, College of Arts and Sciences, University of Colorado at Boulder

'In a field dominated by slogans, mistrust, rhetorical claims and counterclaims, this is a welcome factual account – you do not have to agree with all it contains but it helps the reader towards a better understanding of the issues. That understanding could help create a critical mass of people who want the fair, practical and deliverable changes that will be essential as we move to meet the challenges of more people, climate change, equity and ecosystem conservation. Ownership may not be the issue – but control and choice are.'
Andrew Bennett, Executive Director, Syngenta Foundation for Sustainable Agriculture

'This book is an excellent collection of guideposts for perplexed students and scholars and a handbook for the seasoned diplomat seeking to make the world a better place for future generations.'
Professor Calestous Juma, Kennedy School of Government, Harvard University

'Intellectual Property Rights (IPRs) appear mind-numbingly complex but are fundamentally important. This book outlines what the IPRs and food debates are, and why we should wake up and take notice. As the world enters a critical phase over whether, and how, to feed people healthily, equitably and sustainably, the need to understand IPRs is central. It unlocks the struggle over who controls our food futures.'
Tim Lang, Professor of Food Policy, City University, London

'Vital for everyone who eats, gardens, shops, or farms; indeed anyone who cares how communities, nations and the whole human species inhabit the earth. The authors map changes in control over food taking place through a web of international agreements about 'genetic resources', intellectual property rights, biological diversity, investment and trade. This is a powerful and accessible one-of-a-kind guide to the complex issues, agreements and law surrounding who controls the future of the world food supply and an indispensable tool in the fight for a democratic future.'
Harriet Friedmann, Professor of Sociology, Centre for International Studies, University of Toronto

'The influence of IPRs has increased and is increasing – but ought it to be diminished? Today IPRs increasingly deal with the necessities of life, in particular medicine and food. Read this book to learn how IPRs may affect world food supply and to understand the political battlefield.'
Tim Roberts, Chartered Patent Attorney, UK, and Rapporteur to the Intellectual Property Commission of ICC

'As it informs, it draws attention to the far-reaching implications of international norms that impact on a basic need. I recommend it to all who play a role in the formulation of relevant international norms in whatever capacity, and regardless of the interests they may represent.'
Leo Palma, Deputy Director, Advisory Centre on WTO Law; formerly a Philippines negotiator at WTO, 1996–2001

'A long overdue analysis and critique of the premises underlying the push for a new 'Green Revolution', this book brings together seemingly disparate elements to show how, in combination with new intellectual property rules, they will create new dependencies and increase the marginalization of farming and poor communities. This book presents a cogent rebuttal of the industrialized and privatized model of food production prevalent in international trade and intellectual property norm-setting. An awareness of these elements will greatly assist civil society to participate in international negotiations.'
Daniel Magraw, President and Chief Executive Officer of the Center for International Environmental Law

'*The Future Control of Food* makes an invaluable and much-needed contribution to understanding the international state of play regarding food access, food development and intellectual property laws. The book will be useful not only to intellectual property and trade negotiators, but also to bankers, farmers, food service providers, environmental activists and others seeking to understand how food production is currently regulated and will be regulated in the future.'
Joshua D. Sarnoff, Assistant Director, Glushko-Samuelson Intellectual Property Law Clinic,
Washington College of Law, American University, Washington, DC

'This is a timely book, providing useful insights on how international policies can, directly, indirectly and inadvertently, impact on food security. All stakeholders engaged in policymaking that affects the human food chain have a lot to gain by reading it.'
Emile Frison, Director General, Bioversity International

'This well-researched book condenses the essence of decades of negotiations concerning IPRs into a readable but disturbing narrative which juxtaposes detailed descriptions of the systems that privatize nature with examples of people's defence of agricultural biodiversity. For social movements and activists who want to defend food sovereignty, it is essential reading.'
Patrick Mulvany, Senior Policy Adviser, Practical Action/Intermediate Technology Development Group and Chair,
UK Food Group

'This book unpeels the onion: it shows layer on layer of interests and pressures that will define how we feed, or do not feed, a world of nine thousand million people in 2050. We are in a time of new enclosures and privatization of what were public goods, such as biodiversity and genetic resources, through access and benefit sharing legislation, and of the food chain from gene to plate, through IPRs. If you want to understand the fault lines in our food systems, READ THIS BOOK.'
Clive Stannard, former Officer in Charge, Secretariat of the Commission on Genetic Resources for Food and Agriculture
at the FAO

The Future Control of Food

A Guide to International Negotiations and Rules on Intellectual Property, Biodiversity and Food Security

Edited by Geoff Tansey and Tasmin Rajotte

London • Sterling, VA

QUAKER INTERNATIONAL AFFAIRS PROGRAMME

International Development Research Centre

Ottawa • Cairo • Dakar • Montevideo • Nairobi • New Delhi • Singapore

First published by Earthscan in the UK and USA in 2008

Copyright © The Quaker International Affairs Programme, 2008

ISBN: 978-1-84407-430-3 (hardback)
         978-1-84407-429-7 (paperback)

IDRC publishes an e-book edition of The Future Control of Food (ISBN 978-1-55250-397-3)

For further informtation, please contact:
International Development Research Centre
PO Box 8500
Ottawa, ON K1G 3H9
Canada
Email: info@idrc.ca
Web: www.idrc.ca

Typeset by MapSet Ltd, Gateshead, UK
Printed and bound in the UK by Antony Rowe, Chippenham
Cover design by Clifford Hayes

For a full list of publications please contact:

Earthscan
8–12 Camden High Street
London, NW1 0JH, UK
Tel: +44 (0)20 7387 8558
Fax: +44 (0)20 7387 8998
Email: earthinfo@earthscan.co.uk
Web: **www.earthscan.co.uk**

22883 Quicksilver Drive, Sterling, VA 20166-2012, USA

Earthscan publishes in association with the International Institute for Environment and Development

A catalogue record for this book is available from the British Library

Library of Congress Cataloging-in-Publication Data

The future control of food : a guide to international negotiations and rules on intellectual property, biodiversity, and food security / edited by Geoff Tansey and Tasmin Rajotte.
      p. cm.
Includes bibliographical references and index.
ISBN-13: 978-1-84407-430-3 (hardback)
ISBN-10: 1-84407-430-7 (hardback)
ISBN-13: 978-1-84407-429-7 (pbk.)
ISBN-10: 1-84407-429-3 (pbk.)
  1. Food law and legislation. 2. Plant varieties—Patents—Government policy. 3. Produce trade—Law and legislation. 4. Intellectual property (International law) 5. Food industry and trade—Standards. 6. Biodiversity conservation—Law and legislation. 7. Genetic resources conservation. I. Tansey, Geoff. II. Rajotte, Tasmin.
K3926.F88 2009
346.04'8—dc22

                                                                      2007034792

The paper used for this book is FSC-certified and
totally chlorine-free. FSC (the Forest Stewardship
Council) is an international network to promote
responsible management of the world's forests.

This book is dedicated to Sacha, Christine, Rachel
and all the children of this world.

May you inherit a world filled with hope, peace, food
and a diversity of life that sustains and nourishes
all of the Earth's peoples.

Contents

Part I – A Changing Food System

Part II – The Key Global Negotiations and Agreements

Part III – Responses, Observations and Prospects

List of Figures, Tables and Boxes

Figures

Tables

Boxes

Preface

Intellectual property (IP) rights are a source of hidden wealth worth trillions of dollars, and they impose hidden costs on the same scale. The rules of intellectual property range from confusing to nearly incomprehensible, and the professional practitioners who manage these rights sometimes seem to belong to a secret society. ... The IP system also determines when and how an innovation becomes available for others to use by defining boundaries around what is accessible and what is not. Intellectual property rights help determine which innovations are widely available and which are closed off, separating innovation haves from have-nots. ... Ever-stronger intellectual property protection is surely not a panacea to promote technology progress and wellbeing in all countries and industries ... intellectual property creates winners and losers and on balance it helps in some situations, hurts in others ... intellectual property shapes society – whether for better or for worse.

MICHAEL A. GOLLIN FROM *Driving Innovation: Intellectual Property Strategies for a Dynamic World* (Cambridge University Press, 2008)

In today's world, access to food is highly, and unacceptably, uneven. There is massive overproduction and over-consumption, and yet millions experience scarcity and hunger. This book looks at some of the forces and rules shaping the food system and who has control over it. In particular, it focuses on rules on intellectual property – for example patents, plant breeders' rights, trademarks and copyright – and their relations to other rules on biodiversity, an essential requirement for food security. It looks through the lens of intellectual property (IP) at the future control of food and farming, because rules on IP are central to struggles over the distribution of wealth and power in the 21st century.

When, from the 16th century onwards, the colonial powers reorganized the world to suit their economic interests, drew up state boundaries and secured resources for their use, they set the stage for trade patterns and future conflicts that still ring around the planet. Today, the colonies are mostly gone and there are around 200 nation states, yet through a series of quite unbalanced negotiations among these states, the most powerful countries are still able to shape the rules of the world in their interests. Nowadays, their concerns include intangibles like IP and the use of genetic resources. The new international rules on these, agreed since the early 1990s, will do much to shape the future control of food. Yet these often complex and remote negotiations are little known or influenced by the billions of people who will be affected by them. This book is a guide to both the negotiations and these new global rules. At stake are the livelihoods of 2.5 billion people still directly dependent on agriculture and the long-term food security of us all. The IP regime, a new factor in many countries, along with a changing trade regime and new agreements on biodiversity, will help shape the kind of agricultural development in the future. It may include most of these 2.5 billion people, or it may exclude them. Either way their livelihoods will be affected. Moreover, all of us will be affected by the way these rules are written, since they will also help shape the food system, the kind of products it produces and the structures through which it delivers them. It is important to know about the mix of rules because changes in one affect others, and concerns over IP overshadow many. Some of the questions that arise are:

- Will the rules facilitate and support the worthy but as yet unfulfilled goals of ending hunger and increasing food security espoused at food summits since the 1970s?
- Will they increase the capacity of those who need either more food or better food for a healthy life to produce or procure it?
- Will they promote fairer and more equitable practices among those engaged in ensuring that production reaches all who need it?
- Will they – the IP regime in particular – create incentives for more ecologically sound and culturally and socially appropriate farming, fishing and herding practices among producers of foodstuffs?

Guide to the Book

The decision to produce this book was, in part, a response to concerns negotiators in various multilateral negotiations raised about the need for such a guide as well as the observation that negotiators or groups working in one area were often unaware of, and sometime undermining, what was happening elsewhere, which we encountered in the Quaker programme of work in this area.[1] In part, it is also a response to food security being the more neglected area by many governments and civil society groups compared with the new IP regime's impact on access to medicines and even access to knowledge. As a recent study noted: 'Unfortunately, for agriculture, genetic resources and traditional knowledge the benefit [for NGO involvement] does not seem to be visible and immediate, so … the pressure for policy outcomes is not as great as for public health and access to medicines' (Matthews, 2006).

This guide seeks to inform a wider audience than negotiators so that civil society, researchers and academics, as well as those leading peasant and farmers' groups, small businesses and government officials, can take a more informed and active part in the complex process of negotiations that lead to international agreements. In that way, a broader range of interests will be in a better position to judge if the rules need amending and be better informed to work locally, nationally and internationally to secure global rules that promote a just and sustainable food system.

Part I begins with a brief overview of the contemporary food system, the basics of IP and its role in the food system. The central core of the book is Part II, which provides the background and a guide to negotiations and the key elements of the agreements. The different chapters aim to:

- help readers see how IP has spread into food and agriculture through various agreements;
- provide a short guide to the background and history behind each of the agreements;
- highlight key issues in each of these agreements and emerging trends;
- note connections to other negotiations – multilateral, regional and bilateral – and national laws; and
- discuss the various interconnections and complex webs between the different rules and negotiations.

Part III includes discussion on some of the various civil society reactions to these changing global rules and their impact on research and development in Chapter 8. Chapter 9 reflects on these international negotiations and makes a number of observations that may help those seeking to learn lessons from what has gone on. The final chapter briefly draws together some conclusions about the negotiating processes, alternative futures and the nature of innovation needed to face them. Finally, at the end of the book, we provide a table of further resources and institutions to contact for more information.

Notes on Contributors

Heike Baumüller was Programme Manager, Environment and Natural Resources, at the International Centre for Trade and Sustainable Development (ICTSD) up to the end of 2006. Among other areas, she coordinated ICTSD's project activities on biotechnology, fisheries, trade and environment, and biodiversity-related intellectual property rights from 2000, was the Managing Editor of the ICTSD publication *BRIDGES Trade BioRes*, and has published on a range of issues related to trade and sustainable development. She holds a master's degree in Environmental Studies from Macquarie University, Sydney, and is now working freelance as a consultant in Cambodia.

Susan H. Bragdon is qualified in biology, resource ecology and law. She works on the conservation, use and management of biological diversity; creating compatibility between environment and agriculture; and promoting food security. She was the lawyer for the Secretariat for the Intergovernmental Negotiating Committee for the Convention on Biological Diversity (CBD), providing legal advice to the working group handling intellectual property rights, transfer of technology, including biotechnology, and access to genetic resources. She subsequently joined the treaty Secretariat as its Legal Advisor. From 1997 to 2004 she was a senior scientist dealing with law and policy at Bioversity International (formerly the International Plant Genetic Resources Institute (IPGRI)). She currently works as a consultant for intergovernmental organizations, governments and foundations.

Peter Drahos is a Professor in Law; he is Head of Programme of the Regulatory Institutions Network at the Australian National University (ANU), Director of the Centre for the Governance of Knowledge and Development at the ANU and a Director in the Foundation for Effective Markets and Governance. He also holds a Chair in Intellectual Property at Queen Mary College, University of London. He has degrees in law, politics and philosophy and is qualified as a barrister and solicitor. He has published widely in law and the social sciences on a variety of topics including contracts, legal philosophy, telecommunications, intellectual property, trade negotiations and international business regulation.

Graham Dutfield is Professor of International Governance at the Centre for International Governance, School of Law, University of Leeds. Previously he was Herchel Smith Senior Research Fellow at Queen Mary, University of London, and Academic Director of the UNCTAD-ICTSD capacity-building project on intellectual property rights and sustainable development. He has served as consultant or commissioned report author for several governments, international organizations, United Nations agencies and non-governmental organizations, including the governments of Germany, Brazil, Singapore and the UK, the European Commission, the World Health Organization, the World Intellectual Property Organization, and the Rockefeller Foundation.

Kathryn Garforth is a law and policy researcher and consultant working in the areas of biodiversity, biotechnology, intellectual property rights and health. She has attended numerous meetings of the CBD in a number of different capacities including as an NGO representative, on the Canadian delegation and as part of the CBD Secretariat. She has consulted widely for international organizations, national institutions and donors. She earned a joint law degree and master's in Environmental Studies from Osgoode Hall Law School, York University.

John E. Haapala Jr is an intellectual property attorney based in Eugene, Oregon. He is the former Director of the Farmer Cooperative Genome Project and the former Research Director for Oregon Tilth. He is also the owner/operator of Heron's Nest Farm and has been breeding and producing vegetable and flower seeds for the US organic seed market since 1988.

Michael Halewood is Head of the Policy Research and Support Unit of Bioversity International. He manages policy research projects with a broad range of partners, mostly from developing countries; he also coordinates representation of the International Agricultural Research Centres of the CGIAR at international genetic resources policy making negotiations. He was previously coordinator of the Crucible II Group, a global think-tank analysing genetic resources policy options.

Kent Nnadozie is a lawyer engaged in environmental and sustainable development law and policy issues. He is Director of the Southern Environmental and Agricultural Policy Research Institute (SEAPRI), an initiative of the International Centre for Insect Physiology and Ecology (ICIPE), Nairobi, Kenya. He has been a member of the Nigerian delegation to the CBD and a member of the IUCN Commission on Environmental Law and Co-chair of its Specialist Group on the Implementation of the CBD. He is a specialist legal adviser at the Secretariat of the International Treaty on Plant Genetic Resources for Food and Agriculture. He has also consulted widely for national institutions, international organizations and bodies as well as donors, including Bioversity International (formerly IPGRI), the FAO Commission on Genetic Resources for Food and Agriculture, and the Secretariat of the CBD.

Maria Julia Oliva is a legal consultant on intellectual property-related and other issues for the UNCTAD BioTrade Initiative. She is also one of the lead researchers in the Trade and Environment Research Group at the University of Geneva Faculty of Law. She sits on the board of directors of IP-Watch and is a member of the IUCN Commission on Environmental Law. Previously, she served for several years as Director of the Intellectual Property and Sustainable Development Project at the Center for International Environmental Law (CIEL). She earned an LLM degree in environmental law from the Northwestern School of Law at Lewis and Clark College, USA, and a law degree at the University of Mendoza in Argentina.

Tasmin Rajotte is the Quaker Representative for the Quaker International Affairs Programme (QIAP) in Ottawa, Canada. She has been the primary developer and executor of the work on intellectual property rights since QIAP's inception in 2001. She has a master's degree in environmental studies and has worked in the field of sustainable agriculture, food security and environment for a number of years.

Pedro Roffe is Intellectual Property Fellow at the International Centre for Trade and Sustainable Development (ICTSD). A former staff member of UNCTAD, Geneva, he has also been a consultant to Corporacion Andina de Fomento (CAF), Economic Commission for Latin America and the Caribbean. His work has focused on intellectual property, foreign investment, transfer of technology-related issues and international economic negotiations. He has contributed to several UN reports on these issues and to specialized journals.

Geoff Tansey is a writer and consultant. He helped found and edit the journal *Food Policy*, has worked on agricultural development projects in Turkey, Albania and Mongolia and co-authored the prize-winning book *The Food System: A Guide*. He has consulted for various international organizations and was senior consultant for the intellectual property and development programmes of the Quaker United Nations Office, Geneva, and Quaker International Affairs Programme, Ottawa, from their inception until 2007. He was also a consultant for DFID for the first phase of the UNCTAD-ICTSD TRIPS and Development Capacity Building Project from 2001 to 2003. In June 2005, he received one of six Joseph Rowntree 'Visionaries for a Just and Peaceful World' Awards, which provide support for five years. He is also a member and a director of the Food Ethics Council.

Acknowledgements

We are immensely grateful to a large number of people who have contributed in various ways to publication of this book. It has been a long process in which we have sought feedback throughout the development of the book. This process involved: many one-on-one consultations and discussions with people involved with food, agriculture, biodiversity and intellectual property issues from a variety of backgrounds, including staff in a range of international organizations; dialogues at different stages of the book; and a very broad peer review process. The first dialogue was hosted by the Centre for Rural Economy at the University of Newcastle, UK. The second dialogue was hosted by the Quaker International Affairs Programme (QIAP) in Ottawa. The final dialogue was held in Geneva and was hosted by the Quaker United Nations Office. We are also grateful to the participants in, and farmers we met through, the international gathering 'From Seeds of Survival to Seeds of Resilience' in Ethiopia in November 2006.

We received rich feedback from a wide range of reviewers and had very concrete, insightful and stimulating discussions in the dialogues. At the risk of missing some people out we would specifically like to thank all of those who took part in the dialogues and reviewed some or all the chapters, including: Frederick Abbott, John Barton, Terry Boehm, Sara Boettiger, Eric Chaurette, Carlos Correa, Susan Crean, Soma Dey, Carol Dixon, Caroline Dommen, Andrew Donaldson, Tewolde Berhan Gebre Egziabher, Peter Einarsson, Harriet Friedmann, Felix FitzRoy, Michael Gollin, Jonathan Harwood, Corinna Hawkes, John Herity, Lionel Hubbard, Brewster Kneen, Ted Lawrence, Richard Lee, Carlo Leifert, Lucie Lemieux, Sarah Lieberman, Niels Louwaars, Philip Lowe, Andrew MacMillan, Tom MacMillan, Ron Marchant, Duncan Matthews, Christopher May, Tracey McCowen, Eric Millstone, Gerald Moore, Patrick Mulvany, Davinia Ovett, Barbara Panvel, Ditdit Pelegrina, Jeremy Phillipson, Veena Ravichandran, Dwijen Rangnekar, Chris Ray, Jack Reardon, Tim Roberts, Wayne Roberts, Chris Rodgers, Eric Ruto, Josh Sarnoff, Nicola Searle, Dalindyabo Shabalala, Devinder Sharma, Lucy Sharratt, Carin Smaller, Jim Sumberg, Steve Suppan, Awegechew Teshome, Carl-Gustaf Thornström, Gary Toenniessen, Ruchi Tripathi, Rob Tripp, David Vivas-Eugui, Joachim Von Braun, Kathryn Wilkinson, Hironori Yagi, Neil Ward, the Secretariat staff of several intergovernmental organizations, and Geneva-based WTO and WIPO negotiators.

We are, of course, also deeply indebted to the contributors for sharing their knowledge and insights (and who have stuck with us through the lengthy process). We also thank Sanda Wiens, the QIAP assistant, who assisted in: coordinating the logistics for the dialogues; developing the database for the peer review process; developing the list of organization resources and references; and editing and formatting the draft manuscript. We also pay tribute to the staff at Earthscan for their support and help throughout, in particular Rob West, Alison Kuznets, Hamish Ironside and Gudrun Freese.

This book would not have happened without the support of the Canadian Quakers through the Quaker International Affairs Programme and funding from the International Development Research Centre in Canada as well as support from their officers, in particular Jean Woo, Brian Davy, Bill Carman and Rob Robertson. We would like to thank the Joseph Rowntree Charitable Trust, which, through their Visionaries programme, provided support for some of the time of one of the editors, and the Dutch Ministry of Foreign Affairs, which, through the Quaker United Nations Office (QUNO), provided additional support for QIAP. We are particularly grateful for help from Martin Watson and David Zafar Ahmed at QUNO.

Finally, but not least, we were nourished throughout the process by the support, faith and unwavering love of our Quaker committees, colleagues and families, in particular Norman de Bellefeuille and Kathleen Tansey, as we endured tight timelines, time zones, late nights and the joy of a newly born baby during the making of this book. To everyone, a heartfelt thank you.

Acronyms and Abbreviations

A2K	access to knowledge
AATF	African Agricultural Technologies Foundation
ABIA	American Bioindustry Alliance
ABS	access and benefit sharing
ACP	African, Caribbean and Pacific
AIA	Advance Informed Agreement
AIPPI	Association Internationale pour la Protection de la Propriété Industrielle (International Association for the Protection of Intellectual Property)
AnGR	Animal Genetic Resources
ASSINSEL	Association Internationale des Selectionneurs pour la Protection des Obtentions Végétales (International Association of Plant Breeders)
ASTA	American Seed Trade Association
AU	African Union
BCH	Biosafety Clearing House
BiOS	Biological Open Source
BIRPI	Bureaux Internationaux Réunis de la Protection de la Propriété Intellectuelle (United International Bureaux for the Protection of Intellectual Property)
BSE	Bovine Spongiform Encephalopathy (mad cow disease)
CATIE	Centro Agronómico Tropical de Investigación y Enseñanza (Tropical Agricultural Research and Higher Education Centre)
CBD	Convention on Biological Diversity
CDP	Cooperation for Development Programme
CESCR	Committee on Economic, Social and Cultural Rights
CGIAR	Consultative Group on International Agricultural Research
CGRFA	Commission on Genetic Resources for Food and Agriculture
CHM	clearinghouse mechanism
CIAT	International Center for Tropical Agriculture
CIMMYT	International Wheat and Maize Research Institute
CIPIH	Commission on Intellectual Property Rights, Innovation and Public Health
CIOPORA	International Community of Breeders of Asexually Reproduced Ornamental and Fruit Varieties
CITES	Convention on International Trade in Endangered Species of Fauna and Flora
COP	Conference of the Parties
CRC	Convention on the Rights of the Child
CSO	civil society organization
DFID	UK Department for International Development
DSM	dispute settlement mechanism
EARO	Ethiopian Agricultural Research Organization
EC	European Community
ECOSOC	United Nations Economic and Social Council
EDV	essentially derived variety

EEC	European Economic Community
EFTA	European Free Trade Association
EoF	expressions of folklore
EPAs	economic partnership agreements
EPO	European Patent Office
EU	European Union
FAO	UN Food and Agriculture Organization
FiRST	Financial Resource Support for Teff
FIS	Fédération Internationale du Commerce des Semences (International Seed Trade Federation)
FTAs	free trade agreements
FTO	freedom to operate
GATT	General Agreement on Tariffs and Trade
GEF	Global Environment Facility
GMO	genetically modified organism
GFAR	Global Forum on Agricultural Research
GURTs	genetic use restriction technologies
HPFI	Health and Performance Food International
IBC	Institute of Biodiversity Conservation
IBPGR	International Board for Plant Genetic Resources
ICBGS	International Cooperative Biodiversity Group
ICC	International Chamber of Commerce
ICESCR	International Covenant on Economic, Social and Cultural Rights
ICTSD	International Centre for Trade and Sustainable Development
IFPRI	International Food Policy Research Institute
IGCGRTKF or IGC	Intergovernmental Committee on Genetic Resources, Traditional Knowledge and Folklore (more commonly IGC)
IIFB	International Indigenous Forum on Biodiversity
IMP	intellectual monopoly privilege
INBio	National Biodiversity Institute, Costa Rica
INGER	International Network for Genetic Evaluation of Rice
IP	intellectual property
IPRs	intellectual property rights
ISF	International Seed Federation
ITPGRFA	International Treaty on Plant Genetic Resources for Food and Agriculture (also referred to as the Treaty)
IUPGRFA or IU	International Undertaking on Plant Genetic Resources for Food and Agriculture (also referred to as the Undertaking)
KFC	Kentucky Fried Chicken
LDC	least developed country
LMMCs	Like-Minded Megadiverse Countries
LMOs	living modified organisms
LMOs-FFP	living modified organisms for food, feed and processing
MATs	mutually agreed terms
MDGs	Millennium Development Goals
MEA	multilateral environmental agreement

MFN	most favoured nation
MLS	multilateral system of access and benefit sharing
MOP	Meeting of the Parties
MSF	Médecins Sans Frontières
MTA	material transfer agreement
NGO	non-governmental organization
OECD	Organisation for Economic Co-operation and Development
PBRs	plant breeders' rights
PCDA	Provisional Committee on Propsals related to a WIPO Development Agenda
PCT	Patent Cooperation Treaty
PGRFA	plant genetic resources for food and agriculture
PIC	prior informed consent
PIIPA	Public Interest Intellectual Property Advisors, Inc.
PIPRA	Public Intellectual Property Resource for Agriculture
PVP	plant variety protection
QIAP	Quaker International Affairs Programme
QUNO	Quaker United Nations Office
R&D	research and development
RR	Roundup-Ready
SBSTTA	Subsidiary Body on Scientific, Technical and Technological Advice
SCP	Standing Committee on the Law of Patents
SMTA	Standard Material Transfer Agreement
SPLT	Substantive Patent Law Treaty
TCEs	Traditional cultural expressions
TK	traditional knowledge
TRIPS	Agreement on Trade-Related Aspects of Intellectual Property Rights
UDHR	Universal Declaration of Human Rights
UK	United Kingdom
UN	United Nations
UNCTAD	United Nations Conference on Trade and Development
UNDP	United Nations Development Programme
UNEP	United Nations Environment Programme
UNESCO	United Nations Educational, Scientific and Cultural Organization
UNPFII	United Nations Permanent Forum on Indigenous Peoples Issues
UPOV	International Union for the Protection of New Varieties of Plants [Union Internationale pour la Protection des Obtentions Végétale]
US	United States of America
USDA	United States Department of Agriculture
USPTO	United States Patents and Trademarks Office
WHO	World Health Organization
WIPO	World Intellectual Property Organization
WTO	World Trade Organization

Part I

A Changing Food System

Food connects us all. Yet the oft-repeated pledges to create a well-fed world in which hunger is abolished are still words, not reality. What has changed since the 1990s is the creation of new global rules made in different negotiating fora by groups and ministries dealing with different interests. These are reshaping the framework in which people working in the food system operate. It is a system in which different actors vie for power and control over the area that they work in, seeking to minimize or offload the risks they face and maximize or optimize the benefits they get.

Part I of this book provides a brief guide to the contemporary food system, the range of actors and interests in it, the tools they seek to use for control, and the increasingly important role of laws, rules and regulations, not just nationally but globally. Next, it outlines the basics of 'intellectual property' and then briefly examines the growing importance of rules on patents and other forms of intellectual property in shaping future food systems and certain issues surrounding these.

1

Farming, Food and Global Rules

Geoff Tansey

This chapter first gives a brief overview of today's dominant food system in which four key words – power, control, risks and benefits – are seen as vital for the major actors in the system. It discusses the dynamics of the system and then provides a brief background to the legal fiction that is intellectual property – patents, copyright, plant variety protection, trademarks, and so forth – and associated concerns as global rules on it continue to grow. Finally, the chapter looks at the growing role of intellectual property in food and farming and the concerns surrounding this.

Introduction

Serious doubts have been raised about the long-term viability of the industrial farming model that is spreading from the industrialized world to other countries. Yet the long-term viability of farming is central to ensuring food security for everyone on this planet (Box 1.1). Many now call for more ecologically sustainable approaches to farming built around biodiversity and ecology. Yet others, sure of humankind's inventive capacity or responding to their industry's interests, promote further intensification and industrial approaches to farming as the way forward. Thus the future direction of farming is highly contested (Lang and Heasman, 2004).

What is clear is that there are serious flaws in a food system that globally leaves more than 850 million people undernourished and over 1 billion overweight (300 million of them obese). Some 2 billion people also suffer from vitamin and micronutrient shortages. Undernutrition in pregnant women and young babies can have irreversible effects for life, while obese people's lives are threatened by diet-related non-communicable diseases such as diabetes and heart attacks.

For decades, governments have made fine commitments to end hunger and deal with malnutrition, notably at the World Food Summit held at the UN Food and Agriculture Organization's Headquarters in Rome in 1996 (Box 1.2). They have also recognized, at least since the first global conference on the environment in Stockholm in 1972, that the environmental impact and consequences of human activity on the planet are fundamental to our survival. Yet it took almost 20 years before the central role of biodiversity as the basis for healthy ecosystems was addressed internationally (see Chapter 5).

Agricultural biodiversity, which has been developed through the creative activity of farmers over thousands of years (Chapter 6),

Box 1.1 Levels and elements of food security

Globally, food security depends on a range of things, including:

- our ability to minimize/manage/react to climatic change and disruptions to food production by holding suitable stock levels and having emergency distribution arrangements in place; and
- ensuring new technologies enhance this capacity and do not increase the risk of major disruptions in food supply through unforeseen consequences on ecological viability.

Regionally and nationally it includes:

- maintaining the capacity to produce and/or import the food requirements of a population and ensuring a distribution system or entitlements that enable all people within the borders to produce or acquire the food they need (by production, purchase or special schemes);
- maintaining an R&D (research and development) system that includes farmers and is able to deliver continued improvements to all aspects of production systems used by the full range of farmers in the country and cope with variability (agro-ecological and economic) and climatic changes; and
- ensuring both rural and urban dwellers are able to secure their livelihoods and so have access to the food they need, either from direct production, purchase or barter.

At the community and household levels it requires:

- continued ability to maintain livelihoods that allow production/procurement of food needs in an appropriate manner;
- use of risk management strategies suitable to local needs and customs to prevent impoverishment;
- prevention of conflicts and of the use of food as a weapon;
- support for those in marginal areas/environments to increase productivity, or if they are forced out for there to be alternative livelihood possibilities available; and
- equitable gender and inter- and intra-household distribution.

Source: Adapted from Tansey (2002)

and is a necessity for food security, was discussed in the 1980s and 1990s. Concerns over genetic erosion and the continuing loss of the many varieties of plants important for human survival led to a major conference of the UN Food and Agriculture Organization (FAO) in 1996 and a Global Plan of Action to combat the loss of plant genetic diversity. Unfortunately, similar losses of animal genetic diversity are only now beginning to be addressed (Box 6.6) and action on both is far from adequate.

Another recent change has been the rapid extension of a legal system (patents) developed to encourage innovation in inanimate objects into the area of living organisms. This was led by the US in the 1980s. It is linked to the commercial application of insights from a major revolution in our understanding of biology that allows new techniques such as genetic engineering and its application in medicine and agriculture in particular. For some, the whole idea of extending patents into the living world is intrinsically wrong. For others, problems only arise should there be adverse consequences. The push to extend patents has not only come from commercial interests in biology but also from developments in information science and the ability to digitally encode and manipulate all kinds of information.

Box 1.2 Fine words, poor implementation

Everyone has a right to a standard of living adequate for the health and wellbeing of himself and his family, including food. (Universal Declaration of Human Rights, 1948)

States Parties … recognize the fundamental right of everyone to be free from hunger. (International Covenant on Economic, Social and Cultural Rights, 1966)

Every man, woman and child has the inalienable right to be free from hunger and malnutrition in order to develop fully and maintain their physical and mental faculties. Society today already possesses sufficient resources, organizational ability and technology and hence the competence to achieve this objective. Accordingly, the eradication of hunger is a common objective of all the countries of the international community, especially of the developed countries and others in a position to help. (World Food Conference, 1974)

We pledge to act in solidarity to ensure that freedom from hunger becomes a reality. (International Conference on Nutrition, 1992)

We, the Heads of State and Government, or our representatives, gathered at the World Food Summit at the invitation of the Food and Agriculture Organization of the United Nations, reaffirm the right of everyone to have access to safe and nutritious food, consistent with the right to adequate food and the fundamental right of everyone to be free from hunger.

We pledge our political will and our common and national commitment to achieving food security for all and to an ongoing effort to eradicate hunger in all countries, with an immediate view to reducing the number of undernourished people to half their present level no later than 2015.

Food should not be used as an instrument for political and economic pressure. We reaffirm the importance of international cooperation and solidarity as well as the necessity of refraining from unilateral measures not in accordance with the international law and the Charter of the United Nations and that endanger food security. (World Food Summit, 1996)

In 1970, there were about 960 million hungry people. Today there are just over 100 million less[*]. There are, of course, many more people in the world today than at the time of the first World Food Summit in 1974 – called after a major famine in Ethiopia in the early 1970s, indicating that there has been progress in feeding people since then. However, this progress has not gone far enough. Food production in general – although not in sub-Saharan Africa – has kept pace with or exceeded population growth. Moreover, obesity was not a major global concern then, although it worried some, especially in the US.

The world is in danger of failing to meet the relatively modest aim agreed in the 1996 World Food Summit of halving the *number* of hungry people by 2015. Even this aim was watered down further in the Millennium Development Goals, where it became the more modest goal of halving the *proportion* of hungry people, which may also be missed.

Note: [*] In 1969–1971 there were just over 960 million people undernourished in developing countries. This had fallen to 820 million in 2001–2003, with a further 24.7 million in countries in transition and 9.3 million in industrialized countries making a total of 854 million.
Source: FAO, see www.fao.org/faostat/foodsecurity/index_en.htm for details

In a world with global markets, enterprises and problems, national responses and rules are no longer sufficient to tackle sensitive food, environmental and economic issues. New global negotiating processes have led to a range of new treaties on trade, biodiversity, and plant genetic resources for food and agriculture which were influenced by the concerns of some countries about patents and other forms of intellectual property (IP).

New institutions, new challenges

In the 21st century, new institutions producing global rules are reshaping the framework in which people concerned with food operate – from smallholders and farm families to global corporations. However, because of the political weight which they command in developed countries, the latter have a disproportionate impact in shaping the increasingly changing global rules within which different actors in the food system have to operate.

Some key questions arise from these changes: What will the long-term impact of these global rules be? Whose interests will they serve? Will they help make the food system more functional, in reducing all forms of malnutrition, from under- to over-nutrition, in an ecologically sustainable manner? But to address these we need an understanding of just what the rules are, how they arose and what may be done with them in the future. This book provides a guide to some of the global rules that:

- govern trade, in particular those that link trade rules to those on patents, copyright, trademarks and other forms of IP. These privilege some to the detriment or exclusion of others, in theory for the social and economic benefit of all (Chapters 2, 3 and 4);
- aim to conserve and promote the use of the enormous biodiversity on the planet

and ensure the sharing of the benefits from using this (Chapter 5); and
- make special provision for agricultural biodiversity in the field of plants (but not yet that of animals), dealing with its unique characteristics as a way of safeguarding future food security globally (Chapter 6).

Different interests have been driving the various negotiations on these rules, which have also led to the creation of new global institutions. Perhaps the most important of these is the creation, in 1995, of the World Trade Organization (WTO), which came out of the Uruguay Round of trade talks begun in 1986 under the General Agreement on Tariffs and Trade (GATT). The key difference between the WTO and existing UN organizations – specialized agencies like the World Health Organization (WHO) and the FAO or that dealing with the Convention on Biological Diversity (CBD), which administratively is part of the UN Environment Programme (UNEP) – is that the WTO has a binding dispute settlement mechanism backed by sanctions. This means that countries that fail to follow its rules face real consequences, which is not the case for most other international bodies, except the UN Security Council.

When the WTO was set up, it brought agriculture fully under the trade regime for the first time, as well as introducing rules on plant and animal health (sanitary and phytosanitary standards) and IP. IP rules were introduced into the WTO against the wishes of developing countries, however, and with relatively little involvement of most stakeholders in developed countries. Instead, they were promoted and initially drafted by a small group of transnational actors from four major industries – film, music, software, and pharmaceuticals and biotechnology (Drahos, 1995; Drahos and Braithwaite, 2002; Matthews, 2002; Sell, 2003). This group saw that in global markets they needed global rules on IP if their business model was to survive and they were to capture the benefits arising from exploitation of new technological opportunities. Importantly, the inclusion of IP rules in the WTO meant that IP was introduced into agriculture for the first time for many countries, since the WTO rules require the patenting of micro-organisms and some form of plant variety protection through the Agreement on Trade-Related Aspects of Intellectual Property Rights (TRIPS).

One problem here is that these global-level negotiations take place in different international bodies, are carried out by differing government departments – such as environment, agriculture, commerce, patent offices and trade – and are hard for many stakeholders to understand or influence. It is difficult for low-income and smaller countries to participate in them effectively, because of both the need for special expertise and the high costs. This complexity often makes it difficult to get coherent policies across the different areas (Petit et al, 2001). So, although more and more institutions/treaties/agreements/regimes are required as agricultural, environmental and trade systems become ever more global, problems arise when rules and regimes overlap (requiring legal interpretation and negotiation). Furthermore, when regime remits are similar, but their provisions benefit some more than others, then states 'shop around' for the most beneficial possible outcomes of membership in different regimes.

Before discussing IP further, we need first to look at the changing food system.

Food Policy and a Changing Food System

Enormous challenges face us in ensuring a sustainable, secure, safe, sufficient and nutritious (in other words healthy), equitable and culturally appropriate diet for all, which should be the aim of food policy and a functional food system (Tansey and Worsley, 1995). Yet few governments have consciously tried to link the different elements of national policy to food and produce coherent food policies. One reason is complexity. Food policy is about what influences the set of relationships and activities that interact to determine what, how much, by what method and for whom food is produced and distributed, and by whom it is consumed. It deals with the food economy, which is a subset of the wider economy (OECD, 1981).

Humans are very adaptable and can have a wide variety of diets, as the variety of peasant cuisines, developed from what was locally available, shows. Furthermore, these diets have changed, absorbing new plants and animals and yielding new products as humans have spread across the planet, as empires have waxed and waned, as the rich have sought new delicacies, and as the poor have sought to have what the rich had. Wherever we are today, the food we eat could have been different, and probably was in the past. What we eat has a history, and that history is not simply a history of food but a history of culture and society.

Food is a basic necessity for life. We eat foods, not nutrients, and different foods fulfil a wide variety of roles in our lives, not simply in terms of sustenance but physiological, social and cultural. We use food for reward, for pleasure, to express status, culture and religious preference, and so on. In spite of the overall adequacy of food availability in the world, however, there continue to be huge differences in the amount and quality of food that people eat, as discussed above.

Food comes from our environment – people have to grow or gather it, or fish or hunt it. Continued food supplies depend upon maintaining a healthy environment and upon having a diverse range of plants and animals available to us to make it possible to keep breeding varieties that can cope with the diseases, changes in climate and other stresses that farmers, fishers and herders face. That is why agricultural biodiversity is crucial. And it means that ecological wellbeing is a core requirement for our future food supplies, and that new technological development needs to take it into account (ETC Group, 2004).

Actors and interests

There are many different groups of actors involved in bringing the food we eat to our mouths (Tansey and Worsley, 1995), unless we live a mainly self-provisioning life. Most of the actors found in industrialized countries – farm input suppliers, farmers, food processors and manufacturers, distributors, workers and caterers – may all be in the same household in largely smallholder farming communities. Even then, there is probably a need to have other input suppliers for fuel or fertilizer, traders to sell surplus to, and retailers or wholesalers to buy from. For most town and city dwellers and people in the wealthier countries, or wealthier people in poorer countries, what they can get to eat depends largely on others. The various actors in the food system are engaged in a struggle over who will have *power* and *control* over the production and supplies of food, and how the *benefits* and *risks* arising from different activities will be distributed. Increasingly, the money made out of food does not go to farmers but to those who supply them and who are intermediaries between them and our mouths.

Fortunately, we do not need that much food to live healthily. A healthy diet can be obtained from a relatively simple mix of a staple source of carbohydrate supplemented with some sources of protein and fruits and vegetables – which the great cuisines of the world tend to be based on – although some communities, for example the Inuit, have even more specialized diets linked to special environments. Our limited need for food, however, poses a

problem for businesses working in food in a market economy. To prosper they need to expand their business, especially if they are publicly quoted companies. This limited demand puts greater pressures on food-related businesses than many others. Think, for example, of a pair of shoes, a radio, a CD, a TV or a car. You can increase your consumption of these many times – you can have 10 pairs of shoes, 50 CDs, three radios, two TVs and two cars – without any physical harm coming to you. But you cannot increase your basic food intake two-, three- or fourfold without serious harm – as indeed we are seeing in the obesity epidemic spreading around the world.

The pressure on businesses increases the competition between them, the desire to find new technologies to give them an edge over others, to look for ways to increase the productivity of the money, land or people used in the business, and to diversify from what they started doing into other activities, products – especially high value products – or markets.

Trends and tools

Three key trends have affected how the food system – indeed the economic system more generally – develops. First, a growing economic concentration of power in any of the sectors – from farm input suppliers such as agrochemical, energy or equipment companies to traders, retailers and caterers – means that fewer and fewer firms control more and more of the market. Box 1.3 illustrates this for the agriculture input industry, an area where changing IP rules is important in fuelling the trend. The increasingly concentrated market power enables the ability of these bigger players to affect prices, reduce competition and set standards within a sector (Murphy, 2006; Vorley, 2003). A recent development has been that:

Box 1.3 Tracking the trend towards market concentration: The case of the agricultural input industry*

There is clear evidence suggesting a trend towards greater concentration at several stages in various commodity sectors. Focusing on the agricultural input segment, there has been a process of consolidation in the global agribusiness in recent years (by means of divestitures, mergers and acquisitions), the outcome of which is a few major integrated companies, each controlling proprietary lines of agricultural chemicals, seeds and biotech traits. A significant increase in the concentration of the agrochemical industry has been observed, with three leading companies accounting for roughly half of the total market. An upsurge in seed industry takeovers and changes in rankings (with the acquisition of Seminis in 2005, Monsanto surpassed DuPont in the global seed market) occurred between 2004 and 2005. Some of the largest agrochemical companies have branched out forcefully into plant biotechnology and the seed business, heralding a move towards unprecedented convergence between the key segments of the agriculture market (agrochemicals, seeds and agricultural biotechnology).

Besides mergers and acquisitions, another aspect of structural change of interest in this area is increased 'coordination', which typically refers to contractual arrangements, alliances and tacit collusive practices. At the horizontal level, evidence suggests a trend towards heightened strategic cooperation among the largest competitors in the agricultural biotechnology sector. It is also interesting to note vertical coordination upward and downward along the food chain, with the establishment of food chain clusters that combine agricultural inputs (agrochemicals, seeds and traits) with extensive handling, processing and marketing facilities.

On the one hand, the need to consolidate patent portfolios and thus ensure freedom to operate appears to have created incentives for the extensive mergers and acquisitions that have occurred between agricultural biotechnology and seed businesses, and for other cooperative responses short of full integration (such as cross-licensing). On the other hand, because of the breadth of protection accorded to the patent holder (the seed or biotech company), concentration in agricultural biotechnology is giving the largest corporations unprecedented power vis-à-vis growers and other stakeholders. In particular, the privatization and patenting of agricultural innovation (gene traits, transformation technologies and seed germplasm) have supplanted the traditional agricultural understandings on seed and farmers' rights, such as the right to save and replant seeds harvested from the former crop. In some jurisdictions, the privatization and patenting of agricultural innovation has resulted in a drastic erosion of these traditional farmers' rights, and the assertion of proprietary lines on seed technologies and genetic contents has changed farmers from 'seed owners' to mere 'licensees' of a patented product.

Note: * This is the Executive Summary from a study with this title prepared by the UNCTAD Secretariat, United Nations Conference on Trade and Development, 20 April 2006, available at www.unctad.org/en/docs/ditccom200516_en.pdf (last accessed 29 July 2007).

the plant genetics industry is now heavily concentrated in a half-dozen major firms that hold substantial numbers of key patents on germplasm. They also have IP coverage of the related enabling technologies. ... [T]he control of patents and seed distribution networks exercised by these companies has substantially increased the barriers to entry for new firms in the field of germplasm development. (Falcon and Fowler, 2002, pp204–205).

Second, there is a shift from local to national, regional and global markets, with some larger players increasingly seeing the world as a global market and organizing to be active in it. And the third trend is to look for ever better, more certain, more effective tools to help control the risks faced by the different actors and to secure the desired benefits. The various tools for control used are science and technology, information, management, and laws, rules and regulations.

Science and technology

While science and technology are often talked of together, they are not the same. It is not necessary to have a correct scientific understanding of something to develop a technology that works. Trial and error, treating things as black boxes, where doing X produces Y, without understanding exactly why, is sufficient to develop many forms of technology. Sometimes, however, a revolution in scientific understanding is needed to conceive of new technologies. Such was the shift Einstein brought to physics when he showed matter and energy were interchangeable, which opened up the possibilities of nuclear power. Another such revolution has occurred in biology, with the understanding that living organisms grow and develop through the expression of genes, encoded in DNA, which are built from the same four building blocks. This understanding makes it possible to conceive of ways to re-engineer living organisms and gives rise to genetic engineering and other aspects of modern biotechnology, such as cloning, genomics and marker-assisted breeding. It is now possible, in principle, to mix genes from any species with another and possibly synthesize new life forms (synthetic biology) although the desirability of doing so and the long-term effects are hotly debated. These possibilities are leading to different actors seeking to redesign many living organisms of commercial value in agriculture. The questions arising concern whether they *should* do so; who carries the risk and gets the benefits if they do; and the possible longer-term effects and implications.

Information, management and law

Information is another tool different actors use to affect food habits. Some types of information may be designed to inform or educate, while other forms are used to market or advertise, or in promoting public relations or lobbying for specific policies. The spread of global media, broadcasting similar images across the world, helps fuel product globalization and reinforce brand images, usually protected by trademarks or copyright.

Understanding and influencing consumer behaviour has become a major interest of retail businesses. Today, cognitive science is increasing understanding of human motivations and behaviours, and insights from this may help bigger players to use ever more subtle ways to influence people's attitudes and buying habits. Information technology and data processing methods – which affect the capacity both to carry out basic scientific procedures, such as gene sequencing, and to manage businesses and supply chain logistics and profile customers – are also widely used by many of the bigger actors.

Other management tools, such as logistics, may be used to determine the supply systems most advantageous for the businesses involved. For example, the UK's biggest food retailer and an increasingly global player, Tesco, invested heavily in supply chain logistics in the 1980s. In industrialized countries, work organization has shifted from craft-based, small-scale production to a large-scale, mass-production phase, which now often uses just-in-time manufacturing and stocking techniques. In the US, business methods themselves are patentable.

Information and management activities tend to be the preserve of firms and governments and to focus on children, other businesses or consumers – the people who influence or make decisions about what to buy in market economies. Yet unlike the major actors in the system – the input suppliers and processing, retailing and catering companies that are best able to use information and management tools – consumers are unorganized individuals. Consumers can have a significant effect on policy, however, when they take action en masse, such as stopping buying beef because of fears over mad cow disease (BSE), or work through consumer groups. Otherwise firms can simply open a new niche in the market to cater for a specific group of consumers' tastes or concerns.

Marketing, public relations and advertising go together to influence people's behaviour. Much effort and expense goes on these tools, which are more easily used by the larger players in promoting their particular product, approach or image.

When consumers act as citizens, however, they may be able to shape the environment in which all the other actors operate through influencing the choice of government and the laws, rules and regulations governments put in place to balance the range of interests in society. When laws are developed and applied nationally there is a greater chance that a range of people affected by changes can have a say in shaping such changes. This becomes more difficult as rule-making processes become more global, with rules being set by international intergovernmental organizations. For just and balanced outcomes, both nationally and internationally, it is important that rule-making processes do not become captured by vested interests.

One set of rules that has moved from being set nationally in national economic interests to being promoted globally as minimum standards that all countries must adhere to are those on IP, and it is to this that we now turn in more detail.

A Legal Fiction – Intellectual Property

Origins of IP

So where does IP come from? As P. Drahos points out, '"Intellectual property" is a twentieth-century generic term used to refer to a group of legal regimes [such as patents, trademarks and copyright] which began their existence independently of each other and at different times in different places' (Drahos, 1996, p14). These different forms provide creators and inventors with legal protection from someone copying or using their work or invention without permission. Some protect the intellectual knowledge behind technological innovations (patents) and others protect creative works such as books, films and music (copyright). They also include trademarks such as those connected with branded goods, geographical indications like Stilton cheese and champagne, and trade secrets such as the

formula for Coca-Cola or the parent lines of hybrid plants. These different forms of IP are an invented kind of intangible property – yet just as valuable as oil, gold or land for some. Societies construct the rules governing them through political processes dependent on power plays for their outcomes (May, 2000). They are not like a natural phenomenon such as gravity waiting to be discovered. In today's knowledge-based market economy, control of so-called 'intellectual property rights' (IPRs) helps in controlling markets and influences the distribution of wealth and power (Box 1.4).

The ordinary concept of property itself is not a natural phenomenon but a socially constructed one. For some indigenous peoples or religious groups, for example, the idea of ownership of land or water, a fundamental in most current ideas of tangible property, is literally 'non sense' and does not figure in their way

Box 1.4 What are IP rights?

IP rights are legal and institutional devices to protect creations of the mind such as inventions, works of art and literature, and designs. They also include marks on products to indicate their difference from similar ones sold by competitors. Over the years, the rather elastic (and arguably misleading) intellectual property concept[*] has been stretched to include not only patents, copyrights, trademarks and industrial designs, but also trade secrets, plant breeders' rights, geographical indications and rights to layout designs of integrated circuits. Of these, patents, copyrights and trade marks are arguably the most significant in terms of their economic importance, their historical role in the industrialization of Europe and North America, and their current standing as major pillars of the international law on intellectual property.

Patents provide inventors with legal rights to prevent others from using, selling or importing their inventions for a fixed period, nowadays normally 20 years. Applicants for a patent must satisfy a national patent issuing authority that the invention described in the application is new and susceptible of industrial application (or merely 'useful'[**] in the US) and that its creation involved an inventive step or would be unobvious to a skilled practitioner. Patent monopolies are extremely valuable for business.

Copyrights give authors legal protection for various kinds of literary and artistic work. Copyright law protects authors by granting them exclusive rights to sell copies of their work in whatever tangible form (printed publication, sound recording, film and so on) is being used to convey their creative expressions to the public. Legal protection covers the expression of the ideas contained, not the ideas themselves. The right lasts for a very long time indeed, usually the life of the author plus 50–70 years.

Trademarks are marketing tools used to support a company's claim that its products or services are authentic or distinctive compared with similar products or services of competitors. They usually consist of a distinctive design, word or series of words placed on a product label. Normally, trademarks can be renewed indefinitely, though in most jurisdictions this is subject to continued use. The trademark owner has the exclusive right to prevent third parties from using identical or similar marks in the sale of identical or similar goods or services where doing so is likely to cause confusion. One of the main benefits of trademarks to the wider public is that they help to avoid such confusion.

Notes: * It is important to note that IP does not lend itself to any precise definition that would satisfy everybody. Indeed, a recent document published by the World Intellectual Property Organization expressed some quite reasonable scepticism about its validity:

Intellectual property, broadly conceived, may be seen as a misnomer, because it does not necessarily cover 'intellectual works' as such – it covers intangible assets of diverse origins, which need not entail abstract intellectual work; nor need it be defined and protected by property rights alone (the moral rights of authors and the reputation of merchants are not the subject of property, under a civil law concept). (WIPO, 2002a, p9)

** Although usefulness appears to be a less demanding requirement, it is possible for a claimed invention to pass the test of industrial applicability in Europe but to fail the usefulness text in the US. As Alain Gallochat, adviser to the French Ministry of Technology, explains: 'one can imagine a product or a process giving an answer to a technical problem, or involving steps of a technical nature, but without any utility: such an invention, patentable according to the European system, shall not be patentable according to the America system'(Gallochat, 2002, p5).

Source: Taken from Dutfield, 2003a, pp1–2

of seeing the world. The idea of creating an intangible form of property, which developed in the past few centuries in Europe, is 'entirely a legal construction' (May, 2002). In other words, human beings, at least those with power in society, make it up and then seek to justify it

Box 1.5 Justifying IP – No simple matter

Justifying IP is a formidable task. The inadequacies of the traditional justifications for property become more severe when applied to IP. Both the non-exclusive nature of intellectual objects and the presumption against allowing restrictions on the free flow of ideas create special burdens in justifying such property. … [F]ocusing on the problems of justifying IP is important not because these institutions lack any sort of justification, but because they are not so obviously or easily justi-fied as many people think. We must begin to think more openly and imaginatively about the alternative choices to us for stimulating and rewarding intellectual labour. (Hettinger, 1989, pp51–52)

Patents not only underwrite a scheme of property rights, but they order the process of invention in two ways that could be seen as intrinsically political. One is to designate classes of things that can be considered property. The extension of patents to new domains alters basic notions of what a commodity is and who can assert ownership over it. When a patent is awarded for a biological product, it has the effect of removing the thing being patented from the category of nature to the category of artifice – a profound metaphysical shift that, at least in theory, should invite public deliberation. The second political function is distributive. Patents assign ownership rights within production systems, rewarding some participants in the discovery process more than others. For instance, lab technicians' and research subjects' names are rarely written into patent applications; nor do these individuals normally share in the economic proceeds from specific inventions. The institutions in which inventive work is carried out do, by contrast, earn the lion's share of royalties. In this way, patents act as instruments of economic distribution. (Jasanoff, 2005, p204)

(Box 1.5). To be socially acceptable in European society, for example, the notion of IP also required a society secularized enough to accept that creative genius was a personal trait, not a divine gift, that intellectual products had to have a commercial value in their own right and that private rights had to be distinguishable from those of sovereigns (Lesser, 1997).

Historically, IP rules have been a matter of national decision making based on national economic interests. Countries with a national interest in having strong patent rules, because they produced a lot of technology, for example, did create such rules, those without such a capacity did not. Countries copied technologies from each other, selectively offered patent rights, for example to domestic inventors over foreign nationals, or simply did not allow any patents on some products such as medicines (Chapter 3). International treaties in patents and copyright originated in Europe and the US

and countries signed up to them if it suited them. Some did not fully adopt the existing international rules. For example, until the mid-1980s, the US protected the domestic printing industry by denying copyright to foreign authors unless their books were printed in the US.

Even today, patents still must be applied for in each country, although there are mechanisms to enable companies to apply for them in many countries at the same time through the World Intellectual Property Organization (WIPO – see Chapter 4). WIPO is an international insti-tution where many international discussions and negotiations about IP take place, but it is no longer the only one, following the introduc-tion of the Trade-Related Aspects of Intellectual Property Rights Agreement (TRIPS) as part of the WTO package of Agreements (Chapter 2). In WIPO countries are free to sign up to each of the various agreements individually. It was this that posed a problem for those industries and countries that wanted to safeguard their economic interests with a global IP regime and led them to seek to introduce minimum standards for IP rules through the WTO.

Concerns about IP

The strengthening and extension of the IP regime has led to a range of concerns over the impact of the new IP regime on low- and middle-income countries, especially the effects on health, in particular concerning access to medicines, such as AIDS drugs in Africa or basic diagnostic techniques for screening for breast cancer. Similar concerns about the effects of IP on access to seeds and knowledge needed for research and development are being raised by a range of academics, policymakers and NGOs such as GRAIN and the ETC Group. These include IP's effects on who does what research and development, how and whether smallholder farmers can continue farming, especially in low- and middle-income countries, and the increasing concentration of power in the various sectors of the food system (Chapter 8). Other concerns are over the way in which these rules were agreed and extended globally and the continued pressures for developing countries to adopt ever higher standards of IP protection (Chapter 7). A central issue is whether the new IP regime has the balance of interests right between those who receive the privileges IP affords and those negatively affected by it. Another issue is the need for the IP rules to be embedded in a broader regulatory regime that can curb the tendency to monopoly and abuse (such as cartels) that IP can give rise to:

The immediate impact of intellectual property protection is to benefit financially those who have knowledge and power, and to increase the cost of access to those without. (IPRs Commission, 2002, p47)

The UK government recognized the complexities and concerns about IP in its White Paper on International Development in 2000 and set up a Commission on Intellectual Property Rights (IPRs Commission) to consider 'how intellectual property rules might need to develop in the future to take greater account of the interests of developing countries and poor people'. The Commission reported to the Secretary of State for International Development at the Department for International Development (DFID) in September 2002 and noted that:

Developing countries ... negotiate from a position of relative weakness. ... The immediate impact of intellectual property protection is to benefit financially those who have knowledge and power, and to increase the cost of access to those without. (IPRs Commission, 2002, p47)

It also noted that:

Developing countries should generally not provide patent protection for plants and animals ... because of the restrictions patents may place on use of seed by farmers and researchers. ... [T]he extension of intellectual property protection does carry the risk of restricting farmers' rights to reuse, exchange and sell seed, the very practices which form the basis of their traditional role in conservation and development. (IPRs Commission, 2002, pp66–68)

The Bigger Debate on IP

To have ...

The proponents of a strong global IP regime argue it provides the necessary incentive, proper reward and required security for investment in R&D to produce life-improving innovations. Historically, two main moral and philosophical arguments for rewarding creative and innovative people have been used. One stems from the view of the 19th-century German philosopher Hegel – that an idea belongs to its creator because the idea is a manifestation of the creator's personality or self. The other is drawn from the work on real property by John Locke, the 17th-century English philosopher – that the usefulness of physical or natural objects came about through human effort and that those who had expended that effort had a moral claim to exclusive use of those objects (May, 2000).

Today, in practice in industrialized countries, the rationale for protecting the intangibles created by IP is essentially utilitarian – with the utility focused on promotion of innovation on the assumption this bring benefits for all. For example, knowledge about how to make something, unlike a physical object such as a piece of bread, can be used or consumed by one person without limiting its use by others. Sharing knowledge with others, then, does not reduce the amount you have, unlike sharing a piece of bread. However, it might reduce the advantage you may have had if you were the only one to know something or were allowed to exclude others from using what you know. The problem is that while the widest possible dissemination of new knowledge makes for the greatest economic efficiency, if everybody is free to use new knowledge, inventors have little incentive to invest in producing it. The various forms of IP stop that sharing (usually temporarily) by transforming knowl-

edge from a shared public good into a private good. In other words IP creates scarcity where there need be none. This gives the holders of IP enhanced market power and permits the use of monopoly pricing through which they can recoup their expenditure in research and development. Creative minds and innovative firms thus have an incentive to engage in inventive activities. The IP regime, then, plays an important role in underpinning private sector-led innovation, and also in the ability of firms to establish and maintain market power.

This argument provides the main rationale for the protection given by patents, copyright, plant breeders' rights and other types of IP. However, the various forms of IP in different countries differ in terms of the subject matter that may be eligible for protection, the scope (what can be protected) and duration (length of time) of protection, and possible exemptions to exclusive rights. This reflects the fact that they are a concession granted by a society, through the laws it constructs, which advantage a specific group for broad social goals (increasing creativity and inventiveness) and try to balance the interests of producers and users of intellectual works.

The EU clearly sees IP playing a role in helping to secure its members' economic interests in the development and application of modern biotechnology. Among the measures proposed by the European Commission in a 30-point action plan is creating a 'strong, harmonized and affordable European intellectual property protection system, functioning as an incentive to R&D and innovation' (CEC, 2002, p25) as one support for utilizing the full potential of biotechnology and strengthening the European biotechnology sector's competitiveness.

... or not to have?

In an extensive study reviewing the main justifications for IP – whether for reward to authors or to promote innovation – political scientist Chris May argues that their real purpose today is protecting financial investment. In some countries this is identified with the national interest. May notes that, when negotiating to put new IP rules into the WTO in TRIPS, the US saw them as a way 'to retain its competitive advantage in the global system' (May, 2000, p119). This is not seeing them as a way of transferring up-to-date technology but rather of maintaining the gap between those countries with technology and those without to ensure national advantage. However, May argues that the gap is legitimized by using IP justified on the basis 'not of advantage, but of the rights of the individual knowledge innovators'. This view of the expanding IP regime as one of the ways of preventing development is put more graphically by University of Cambridge economist Ha Joon Chang, who talks of 'kicking away the ladder' (Chang, 2002).

James Boyle, a professor of law at Duke Law School, argues that the effects of a global IP regime will be widespread and not as beneficial as its proponents suggest. He helped draft a declaration which suggested that:

> *The blandishments of the international information industries notwithstanding, more intellectual property rights may actually mean less innovation, less heterogeneity in culture and environment and a less informed world of public debate.* (Boyle, 1996, p197)

This is basically because they may underpin a highly concentrated market structure dominated by large firms that use these rules to inhibit others from threatening their position. IPRs, he argues, are being used as part of a new round of enclosures in what were formerly the 'global commons' – including genetic information encoded in the genes of people, plants, animals and micro-organisms (Boyle, 2001). This is part of what Peter Drahos sees as a trend towards 'proprietarianism – a creed which says that the possessor should take all, that ownership privileges should trump community interests and the world and its contents are open to ownership' (Drahos, 1996, p202).

Drahos warns against thinking of IPRs as rights. Instead we should think of them as *privileges*:

> *Unlike real property law, intellectual property law posits rights in abstract objects ... IPRs are rule-governed privileges that regulate the ownership and exploitation of abstract objects in many fields of human activity ... [they] are liberty-intruding privileges of a special kind ... they promote factionalism and dangerous levels of private power. From the point of view of distributive justice, their scope should be limited ... there are strong reasons for supporting private property rights, but we should do so in a contingent, consequentially-minded way ... guided by a philosophically defensible view of the role of property in social life and democratic culture.* (Drahos, 1996, pp1, 5)

Drahos sees stronger, global IPRs resulting in a new form of 'feudalism'. This is because they will alter social relations in ways that mean individuals never 'own' entities like software or seeds. Instead purchasers are only licensed by their corporate rights holders to use them in very limited ways and are excluded from socially important acts normally associated with real property – the ability to lend, share, give away or sell (Drahos and Braithwaite, 2002). Thus the issues surrounding IP go far beyond the focus here on food and agriculture.

Not rights but privileges

It would be a more accurate reflection of reality if we stopped using the term 'intellectual property rights' and instead talked of 'business monopoly (or exclusionary) privileges'. Using more accurate language would also avoid any confusion with human rights discussions (see Chapter 7). The language of privilege, even if these privileges are enshrined in law rather than custom, helps make clearer the political and power-based mechanisms that lead to some being privileged over others. They also make clearer their instrumental purpose, which is geared to market-based creative and inventive business operation across a wide range of fields, among which agriculture has become a recent target.

It may also make it easier to unpick the rather mystifying terminology of IPRs. This terminology has conflated what used to be called 'industrial property', such as trademarks, patents and industrial designs, with copyright. This latter is connected, especially in Europe, with notions of the moral rights of authors to be identified with their work and not have that work distorted.

Patent problems

Of particular concern to many is the extension to developing countries, through the WTO TRIPS Agreement (Chapter 3), of minimum requirements on patenting. This issue is made more complicated because a system that was developed for innovation in inanimate objects has, in some countries, been extended to cover living organisms and parts of them. Patents are supposed to provide benefits to their owners and society at large. Patents are granted in the US on the basis that there has been an invention of something new, useful and non-obvious; in Europe on the basis of being novel, having industrial application and involving an inventive step. A major concern today even in the US and

EU is that the meaning of these words has been devalued and poor quality patents are being granted for 'inventions' that lack novelty and an inventive step.

Moreover, in reality, 'the basic patent bargain works only in theory. In practice, both sides cheat', argues Professor of Information and Organization at Sheffield University, Stuart Macdonald:

> *Most obviously, the patent affords protection only when the patentee can afford to enforce his rights, which may mean that the poor have no protection at all. ... And if society cheats in not providing the protection the inventor has a right to expect from the patent system, the inventor cheats too. Only in theory does the inventor provide society with the information of invention: in practice, he discloses the information required by the patent system, not the information required by society to replicate and develop his invention.* (Macdonald, 2001)

This raises questions both about the justice of the system, if it is not equitable in its functioning, and about whether its application fails to meet the objectives for which it is designed. Currently, patents are also very unevenly distributed globally, as 'industrialized countries hold 97 per cent of all patents worldwide' (UNDP, 1999, p68).

US economist Keith Maskus writes:

> *There are legitimate reasons to be concerned about the highly protective standards that have emerged recently in the US and the EU. These laws and judicial interpretations provide broad patent protection for software and biotechnological inventions. They also promote extensive rights in the formulation of databases, which could have a negative effect on scientific research. It remains to be seen whether such standards tilt the balance within those jurisdictions toward the private rights of*

inventors and away from the needs of competitors and users. It is not too early to claim that they are inappropriate for developing economies and net technology importers. (Maskus, 2000, pp237–238)

Clear evidence that the patent system has stimulated the development of new products and technologies, which otherwise would not have been developed, is only available for a few sectors, such as pharmaceuticals – and even here basically 'for those diseases where there is a large market in the developed world' (IPRs Commission, 2002, p33). The rationale for patents in the pharmaceutical industry, for example, is that the exclusive rights they confer allow the industry to charge high prices for products and so recoup its research and development (R&D) costs. Once drugs go off-patent and generic suppliers enter the market, prices fall, often dramatically, making medicines more accessible to the poor. In pharmaceuticals, however, where most R&D is commercially led, the industry has not produced drugs aimed at diseases of the poor, nor at those with relatively few sufferers, without some form of government incentive. Much basic research is also done by government and then turned over to companies for commercialization. In effect, consumers pay for it twice, first through taxes that fund government research and then via

high prices for drugs under patents that fund corporate activities. These problems have led to much debate in the health sector about the patent regimes' effect on access to medicines, especially in developing countries (MSF, 2004; Roffe et al, 2006).

In other sectors, patents are sometimes considered to have anti-competitive effects: they serve to secure and strengthen the position of market leaders and limit the entry of new competitors. Indeed, they were used in this way in the 19th century (Jenkins, 1975). In the extreme, they may actually slow the pace of innovation if a dominant firm possesses a powerful pool of patents that limits the ability of other firms to further improve existing products and technologies and acts in an anti-competitive way.

Although policymakers have sought to limit the adverse effects of patents through revised IP legislation, competition policy and other business regulations, the anti-competitive implications of patents remain a cause of concern, for example patent pooling and cross-licensing between a few firms in effect creates a cartel keeping others out. Such concerns have regained momentum with the emergence of patents on biotechnology products and processes that cover fundamental research tools, human genes, genetically engineered plants and other living organisms.

IP in Food and Farming

IP pervades today's industrialized food system. The Gowers review of IP in the UK gave the example of a jar of a well-known brand of coffee:

The contents of a jar, the lid and seal may be protected by patents. Registered and unregistered design rights can also protect the lid and shape of the jar. Copyright can protect the artwork in labels, and trademarks can protect

the shape of the jar, labels, colours used and brand names. (Gowers, 2006, p1)

From consumers ...

Broadly speaking, the various kinds of IP are used more by some firms than others, often based on whether they are selling to a final consumer or producing for intra-firm trade or farmers. Trademarks, geographical indications and trade secrets are widely used by firms and actors dealing with the final consumer. The use of trademarks is often linked to other tools for control, such as brand advertising. Greater efforts to protect brands and increase market share are increasingly likely. In 1993, the chairman of Unilever, the Anglo-Dutch multinational, called brand equities 'the most valuable items in our stewardship' and saw 'the power of our brands as the engine of long-term growth' (Tansey and Worsley, 1995, p115). During that year, the company spent almost 12 per cent of turnover (£3284 million) on advertising and promotional investment. In 2000, Unilever announced plans to dispose of three-quarters of its 1600 brands to focus on just 400 around the world. In 2002, its chairmen said, 'We are focused increasingly on driving the growth of our leading brands and dealing with other brands in ways which create value for shareholders' (Burgmans and Fitzgerald, 2002). Other global companies with many fewer or single brands also spend heavily on advertising and marketing. In 2006, for example, over US$2.5 billion was spent advertising Coca-Cola while McDonald's selling, general and administrative expenses amounted to over $2.3 billion. These figures are much more than the annual budget of the WHO and around three years of the FAO's budget.[1] Yet, as research by the Food Commission in the UK illustrates, there is an inverse relationship between what is advertised and what is recommended as a healthy diet (Dalmeny et al, 2003).

As the reach of the market and mass marketing techniques, especially in an increasingly globalized market, go further into low- and middle-income countries, so too will the major actors make use of various forms of IP as part of their business development strategy. In urban societies served by multiple retailers – supermarkets are also spreading rapidly in many rapidly urbanizing developing countries today – advertising and media images become more important and unless farmers or producers

have a major brand they will not get their goods on the retailers' shelves. Normally, only the top two or three brands of a given product actually do.

For some products, a combination of widely advertised branded products (which are based on trademarks) and trade secrets – the recipe for Coca-Cola being the most famous – are used. For others, producing a product in a particular way or region, a designated name, linked to the region and method of production, provides a marketing tool that allows them to capitalize on their uniqueness. These geographical indications (another form of IP) are of considerable importance in some foods, for example Roquefort cheese or Parma ham. Such designation normally comes out of a well-established activity that has national recognition and produces products sought after by consumers. The ability of small producers to find markets for their often unadvertised products or to develop new geographical indications which they have little capacity to promote is very different from those whose supply chains lead into nationally, regionally and globally promoted branded products.

... to producers

If gardeners buy a rose or other ornamental plant from a garden centre, they may find a note attached saying they are not allowed to take cuttings or otherwise propagate the plants they buy. The same may be the case for some farmers and vegetable growers, with restrictions placed on their saving seed. This is possible because the holders of another form of IP, in this case plant breeders' rights or, in a few places, patents, can legally exclude people from doing things they might otherwise have done, like replanting seed saved from a previous crop that they have grown.

For farmers in the wealthier parts of the world who buy seed, fertilizer, feeds, agrochemicals and equipment, and for researchers developing new breeds, varieties and products for them to use, the key forms of IP are plant breeders' rights (Chapter 2) and patents (Chapter 3). These forms of IP will increasingly influence control of food production in a world where genetic engineering and commercial breeding becomes more prevalent. Where farmers in developing countries are the focus of seed sales, however, it seems that commercial horticultural seed producers consider trademarks to be as important as plant variety protection, at least according to the author of a recent study (Louwaars, personal communication, 2006), which examined the impact of plant variety protection on the breeding and seed sector in developing countries (Louwaars et al, 2005). Trade secrets are potentially also important as they are used to protect hybrids, with the parent lines kept secret, but these are difficult to enforce in most countries. While these forms of IP have been used in the urbanized, industrialized countries for a few decades, they are still very new in many low- and middle-income countries.

Patent power

Patents are very important for the development of agrochemicals and many controversial developments in modern biotechnology (Barton, 2003; Box 1.3), especially genetic engineering and now nanotechnology. Agrochemicals have long been patentable, but it was only recently – in 1980 – that a genetically-engineered microorganism was first allowed to be patented in the US, following the *Diamond v. Chakrabarty* Supreme Court case in 1980 (Dutfield, 2003a, 154ff). Within a few years plants and animals, and parts thereof, such as genes, were also allowed to be patented in the US (although a special form of plant patent on asexually reproducing plants had been available in the US since the 1930s). Once patent law was extended to cover living organisms in the US, companies were then able to move into and work in this

area as they would now be able to capture the benefits by excluding others from using such organisms through the patent system. It also led to pressures in other industrialized countries to allow similar extensions in their patent law, although many restricted patentability to genetically engineered organisms, not allowing naturally occurring ones to be patented.

The potential of genetic engineering to open up new market opportunities all over the world fuelled an expansion of private sector interest in agricultural research in industrialized countries. This happened at the same time as public sector-financed R&D in agriculture declined and moved away from research of practical benefit to farmers. Instead, public sector-financed R&D increasingly focuses on more basic research that produces results that can only be used by the larger corporate players that have R&D facilities (Millstone and Lang, 2003, p40; see also Chapter 8).

The firms involved in the private sector-led transformation of the basic inputs into agriculture want a set of rules and regulations to permit them to secure benefits from their R&D and avoid costs. If they can, companies naturally want to stop others from copying – or buyers reproducing – their new products. This can be done in two ways. One is by legal means, through patent and other IP rules. This has led to a clash between real property rights of farmers about how they use their land and the rights of patent holders (Box 1.6). The other means is technological. Breeding hybrids, for example, which do not reproduce truly and lose their yield characteristics in subsequent generations is one such method (Lewontin, 1993). This creates a kind of 'economically sterile' seed and also promotes a planned obsolescence approach to variety production (Rangnekar, 2002a). Breeders also use trade secrets protection to keep the parents of the hybrids secret, thus making it difficult for competing breeders to get a similar cross onto the market. Another approach is to attempt to develop technologies that will stop seeds germinating or specific

Box 1.6 Regulating agricultural biotechnology: Prioritizing real or intellectual property?

Christopher Rodgers[a]

The rise of agricultural biotechnology, and the patenting of genetically modified organisms (GMOs) for use in crop production – initially in the US and Canada, but now much more widely – raises a number of very difficult legal issues. There is an inherent conflict between the traditional role of the law in protecting private property (categorized by lawyers as 'real property'), and the use of intellectual property law to protect innovations in GM technology. This is not simply a matter of legal principle – the issues at stake have dramatic implications for the future of farmers in the developing countries and for food security.

In the common law world, the primary mechanism for protecting a property owner's rights is the law of nuisance and trespass. Can non-GM farmers use the law of nuisance to claim damages for alleged 'contamination' of their crops by cross-pollination from GM crops and further remedies (for example injunctions) to prevent further cross-pollination? This contentious issue has been rehearsed in the courts in Canada (in *Hoffman, LB Hoffman Farms Inc. and Beaudoin v. Monsanto Canada and Aventis Crop Science Canada Holding Inc* (2005)[b]) and in the US (in the *Star Link Corn Products Liability Litigation* (2002)[c]), without a conclusive resolution. The only English case in which the issues have been discussed was *R v. Secretary of State for the Environment ex parte Watson* (1999)[d]. In this case the grant of a licence for field trials of GM maize was challenged on judicial review by a neighbouring organic sweet corn producer. The challenge was unsuccessful due to the court's unwillingness to interfere with the risk assessment undertaken by the UK government's specialist scientific advisers, the Advisory Committee on Releases to the Environment (ACRE). The environmental risk assessment carried out by ACRE indicated that the danger of cross-contamination was so small as to be statistically insignificant. In the course of a short judgement dismissing the claim, Lord Justice Buxton commented that the applicant's case 'sounded like one of private nuisance' and should have been pleaded as such, as the claim was ultimately aimed at restricting the research institute's right to use its property for an otherwise legitimate purpose. The court characterized organic farming as a 'hypersensitive' land use that would not be protected by the common law of nuisance.

Although the issues were not explored in depth, this case illustrates the considerable difficulties for any organic farmer seeking to establish legal liability for alleged GM 'contamination' of his land or crops in nuisance. There are difficult problems of causation, and in establishing that the cross fertilization of a non-GM crop constitutes either property 'damage' in the required sense, or is causing an unreasonable interference with the farmer's use of his land.

On the other hand, the courts have adopted a radically different stance to the protection of *intellectual* property. One of the *causes célèbres* in the recent history of biotechnology law is the decision of the Canadian courts in *Monsanto v. Schmeiser* (2004).[e] Monsanto successfully sued a Saskatchewan canola farmer, Percy Schmeiser, for damages and an injunction, in circumstances where Schmeiser's crop had acquired (without his consent) Monsanto's patented RT73 gene. This gives crops resistance to Monsanto's 'Roundup' glyphosate broad-spectrum herbicide. The legal basis for Monsanto's successful claim for patent infringement was the courts' recognition that they could maintain patent protection in the patented gene even when it had passed by cross-fertilization into Schmeiser's canola crop. The Supreme Court of Canada saw nothing to prevent the recognition of two sets of property rights subsisting simultaneously in Schmeiser's crop; that of the farmer in the land and the crops it produced, and that of Monsanto in the gene giving resistance to its Roundup herbicide.[f] Unlike nuisance (which requires the proof of 'unreasonable' interference with real property rights), the law protecting patent rights is based on strict liability: Schmeiser was in breach of patent law simply because he had harvested a crop in which he knew or should have known that the patented gene was present, and had (as is common agricultural practice the world over) kept back a proportion of the seeds, and had then planted them the following year.

In protecting Monsanto's patent rights, the Canadian courts accorded priority to the *intellectual property* rights of the corporation over the *real property* rights of the farmer. This is not only arguably in contravention of the 'polluter pays' principle of environmental law – if this approach were to be adopted in other jurisdictions it would compromise the legal rights of non-GM farmers, who would find it much more difficult to maintain organic and/or traditional farming methods in the face of the spread of GM technology across traditional sectors of agriculture – it also illustrates a wider issue, namely the way in which intellectual property rights can be used by their owners to acquire control over the food production system, and to override the land use rights of farmers and their ability to save seed. The decision clearly gives support to the biotechnology companies to try to protect their patent rights, but jurisdictions outside Canada and the US may choose to fix a different balance between real property and intellectual property rights.

Notes:
[a] Professor of Law, Newcastle University, UK.
[b] 2002 SKQB No 67, 2005 SKQB 225 (Saskatchewan Court of Appeal);
[c] 2002 212 F. Supp. 2d 828 (US District Court, Northern District of Illinois);
[d] 1999 Env. L. R.310 (Court of Appeal, England);
[e] 2004 SCC 34 (Federal Supreme Court);
[f] See 2004 SCC 34 at paragraph 96, per McLachlin, C. J. and Fish, J. This point was also made forcibly in the Federal Court of Appeal ruling in Schmeiser: '...there is no authority for the proposition that ownership of a plant must necessarily supersede the rights of the holder of a patent for a gene found in the plant. On the contrary, the jurisprudence presents a number of examples in which the rights of ownership of property are compromised to the extent required to protect the patent holder's statutory monopoly. Generally, the existence of such a conflict of rights is not relevant to the determination of infringement [of patent] but only when fashioning the remedy if infringement is found' (Sharlow, J. A., 2002 FCA 309 judgement at paragraph 51). See also Bruce Ziff (2005) 'Travels with my plant: *Monsanto v. Schmeiser* revisited', *University of Ottawa Law and Technology Journal*, vol 2, in particular pp501–503 available online at www.uoltj.ca/articles/vol2.2/2005.2.2.uoltj.Ziff.493-509.pdf; Jennifer Chandler (guest ed) (2007) 'Law and technology: Exploring the role of the law in the conflict between organic farming and biotechnology', *Bulletin of Science, Technology and Society*, special issue, part one, vol 27, no 3, pp187–25.

traits being activated without a purchased input – so-called genetic use restriction technologies (GURTs), also dubbed 'terminator' and 'traitor' technologies (Chapter 5, Box 5.5).

As the various competing businesses developing products and processes in this area make growing use of IP, such as patents and plant breeders' rights (PBRs), to protect their investments, there has been more litigation to settle disputes (Barton, 1998). Without these forms of IP, while research would undoubtedly go on, the way and speed with which its results were developed and commercialized would almost certainly be different.

The potential of genetic engineering to manipulate plants which could be patented drew new players into the business of seed production, largely from the chemical and pharmaceutical industries. They have invested billions of dollars over the past two decades in agricultural biotechnology R&D and want to see returns on this investment, which means that the crops they have developed have to be grown commercially sooner rather than later. These companies have a long history of using patents as business tools and require some form of control over their rights to the research tools they have developed and rights to prevent reuse of their products, such as seeds, without their permission or further payment. They were one of the important interest groups keen to allow for patenting of living organisms and are supporters of the main players pushing for stronger IP rules internationally.

There are growing concerns on the part of some researchers and NGOs that exposure to the full range of IP tools being wielded by the large firms, which are sophisticated in their use thereof, may have a major adverse impact on people's livelihoods and food security in devel-oping countries in particular. In part this is felt to be a result of increased corporate control, undermining livelihoods and local farming systems and promoting undesirable consump-tion patterns (ActionAid International, 2005). When IP tools are combined with other requirements by buyers (for example identifica-tion of place of origin), the pressures for exclusion of small-scale suppliers can become even greater. Of particular concern to many is the pressure to allow patents on everything, everywhere.

Going Global

Extending IP rules globally will have wide-ranging implications for the future control of food, many of which are still to be felt. It will affect access to seeds, knowledge and anything else protected by IP. Yet access to and exchange of genetic resources is the basis of agriculture. At the same time as IP regimes are expanding, other international regimes, concerning biodi-versity and agriculture biodiversity, are still being worked out in practice on the ground and in conference halls around the world. It is to these different regimes that we turn in Part II, before returning to look at the experiences and implications of these regimes for our future food security, however that is understood (Box 1.7).

Whatever people try to achieve locally in managing their food and farming, they need to know about the mix of global rules because these rules will increasingly constrain local and national action. Moreover, changes in one area tend to affect others. Part II of this book examines these new rules, the negotiations that surround them, how they interconnect and the complex web they create.

Box 1.7 Food security, insecurity, the right to food and food sovereignty

A range of terms is used in discussions about ensuring everyone in the world has enough good food to eat, produced from a sustainable food system.

According to the UN's FAO:

- **Food security** is a 'situation that exists when all people, at all times, have physical, social and economic access to sufficient, safe and nutritious food that meets their dietary needs and food preferences for an active and healthy life'.
- **Food insecurity** is a 'situation that exists when people lack secure access to sufficient amounts of safe and nutritious food for normal growth and development and an active, healthy life. It may be caused by the unavailability of food, insufficient purchasing power, or the inappropriate distribution or inadequate use of food at the household level. Food insecurity, poor conditions of health and sanitation, and inappropriate care and feeding practices are the major causes of poor nutritional status. Food insecurity may be chronic, seasonal or transitory.'
- The **Right to Food** is a legally-binding right and was recognized in the Universal Declaration of Human Rights in 1948 and the International Covenant on Economic, Social and Cultural Rights in 1967 (now ratified by 156 countries). In 2004, governments at the FAO adopted a set of 'Voluntary Guidelines to support the progressive realization of the right to adequate food in the context of national food security'. These guidelines aim 'to provide practical guidance to States in their implementation of the progressive realization of the right to adequate food in the context of national food security, in order to achieve the goals of the Plan of Action of the World Food Summit'.

Many farmers, pastoralists, fishermen, indigenous peoples and non-governmental organizations (NGOs) are calling for adoption of a broader concept of:

- **Food sovereignty** that is 'based on the human right to food, to self-determination, on indigenous rights to territory, and on the rights of rural peoples to produce food for local and national markets. Food sovereignty defends agriculture with farmers, fisheries with artisanal fishing families, forestry with forest communities and steppes with nomadic pastoralists.' At the Nyéléni 2007 Forum for Food Sovereignty in Mali (see www.fao.org/righttofood/; www.nyeleni2007.org), the participants identified six pillars of food sovereignty: it focuses on food for people, values food providers, localizes food systems, puts control locally, builds knowledge and skills, and works with nature (see Chapter 8, Box 8.2).

Sources: FAO (2001); Mulvany (2006); Windfuhr and Jonsén (2005).

Part II

The Key Global Negotiations and Agreements

International agreements often seem hard to understand and legalistic. In reality, they are very difficult to arrive at and involve complex, long negotiations among states with different interests. It is the outcome of these machinations that produce agreements that come to have legal force and affect all our lives.

The following chapters discuss several key texts to show how various international agreements arose and some of the power plays and interests that lay behind them. Key points from the agreements are discussed, along with how they relate to each other and the complex connections that are developing. The aim is to inform and so help facilitate wider participation in shaping the rules that govern us and affect our food future.

2

Turning Plant Varieties into Intellectual Property: The UPOV Convention

Graham Dutfield

The first international treaty bringing intellectual property (IP) into agriculture was drawn up in Europe to harmonize and support existing national systems that give commercial plant breeders' rights over the plant varieties they breed, and to promote the system in other countries. This system of plant breeders' rights was a newly created alternative to the US approach of allowing plant patents, itself a special regime designed to protect vegetatively reproduced ornamental and fruit varieties. Since the TRIPS Agreement, all WTO Members must provide some form of IP protection for plant varieties, but it is up to them how to do it. This chapter examines the development of plant breeders' rights and some issues that arise from them today.

Background and History

For almost all of human history, farming and crop improvement were carried out by the same people and in the same places, by farmers and indigenous peoples on their own land. The separation of the two activities is very recent, starting in the 19th century. In this chapter I explain what scientific breeders do (see also Chapter 6) and then briefly trace the history of this separation between farming and breeding, which began in Europe and North America, where the first professional breeders emerged, and farmers abandoned or were forced out of breeding as an activity. This separation is an ongoing process in many developing countries and in some areas has hardly even begun.

Since Neolithic times, farmers have set aside some of their harvested seeds for replant-

ing. They selected such seeds, whether consciously or unintentionally, on the basis that the plants producing them possessed desirable traits such as high yields, disease resistance, or drought or frost tolerance. Over the generations, this practice resulted in ever increasing quantities of locally adapted varieties known as 'landraces', 'folk varieties' or 'farmers' varieties'.

Breeding as a science

This situation changed in North America and Europe from the late 19th century as the profession of farming became a separate one from seed production. The emerging seed producers started to select from the existing materials to increase their share in the market. This commercial crop improvement remained merely empirical and experimental but with a growing scientific basis in mathematics applied to selection methods. Very soon after the 1900 rediscovery of Mendel's insights into the laws of heredity, scientists sought to apply genetics to crop improvement. This led to the directed development of 'pure lines' of self-pollinating crops. Pure lines are uniform, breed true to type and contain consistent and identifiable traits that can be transferred to other plants. According to two experts on the politics of modern agriculture, Robin Pistorius and Jeroen van Wijk (1999), 'while Mendelian breeding allowed for a controlled mixing of genetic characteristics, pure line breeding offered a practical method to "fix" them in succeeding generations'.

Breeding new plant varieties is a laborious and time-consuming process. It takes about 7–10 years to get from the first cross to the marketable variety. The first task is to determine the objectives of the breeding programme. One obvious goal is to produce varieties with higher yields, but there are many other possible objectives such as the development of varieties with added or improved characteristics such as pest resistance, disease resistance or drought tolerance, compatibility with inputs such as fertilizers and pesticides, and improved consumption or food-processing characteristics. A major challenge for breeders is to respond both to the requirements of varying farming conditions and to the need to develop varieties that can be sold widely. Furthermore, they increasingly have to respond to the ever-changing demands of conglomerate seed and chemical companies, food processing companies and supermarket chains.

The basic conventional technique is known as 'crossing and selecting', which involves crossing two or more parent lines or varieties with desirable traits to produce multiple offspring. Of these, the best plants are selected and allowed to breed again. Again, the best

ones are selected for breeding and the process is repeated a number of times. After 8 to 12 generations, an improved variety is produced that breeds true and is ready to be planted by farmers.

But breeding is rarely this simple. For one thing, a new variety may be derived from 50 or more parental lines. For another, a variety used in the breeding programme may be the source of only one desirable trait and many undesirable ones. So how does the breeder incorporate this single trait into his or her new variety while excluding the others? Very simply, let us call plants from the parent line or new variety into which the single trait is to be introduced 'Group A' and call members of the 'donor' plants (which could well be a wild or semi-domesticated relative) 'Group B'. These Group B plants are the source of just one desirable trait, among many unwanted ones, for which as little as one allele (a DNA sequence that codes for a gene) may be responsible. For the breeder to transfer this allele without the undesirable traits, he must first cross Group A and Group B plants and then 'back-cross' those offspring containing the trait with plants from Group A. This is repeated through the generations, selecting plants that retain the trait and back-crossing them with Group A plants. In time, the proportion of genes from Group B plants contained in the offspring goes down in conventional selection systems from 50:50 in the first generation to a negligible figure.

These approaches generally work well with crops like wheat, rice and sorghum that self-fertilize. These tend to be genetically stable and consequently breed true. But, as with humans and animals, inbreeding can be deleterious for cross-pollinators such as maize, pearl millet and cruciferous crops like cabbages and oilseed rape. This is not such a problem for plants that can reproduce asexually, such as vines, apple trees and potatoes, where the genetics are fixed through this reproduction system: once a new variety has been bred, it can be multiplied through vegetative forms of propagation, whether cuttings, grafts or tubers. But for cross-fertilizing seed crops, the breeder must find another approach.

Maize breeders in the early 20th century came up with a solution by applying the rediscovered principles of Mendelian genetics. George Shull, a breeder working at a US government research centre, managed to induce the characteristic of what he called 'heterosis' in the corn plants, resulting from his cross-breeding of inbred lines. This phenomenon, commonly referred to as 'hybrid vigour', is manifested in heightened yields. But because they are hybrids, the offspring cannot breed true and the maximum yield enhancements thus last only for a single generation. The additional advantage that hybrid varieties provide a uniform crop compared to the open-pollinated populations became apparent with large-scale agricultural mechanization. So while farmers stand to benefit from seeds providing this hybrid vigour, they need to buy seeds at the beginning of every planting season to enjoy equally productive future harvests. If farmers replant the seeds from hybrid crops, the resulting plants tend to be 'segregated', reflecting the characteristics of the grandparents. This necessity to buy seed was and continues to be a boon for the seed companies, which could correct a major risk factor in seed production, namely that seed markets are generally anti-cyclic, in other words after a good harvest – when the seed producer has good stocks – farmers save their seed, whereas the demand for seed is high when seed production conditions have been poor. Hybrids create a stable seed market.

The hybrid route to the breeding of better seeds is generally assumed to be a very good thing for farmers and for the development of the seed industry, but sceptics argue that the massive investments in the development of hybrid varieties that were made in the 1920s and 1930s could have been allocated to breeding based on more conventional techniques using open-pollination that would have achieved similar yield increases but without preventing farmers from being able to replant their harvested seeds (Lewontin, 1993).

Other breeding techniques, such as tissue and cell culture development, have also been used for several decades. These enable scientists to regenerate large numbers of plants that are genetically identical and free from disease. These techniques do not replace conventional breeding but can improve its efficiency. More recently, molecular biology introduced new opportunities in breeding, either to make conventional breeding more efficient and effective (marker-assisted selection) or by moving foreign genes into the breeding materials (genetic engineering), not just from other plant species, but sometimes from completely different forms of life. For example, scientists have succeeded in inducing insect resistance in crops like corn and cotton by inserting genes from a soil microbe called *Bacillus thuringiensis* (Bt) that is toxic for certain insects. These techniques include direct gene transfer into tissue cultures using bacteria or viruses as carriers of the foreign DNA, and such devices as high-velocity 'gene guns' which shoot DNA-containing 'bullets' into cell nuclei. The new science of genomics is being used to identify useful genes and the plants which contain them.

The emergence of the modern seed industry

During the 19th-century westward expansion of the US, the government sought to encourage settlement. One way to do this was to entrust the farmers themselves with the selection, breeding and multiplication of seed. To this effect, first the Patent Office, and then the US Department of Agriculture (USDA), provided farmers with free seed packets for them to experiment with. At the time the seed industry was small and insignificant. Farmers used these seeds and those introduced by the immigrants arriving in the US to breed varieties adapted to suit their own needs and the local ecological conditions. The number of such varieties increased enormously. Later these farmer-bred and selected crop varieties formed the basis of the public and private sector breeding programmes.

Cary Fowler (1994) argues that the separation of farming from breeding, the undermining of the customary practice of seed saving in the case of hybridized crops and the commodification of the seed cannot be explained by advances in plant breeding science and technology alone. When scientifically bred seeds came onto the market, subsistence agriculture had largely been replaced by commercial farming anyway. Mechanized harvesting and the consolidation of landholdings had made seed selection non-viable compared to the greater convenience of purchasing mechanically-cleaned seed from dealers. And, since most farmers were no longer improving seeds themselves, the attraction of selecting and replanting was declining even before scientifically bred varieties became widely available.

In 1890, 596 US firms were involved in commercial seed production. Having formed a business association called the American Seed Trade Association (ASTA) a few years earlier, they were becoming active in defending their interests. One of ASTA's early campaigns was to stop the government from providing farmers with seeds. This failed for lack of support from the public and Congress, many of whose members sent seed packets to constituents. However, during the first two decades of the 20th century, the government increasingly sent seeds only of the most common varieties to farmers, while passing on the more exotic germplasm to the government experimental stations and colleges. A later campaign by ASTA from the First World War onwards was to oppose the saving of seed by farmers.

Shortly after the First World War, the US Secretary of Agriculture decided that the USDA would henceforth support research aimed at the development of hybrids and ending farmer participation in breeding programmes. The Secretary's son, Henry A. Wallace, was sent by his father on a tour of experimental stations and recommended his father appoint a devotee of hybrids as head of research. Henry subsequently founded the Pioneer Hi-Bred Seed Company and was himself appointed Secretary of Agriculture in 1932 (Lewontin, 1993, pp55–56).

The implications of the emergence of corn hybrids for private-sector breeding cannot be underestimated. Several of the world's major 20th-century seed companies first came to prominence through their successful breeding of hybrid corn varieties. Many of these old seed companies are now owned by companies like Monsanto, Syngenta, Dupont and Delta & Pine Land, which was itself bought by Monsanto in 2006. According to Jack Kloppenburg (1988), 'hybridization is … a mechanism for circumventing the biological barrier that the seed had presented to the penetration of plant breeding and seed production by private enterprise'. This was well understood by some of the pioneering scientists involved in the development of hybrid corn, who realized that the absence of genetic stability in the harvested seed gave them a kind of virtual IP protection which they could back up by using trade secrecy law. Indeed, the determination of companies to prevent unauthorized access to their inbred parent lines could be very intense. Unfortunately for breeders (and presumably for farmers), though, hybridization does not work for some of the most economically important crops such as wheat. Clearly, this presents problems for breeders. Plants are self-reproducing. With no law to prevent it, there is nothing to stop farmers from replanting harvested seed, or even multiplying seed and selling it in competition with the breeder (assuming this would be more profitable for them than selling harvested produce). This is where IP rights come in.

As opposed to the US situation of expansion by settlers into new land for cultivation, albeit into land often taken from the indigenous peoples, virtually all the cultivable land in 19th century Europe had been farmed for a very long time. Most of the major European crops whose origins were exotic, like wheat, rye, maize, potatoes and tomatoes, had become well-established and integrated into local farming systems for centuries or even millennia. Although some crops were vulnerable to devastating diseases due to widespread genetic uniformity (most notoriously potatoes), European farmers developed a huge range of varieties over the centuries to suit local conditions. European governments generally did not find it necessary to encourage farmers to breed new varieties themselves as in the US case.

Agricultural intensification took place under different circumstances and with different aims. In Europe, land was in short supply but labour was plentiful, rather than the other way round as was the case in the US. Farms tended to be smaller and did not lend themselves so easily to mechanization. Attempts to increase productivity came through other techniques to grow more food on existing land.

Introducing new species and formal experimental breeding were carried out first by wealthy landowners, and from the second half of the 19th century by small family seed firms. These firms descended from farmers that made it their main business to provide seed for other farmers and who then started breeding programmes to better meet the requirements of their customers. As in the US, in the early 20th century public research institutions and universities were also carrying out breeding work, which benefited the emerging private plant breeding sector. By the time of the Second World War, Germany, the US, The Netherlands, Sweden and the Soviet Union were the leading plant breeding nations for field crops. In countries like Britain and France, government-supported research during the first half of the century was often directed to tropical agriculture rather than temperate-zone crops. This was

to develop and improve the production of certain crops in the colonies. Both countries reoriented their breeding efforts as these colonies became independent, and France subsequently developed the world's second largest private seed sector. Britain, though, had few seed firms until the 1960s, and most breeding, especially of major crops like wheat, was left to the public sector. This situation has changed, but the seed sector is still much smaller than that of France – the birthplace of the UPOV Convention.

From the 1960s, the use of modern high yielding varieties of major food crops like rice and wheat became increasingly common in developing countries, particularly in Asia and Latin America. Nonetheless, the extent of private sector involvement in breeding for developing country farmers was quite modest during that era. Since then, though, US and European plant breeding companies have become much more active in the developing world. This is happening at a time when public sector agricultural research investments targeted at the needs of developing country farmers, especially those with few resources, are considered by many to fall well short of what is needed.

As already mentioned, several economically valuable crops do not lend themselves to hybridization. For these, breeders needed to find other means to control the use and production of their varieties. This is where lack of IP protection became an issue several decades ago, leading to the development of an international regime designed specifically to protect plant varieties whose seeds could otherwise be easily saved, replanted and sold, namely the UPOV Convention. Before looking into the particular solution devised, Table 2.1 places the discussion in context by presenting the legal and technological problems and solutions faced by companies seeking to capture the rewards from their investments in plant improvement according to how the plants normally reproduce (Dutfield, 2007).

Table 2.1 *Appropriating plant breeding innovations: Legal and technological problems and solutions*

	Self-pollinators	Cross-pollinators	Asexual reproducers
Examples	Wheat, rice, sorghum	Maize, millet, pulses	Fruit trees, potatoes
Key features	Breed true	Do not breed true	Can be rapidly reproduced
Obstacle to appropriation	Harvested seed can be replanted	Deleterious effects of inbreeding	Easy to copy
Legal solution	PVP, contracts/licences	Trade secrecy, contracts/licences	PVP, contracts/licences
Continuing obstacles to appropriation	• Farmers' privilege • Research exemption • Difficult to enforce rights		• Farmers' privilege • Research exemption • Difficult to enforce rights
Technological solution	Terminator technology (under development)	Hybrids	

The UPOV Convention

The form of plant variety protection (PVP) under UPOV, otherwise known as plant breeders' rights (PBRs), is commonly described as a 'patent-like' regime. In fact, this is not quite accurate, as an understanding of the background to the UPOV Convention should clarify. Admittedly, though, the increasing strength of the PVP right of recent years is beginning to approximate that of the patent.

The UPOV Convention was adopted in Paris in 1961 and entered into force in 1968 once it had been ratified by three countries – The Netherlands, the UK and West Germany. It was revised slightly in 1972 and more substantially in 1978 and 1991. The 1978 Act entered into force in 1981, the 1991 Act in 1998. All members, with the exception of Belgium, are parties either to the 1978 or the 1991 Acts. New members are required to accept UPOV 1991, although exceptions allowing membership on the basis of the 1978 Act have been made.

The Convention established an organization called the Union Internationale pour la Protection des Obtentions Végétales (UPOV). The official English translation is International Union for the Protection of New Varieties of Plants. UPOV has a close association with the World Intellectual Property Organization (WIPO – see Chapter 4) to the extent that the latter organization's director general is also secretary general of UPOV. As of April 2006, the Union had 60 member states plus the European Community. Unlike WIPO, UPOV is a lean organization with a small office in Geneva. The supreme decision-making body is the Council, which consists of representatives of each member and has one ordinary session a year.

The existence of UPOV can be attributed largely to two international organizations. One is the Association Internationale pour la Protection de la Propriété Industrielle (International Association for the Protection of Intellectual Property) (AIPPI), which was founded in 1897 and consists of activist legal practitioners, patent attorneys, trademark agents, scientists, engineers and corporations. The other is the Association Internationale des Selectionneurs pour la Protection des Obtentions Végétales (International Association of Plant Breeders) (ASSINSEL).

At the 1952 AIPPI Congress, the delegates, partly at the urging of ASSINSEL, discussed the issue of plant varieties. There was general agreement that plant varieties should be protected in some way. The most concrete ideas came from the German AIPPI group, which submitted a detailed technical report arguing that both patents and an alternative system should be available to breeders. As the authors, Franz and Freda Wuesthoff, explained, it is a normal requirement of patentability that other people skilled in the art should be able to reproduce the invention described in the specification (Wuesthoff and Wuesthoff, 1952). That is to say, following the instructions provided in the specification should result in the invention as claimed. But, as they explained, when it comes to plant breeding, being able reliably to reproduce the new variety from the beginning is difficult because it depends on natural processes over which breeders do not have total control and which are to some extent random. However, repeating the whole breeding process is not necessarily important or even necessary. What really matters is that the new plant that has been brought into existence can be directly propagated. For sexually reproducing plants, this means that they must breed true so that the offspring are identical to their parents.

As the two authors saw it, the solutions were to change the patent system by taking a permissive view of the reproducibility requirement and to extend the range of patentable subject matter in those countries where plants were not considered to constitute inventions, and to develop a new or modified IP system for the more incremental plant breeding-derived innovations. They considered that patents in their present form would accommodate a certain amount of innovation in plant breeding and should be made available to breeders, but that for many new varieties, workable IP protection would require a relaxation of the novelty and inventive step requirements so that varieties reflecting incremental improvements

on existing ones and that were already known about could nonetheless be protected.

The AIPPI Congress could not reach a consensus on the means of protection, and a 1954 Congress also failed to do so. One of the main reasons was that some of the patent lawyer members of the AIPPI opposed the patenting of plant varieties on the grounds that doing so would stretch basic patent law concepts like inventiveness to the point of undermining the credibility of the patent system (see Chapter 3).

In the event, ASSINSEL's members decided at their own Congress in 1956 to abandon the patent route and to call for an international conference to consider the possibility of developing a new international instrument for protecting plant varieties. ASSINSEL requested the French government to organize what became the International Conference for the Protection of New Varieties of Plants. The Conference, which convened in May 1957 in Paris, established the basic principles of PBRs that were later incorporated into the UPOV Convention. Only European governments were invited to participate or attend as observers. A Committee of Experts was set up to:

- study the legal problems arising out of the protection of the breeder's right as defined by the Conference;
- give as precise formulations as might be appropriate of the basic technical and economic principles laid down by the Conference; and
- prepare the first draft of an international convention for submission to a later session of the Conference itself.

The Committee met twice before appointing a Drafting Group to develop a legal text. One of the important issues the Committee had to decide upon was whether the convention would be incorporated into the general framework of the Paris Convention, which dealt with industrial property, primarily patents, or whether a separate convention was necessary. It decided in favour of the latter, but recommended that the new office administering the convention should work closely with the Bureaux Internationaux Réunis de la Protection de la Propriété Intellectuelle (BIRPI – see Chapter 4), the forerunner to WIPO.

The second meeting of the International Conference for the Protection of New Varieties of Plants took place in November 1961, with 12 European countries invited along with BIRPI (now WIPO), the FAO, the European Economic Community, the Organisation for Economic Co-operation and Development (OECD), the AIPPI, ASSINSEL and two other business associations: the Communauté Internationale des Obtenteurs de Plantes Ornementales et Frutières de Reproduction Asexuée (CIOPORA) and the Fédération Internationale du Commerce des Semences (FIS). Since then, ASSINSEL, the FIS and the new International Seed Federation (ISF), along with CIOPORA and the International Chamber of Commerce, have played key roles in shaping the evolution of the UPOV Convention through its various revisions. UPOV was created and shaped by plant breeders for plant breeders and they have a strong sense of ownership of the Convention. Public interest organizations have had minimal involvement. The UPOV office is an active proselytizer of plant variety protection around the world and strongly defends the Convention from those who question its value to developing countries or its continued relevance in the age of biotechnology.

Just as the UPOV Convention was being adopted, the Council of Europe was actively working to promote the harmonization of patent rules, procedures and principles among the Western European countries. One key result of this was the signing of the 1963 Convention on the Unification of Certain Points of Substantive Law on Patents for Invention. The Convention had to accommodate wide differences in national patent rules relating to pharmaceuticals, food, agriculture and horticulture while encouraging states to harmonize their rules within a realistic timeframe at the level of the most expansive rights available at that time in any one country. Accordingly, parties were not required to grant patents in respect of '(b) plant or animal varieties or essentially biological processes for the production of plants or animals'.

The terms 'essentially biological' replaced 'purely biological' from an earlier version of the text. The Council's Committee of Experts on Patents, which was responsible for drafting the convention, changed the wording to broaden the exclusionary language to embrace such 'essentially biological' processes as varietal selection and hybridization methods even if 'technical' devices were utilized to carry out the breeding processes. The Convention's text reflects, as of course does UPOV, the decision in Europe made in the late 1950s to keep plant breeding out of the patent system. There is much similarity between the wording of the Convention and that of the European Patent Convention and the TRIPS Agreement (Chapter 3).

The Convention's Provisions and Issues Arising

Compared to some other important international agreements on intellectual property, such as TRIPS and the Paris Convention for the Protection of Industrial Property, the UPOV Convention's provisions are extremely detailed and specific. They deal with the plant varieties covered, the requirements for protection, the length of the protection term, the scope of protection, breeders' exemption, farmers' privilege, and whether or not both patents and PVP can be held on the same variety. They have been subject to several revisions since 1961. In order to join the Union, countries are supposed to have PVP regimes already in place, and these are normally scrutinized by UPOV to see that they are in harmony with the Convention's provisions.

The most substantial revisions took place in 1978 and 1991; these are discussed and compared below. Note, however, that the French word *obtention* in the name of the Union and the Convention is significant since it indicates that rights can be acquired not just by those who breed new varieties in the classic sense of creating new varieties by crossing and selecting sexually reproducing plants, but also by those who improve plants based on the discovery and selection of mutants or variants found in a population of cultivated plants. Thus UPOV 1991 clarifies that a breeder is a person 'who bred, or discovered and developed, a variety'. This is consistent with the original intent of the Convention to protect varieties that may not entirely be attributable to the application of scientific breeding. At the same time, however, it represents a divergence from patent law, which professes not to allow mere discoveries to be protected. Table 2.2 compares the key provisions of UPOV 1978 and 1991 and patent law.

What qualifies for protection?

To be eligible for protection under the UPOV system, plant varieties must be new, distinct, stable and uniform:

- To be new, the variety needs to be so not necessarily in the absolute sense, but not to have been offered for sale or marketed, with the agreement of the breeder or his successor in title, in the source country, or for longer than a limited number of years in any other country.

- To be distinct, the variety must be distinguishable by one or more characteristics from any other variety whose existence is a matter of common knowledge anywhere in the world, implicitly including among traditional farming communities. Compared to UPOV 1978, the requirement in the most recent version has been relaxed somewhat. It does this by dropping the phrase 'by one or more important characteristics' after the word 'distinguishable'.

- To be considered as stable, the variety must remain true to its description after repeated reproduction or propagation. In other words it must have a certain level of uniformity which avoids the change of the variety through genetic drift.

The uniformity requirement also shows the specific nature of the UPOV system, since this requirement cannot practically be the same for species with different ways of reproduction; self-fertilizing species can be much more uniform than cross-fertilizing crops. Therefore the uniformity requirement is made relative instead, in other words a new variety should be uniform when compared to the varieties of the same species. This means that when plant breeding techniques were refined, the uniformity requirement gradually increased, making it beyond the reach of farmer-breeders who may select in landraces, which are not genetically uniform, to develop new varieties. Unlike patents, there is no disclosure requirement. Instead, applicants are required to submit evidence that the variety meets the protection requirements (in the US, for example) or to submit the plant material for which protection is sought to the responsible governmental authority for testing to ensure that the above eligibility requirements have been met.

While it is logical to require that protected varieties are genetically uniform, there are dangers with widespread planting of crop varieties that are genetically similar to each

Table 2.2 *Comparison of main provisions of UPOV 1978/1991 and patent law*

Provisions	UPOV 1978	UPOV 1991	Patent law under TRIPS
Protection coverage	Plant varieties of nationally defined species	Plant varieties of all genera and species	Inventions
Requirements	Commercial novelty Distinctness Homogeneity Stability Variety denomination	Commercial novelty Distinctness Uniformity Stability Variety denomination	Novelty Inventive step (or non-obviousness) Industrial application Enabling disclosure
Protection term	Min 15 years from issue (Min 18 years for vines and trees)	Min 20 years from issue (Min 25 years for vines and trees)	Min 20 years from filing
Protection scope	Minimum scope: producing for purposes of commercial marketing; offering for sale and marketing of propagating material of the variety	Minimum scope: producing, conditioning, offering for sale, selling or other marketing, exporting, importing or stocking for purposes of propagating material of the variety. Plus, some acts in relation to harvested material if obtained through an unauthorized use of propagating material and if the breeder has had no reasonable opportunity to exercise his right in relation to the propagating material	In respect of the product: making, using, offering for sale, selling or importing In respect of a process: using the process; doing any of the above-mentioned acts in respect of a product obtained directly by means of the process
Breeders' exemption	Yes	Yes. Plus, essentially derived varieties cannot be exploited in certain circumstances without permission of holder of rights in the protected initial variety	Up to national laws; but likely to be limited to scientific and/or experimental use
Farmers' privilege	In practice: yes	Up to national laws	Up to national laws[a]
Prohibition of double protection	Any species eligible for PBR cannot be patented	No	Up to national laws

Note: [a] Article 11 of the EU biotechnology inventions directive provides for farmers' privilege under patent law.
Source: Based upon a table in van Wijk et al (1993)

other. Kloppenburg (1988, p93) provides a good illustration of what can go wrong when there is 'genetic vulnerability accompanying dependence on a narrow base of germplasm'. In 1970, '15 per cent of the corn crop in that year was lost to an epidemic of southern corn leaf blight. Corn prices rose 20 per cent, and losses to consumers and farmers totalled some US$2 billion.'

What is a 'plant variety', and how may it be distinguished, for the purposes of IP protection, from a 'plant'? This is very important given the increased application of genetic engineering to crop research and the fact that in some jurisdictions, plants are patentable but plant varieties are not. The original 1961 version of the UPOV Convention defined 'plant variety' as including 'any cultivar, clone, line, stock or hybrid which is capable of cultivation'. The 1991 revision contains a more detailed definition, according to which a plant variety is:

> *a plant grouping within a single botanical taxon of the lowest known rank, which grouping, irrespective of whether the conditions for the grant of a breeder's right are fully met, can be:*
>
> - *defined by the expression of the characteristics resulting from a given genotype or combination of genotypes;*
> - *distinguished from any other plant grouping by the expression of at least one of the said characteristics; and*
> - *considered as a unit with regard to its suitability for being propagated unchanged.*

Scope of protection

UPOV 1978, which several countries are still contracting parties to, defines the scope of protection as the breeder's right to authorize the following acts: 'the production for purposes of commercial marketing; the offering for sale;

and the marketing of the reproductive or vegetative propagating material, as such, of the variety'. The 1991 version extends the scope of the breeders' rights in two ways. First, it increases the number of acts for which prior authorization of the breeder is required. These include 'production or reproduction; conditioning for the purpose of propagation; offering for sale; selling or other marketing; exporting; importing; and stocking for the above purposes'. Second, such acts do not just concern the reproductive or vegetative propagating material, but also encompass harvested material obtained through the illegitimate use of propagating material and so-called essentially derived varieties.

Breeders' exemption

However, the right of breeders both to use protected varieties as an initial source of variation for the creation of new varieties and to market the resulting varieties without authorization from the original breeder (the 'breeders' exemption') is upheld in both versions. This represents a major difference with patent law, which normally has a very narrow research exemption. Many plant breeders are concerned about the effects of patents on free access to plant genetic resources, including varieties bred by others. One difference between UPOV 1978 and UPOV 1991 is that the latter extends rights to varieties which are essentially derived from the protected variety. So the breeder of PVP-protected variety A has the right to demand that the breeder of variety B secure his or her authorization to commercialize B if it was essentially derived from A. The main idea here is that breeders should not be able to acquire protection too easily for minor modifications of extant varieties produced perhaps through cosmetic breeding or genetic engineering, or free-ride without doing any breeding of their own, problems that the increased application of biotechnology in this field appeared likely to exacerbate.

PVP *and patents*

Beyond resolving these particular issues, but related to them, the provision on the scope of protection was also intended to ensure that patent rights and PVP rights operate in a harmonious fashion in jurisdictions where plants and their parts and genes are patentable and access to these could be blocked by patent holders. Such a practice would undermine one of the main justifications for PVP protection, which is that breeders should be able to secure returns on their investments but without preventing competitors from being able freely to access breeding material. An example here might be useful. Consider the case of a PVP-protected variety, variety A, and a patented genetic element owned by another company (Jördens, 2002, p6). The owner of a patent on this genetic element is free to use A to produce his or her variety B and, in the absence of the essential derivation provision, place B on the market with no obligations to the owner of A, despite the fact that B differs from A only in the addition of the patented genetic element. However, the owner of A would need a licence from the producer of B to use the patented genetic element in the breeding of further varieties. In such a situation, then, patents can have the effect of blocking the breeders' exemption that PVP rights normally provide. The PVP-issuing office, however, will not itself determine whether a variety is essentially derived from an earlier one. This will be left to the courts. So far, only one court, in The Netherlands, has been called upon to make such a determination and it found in favour of the defendant (Fikkert, 2005). According to the court, the general rule is that distinguishable varieties are normally independent, the essentially derived variety (EDV) provision being an

exception to this rule that ought to be construed narrowly. Given that one of the two varieties at issue differed in several ways in shape and form from the variety from which they were allegedly essentially derived, the exception was not applicable. As for the other variety, no convincing case had in any case been made that it was an EDV, besides which the Community Plant Variety Office made no mention of its similarity to the already registered original variety or found any grounds to investigate such a possibility.

In the EU, the 1998 EC Directive on the Legal Protection of Biotechnological Inventions seeks to make PVP and patents operate more harmoniously by providing that where the acquisition or exploitation of a PVP right is impossible without infringing a patent, or vice versa, a compulsory licence may be applied for to allow for its use. If issued, the licensor party will be entitled to cross-license the licensee's patent or PVP right. Subsequent legislation in Germany and France restore the breeder's exemption in that it explicitly allows breeders to use genetic materials that include patented components for further breeding. When the new variety contains the patented component, however, consent has to be sought for the marketing of that new variety; when the patented component is 'bred out' of the material, the patent holder has no rights on the new variety.

Farmers' privilege

There is no reference in the 1978 version to the right of farmers to re-sow seed harvested from protected varieties for their own use (often referred to as 'farmers' privilege'). The Convention establishes minimum standards such that the breeder's prior authorization is required for at least the three acts mentioned above, namely the production for purposes of commercial marketing; the offering for sale;

and the marketing of the reproductive or vegetative propagating material, as such, of the variety. Thus, countries that are members of the 1978 Convention are free to either uphold farmers' privilege or eliminate it. All UPOV member countries implemented the exemption for 'private and non-commercial use' under the UPOV Act of 1978 to include the re-sowing and in some cases the local exchange or sales of seed. However, this was not the case for ornamental crops in The Netherlands, where a stronger protection was deemed necessary. In the US this was interpreted very liberally, so that in practice sales of farm-saved seed were allowed provided that they contributed less than 50 per cent of total farm income. This resulted in large quantities of seed being 'brown bagged' to the detriment of the commercial interests of the breeder.

The 1991 version is more specific. Whereas the scope of the breeder's right includes production or reproduction and conditioning for the purpose of propagation (Article 14), governments can use their discretion in deciding whether to uphold the farmers' privilege which includes only the use of saved seed on the same farm (and thus excludes any type of exchange or sale of such seed). According to Article 15, the breeder's right in relation to a variety may be restricted 'in order to permit farmers to use for propagating purposes, on their own holdings, the product of the harvest which they have obtained by planting … the protected variety'. Even though the Act states that the legitimate interest of the breeder explicitly has to be taken into account, the seed industry generally dislikes farmers' privilege. The EC Regulation 2100/94 on Community Plant Variety Rights, which was adopted in 1994, restricts farmers' privilege to certain crops, and breeders must be remunerated through the payment of royalties unless the users of the farmers' privilege are small farmers, in which case they are exempted. Interestingly, the European Community's patent rules also require that farmers' privilege be provided and

defined under the same terms as the above regulation. The US's PVP rules are less strict in this regard: seed saving must be restricted to the amount necessary for on-farm replanting, but it is not clear how the legitimate interests of the breeder are implemented since royalty payments on farm-saved seed are not required.

Length of protection and double protection

UPOV 1991 extends protection from at least 15 years to a minimum of 20 years. This later version is silent on the matter of double (that is, both patent and PVP) protection, whereas the 1978 version prohibited such double protection on the same variety. Allowing double protection without any restriction was to ensure the intellectual property practices of the US and Japan, which allowed such double protection, would be fully compliant with UPOV. Nonetheless, most countries, including all European countries, expressly forbid the patenting of plant varieties. In 1995, in *Greenpeace v. Plant Genetic Systems NV*, the European Patent Office's (EPO) Technical Board of Appeal ruled on an appeal against the upholding of a plant-related patent. The board determined that a patent claim for plant cells contained in a plant is unpatentable since it does not exclude plant varieties from its scope. This implied that transgenic plants per se were unpatentable because of the plant variety exclusion. Consequently, for the next four years, the EPO stopped accepting claims on plants per se. However, in December 1999, the EPO Enlarged Board of Appeal decided in *Novartis* that, while genetically modified plant varieties are unpatentable, 'a claim wherein specific plant varieties are not individually claimed is not excluded from patentability under Article 53(b), EPC, even though it may embrace plant varieties'. This reopened the door to the patenting of plants as long as the claims in the patent specification do not refer to individual varieties.

UPOV

Changing membership

Until the late 1990s, the overwhelming majority of UPOV members were developed countries, reflecting the fact that in many developing countries, especially in Africa, private sector involvement in plant breeding and seed supply is quite limited. Moreover, in many of these countries small-scale farming communities are responsible for much of the plant breeding and seed distribution, as they have been for centuries. Consequently, until recently there would have been few domestic beneficiaries of a PVP system in these developing countries apart from the public institutes for agricultural research.

However, many developing countries are now joining UPOV. In many, if not most, cases, this is not because of any strong domestic demand for PVP, but because of their obligations under Article 27.3(b) of TRIPS (see Chapter 3) or trade agreements (see Chapter 7). The UPOV system is the only *sui generis* system for plant varieties that exists in international law and is currently being actively promoted worldwide by the organization itself, as well as by the US and the EU though bilateral free trade agreements that tend to require developing country parties to join UPOV. However, developing country WTO Members that prefer not to allow plant varieties to be patented do not need to join UPOV. In principle they can devise their own system without reference to UPOV's standards. Alternatively, they could simply use one of the UPOV Acts as a model but opt not to join the organization, an approach that many Asian countries currently follow, choosing to use the 1978 version of UPOV as a model, mainly because of the greater freedom to formulate farmers' privilege.

PVP versus patents

Despite the increasing membership of UPOV, the question arises of why breeders still tend to prefer PVP to patents, and also of whether this particular intellectual property right has a future. After all, patents provide much stronger legal protection (Table 2.2). Moreover, breeders nowadays tend to work not for small independent seed firms, but for large life science corporations that invest huge amounts of money in biotechnological research and hold massive patent portfolios. Probably the main reasons for this preference for PVP is the breeders' exemption, which allows them such broad access to breeding material, and their concerns that the patenting of biotechnological research tools may jeopardize this access. Breeders, especially those in smaller companies, also fear the complexity of rights in the patent system, compared to the simple 'one variety, one right' system of PVP, leading to complex legal battles for which they fear they do not have the financial or legal resources. This suggests that as long as there is profit-motivated plant breeding, PVP rights will continue to exist alongside patents, and sometimes in tension with them.

Critical Concerns

Concern has been raised that the UPOV system was drawn up mainly by European countries, and is designed to accommodate the specific characteristics of the capital-intensive large-scale commercial agricultural systems that generally prevail on that continent. As a result, it is often argued, the system is unsuitable for most developing countries. Among such critics, the current system of IPRs protection for plants has raised concerns over their impact on food security in three areas: (i) PVP and research priorities; (ii) the interests of poor farmers; and (iii) the availability of genetic resources for further breeding. Note, however, that, while a few studies have been carried out on the impacts of PVP in developing countries (see below), the overall effects of plant intellectual property in developing countries are difficult to discern conclusively and researchers find themselves having to rely to too great an extent on the experiences of developed countries.

PVP and research priorities

Does the UPOV Convention encourage breeders to investigate minor crops and to bring whole new species into cultivation? Empirical evidence casts doubt on whether PVP (as well as patents) does much to encourage investment in plant breeding except in just a few commercially important crop species such as wheat and soya bean and ornamentals, although UPOV's own studies are, perhaps unsurprisingly, much more positive about the overall impacts of PVP (UPOV, 2005a). Critics also argue that even if breeders did turn to neglected crops, many of the small farmers that grow them would not be better off if their freedom to use saved seed as they wished were diminished. In most developing countries a very large proportion of the farming population consists of smallholders, and for these people saving, selling and exchanging seed is common practice and essential for their survival.

Many smallholder farmers cultivate minor food crops that enable them to meet the nutritional needs of rural and urban communities much better than if major crops such as wheat, rice and maize alone were cultivated. In many parts of the world, farmers may grow more than 100 crop species and cultivated varieties. However, PVP does not encourage breeding related to minor crops with small markets. This

is because the likelihood of good returns on breeders' research investment is small even with the legal protection provided by PVP. Rather, it encourages breeding targeted at major crops with significant commercial potential. Moreover, protected varieties of plants may not even be food crops. In Kenya, for example, from 1997 to 2003, out of a total of 611 PVP applications, 247 were for foreign-bred roses. This is not necessarily a bad thing, since such exports of cut flowers are a good source of foreign exchange, but some argue that the production methods used damage the environment and the health of the growers (War on Want, 2007).

It is conceivable, then, that PVP may contribute to a trend whereby traditional diverse agro-ecosystems, containing a wide range of traditional crop varieties, are replaced with monocultures of single agrochemical-dependent varieties, with the result that the range of nutritious foods available in local markets becomes narrower. Admittedly this trend is a global phenomenon whose beginning predates the introduction of PVP systems; nevertheless, it is one that the existence and increasingly widespread use of PVP may indirectly encourage.

PVP and smallholder farmers

In most developing countries a large proportion of the population depends on agriculture for employment and income. Many of these farmers are smallholders for whom the saving and across-the-fence and inter-community exchanging of seed are common practices. This is especially the case in countries and regions where neither the public nor private sectors play a significant role in breeding, producing or distributing seed. Although the UPOV system may allow on-farm replanting, its rules restrict farmers' freedom to buy seed from sources other than the original breeders or their licensees.

Seed companies argue in response that farmers do not have to purchase PVP-protected seed just because it is available. They point out that the farmers are free to continue cultivating seed that is not plant variety protected, including traditional local varieties, if they so wish, and that therefore their basic freedoms are unaffected by PVP. While this is likely to be true, traditional varieties are often disparaged and are likely to be excluded from government-approved seed lists that some countries maintain under their seed regulations. While finding non-PVP seed may not yet be a serious difficulty for developing country farmers, this situation may change. In some developed countries, it is becoming difficult for farmers to find non-PVP varieties of some crops.

Seed laws

PVP is not the only issue, as seed laws may sometimes unduly limit the choice of varieties that farmers are allowed to bring into commercial production. Seed regulations were introduced for very good reasons. From the late 19th century a number of European governments became alarmed about the unregulated nature of the seed trade and the extent to which poor quality seed got onto the market. This situation was problematic for farmers, legitimate breeders and governments, which had become concerned about the need to increase agricultural productivity. In the early decades of the 20th century, many governments responded first by establishing seed testing stations, and then by certifying seed. The latter also provided to a certain limited extent a kind of IP protection for breeders, and as such was a kind of barrier to market entry. Indeed, UPOV largely grew out of such seed certification regimes. In many developing countries, governments concerned about rural poverty and convinced, even if mistakenly, that

traditional agriculture is unproductive support farmers in rural credit schemes by promoting particular crops and types of seed, such as hybrids, which tend to require expensive inputs and may not be suitable for the local agronomic conditions (see also Chapter 8, Box 8.9). Furthermore, seed aid is often used by providers as a way to promote the use of modern varieties that may not necessarily be the most appropriate ones to plant. As Sperling et al (2006) explain:

> *while formal sector varieties are referred to as 'improved' and the quality of the seed is certified, these varieties often yield poorly in many smallholder cropping systems. Such new varieties may not be adapted to the local agro-ecological conditions and farmers may not possess the management inputs (for example fertilizers and pesticides) crucial for their growth.*

Seed saving, however, is not always a cost-effective option for farmers since saved seed deteriorates over generations. Moreover, seed is one among several agricultural inputs that farmers may have to pay for. Even poor farmers may decide to pay a higher price for better quality seed if they expect a bigger harvest to result.

IPRs and genetic resources for breeding

Plant breeders and other supporters of UPOV tend to stress the necessity of being able to freely access genetic material, including that which is IPR protected. This is why the UPOV Convention contains such a broad breeders' exemption. Patent law tends to have a much narrower research exemption, which is often limited to non-commercial scientific or experimental use. Moreover, while a protected plant variety is covered by a single title, plant-related biotechnological inventions are likely to be protected by a patent, in some cases by several patents. These patents may cover not just plants, but also seeds, genes and DNA sequences. The effect of patents is to restrict access to the patented 'products'. It has been argued that 'locking up' genetic resources with patents is a bad thing because innovation in plant breeding is cumulative and depends on being able to use as wide a stock of material as possible. This is a plausible concern and one that many plant breeders share with public interest NGOs such as GRAIN. It was to deal with this concern that the FAO International Treaty introduced a number of provisions; these are discussed in Chapter 6.

However, the restrictions on access to breeding material may have other causes than IPRs. For one thing, some countries have chosen to exclude certain categories of plant genetic resources they consider to be strategically important from the multilateral system set up under the International Treaty. Furthermore, some developing countries have been exercising their rights under the Convention on Biological Diversity (CBD – see Chapter 5) to regulate access to their genetic resources in ways that unduly restrict their movement. This may well be detrimental to long-term food security even in their own countries.

Research, development and ownership

Beyond these issues about how specific intellectual property rights privatize genetic material needed for breeding is the association of IPRs generally with the shrinkage of non-proprietarian public sector research, and the increased concentration of ownership of breeding material, research tools and technologies in the hands of a small number of giant corporations. While IPRs are not directly responsible for this shrinkage of public sector research, they do appear to contribute to this concentration effect. For one thing, the expense of acquiring large IPRs portfolios can operate as a barrier to market entry. For another, the advantages of owning lots of patents and PVP titles are such that large firms have an incentive to buy up or merge with rival companies that also own such rights (see also Chapter 8).

Are these trends a bad thing? One consequence is a reduction in the free circulation of breeding material. This may lead to a reduced level of welfare-enhancing breeding activity, especially if rights are asserted against the public sector. In addition, they may make public policymaking aimed at enhancing food security harder to put into practice. This is because it is much more difficult for governments to influence companies than the public institutions they partly or wholly fund. Cash-strapped governments, however, may have to reduce their research expenditures out of necessity, and the private sector can and sometimes does play a useful role in taking up the slack.

Empirical Evidence

This discussion on how PVP affects food security and nutrition in developing countries leads one to consider in more general terms the applicability of such an IPR to these countries. Unfortunately, few comparative empirical studies exist, but one such was conducted by UPOV (2005a). It covered five countries experiencing highly varied levels of development (Argentina, China, Kenya, Poland and South Korea) and argued that PVP brought economic benefits.

Two other studies were published in 1994

UPOV

by the Inter-American Institute for Cooperation in Agriculture and the University of Amsterdam (Jaffé and van Wijk, 1995), and in 2005 for the World Bank by various researchers (Louwaars et al, 2005).

Taking the 1994 study first, the research aimed to examine the expected impact of PVP on developing countries in the areas of 'private investment in plant breeding, breeding policies of public institutes, transfer of foreign germplasm and diffusion of seed among farmers'.

Five countries were used as case studies, of which three (Argentina, Chile and Uruguay) had PVP systems already in place and two (Colombia and Mexico) were about to introduce them. These countries are similar in the sense that each has basically two seed markets. The hybrid seed market is controlled by transnational corporations, whereas the seed market for self-pollinating varieties is dominated by domestic firms.

However, Argentina differs from the others in that it is the only country in which owners of PVP rights have successfully enforced their rights to the extent that their control over seed supply for wheat and soya is comparable to that of their counterparts in the US. This leads the authors of the study report to conclude that, in all probability, PVP in that country has 'prevented the local wheat companies from reducing or even terminating their breeding activities and triggered the reactivation of some soya bean breeding programmes'.

For exotic genetic resources, there is little evidence to show that PVP has led to any significantly improved access for domestic seed companies to modern cultivars, special genetic stocks and genomic material from abroad. Moreover, companies with licences from overseas breeders to use proprietary varieties may sometimes have to contend with restrictions on where they can export to. For example, in 1994 Argentinean strawberry plant growers were prevented from exporting their plantlets

to Europe because the US breeder and the European licensees did not want these plantlets to compete with those that were already produced in Europe.

In Argentina and Chile, public agricultural research centres are using PVP to secure income and collaborate with companies. According to the report, this is shifting the orientation of public research and reduces the public availability of their genetic resources.

How are farmers affected? First, Argentinean seed dealers must now pay royalties and taxes on the seed they trade. So far these costs have not been passed on to the farmers. Second, PVP legislation in the three countries where it is well established has not prevented the replanting of farm-saved seed. Third, as the report indicates, 'since many modern plant varieties are not appropriate for resource-poor farmers, PBRs predominantly favour plant breeding for those farmers who operate under relatively prosperous conditions'.

The study for the World Bank covered China, Colombia, India, Kenya and one country that still does not have a PVP regime, Uganda. Among the study's numerous findings is that the availability of PVP is not an absolute prerequisite for the existence of a thriving plant breeding sector. India had quite a large number of private plant breeding firms many years before PVP legislation was passed. Rather cautiously, among the report authors' findings are that 'the ease of implementing PVP seems to be overestimated. In all cases, the effectiveness of PVP is still being tested and refined, and the cases illustrate that establishing a PVP law and putting it into practice are two separate challenges.'

Moreover, as the authors conclude:

not only do IPRs in plant breeding have to be seen in the context of a wider range of agricultural policies, but IPR regimes themselves must be carefully tailored to specific situations. It is important that countries recognize that they have choices in designing legislation consistent with the TRIPS Agreement and that there are still opportunities for debating and interpreting the Agreement itself. The UPOV Conventions offer some important advantages for fulfilling the requirements for a sui generis *system but they do not exhaust the possibilities.*

Emerging Issues – Harmonization

The big emerging issue is harmonization. UPOV and the associations representing the plant breeders are very keen to see a situation in which PVP is not only available throughout the world but follows the same standards of protection. At present, many countries are still parties to the 1978 version of UPOV, and some countries (for example India) have laws that diverge from any version of UPOV. In the longer term, the associations would probably like to see more regional regimes, such as that in Europe, which has a Community Plant Variety Rights Office. The office, which was established under Council Regulation (EC) No 2100/94 of 27 July 1994, provides a single unitary right covering the whole EU. A certain amount of administrative harmonization may be a good thing for developing countries in terms of cutting the cost of managing the PVP system. But holding an incredibly diverse range of countries to the same substantive rules is inadvisable for similar reasons that harmonized patent rules tend to benefit countries that are 'leaders' and may well hold back the 'followers' (Dutfield and Suthersanen, 2005). Each country should be free to tailor IP systems to their economic conditions and in ways that promote their wider development objectives and strategies.

National Instruments

Realistic proposals for non-UPOV PVP systems have been few and far between. Most countries that do not want to join UPOV use legislation that is based on the 1978 version of the Convention. This is probably one reason why more developing countries are joining UPOV. Nonetheless, it is important to consider alternatives to UPOV so that informed decisions can be made.

To help countries devise an appropriate *sui generis* system, the International Plant Genetic Resources Institute (IPGRI – now called Bioversity International) came up with a list of key questions that decision makers should take into account:

- What kind of domestic seed industry exists?
- What kind of public breeding sector exists?
- What kind of seed supply system is in place?
- To what extent is farm-saved seed used in the country?
- What is the current capacity of breeders?
- What do local breeders want to do in the next 5–10 years?
- Are external inputs to agriculture low or high?
- What are the country's production needs and objectives?
- What is the country's biotechnology capacity?
- What are the goals and realistic expectations of the biotechnology sector?
- What kinds of strategic alliances will the country want to enter into in the next 5–10 years and how involved will other countries be?

The answers to these questions will vary widely from one country to another, which suggests

UPOV

Box 2.1 An Indian alternative?

India's Protection of Plant Varieties and Farmers' Rights Act, passed by parliament in 2001, has four main objectives:

1 To provide for the establishment of an effective system for the protection of plant varieties and the rights of farmers and plant breeders, to encourage the development of new varieties of plants.
2 To recognize and protect the rights of farmers in respect of their contribution made at any time in conserving, improving and making available plant genetic resources for the development of new plant varieties.
3 To protect plant breeders' rights, to stimulate investment for research and development, in both the public and private sectors, for the development of new plant varieties.
4 To facilitate the growth of the seed industry in the country, which will ensure the availability of high quality seeds and plant material to the farmers.

While sharing similarities with UPOV 1978, additional provisions are included to protect the interests of public sector breeding institutions and farmers. For example, the Act upholds 'the right of a farmer to save, use, exchange, share or sell his farm produce of a [protected] variety' except 'in case where the sale is for the purpose of reproduction under a commercial marketing arrangement'. It also includes provisions for farmers' varieties to be registered, with the help of governmental or non-governmental organizations. The applicant for registration of a variety must disclose information regarding the use of genetic material conserved by any tribal or rural family. Any village or local community may claim compensation for the contribution made in the evolution of a variety.

that, as with patents, one size is unlikely to fit all. A detailed discussion on all the issues involved falls outside the scope of this chapter, but it is important at least to discuss the requirements for protection and the scope of the systems.

The *sui generis* clause in TRIPS (see Chapter 3) does give governments a certain amount of freedom to tailor their PVP systems to address such concerns. Thus, while an increasing number of developing countries are joining UPOV, some countries are devising alternative PVP systems that aim in part to strengthen food security. They do this, for example, by allowing farmers to acquire protected seed from any source and/or requiring protected varieties to display qualities that are genuinely superior to existing varieties.

The Indian parliament has passed legislation that would maintain farmers' freedom to save, sell and exchange all produce of a protected variety (Box 2.1), and the African Union (formerly the Organization of African Unity) has developed a model law, for the consideration of member governments, known as the African Model Legislation for the Protection of the Rights of Local Communities, Farmers and Breeders, and for the Regulation of Access to Biological Resources. In both cases, as much emphasis is placed on the interests of farmers as on those of breeders.

The Indian Act appears to reflect a genuine attempt to implement TRIPS in a way that supports the specific socioeconomic interests of all the various producer groups in India, from private sector seed companies to public corporations and research institutions and resource-poor farmers. However, India is in the process of joining UPOV under its 1978 Act, and the 2001 legislation may need to be modified. The Indian case also shows the interaction between PVP and seed legislation, since a new seed bill seems to restrict the same farmers' right to sell seed by requiring compulsory certification.

Conclusion

It is actually very difficult for developing countries to design and implement their own systems of PVP if, as is likely, these would diverge at all from the latest version of the UPOV Convention. Intellectual property reform has always been political as much as technical, never more so than in the present day. As this book and others amply demonstrate, both the EU and the US impose various forms of 'soft' and 'hard' pressure on developing countries to introduce IP rules that they approve of. And for PVP, UPOV provides the approved standards, with no alternatives acceptable to those standards. While India may be strong enough to resist pressure from the EU, US and UPOV, it seems most other countries are too small and weak to have much room for manoeuvre.

The importance of PVP globally, and pressures to introduce the UPOV model into developing countries, stems from the extension of IP requirements into agriculture through the TRIPS Agreement in the WTO, which is the subject of the next chapter.

Resources

Apart from UPOV, other key organizations of importance in this area are the International Community of Breeders of Asexually Reproduced Ornamental and Fruit Tree Varieties (CIOPORA), GRAIN, and the International Seed Federation (ISF) (see Appendix 1).

3

Bringing Minimum Global Intellectual Property Standards into Agriculture: The Agreement on Trade-Related Aspects of Intellectual Property Rights (TRIPS)

Pedro Roffe

The biggest shift in the intellectual property (IP) regime occurred at the end of the 20th century with the introduction of IP into the international trade regime. This de facto made IP rules global and extended the reach of IP into new countries and sectors, notably agriculture. This chapter charts that history and examines the key elements of the new regime under TRIPS, which introduced the requirement for WTO Members to have plant variety protection and extend patentability to micro-organisms. It also looks at the links between TRIPS rules, genetic resources, traditional knowledge and food security.

Background and History

From a formal legal point of view, IP was until recently unrelated to the trading system. Its formal incorporation in the Uruguay Round trade negotiations in 1986 was a controversial North–South issue and also a major novelty.[1] It also coincided with the bringing of agriculture and plant and animal health (sanitary and phytosanitary regulations) into the trade regime. All of these became incorporated into the World Trade Organization (WTO), formally established as an outcome of the Uruguay Round.

The relationship between IP protection and international trade was also controversial at the birth of the modern international IP system. When the first attempt to negotiate an international understanding on the protection of patents was made in the last quarter of the 19th century it found Europe in the middle of a major controversy between patent advocates and free traders. The free traders argued that the recognition of patents in different national jurisdictions constituted trade barriers. The compromise made in those days was around the recognition that each member country of the 1883 Paris Convention for the Protection of Industrial Property (patents, trademarks, utility models, industrial designs and unfair competi-

48

tion) would have the freedom to subject the recognition of patents to the local exploitation of the invention. In other words, countries could decide that if you did not produce what was patented in the country where the patent was sought, then the patent could be revoked or be subject to use by third parties via a compulsory licence. It was then understood that trade and patent protection were not necessarily related.

The international governance of IP was further reinforced in the late 19th century with the adoption of another major instrument, the Berne Convention (1886) dealing with copyright. Unlike the Paris Convention, the US was not an active advocate for the Berne Convention, which responded more to the European continental tradition on the treatment of authors and the respect for their moral rights. It was not until 1989, during the Uruguay Trade Round negotiations, that the US joined the Berne Convention.

The international IP architecture grew in the 20th century to specific areas of IP, mainly in copyright and related rights, patents, trademarks, industrial designs and geographical indications, and agreements on the facilitation of IP protection in third countries, like the Patent Cooperation Treaty and the Madrid System for trademarks (see Chapter 4).

A major dislocation to the system occurred in the 1970s, when a number of developing countries, including newly independent countries in Africa and Asia, questioned the international system and its relevance in developing countries for the dissemination of knowledge, access to advanced technologies and control of abuses of intellectual property by right holders. The Berne Convention was amended to respond to some of those concerns by establishing methods for preferential arrangements in the translation of works. A group of developing countries initiated a revision process for the Paris Convention, to respond to their concerns, in the World Intellectual Property Organization (WIPO – see Chapter 4). However, the various diplo-

matic conferences convened for that purpose failed to achieve the objectives of the revision as proclaimed in the Declaration of Objectives of 1979.

Around that time, major changes were taking place in the US. In the mid-1970s, and more clearly during the Reagan Administration, a link was made in its Trade Act between international trade and the protection of the interests of US firms in their IP dealings in third countries. Countries that did not adequately protect intellectual property rights (IPRs) from US titleholders could be candidates for commercial sanctions. The US system of protection was later reinforced in 1982 by the creation of the US Court of Appeals for the Federal Circuit, which was supposed to bring coherence and consistency in cases dealing with IPRs.

The shortcomings of WIPO in dealing with the enforcement of IPRs and the paralysis produced in the attempt by developing countries to revise the Paris Convention, together with the active organizing by industrial groups for global IP rules, mainly related to the pharmaceutical-chemical, entertainment and software sectors, in the US, Europe and Japan offered the opportunity for the major industrialized powers to claim that the IP system should be fully integrated in the new multilateral trading system that was taking shape in the second half of the 1980s.

Another important antecedent to including IP within the WTO and in general in the pressures for patent reform was the Draft Treaty Supplementing the Paris Convention as far as Patents are Concerned. In 1983, the Director General of WIPO launched a negotiating process for a patent law treaty within an expert committee, a process that continued from 1984 to 1991. The committee gradually expanded the limited initial scope of the treaty to cover other areas of patent harmonization. This process culminated in a diplomatic conference held in The Hague by the end of 1991. It did not succeed, mainly because of the opposition of developing countries that were still sustaining their own initiative for revision of the Paris Convention. However, many of the issues opposed by developing countries in The Hague Diplomatic Conference were finally accepted in the Uruguay Round negotiations on TRIPS. This became possible because the Uruguay Round, although dealing with many different areas, was conducted on the basis that the final deal would be a single undertaking – which meant that countries had to accept all elements of the packets agreed (such as agriculture, services and textiles), even if they really only wanted some of them.

Developing countries initially resisted the initiative of including IP matters in trade negotiations, claiming that WIPO was the specialized agency of the UN and solely responsible for IP matters. The concept of the single undertaking of the Uruguay Round prevailed, however, and this meant developing countries had to agree to everything in the negotiating package. And so, finally, IP matters were fully incorporated in the newly established WTO. The Agreement on Trade-Related Aspects of Intellectual Property Rights (TRIPS) was part of the Marrakesh Final Act of 1994. TRIPS, with different modalities of application, entered into force on 1 January 1995.

The TRIPS Agreement

The negotiations towards an accord on IPRs, in the context of the Uruguay Round, were led by a core group of developed countries. This group had a dominant role not only during the negotiations of the TRIPS Agreement and in the preparatory process which concluded with the Punta del Este Ministerial Declaration adopted in December 1986, launching the process of negotiations, but also in the mid-term review initiated at Montreal two years later. From the outset, among that core group, the US clearly advocated a strong position on including IP issues in the GATT system. In fact, during the previous trade round (the Tokyo Round), the US had floated a proposal for an Anti-Counterfeiting Code, although it was not actively pursued. From the US perspective the improvement of IP should be a GATT objective because inadequate protection of IPRs in a number of countries posed serious and growing trade-related problems. The US views of the scope of the upcoming IP negotiations – not completely shared at the beginning by all developed countries, particularly those of the EC, which at that time did not have a community position on this matter – were ambitious, going beyond the mere establish-

ment of rules on anti-counterfeiting goods. The US position essentially represented the interests of a number of large corporations from a few sectors, some of whose lobbyists helped draft the initial proposals (Sell, 2003). These lobbies also mobilized industry groups in the EU and Japan to support the TRIPS proposals.

This expansive approach to IP was very much opposed by developing countries, led by Brazil and India. They believed that the protection of IPRs was a non-GATT issue and that consequently it was outside the realm of trade negotiations and therefore had no place in the deliberations of the Preparatory Committee of the Ministerial Conference. This view was reflected in the proposal submitted for the Ministerial Declaration to be adopted at Punta del Este and forwarded to the Committee by Brazil jointly with nine other developing countries (Argentina, Cuba, Egypt, India, Nicaragua, Nigeria, Peru, Tanzania and Yugoslavia),[2] where no reference to intellectual property matters was included.

From the outset of the Uruguay Round negotiations in 1986, and until early 1989, developing countries were opposed to incorporating substantive standards of IPR protection

Box 3.1 The evolution of TRIPS negotiations

The negotiations on a future arrangement on IP began in the Negotiating Group on Trade Related Aspects of Intellectual Property Rights, including Trade in Counterfeit Goods (the Negotiating Group). Its original mandate under the terms of the Punta del Este Ministerial Declaration of 1986 stated that 'negotiations shall aim to develop a multilateral framework of principles, rules and disciplines dealing with international trade in counterfeit goods'. At the so-called mid-term review of the negotiations of the entire Uruguay Round, the Trade Negotiation Committee, which met in Montreal and Geneva in December 1988 and April 1989, respectively, expanded the mandate of the Negotiating Group. Trade Ministers agreed to include:

- the applicability of GATT's basic principles and of relevant IP conventions;
- the provision of adequate standards concerning availability, scope and use of IPRs;
- the provision of adequate means for the enforcement of IPRs; and
- the provision of procedures for multilateral prevention and settlement of disputes.

Ministers also agreed to give due consideration to concerns raised by participants related to underlying public policy options of national IP systems, including developmental and technological objectives.[a] The composite text, the Anell Draft, prepared by the Chairman of the Negotiating Group in late 1989, was the first attempt to cover all proposals made to date; it suggested the future shape of an agreement on trade in counterfeit and pirated goods, including specific rules on substantive IP matters.[b] This composite text was superseded by the Brussels Draft of 1990 and finally by the Dunkel Draft of 1991, which is the text that, with minor changes, was finally adopted as the TRIPS Agreement.

Note: [a] GATT document MTN.TNC/11, dated 24 April 1989; [b] Chairman's Report to the General Negotiating Group, GATT document MTN.GNG/NG11/W/76, July 1990.

in GATT. However, based on the Punta del Este Declaration, there was acceptance of basic protection against trademark counterfeiting and copyright piracy. The initial resistance of developing countries to broader IPR standards was overcome through a combination of concessions offered by developed countries in areas such as agriculture and textiles and by threats of trade sanctions (Box 3.1).

Main elements

The TRIPS Agreement was incorporated as Annex 1C of the Marrakesh Agreement Establishing the World Trade Organization (WTO), which was concluded on 15 April 1994, more than three years later than originally planned. TRIPS has 73 provisions organized in seven parts:

1 general provisions and basic principles;
2 standards concerning the availability, scope and use of IPRs;
3 enforcement;
4 acquisition and maintenance of rights and related *inter partes* procedures;
5 dispute prevention and settlement;
6 transitional arrangements; and
7 institutional arrangements and final provisions.

The TRIPS Agreement is particularly relevant in the history of IP because it breaks with the tradition of the classical conventions of the 19th century. *No longer is the harmonization of standards a bottom–up approach, but it is now based on the principle of minimum standards of protection.* Before TRIPS, countries could exclude some industrial or technological sectors from patentability (as the Paris Convention does not contain any obligation in this respect) and also discriminate against the patentability of process and products. The pharmaceutical and food and beverages sectors were among the most excluded among countries regarding the patentability of both products and/or processes. The German industrial property law of 1877 was the first to exclude food products from patentability, to avoid price increases associated with monopolistic protection, particularly in a country which, at that time, was suffering from food shortages. By the mid-1950s, at least Austria, Bulgaria, Canada, Chile, Colombia, Czechoslovakia, Denmark, Ecuador, Estonia, Iceland, Japan, Luxemburg, Norway, Sweden, Switzerland and Yugoslavia had the same exclusion.

The minimum standards of protection in disciplines such as copyright and related rights, trademarks, geographical indications, industrial designs, patents, layout designs of integrated circuits, protection of undisclosed information and control of anti-competitive practices in contractual licences, listed in Part II of the Agreement, are supplemented by those of the Paris and Berne Conventions, which are explicitly imported into TRIPS (with the exception of the moral rights of authors under the Berne Conventions). In addition, TRIPS also breaks with the tradition that IP matters were dealt with primarily by WIPO, which already administered the most important international treaties on different IP-related issues in force at that time (see Chapter 4).

The main features of the Agreement, compared to earlier instruments on IP, are:

- Its comprehensive coverage. One single instrument covers the major IP disciplines through the establishment of minimum standards in each of them.
- The inclusion, for the first time, of disciplines related to the enforcement of IP rights. WTO Members should not only recognize and protect those rights but set up mechanisms that would guarantee, through administrative procedures and civil and criminal procedures, including border measures, the appropriate means for the domestic enforcement of those rights.

- The full incorporation of IP into the international GATT-style trading system. This means that the main pillars of the system – national treatment and most favoured nation (MFN) treatment, among others (see definitions below) – should apply in the relationships among Members. Of these two core principles, MFN is an absolute novelty to IP international treaties. The second major consequence of this formal incorporation of IP in the trading system is the application of the WTO principles for effective and expeditious procedures for the multilateral prevention and settlement of disputes between governments. The application of these procedures could justify measures of commercial retaliation, including cross-retaliation (a retaliation adopted by the complaining party in another sector from that in which the infraction was made: goods, services or IPRs), in the event of non-compliance by Members of their obligations under TRIPS. The cross-sectoral, sanctions-backed dispute settlement mechanism (DSM) in the WTO is quite different from that under GATT. This DSM could be extended to violations of the Agreement or to cases described in the WTO system as non-violation complaint situations. Non-violation complaints were conceived in the GATT system to protect parties against nullification or impairment of their trade in goods expectations by possible actions by a Party that, without contravening a particular trade obligation, might nonetheless impair another Party's trade expectations or benefits (Box 3.2).

Box 3.2 Non-violation complaints

WTO Members bringing non-violation cases might argue that certain public policies restricting market access of IPR-protected products deprive rights holders of certain expectations arising from the TRIPS substantive rules. For example, the recourse by developing countries to price controls, particularly in the area of pharmaceutical products, could be considered as impairing marketing expectations on the part of foreign patent holders. Also, the use by governments of TRIPS flexibilities such as the general exceptions clause (Article 30), the granting of compulsory licences (Article 31) or even the narrow design of patentability criteria could be the target of non-violation complaints. In addition, although TRIPS grants considerable discretion about the enforcement of IPRs, Members could seek to challenge another Member's choice of remedies as not being sufficiently stringent. Finally, public policy choices pursued through internal taxes, packaging and labelling requirements, consumer protection rules and environmental standards may affect the profitably of IPRs and thus nullify or impair benefits expected from such rights. Although these are possibilities, there is no agreement in the WTO about whether or not non-violation complaints are applicable to TRIPS. Most Members, with the notable exception of the US, oppose their use and support a moratorium on the issue.

Source: UNCTAD-ICTSD (2005), p681

TRIPS

General provisions and basic principles

The first part of TRIPS outlines the general provisions, its basic principles and objectives, namely:

- The minimum standard of protection. *The Agreement specifies that Members are not obliged to implement in their laws more extensive protection than is required in the Agreement*, provided that such protection does not contravene the provisions of the Agreement. This means that Members could provide more extensive protection if they so wish. This is happening in the new generation of free trade agreements with special chapters on IP, characterized as TRIPS-plus agreements (see Chapter 7). The provisions of the TRIPS Agreement, however, are not always drafted in a mandatory way. The Agreement leaves space for some flexibility in the implementation of its provisions as was reiterated in the Doha Ministerial Declaration on TRIPS and public health (see below and

also Chapter 9). Part II of TRIPS gives details of the minimum standards provided for the different disciplines covered by the Agreement. The Agreement, within this flexibility, provides for the freedom of implementation of its provisions, in the sense that Members are free to determine the appropriate method of translating the Agreement within their own legal system and practice.

- The national treatment principle incorporated in the classical WIPO-administered conventions sanctions the non-discrimination between nationals and foreigners. Thus foreign IP right holders should receive in other Members a treatment similar to that accorded to own nationals. But, compared to the classical conventions and influenced by a US–Korea IP-related agreement in the late 1980s, the national treatment principle in TRIPS is expressed as 'treatment no less favourable' than that accorded to own nationals.
- The most favoured nation (MFN) treatment is a major novelty compared with the classical IP conventions. The

MFN requires non-discrimination among foreigners. Through this principle, which accepts very limited exceptions, countries cannot be treated differently over the protection of IP. The principle means that any advantage, favour, privilege or immunity granted by a WTO Member to a national of any other country (for example in a bilateral agreement) – whether a WTO Member or not – is immediately and unconditionally extended to the nationals of all other WTO Members.

- Finally, Part I of the Agreement spells out the guiding objectives and principles underpinning the protection and enforcement of IPRs. Article 7 states that 'intellectual property rights should contribute to the promotion of technological innovation and to the transfer and dissemination of technology, to the mutual advantage of producers and users of technological knowledge and in a manner conducive to social and economic welfare, and to a balance of rights and obligations'. While Article 8.1 provides that 'Members may, in formulating or amending their laws and regulations, adopt measures necessary to protect public health and nutrition, and to promote the public interest in sectors of vital importance to their socioeconomic and technological development, provided that such measures are consistent with the provisions of this Agreement'.

Substantive minimum standards

The fundamental principle in TRIPS of minimum standards differentiates this Agreement from the classical IP conventions. All WTO Members, without differentiation, are obliged to implement and observe these minimum standards in their national legislation. The Agreement recognizes, however, some differentiation among groups of Members in the degree and timing of this implementation,

an idea that was first formally introduced in a proposal by Switzerland to the TRIPS Negotiating Group in May 1990.[3] Transitional periods were recognized in several proposals and in the final text given to developing countries and countries with economies in transition. These transitional periods expired for all these countries on 1 January 2005. However, for the least developed countries, subsequent decisions of the WTO Council for TRIPS have waived the obligation of implementation until June 2013 and for pharmaceutical products until 1 January 2016.

The substantive standards are spelt out in Part II of TRIPS for all the categories of IP covered by the Agreement. Probably the most far-reaching changes brought about by TRIPS, particularly compared with the situation prevailing before the Agreement, concern patents (UNCTAD, 1997, p30) and undisclosed information, this latter area being included for the first time in a multilateral IP-related agreement. In all the other areas covered by the Agreement, TRIPS in many respects imported and expanded the main standards covered already in pre-existing WIPO-administered treaties. However, it gives to these imported standards the benefit of the enforcement provisions and the dispute settlement mechanism provided under TRIPS.

Key patent rules

For patents, the Agreement includes a number of important features; these are described in the following sections.

Scope and duration

In a major departure from the Paris Convention, TRIPS provides that *patents shall be available for products and process, and patents rights enjoyable without discrimination as to the place of inven-*

tion, the field of technology and whether products are imported or locally produced. This major feature of the Agreement was not free of controversy (Box 3.3), nor is there agreement on the obligations it imposes. Some argue that this means that countries are no longer free to grant patent protection in some sectors while excluding others – which was normal for pharmaceuticals, chemicals and food products before TRIPS. For example, at the time of the negotiations of the Uruguay Round almost half of the known patent laws excluded pharmaceutical products from protection. In some cases – in Brazil, for example – exclusion from patentability included the entire sector. One third of those laws excluded inventions on food products. Others assert that this TRIPS provision does not require patents for all sectors. For example, even though business methods and software are not specifically excepted from this provision, at the time the TRIPS Agreement was negotiated even proponents of this provision did not believe that patents should generally be issued for them.[4] In addition, the WTO in one of its dispute panels held that 'discrimination' under this provision means unjustified differentiation, and thus differential treatment may be normatively justified.[5]

The principle of non-discrimination not only means that patents are available for any inventions, whether products or processes, in all fields of technology, but also that the *granting period* was standardized to *no less than 20 years* (see below). Note too the intrusive nature of the Agreement compared to the prevailing situation before TRIPS. The bottom–up approach to harmonization that characterized the international regimes under the classical conventions left each country with the freedom to determine the patentability criteria to be applied and the term of the patent protection. The TRIPS Agreement, however, reflects the broad parameters of patentability applied in major developed countries, namely that patents are available for inventions, whether products or processes, provided that they are new,

involve an inventive step and are capable of industrial application.

Exclusions

Before TRIPS, countries could exclude from patentability any inventions, but according to the new minimum standard of non-discrimination under TRIPS, Members may only exclude from patentability certain inventions, 'necessary to protect *ordre public* or morality, including to protect human, animal or plant life or health or to avoid serious prejudice to the environment, provided that such exclusion is not made merely because the exploitation is prohibited by their law' (Article 27.2).

One of the most controversial provisions of the Agreement, and of great importance for agriculture, biodiversity and the future of food, concerns whether or not living organisms are patentable. Article 27.3(b) states:

> *Members may also exclude from patentability: plants and animals other than micro-organisms, and essentially biological processes for the production of plants or animals other than non-biological and microbiological processes. However, Members shall provide for the protection of plant varieties either by patents or by an effective* sui generis *system or by any combination thereof.*

It also says its provisions will be reviewed four years after entry into force of the Agreement.

Rights of patent holders

In another major departure from the prevailing system before TRIPS, the Agreement provides an exhaustive definition of the exclusive rights conferred by a patent on its owner. These include the right to prevent third parties not

TRIPS

Box 3.3 A brief legislative history of patentability under TRIPS

The patentability of inventions in all fields of technology, a key feature of TRIPS, was one of the issues whose negotiation remained pending until the final phases of the Uruguay Round.[a] Article 27 of the TRIPS Agreement deals with patentable subject matters. Its first paragraph – based on the WIPO Draft Treaty Supplementing the Paris Convention as far as Patents are Concerned[b] – establishes the main criteria for patentability: inventions, whether products or process, in all fields of technology, and subject to fulfilling the classical three requirements for patentability: novelty, inventive step and industrial applicability. Paragraphs 2 and 3 of Article 27 contain exclusions to patentability. Paragraph 2 refers to general exclusions which at the time the TRIPS Agreement was negotiated were included in various domestic legislation, but subject to certain conditions. Paragraph 3, however, includes two more specific exceptions to patentability in sub-paragraphs (a) and (b) which need no justification to be applied.

The idea of having worldwide-accepted provisions about patentable subject matter, conditions for patentability and exclusions incorporated in an international treaty was not new in IP negotiations. These components of IP reform were important elements of the negotiations of the WIPO Draft Treaty Supplementing the Paris Convention as far as Patents are Concerned.

During the WIPO negotiation process and The Hague Diplomatic Conference, the patentability was a heated issue. Two different options about the field of technology were presented to the Diplomatic Conference. One (Option A), was presented by a group of 23 developing countries. This option included many of the elements contained in the current Article 27 of the TRIPS Agreement (inventions contrary to public order, law or morality, or injurious to public health; plant or animal varieties or essentially biological processes and methods for medical treatment). Option B referred to the patentability of inventions in all fields of technology, without indication of any criteria of patentability or exclusions from patentability.

During the TRIPS negotiations, the first consolidated text of a trade-related IPR agreement[c] was prepared by the chairman and presented in his report to the Negotiating Group in July 1990. This text (the composite text) was mainly based on different proposals previously presented by the European Communities, the US, Japan, Switzerland and a group of 11 developing countries. All these proposals contained a provision about patentable subject matter, though they differed in scope. For instance, all of them, except the one presented by the US, contained exclusions. Among those proposals that incorporated exclusions, the emphasis was quite different. The exclusion of inventions contrary to the public order or morality was included in the proposals presented by the EC, the group of developing countries, Switzerland and Japan; the plant or animal varieties exclusion was included in the proposals of the EC and the group of developing countries, but not in the others. The reference to a *sui generis* protection system for plant varieties was included for the first time in the proposals made by the EC and Switzerland and was kept in the chairman's consolidated text of July 1990 and in the subsequent texts (the Brussels text of December 1990[d], the Dunkel text of December 1991[e] and the final version of the Agreement).

The final drafting of Article 27 contains a built-in review mechanism that was included at the very end of the negotiations in the Brussels text of December 1990, without a time-frame. The four-year term was added to the Brussels text a year later. This built-in review process started in 1999 in the TRIPS Council and has not yet been finalized.

Notes: [a] GATT document MTN.TNC/W/89/Add.1, p5; [b] Articles 10 (fields of technology) and 11 (conditions of patentability) of the Draft Treaty; [c] MTN-GNG/NG11/W/76; [d] MTN.TNC/W/35.Rev.1; [e] MTN.TNC/W/FA.

having the owner's consent from the acts of making, using, offering for sale, selling, or importing for these purposes the product, in the case of a product patent, or the product obtained directly by that process, in the case where the subject matter of a patent is a process. Also important in TRIPS is the definition of the term of protection that shall not end before the expiration of a period of 20 years counted from the filing date. The practice prior to TRIPS varied between countries, with some recognizing the 20 years and others discriminating according to sectors. In India, for example, the general rule was a patent duration of 14 years, while for pharmaceutical and food products the duration was only 7 years.

As explained, patents confer an exclusive right to prevent others from using the invention without the authorization of the patent holder. However, the conferred rights are not absolute. Under most patent laws, such rights may not be exercised with regard to certain acts by third parties. Thus, under certain specified circumstances, there may be exceptions to the exclusive rights. However, the Agreement limits the establishment of exceptions to those exceptions that 'do not unreasonably conflict with a normal exploitation of the patent and do not unreasonably prejudice the legitimate interests of the patent owner, taking account of the legitimate interests of third parties' (Article 30). The purpose of the exceptions, as well as their scope, may vary significantly among national laws, depending on the policy objectives pursued in each country. Such exceptions may apply to non-commercial acts (for example private use or scientific research) or to commercial acts. In some cases, they aim at increasing static efficiency by speeding up competition (for example the early working exception), while in others the main concern is enhancing dynamic efficiency by avoiding barriers to future research (for example experimental exception) (UNCTAD-ICTSD, 2005, p430).

Compulsory licensing

On the granting of compulsory licensing, the Agreement sets up 14 conditions or modalities in cases where the law of a WTO Member allows for other use of the subject matter of a patent without the authorization of the right holder, including use by the government or third parties authorized by the government. These conditions are:

- the need for the proposed user to negotiate beforehand with the right holder on reasonable commercial terms and conditions for a licence to use the invention. This requirement may be waived in the case of a national emergency or other circumstances of extreme urgency or in cases of public non-commercial use;
- the scope and duration of such use shall be limited to the purpose for which it was authorized;
- such use shall be non-exclusive;
- any such use shall be authorized predominantly for the supply of the domestic market of the Member authorizing such use;
- authorization for such use shall be terminated if and when the circumstances which led to it cease to exist and are unlikely to recur;
- the right holder shall be paid adequate remuneration in the circumstances of each case, taking into account the economic value of the authorization; and
- the legal validity of any decision relating to the authorization of such use shall be subject to judicial review or other independent review by a distinct higher authority in that Member.

The Agreement, as confirmed by the Doha Declaration on TRIPS and Public Health of 2001, does not interfere with the right of Members to define the grounds for the granting of compulsory licences.

Burden of proof in process patent infringement cases

The TRIPS Agreement includes a special provision about civil proceedings in process patents where the judicial authorities shall have the authority to order the defendant to prove that the process to obtain an identical product is different from the patented process. Process patents are a weak form of protection because of the difficulties involved in proving infringement. This provision reverses the burden of proof and facilitates proceedings in cases, particularly of pharmaceuticals and food products, that in most cases prior to TRIPS could only be protected as processes and not as products as now allowed by the Agreement. The effect was that for practical purposes pharmaceutical products were not fully protected, because the key feature of a pharmaceutical product is usually its molecule, and in practice the composition of this is fairly easy to analyse, though the same molecule must be manufactured by an alternative method in order not to infringe the process patent. The Agreement attempts to deal with this perceived weakness by reversing the obligation of the holder of the patent process to prove that there is an infringement, so that if the defendant has produced an identical product to that produced by the process patent, the onus shifts to the defendant to show that the product was produced without use of the process covered by the patent (UNCTAD-ICTSD, 2005, p503).

Data protection for pharmaceuticals and agrochemicals

Finally, related to patent protection particularly of pharmaceutical and chemical entities, the Agreement prescribed that Members, 'when requiring, as a condition of approving the marketing of pharmaceutical or of agricultural chemical products which utilize new chemical entities, the submission of undisclosed test or other data, the origination of which involves a considerable effort, shall protect such data against unfair commercial use' (Article 39.3). The scope of this requirement is subject to dispute. The same article continues: 'In addition, Members shall protect such data against disclosure, except where necessary to protect the public or unless steps are taken to ensure that the data are protected against unfair commercial use.'

The powerful pharmaceutical 'research-based industry' considers the protection of data submitted for the registration of medicines to be of considerable economic importance. The reasoning is that the manufacturer has invested, often heavily, in the research necessary to develop the relevant data, and where patent law fails to provide protection (for example because the active component was shortly to be out of patent, or because the drug was based on a combination of known substances used in novel manner), the secrecy of the testing work would provide the only barrier to a competitor rapidly producing and registering an exact copy of the drug. From a public health perspective, however, the early entry of generic competition is also seen as an important policy objective, whose realization is facilitated by regulations that allow health authorities to rely on existing test data to approve subsequent applications for generic products (see UNCTAD-ICTSD, 2005, p538). This important provision of TRIPS did not fully capture a requirement specifically to provide exclusive protection of test data for a number of years, although it was arguably the intention of some of the promoters of the provision.[6] The Agreement recognized that undisclosed information should be protected against unfair competition, thus against dishonest industrial or commercial practices. Under traditional treaty interpretation principles, countries may choose how to implement a provision having no clearly specified meaning.[7] However, recognition of exclusive protection of the data for a number of years (for example for at least five years from the date of approval of the pharmaceutical product) has been achieved in recent free trade agreements signed by European Free Trade Association (EFTA) countries and the US with a number of developing countries (see Chapter 7).

TRIPS and Genetic Resources, Traditional Knowledge and Food Security

As already pointed out, the Agreement deals with all the major IP disciplines, incorporating and expanding the coverage of protection to all areas and industrial sectors. With patents this is made explicit in the Agreement because a number of sectors, including food products, were, prior to the advent of TRIPS, not required to be under patent protection. As also described above, the exceptions to patentability are limited to particular cases and 'exclusion is not made merely because the exploitation is prohibited' by domestic law. Given the far-reaching nature of the changes, their full impact, especially since developing countries only had to become fully compliant in 2005 (least developed countries have until 2013), will take some time to emerge.

Under the principles of the Agreement (Article 8), Members may, in formulating or amending their laws and regulations, adopt measures necessary to protect nutrition, provided that such measures are consistent with the provisions of TRIPS. Article 8 of the Agreement refers to nutrition as well as to health. This provision, in the case of health, was reaffirmed by WTO Members in the Doha Ministerial Declaration on Health and TRIPS in emphatic terms:

We agree that the TRIPS Agreement does not and should not prevent Members from taking measures to protect public health. Accordingly, while reiterating our commitment to the TRIPS Agreement, we affirm that the Agreement can and should be interpreted and implemented in a manner supportive of WTO Members' right to protect public health and, in

particular, to promote access to medicines to all. In this connection we reaffirm the right of WTO Members to use, to the full, the provisions in the TRIPS Agreement, which provide flexibility for this purpose.

The reasons provided in the case of health could be extended to nutrition. However, this principle could not be interpreted in a loose way, simply authorizing Members to override patent protection. In both the TRIPS Agreement and the Doha Declaration the language is qualified. Such measures should be consistent with the Agreement. However, a sound interpretation of these provisions should reaffirm the notion that 'discretion to adopt measures is built into the Agreement. Challengers should bear the burden of establishing that discretion has been abused' (UNCTAD-ICTSD, 2005, p127).

Article 27.3(b)

Article 27.3(b) of TRIPS deals with one of the most controversial issues covered by the Agreement. Sometimes called the 'biotechnology clause', it describes inventions that Members *may* exclude from patentability while, at the same time, specifically obliging them to protect micro-organisms and certain biotechnological processes.

The final drafting of this clause reflected, on the one hand, the strong interests of some developed countries in ensuring protection of biotechnological innovations and, on the other, the differences existing among such countries

Table 3.1 *WTO Members' obligations under Article 27.3(b) of TRIPS*

Members need to provide patent protection to	Members may exclude from patent protection
Micro-organisms	Plants
Non-biological processes	Animals
Microbiological processes	Essentially biological processes for the production of plants or animals
Plant varieties (by IP system which may be patents, a *sui generis* alternative, or a combination)	Plant varieties

Source: UNCTAD-ICTSD (2003), p30

over the scope of protection, as well as the concerns expressed by a number of developing countries about the patentability of life forms. The ambiguous terminology of Article 27.3(b) (see also Table 3.1) is not easy to grasp:

> *Members may also exclude from patentability ... plants and animals other than micro-organisms, and essentially biological processes for the production of plants or animals other than non-biological and microbiological processes. However, Members shall provide for the protection of plant varieties either by patents or by an effective* sui generis *system or by any combination thereof. The provisions of this subparagraph shall be reviewed four years after the date of entry into force of the WTO Agreement.*

Many developing countries have reiterated their discomfort with the implications of this provision, particularly on the need to reconcile TRIPS with the relevant provisions of the Convention on Biological Diversity and on prior informed consent and benefit sharing (see Chapter 5). The African Group in the WTO has consistently raised concerns about the implications of this provision of the Agreement on life forms. In their view there should not be a possibility, within the framework of the TRIPS Agreement, of granting patents on micro-organisms as well as on non-biological and microbiological processes for the produc-

tion of plants and animals (Box 3.4).

TRIPS leaves flexibility for Members to adopt different approaches on the patentability of inventions relating to plants and animals, but unambiguously requires the protection of micro-organisms although, as with other terms in TRIPS, the meaning of micro-organism is not defined, leaving space for flexibility. In addition, this article obliges Members to provide protection for 'plant varieties':

> *While the Agreement is flexible about the form of protection of plant varieties, it is definite on the introduction of protection in an area in which most developing countries had none before the adoption of the Agreement. This obligation has raised concerns in some of those countries about the impact of IPR protection on farming practices (particularly the reuse and exchange of seed by farmers), genetic diversity and food security.* (UNCTAD-ICTSD, 2005, p390)

TRIPS allows for the exclusion from patentability of 'plants and animals' in general. Consequently, Members may exclude plants as such (including transgenic plants), plant varieties (including hybrids), as well as plant cells, seeds and other plant materials. They may also exclude animals (including transgenic) and animal breeds.

On the other hand, the Agreement states that Members 'shall provide for the protection

Box 3.4 African views in TRIPS Council on patenting life forms

The view has been expressed that patenting of life forms is in itself unethical and harmful and therefore should be unconditionally prohibited. Article 27.2 is not sufficient for this purpose as the conditions it imposes on action to protect *ordre public* or morality are unnecessary and cumbersome, for instance that the commercial exploitation of the invention must also be prevented. The qualifications included in Article 27.2 amount to redefining morality for Members. The view has also been expressed that patents on life forms make the exceptions in Article 27.2 for protecting *ordre public* and morality meaningless for those Members that consider patents on life forms to be immoral, contrary to the fabric of their society and culture, and would want to invoke these exceptions in this regard. The minimum that was acceptable in this regard is to clarify that paragraph 3 does not in any manner restrict the rights of Members to resort to the exceptions in paragraph 2.

It has been said that ethical and moral matters are not matters for commercial calculations and their force should not be affected by reasoned commercial concerns. Cultural and social values of many societies cannot countenance the appropriation or marketing of life in any form or at any stage. The preponderance of such inherent values in particular countries is a matter for democratic domestic legislative process to determine and not for the WTO, whose trade mandate is narrow and insufficient to decide on these matters.

Source: Taken from WTO Secretariat (2006)

TRIPS

of plant varieties either by patents or by an effective *sui generis* system or by any combination thereof.'

The reference to patents is straightforward, due to the detailed treatment of them in TRIPS. The reference to an 'effective *sui generis* system' is not so obvious. It might suggest the breeders' rights regime, as established in the UPOV Convention, but the text very deliberately did not refer to UPOV. The possibility is open to combine the patent system with a breeders' rights regime, or to develop other 'effective *sui generis*' forms of protection.

In recent bilateral free trade agreements (FTAs) concluded between on one side the US, EU and EFTA and on the other a number of developing countries, the UPOV Convention has been listed as one of the international IP treaties that the parties should subscribe to in the near future. In these cases protection of plant varieties will follow the breeders' rights model. Moreover, in FTAs where the US is a party, countries undertake further commitments to make efforts to introduce legislation

concerning the patenting of plants. For example, although Chile is a member of the 1978 UPOV Convention, the FTA with this country provides for a 'best effort' clause in order for each party to undertake reasonable efforts, through a transparent and participatory process, to develop and propose legislation, within four years from the entry into force of the agreement, to make available patent protection for plants which are new, involve an inventive step and are capable of industrial application. In other FTAs, such as that between the US and Morocco, there is a straightforward obligation for the parties to grant patents to inventions on animals and plants (see Chapter 7).

On this specific issue, the report of the UK Commission on Intellectual Property Rights (IPRs Commission, 2002, p66) concluded that developing countries should explore all the flexibilities provided by TRIPS. It favours different forms of *sui generis* systems for plant varieties. It recommended that:

Box 3.5 The Council for TRIPS

The Council for TRIPS shall monitor the operation of this Agreement and, in particular, Members' compliance with their obligations hereunder, and shall afford Members the opportunity of consulting on matters relating to the trade-related aspects of intellectual property rights. It shall carry out such other responsibilities as assigned to it by the Members, and it shall, in particular, provide any assistance requested by them in the context of dispute settlement procedures. In carrying out its functions, the Council for TRIPS may consult with and seek information from any source it deems appropriate. In consultation with WIPO, the Council shall seek to establish, within one year of its first meeting, appropriate arrangements for cooperation with bodies of that organization.

Source: Article 68, TRIPS, Council for Trade-Related Aspects of Intellectual Property Rights

Developing countries should generally not provide patent protection for plants and animals, as is allowed under Article 27.3(b) of TRIPS, because of the restrictions patents may place on use of seed by farmers and researchers. Rather they should consider different forms of sui generis *systems for plant varieties.*

Those developing countries with limited technological capacity should restrict the application of patenting in agricultural biotechnology consistent with TRIPS, and they should adopt a restrictive definition of the term 'micro-organism.'

Countries that have, or wish to develop, biotechnology-related industries may wish to provide certain types of patent protection in this area. If they do so, specific exceptions to the exclusive rights, for plant breeding and research, should be established. The extent to which patent rights extend to the progeny or multiplied product of the patented invention should also be examined and a clear exception provided for farmers to reuse seeds.

The continuing review of Article 27.3(b) of TRIPS should also preserve the right of countries not to grant patents for plants and animals, including genes and genetically modified plants and animals, as well as to develop *sui generis* regimes for the protection of plant varieties that suit their agricultural systems. Such regimes should permit access to the protected varieties for further research and breeding, and provide at least for the right of farmers to save and plant-back seed, including the possibility of informal sale and exchange.

The WTO review process of Article 27.3(b)

Article 27.3(b) provides for a review process. This built-in review started in the TRIPS Council in December 1998 (Box 3.5). At that time the Council invited Members that were already under the obligation to fully implement the Agreement to provide information on how the obligations under Article 27.3(b) had been addressed in their domestic legislation. Pursuant to the Doha Ministerial Declaration of 2001, two new related issues were incorporated into the agenda of the TRIPS Council, namely the relationship between the TRIPS Agreement and the Convention on Biological Diversity (CBD) and the protection of traditional knowledge and folklore. Further discussions on the same issues have also taken place within the WTO Committee on Trade and Environment and the WTO General Council.

Within the TRIPS Council the review of Article 27.3(b) has focused on three main issues:

1   patents;
2   *sui generis* protection of plant varieties; and
3   transfer of technology.

Patent issues

A major contentious issue is the case for and against providing patent protection for plant and animal inventions, particularly from a development perspective. Australia, China, Japan, Singapore, Switzerland and the US have put forward arguments in favour. India and Kenya, generally expressing the views of the African Group, have been the main exponents of the case against (Table 3.2). Singapore and the US maintain that exceptions to patentability authorized by these provisions are unnecessary

and that patent protection should be extended to all patentable inventions for plants and animals.

The deliberations in the Council for TRIPS about Article 27.3(b) have focused on four different approaches:

1   Exceptions to Article 27.3(b) are unnecessary and patent protection should be extended to all patentable inventions of plants and animals (US, Singapore).
2   Article 27.3(b) should be maintained as it permits countries to exclude plants and animals from patentability (Australia, Canada, China, Korea, the EC, Japan, Switzerland, Brazil).
3   Exceptions to Article 27.3(b) must be retained but subject to clarification or definition of certain terms, including the

TRIPS

Table 3.2 *Main arguments in the TRIPS Council for and against patent protection for plants and animals*

Arguments favouring the patentability of plants and animals	Arguments against the patentability of plants and animals
Biotechnological inventions, including plants and animals, should be accorded the same patent protection as inventions in other fields, to promote private sector investment in inventive activities to contribute to solve problems in areas such as agriculture, nutrition, health and environment.	There are implications for access to and the cost, reuse and exchange of seeds by farmers as well as displacement of traditional varieties and depletion of biodiversity.
For the above it is necessary to have international accepted rules for the protection of plant and animal inventions rather than relying on different national approaches.	Protection may grant excessively broad patents which do not fully meet the tests of patentability and the consequent problems of biopiracy in respect of genetic resources and traditional knowledge, in addition to the associated costs for the revocation of such patents.
Patent protection for plants and animals facilitates the transfer of technology and the dissemination of state-of-the-art research by providing incentives for licensing and discouraging confidentiality and trade secrets arrangements.	Current international agreements protect the interest of innovators but do not adequately protect the countries and local communities that supply the genetic material and traditional knowledge.
Patents' disclosure requirements can facilitate the operation of laws aiming to protect public morality, health and the environment.	

Source: WTO document IP/C/W/369/Rev.1

difference between plants, animals and micro-organisms (Brazil, India, Peru, Thailand, Zimbabwe).

4 Article 27.3(b) should be amended or clarified to prohibit the patenting of all life forms (Bangladesh, India, African Group (see Box 3.4)).

In order to finalize the review of Article 27.3(b) it has been proposed that some areas of possible agreement need to be identified, including:

- freedom to adopt appropriate regimes to protect plant varieties;
- TRIPS and the CBD should be implemented in a mutually supportive manner;
- TRIPS does not prevent the protection of traditional knowledge; and
- recognition of the importance of genetic resources and traditional knowledge documentation to help patent examination.

Where it seems that a common understanding does not exist is in relation to:

- eliminating the patentability of life forms;
- the need to clarify certain terms of Article 27.3(b);
- the protection of traditional knowledge; and
- the way TRIPS and the CBD should be mutually supportive.

Other issues raised during the review of Article 27.3(b) concern the:

- scope of exceptions to patentability in Article 27.3(b);
- ethical exceptions to patentability under this provision; and
- conditions of patentability for plant and animal inventions.

In fact, discoveries of naturally occurring organisms, and isolated and purified naturally occurring materials (including genetic resources), have a long history of exclusions based on religious grounds, and ethical concerns remain about such patents and patents on non-technological inventions.

At the time of writing, the deliberations in the Council for TRIPS continue with no major changes in the positions adopted by Member countries.

Sui generis *protection*

Various arguments in favour of and against the *sui generis* protection of plant and animal varieties have been raised during the discussions. Some suggest that a reference to the UPOV Convention could be included under Article 27.3(b) while others suggest that the minimum protection provided should be by any 'effective' *sui generis* system. Other issues include the relationship between the TRIPS requirement to have an effective *sui generis* protection system and the UPOV Convention and the relationship between the *sui generis* protection of plant varieties and traditional knowledge and farmers' rights.

Transfer of technology

The TRIPS Council has also focused on the implications of patent protection for life forms and *sui generis* plant varieties protection for access to and transfer of technology. This latter point is seen as one of the basic objectives of the protection of IPRs in TRIPS:

The protection and enforcement of intellectual property rights should contribute to the promotion of technological innovation and to the transfer and dissemination of technology, to the mutual advantage of producers and users of technological knowledge and in a manner conducive to social and economic welfare, and to a balance of rights and obligations. (Article 7)

The relationship between TRIPS and the CBD

The built-in review of Article 27.3(b) of TRIPS clearly has not yet generated consensus and is one of the outstanding negotiating issues of the Doha Round, which includes 'the relationship between the TRIPS Agreement and the Convention on Biological Diversity (CBD), the protection of traditional knowledge and folklore'.

The CBD requires each Contracting Party to implement several measures in order to ensure the *in-situ* and *ex-situ* conservation of genetic resources. It recognizes the authority of national governments to determine access to genetic resources, subject to national legislation. Under the CBD, access, where granted, shall be on mutually agreed terms and subject to prior informed consent of the Contracting Party providing genetic resources and on the basis of benefit sharing. (The CBD is discussed in detail in Chapter 5.)

The relationship between the provisions of TRIPS and the CBD has given rise to different opinions as to their compatibility or inconsistency. The latter have been associated with the possible granting of IPRs, based on or consisting of genetic resources, without observing the prior informed consent and benefit sharing obligations established by the CBD. Since the adoption of the WTO Doha Ministerial Declaration the issue has been included in the agenda of the TRIPS Council and is the subject of parallel 'dedicated consultations' under the responsibility of the Director General of the WTO.

Different views on the TRIPS–CBD relationship have been expressed at the WTO in relation to the review of Article 27.3(b). While a number of developed countries have

found no inconsistencies between the two treaties, several developing countries have indicated the need to reconcile them, possibly by means of a revision of TRIPS.

The main concern of developing countries is that TRIPS does not require patent applicants whose inventions incorporate or use genetic material or associated knowledge to comply with the obligations of the CBD. As pointed out, the CBD makes access to genetic material subject to prior informed consent of and equitable benefit sharing with the Contracting Party providing the genetic resources. Developing countries have repeatedly voiced concern about possible misappropriation of their genetic resources by developed country patent applicants.

During the negotiations of the WIPO Patent Law Treaty this issue was raised by Colombia and supported by a number of developing countries. It was not finally included in the Treaty largely because developed countries argued that this would imply adding a new basic requirement to patentability, in addition to novelty, inventive step and industrial applicability. It has been suggested that an unintended outcome of the Colombian proposal has been the establishment of WIPO's Intergovernmental Committee on Intellectual Property and Genetic Resources, Traditional Knowledge and Folklore (IGC) (see Chapter 4).

To address these concerns, developing countries have proposed in the WTO[8] to amend TRIPS so as to require an applicant for a patent relating to biological materials or traditional knowledge to provide, as a condition for obtaining the patent:

- disclosure of the source and country of origin of the biological resource and of the traditional knowledge used in the invention (see Chapter 7);
- evidence of prior informed consent through approval by authorities under the relevant national regime; and

- evidence of fair and equitable benefit sharing under the relevant national regime.

The approach to enforce CBD obligations through the TRIPS patent system is gaining support among developing countries but is opposed by a number of developed countries that see no conflict between the TRIPS Agreement and the CBD. For example, in the view of the US, the proposed disclosure requirement is not an appropriate solution; rather Members should focus on remedies such as the use of organized databases, information material to patentability, and the use of post-grant opposition or re-examination systems as an alternative to litigation.[9] Norway, on the other hand, supports an amendment to the Agreement by introducing a mandatory obligation to disclose the origin of genetic resources and traditional knowledge in patent applications. In the view of Norway, this amendment should provide that patent applications should not be processed unless the required information has been submitted. However, conversely to the approach of developing countries, non-compliance with the disclosure obligation discovered post-grant should not affect the validity of the patent.[10] The US and most developed countries support efforts in WIPO to ensure that prior art related to traditional knowledge is better integrated into the international patent system (see Chapter 4).

The protection of traditional knowledge (TK) and folklore

Discussions in the WTO have mainly focused on the questions of the right forum or fora for TK protection and the real need for international action on this matter. Developing countries support the creation of international rules and TK protection being principally negotiated in the WTO. In these countries'

view, any other forum, including WIPO, would not provide the appropriate means for the enforcement of rights. The argument being used here is the same that developed countries used when deciding to introduce IP issues in the multilateral system in view of the lack of effective enforcement obligations in WIPO.

Developed Members are not yet convinced that the issue is ripe for international action and mainly oppose treating TK in the WTO and insist that the matter should be dealt with under WIPO auspices (in the Intergovernmental Committee on Genetic Resources, Traditional Knowledge and Folklore – IGCGRTKF or, more commonly, IGC). Some of the arguments relate to the expertise of WIPO as well as to the need to explore further the many complexities of the issue.

Table 3.3 summarizes the main arguments advocated in favour of or against the protection of TK in the Council for TRIPS. Other issues that have been discussed in the TRIPS Council on the protection of TK include the granting of patents to TK and prior and informed consent and benefit sharing.

National implementation of the TRIPS obligations

Considerable differences exist in national laws about the patentability of biotechnological inventions and life forms. For most developing countries, Article 27.3(b) called for a substantial change in national law, since the majority did not protect plant varieties and life forms such as micro-organisms at the time of negotiation and adoption of the Agreement.

Bilateral free trade agreements signed in recent years, as outlined earlier, have adopted certain models for the implementation of Article 27.3(b), including the subscription to and ratification of UPOV and the protection of life forms via patents (see Chapter 7).

Table 3.3 *Arguments in the TRIPS Council for or against international rules on the protection of TK*

Arguments for	Arguments against
TK is a valuable global resource and hence international protection should be given.	Using domestic laws will enable TK holders to protect their knowledge immediately.
Given the economic importance of TK, holders should have a share in the economic benefits derived from that knowledge, which should become a protectable subject matter internationally.	There is no concrete evidence that national regimes are insufficient to deal with the misappropriation of TK.
It would help to maintain and promote knowledge systems for the conservation and sustainable use of biological diversity.	It is prudent to share national experiences, determine areas of inadequacy and conduct cost–benefit analyses before considering international action on the protection of TK.
It would help to sustain the culture of traditional communities, which use TK in their day-to-day life.	A national system can be international in its outlook and may contain, inter alia, choice of forum, choice of law or international arbitration.
The TK of indigenous peoples and local communities is central to their ability to operate in an environmentally sustainable way and to conserve genetic resources.	International regimes need to be supported by the widespread implementation of national regimes.
It would contribute to the fulfilment of development objectives.	
International recognition of TK would be in conformity with the obligations to respect, preserve and maintain knowledge and practices of indigenous and local communities.	
Transboundary use of TK requires international protection and enforcement.	

Source: WTO document IP/C/W/370/Rev.1 (9 March 2006); see also Dutfield (2006b)

Thus many developing countries have joined or are in the process of joining UPOV. Other countries have explored the development of non-UPOV modes of protection such as the Indian Plant Variety Protection and Farmers' Rights Act passed in 2001 (Chapter 2, Box 2.1).

Peru has established a legal system for the protection of TK associated with biodiversity, including the setting up of a National Anti-Biopiracy Commission. The law reflects the CBD requirements of prior informed consent and benefit sharing. It enables indigenous and local communities to assert their rights over collectively held knowledge. For this purpose, the law obliges interested parties to obtain the prior informed consent of those communities providing the biodiversity-related knowledge.

Conclusion

TRIPS impinges on many other areas of activity, not least food and agriculture. It also deals with issues under negotiation and covered by agreements in other places, the interactions between which are discussed further in Chapter 7. The next chapter discusses the UN body devoted solely to IP, which was initially eclipsed by TRIPS.

Resources

Four organizations with a wealth of web-based resources to tap are the International Centre for Trade and Sustainable Development (ICTSD), The United Nations Conference on Trade and Development (UNCTAD), WIPO and WTO.

A great resource is also found on both the ICTSD website and www.iprsonline.org, where all the papers on IP and development from the UNCTAD-ICTSD TRIPS and Development Capacity Building Project and the full content of the Resource Book on TRIPS and Development *are available.*

4

Promoting and Extending the Reach of Intellectual Property: The World Intellectual Property Organization (WIPO)

Maria Julia Oliva

The TRIPS Agreement was the first international instrument to introduce minimum standards for intellectual property (IP) protection at the global level, but – even before the WTO was established – WIPO agreements and activities were critical in shaping IP protection. WIPO is even more significant now, with ongoing discussions and negotiations representing the tension between efforts to increase levels of international IP protection and efforts to balance IP protection with other public policy objectives. In addition, WIPO has a key role in the dynamic of the shifting and cross-cutting negotiation of IP issues in a variety of fora. Not only is WIPO closely linked to the implementation of the TRIPS Agreement, for example, but WIPO treaties are also increasingly included in a number of bilateral trade agreements. This chapter examines the origins and activities of WIPO and how its work relates to the concerns about IP and biodiversity, food and other aspects of sustainable development, including traditional knowledge.

Introduction

Its first predecessor, the Bureaux Internationaux Réunis pour la Protection de la Propriété Intellectuelle (BIRPI – the United International Bureaux for the Protection of Intellectual Property), was created in 1893 to administer the Berne and Paris Conventions, but the World Intellectual Property Organization (WIPO) has been – until recently – little known and understood outside intellec-

tual property (IP) offices. Its broad range of norm setting, administrative and technical assistance activities, however, fundamentally affect IP rules at both the international and national levels. As a result, and given a growing acknowledgement of the links between IP and sustainable development, awareness of the relevance of WIPO is increasing.

As the international IP regime expands to

include a diversity of multilateral agreements, international organizations, regional conventions and bilateral arrangements, WIPO remains one of its cornerstones. Indeed, the strategic importance of WIPO has only increased. For a certain time, as was discussed in Chapter 3, industrialized countries seeking higher levels of IP protection favoured putting IP discussions into the multilateral trade system to achieve minimum standards enforceable through its dispute settlement system. Nevertheless, WIPO has recently regained its role as the leading organization in multilateral IP norm setting, with several treaties currently being considered under its auspices. WIPO agreements, moreover, are often incorporated in other norms, as happened with the incorporation of the Paris and Berne Conventions into the Agreement on Trade-Related Aspects of Intellectual Property Rights (TRIPS Agreement). It is now more and more common for them to be included in regional and bilateral trade agreements. Some of these commit signatories to sign up to future agreements to be concluded at WIPO (see Chapter 7).

In addition, WIPO is highly influential, given the extensive technical assistance it provides or facilitates. The scope of such technical assistance is not limited to WIPO agreements, but extends to all IP concerns and implementation on which WIPO Member States may request support. In addition, on the basis of an agreement between WIPO and the WTO, WIPO provides legal and technical assistance to implement the TRIPS Agreement. Finally, as WIPO is the UN specialized agency on IP-related issues, it also collaborates with other UN agencies, which generally seek its guidance on these issues. The relationship,

often controversial, between WIPO and other international organizations, particularly in relation to biodiversity and food security issues, will be discussed in Chapter 7.

Through all these activities, WIPO has a profound impact on IP rules at both the international and national levels and thus on how these rules affect the conservation and sustainable use of biodiversity, the promotion of food security and other international sustainable development objectives. Nevertheless, these links have only recently begun to be considered in WIPO, an organization that has traditionally regarded its objective to be to increase levels of IP protection around the world. Current efforts to promote a more balanced approach to WIPO objectives, strategies and activities – including on biodiversity and food security issues – have necessarily had to address not only specific topics and discussions, but the organizational structure, culture and dynamics that limited WIPO's consideration of the links between IP and sustainable development. As discussions mount on WIPO reform, biodiversity concerns are at the forefront of some of the central demands for a more development-oriented approach to IP, including:

- rejecting IP provisions and agreements that would limit a country's ability to establish and implement key social, cultural and environmental policies;
- calling for an international instrument to prevent the misappropriation of traditional knowledge (TK) and folklore; and
- demanding all WIPO activities to adequately consider and address their impact on sustainable development.

Background

Intellectual property rights (IPRs) are established solely by national laws and are therefore, in principle, only effective in their respective

national territories. International recognition and protection of IPRs, however, is relevant for holders of IPRs seeking to exploit their protected products and works across national boundaries. International agreements, therefore, have traditionally responded to calls by industrialized countries for certain minimum levels of IP protection and for recognition of the IPRs of their nationals in other countries.

WIPO, whose history dates back to the Paris Convention for the Protection of Industrial Property of 1883 and the Berne Convention for the Protection of Literary and Artistic Works of 1886, has been instrumental in facilitating these efforts towards increased international protection of IP. WIPO replaced BIRPI in 1970, undergoing structural and administrative reforms, but primarily reflecting the growing importance placed on IP, which Member States agreed should be promoted throughout the world. Its work programme and activities have thus focused on the progressive development of IP rules. Indeed, as the US, the EU and other exporters of IP shift the standard-setting agenda to various fora in order to establish more extensive IP protection, WIPO's responsiveness to the needs of the industry and business sectors have made it a focal point of the process towards globalization of IPRs.

In part, the close links between WIPO and IPR holders respond to a characteristic that distinguishes WIPO from most intergovernmental organizations and has a direct impact on its approach. About 90 per cent of WIPO's funding comes not from Member States but from the private sector, through the fees paid for the use of global IP protection systems which facilitate the registration of or filing for an IP right in several countries (IPRs Commission, 2002). The Patent Cooperation Treaty (PCT), one such system, for instance, accounts for 75 per cent of WIPO's total income. The largest users of the PCT system come from the US, Japan, Germany, the UK and France (WIPO, 2005). Although, as an intergovernmental organization, WIPO is answerable only to its Member States, concerns remain that, given its dependence on the business community for funding, WIPO tends

to pursue the agenda of increasing IP protection and harmonization as its own (Shyamkrishna et al, 2004). Box 4.1 outlines WIPO's mandate, governance structure and operation and Appendix 2 (page 247) lists the three types of treaties it administers.

Since 1974, however, WIPO has also been a UN specialized agency. As such, it has responsibility 'for promoting creative intellectual activity and for facilitating the transfer of technology related to industrial property to the developing countries in order to accelerate economic, social and cultural development'. Ongoing discussions about the WIPO Development Agenda, which will be discussed below, have questioned whether the links between IP and sustainable development are indeed considered in WIPO activities. Its publications and activities continue to espouse the view of IP as a 'power tool' for development, a 'universal value' that unreservedly contributes to the progress of societies. Technical assistance programmes of the Economic Development Sector at WIPO are aimed primarily at building up the legal and administrative infrastructure required to protect IPRs. As a result, civil society organizations have criticized WIPO for often acting as a 'church of intellectual property' rather than looking at IP as an instrument of public policy.

A limited perspective on IP and sustainable development could be particularly problematic because, as opposed to early international IP rules that mostly codified already existing state practices and left many central concepts open for national interpretation, current efforts for increased international protection of IP rules seek provisions that significantly limit countries' policy space. As will be explained below, several instruments established or currently being negotiated in WIPO will result in significantly superior scope and levels of protection for IPRs. They will thus impact on national discretion to determine the types and scope of IPRs recognized, the limitations and exceptions to these rights, and the manner in which these rights are enforced. Several initia-

WIPO

Box 4.1 WIPO basics

The WIPO Convention sets out the objectives of WIPO in Article 3:

- to promote the protection of IP throughout the world through cooperation among states, and, where appropriate, in collaboration with any other international organization; and
- to ensure administrative cooperation among the unions (such as Berne and Paris) which are administered by WIPO.

Article 4 of the Convention lists the functions of WIPO, which, as well as a variety of administrative functions, include a number of substantive functions such as:

- promoting the development of measures designed to facilitate the efficient protection of IP throughout the world and harmonizing national legislations in this field;
- encouraging the conclusion of international agreements designed to promote the protection of IP; and
- assembling and disseminating information concerning the protection of IP, carrying out and promoting studies in this field, and publishing the results of such studies.

Under the Agency's Agreement of 1974 with the UN, through which it became a specialized agency of the UN system, it agreed to 'take appropriate action … to accelerate economic, social and cultural development'. WIPO officials, however, usually seem to prefer to cite the WIPO Convention, a document of 1967 mostly designed to cater to the interest of IP rights holders.

WIPO carries out many tasks related to the protection of IPRs, such as administering international treaties, assisting governments, organizations and the private sector, monitoring developments in the field, and harmonizing and simplifying relevant rules and practices. In brief:

- WIPO has 183 Member States.
- Its main decision-making bodies are the General Assembly, the Conference and the Coordination Committee.
- The WIPO Secretariat has 938 staff from 95 countries.
- 23 international treaties are administered (15 on industrial property and 7 on copyright, plus the convention creating WIPO).
- 172 non-governmental organizations, which include industry and business associations and groups, and 65 intergovernmental organizations have observer status.

Sources: www.wipo.int and Musungu and Dutfield (2003).

tives for international rules currently being debated at WIPO would indeed establish 'TRIPS-plus' standards, requiring signatories to implement more extensive standards and eliminating options and flexibilities currently provided by the TRIPS Agreement.

Selected WIPO Work Affecting Genetic Resources and TK

Although the highest decision-making powers, particularly for norm setting, are held by the General Assembly, one of WIPO's governing bodies, substantive discussion and consideration of proposed rules or specific IP issues takes place in a range of WIPO committees. Discussions in three committees are particularly relevant for genetic resource and TK issues: the Standing Committee on the Law of Patents (SCP), the Intergovernmental Committee on Intellectual Property and Genetic Resources, Traditional Knowledge and Folklore (IGC), and the Provisional Committee on Proposals Related to the WIPO Development Agenda (PCDA).

The Standing Committee on the Law of Patents (SCP)

Since 2000, work in the SCP has focused on the harmonization of substantive aspects of patent law; that is on the global standardization of substantive patentability requirements and criteria. In particular, some industrialized countries had put forth a proposal for a Substantive Patent Law Treaty (SPLT). The proposed SPLT would harmonize fundamental areas of patent law on which there are so far no international standards. The SPLT would eliminate the flexibility that WIPO Members enjoy, under existing international intellectual rules such as the TRIPS Agreement, to legislate in such areas. In this sense, its provisions can be considered 'TRIPS-plus', in other words going beyond the requirements agreed to in the WTO TRIPS Agreement. As a result, there has been significant opposition to such patent harmonization efforts by developing countries, with discussions now indefinitely suspended in the WIPO context. Nevertheless, substantive patent harmonization is still being addressed in formal meetings by the so-called Group B-plus

– developed member States of WIPO plus other countries in the European Patent Organisation.

Substantive patent standards define, for example, the concept of 'invention' and the scope of protection granted by a patent. As a result, the proposed SPLT would, for example, by including a mandatory definition for the term 'invention', eliminate the available freedom for countries to determine the patentability for biological materials, including genes (Correa and Musungu, 2002). Currently, for example, living beings or 'biological materials found in nature' are not considered to be inventions in Brazil – even if isolated from the organism. In the US, on the other hand, an isolated and purified form of a natural product is considered an invention and can be patented. Such positions are perfectly consistent with TRIPS, which does not include definitions of any of the terms used in the Agreement.

For multinational companies with global markets, harmonized substantive patent law standards – and eventually a global patent system – would facilitate obtaining patents in different countries. In his 2005 written testimony on patent harmonization before the US Senate, Marshall C. Phelps, Jr, Corporate Vice President and Deputy General Counsel for Intellectual Property of the Microsoft Corporation, stated that:

> *Inventors who desire protection in a particular country must take steps to obtain protection within that jurisdiction. The costs and barriers to access posed by a multiplicity of national patent regimes – all sharing the same basic goal, but each imposing disparate administrative burdens on inventors – is something that industry and policymakers should care deeply about.* (Phelps, 2005)

WIPO

The Director General of WIPO, Dr Kamil Idris, in the memorandum that launched discussions on the proposed SPLT, noted that:

> ... *technology-based, internationally focused, export-oriented enterprises need patents in a number of countries, which in turn need to provide effective patent systems if they are to attract investment and encourage technological development. ... The current framework of the patent system consists of a national and regional patchwork of legal, organizational and administrative arrangements for obtaining and enforcing patents. It is evident that international trade and commerce and the movement of technology are hampered by a tangle of inconsistent regulations across national boundaries. ... A more unified framework for obtaining patents worldwide would encourage more users to develop and commercialize their inventions on a truly international basis, with less fear that their work would not be evenly and effectively protected, thus fostering innovation and economic growth more effectively and at lower cost.* (WIPO, 2001)

Early discussions of the SPLT were characterized by an asymmetrical participation of developing countries. Topics such as the costs and benefits of harmonization, the balance between right holders and the public interests in the proposed provisions, and the relationship between the patent system and other policy and regulatory issues, however, have become increasingly raised by developing countries and civil society organizations. In particular, developing countries have emphasized the importance of adequately addressing issues related to genetic resources and TK. For example, in discussions on the requirements of patent applications involving genetic resources, proposed text has been submitted to require applicants to disclose source and country of origin, as well as compliance with prior informed consent.

As discussed in other chapters, a major concern of developing countries about the international patent system is that it allows the granting of patents for inventions that use genetic material and associated knowledge without adequate consideration of the provisions of the Convention on Biological Diversity (CBD – see Chapter 5). The need for disclosure requirements that would increase transparency, enhance patent examination and quality, and prevent the misappropriation of genetic resources and TK have come up in various fora, including the SCP. Nevertheless, given the broader concerns about the impact of patent harmonization on sustainable development, the focus of SCP discussions has not been on the issue of disclosure. Moreover, the discrepancies between developing countries and the countries home to the Trilateral Patent Offices – the European Patent Office, the Japan Patent Office and the United States Patent and Trademark Office, where more than 85 per cent of all patent applications filed worldwide are processed – eventually led to a deadlock in negotiations. As mentioned, discussions on the proposed SPLT are thus effectively suspended in the WIPO context.

The Intergovernmental Committee on Intellectual Property and Genetic Resources, Traditional Knowledge and Folklore (IGC)

WIPO began work in 1998 on the IP aspects of access to and benefit sharing in genetic resources and of the protection of TK and folklore, through consultations with stakeholders, such as indigenous peoples and other local communities, civil society, governmental representatives, academics and the private sector. When issues related to genetic resources were raised by developing countries in the context of other WIPO negotiations and discussions, however, some Members considered these issues required further exploration and discussion that could not take place in existing bodies in the organization (see also Chapter 3). As a result, in 2000 the WIPO General Assembly established the IGC as a forum in which discussions could proceed among Member States on IP issues that arise in the context of

- access to genetic resources and benefit sharing;
- protection of TK, whether or not associated with those resources; and
- the protection of expressions of folklore.

Once their links with IP were defined and examined, the understanding was that they would be mainstreamed in broader WIPO negotiations.

The IGC was welcomed by developing countries as a possibility to examine these issues and find solutions to satisfy Member States, and by indigenous peoples and other local communities (GRULAC, 2001). In particular, developing countries proposed that the IGC examine the extent to which IP systems could be adapted to improve their protection of genetic resources, TK and folklore; look at what new disciplines and provisions needed to be developed for a comprehensive protection of these resources at the international level; and devise and draft the necessary international instruments and model provisions for national legislative texts (African Group, 2001). The WIPO General Assembly eventually broadened the mandate of the IGC, instructing it to 'accelerate its work' and 'focus on the international dimension of IP, GR [genetic resources], TK and folklore', excluding 'no outcome, including the possible development of an international instrument or instruments in this field' (WIPO General Assembly, 2003).

The work of the IGC has proven a valuable source of information, enhancing the understanding of the different dimensions and implications of the issues of genetic resources, TK and folklore. The IGC has examined various technical matters concerning IP issues in mutually agreed terms for the fair and equitable sharing of benefits arising from the use of genetic resources, including through model IP clauses for contractual agreements on access to genetic resources and benefit sharing. It has also focused on the defensive protection of genetic resources – measures to ensure that IPRs do not allow the misappropriation of genetic resources. Its work has included technical studies on methods for requiring disclosure within patent applications consistent with WIPO obligations and the interrelation of access to genetic resources and disclosure requirements. This latter included options for model provisions and for procedures with regard to triggers of these requirements, prepared at the request of the CBD, as discussed in Chapter 7.

On TK, the work plan has included terminological and conceptual issues, the use of IPRs for the protection of TK and the defensive protection of TK (Box 4.2). For example, a toolkit was developed for managing the IP implications of the documentation of TK. TK is being documented for a variety of reasons, including preservation, but documented TK may also be more readily accessed and used without authorization if certain safeguard measures – which the toolkit explains – are not foreseen. Moreover, the IGC is currently discussing draft provisions on the protection of TK from misappropriation that offer in a 'coherent and focused form the kind of specific questions that may need to be weighed by policymakers at national, regional and international level, when considering the appropriate form and means of protection' (WIPO, 2006b).

However, there are increasing concerns on the part of developing countries that the work has not been successful in its primary objective, as it has not contributed to mainstreaming these issues, indeed that it may have proven a way to 'push them out of the way' both in WIPO and in other fora. Developing countries are still calling for an increase in the pace of negotiations and

WIPO

Box 4.2 Defining TK

A working concept of TK has been defined by the WIPO Secretariat as 'tradition-based literary, artistic or scientific works; performances; inventions; scientific discoveries; designs; marks, names and symbols; undisclosed information; and all other tradition-based innovations and creations resulting from intellectual activity in the industrial, scientific, literary or artistic fields' (WIPO, 2002b). TK subject matter may include herbal classification, location and properties; geographical assets in territories, such as timber or underground deposits, animal domestication and hunting; and land management and use.

WIPO further divides TK into public and non-public knowledge, which in turn determines how the TK may be protected. For example, secret or sacred knowledge may be a subject matter excluded from a system of publication-based protection. Subject matter and products derived from TK, such as use of medicinal plants, may be distinguished from the TK from which the subject derives, and TK and products derived from TK may be protected under similar or different statutes.

The WIPO IGC has also considered 'traditional cultural expressions' or 'expressions of folklore' (EoF). These 'are integral to the cultural and social identities of indigenous and traditional communities, they embody know-how and skills, and they transmit core values and beliefs. As cultural and economic assets, their protection is linked to the promotion of creativity, enhanced cultural diversity and the preservation of cultural heritage. Traditional cultural expressions (TCEs) include music, art, designs, names, signs and symbols, performances, architectural forms, handicrafts, and narratives' (WIPO, no date).

WIPO

more focused and result-oriented debates. In addition, there are worries that the drawn-out discussions in the IGC are being used by some developed countries to detract from initiatives on IP and genetic resources and TK undertaken in other WIPO bodies and international fora. For example, interventions by the US at the WTO recognize the importance of the issues of genetic resources and TK, but insist they must be addressed in the IGC. Moreover, from other perspectives, there is concern from some that this is drawing indigenous groups into an IP approach that is inappropriate for dealing with the substantial social and economic concerns they have.

Nevertheless, the IGC has developed extensive expertise on some aspects of the relationship between IP and genetic resources and TK, and its work has contributed significantly to the awareness and knowledge available on these issues. It has also engaged a wide range of stakeholders in its work. Over 120 organizations – including groups representing indigenous peoples and other local communities, non-governmental organizations, and groups representing industry and the private sector – have been accredited to the IGC as ad hoc observers. Member States of WIPO, moreover, have set up a voluntary fund to facilitate the participation of indigenous and local communities in the work of the IGC. WIPO Member States also contribute to the work through IGC activities such as the analysis of relevant national and regional legal frameworks, case studies, surveys, and comments on various substantive documents, as well as through occasional proposals and submissions.

As a result, the work of the IGC would play an important role in any comprehensive and effective steps to promote a mutually supportive relationship between the international IP regime and the protection of genetic resources and TK. To advance such steps, however, the work of the IGC requires increased focus on concrete measures to be taken at the international level and on supporting, rather than hindering, the related work taking place in other WIPO committees and other organizations.

The WIPO Development Agenda

The WIPO Development Agenda was launched in 2004 as an attempt to ensure WIPO activities and IP discussions are driven towards development-oriented results. Given the relevance of the organization's mandate and governance to its work, as seen above, it is not surprising that these are key elements of the WIPO Development Agenda proposals. The Group of Friends of Development, which has spearheaded the Development Agenda process and includes Argentina, Bolivia, Brazil, Cuba, Dominican Republic, Ecuador, Egypt, Iran, Kenya, Peru, Sierra Leone, South Africa, Tanzania and Venezuela, has presented a number of relevant proposals (Friends of Development, 2005). One suggestion, for example, is to critically analyse and, if necessary, review the mandate to overcome any possible impediment to the Development Agenda's balanced implementation. The disparity between the WIPO Convention and the organi-zation's mandate as a UN specialized agency, the misinterpretation of the development dimension as technical assistance, and the lack of guidelines for incorporating development concerns into all WIPO activities were proposed as some of the specific issues to consider.

The Group of Friends of Development has also raised the need to strengthen the role of Member-driven structures in WIPO to avoid undue influence of IPR holders. Discussions have thus addressed potential changes to the current governance and oversight structures of WIPO, including through an independent evaluation and research office. More transparent and inclusive discussions would also require the increased participation of public interest non-governmental organizations in WIPO, which has traditionally focused its engagement with private sector groups (Figure 4.1).

Initiatives such as the WIPO Development Agenda also highlight some of the institutional advantages of WIPO as a forum for IP and

Balance in the WIPO Development Agenda?

Hardly. Of the 193 non-governmental organizations (NGOs) eligible to attend WIPO's Development Agenda summit, only 24 work explicitly on improving conditions in developing countries. So when WIPO holds a meeting about intellectual property in the developing world, the groups that actually work there will be outnumbered 7 to 1.

Source: Ren Bucholz

Figure 4.1 *Perspectives on civil society participation in WIPO*

sustainable development issues. As the US and other developed countries shift to bilateral trade negotiations for IP standard setting, the collaboration among developing countries and civil society organizations that promoted sustainable development issues and culminated in the WIPO Development Agenda process becomes more difficult.

The WIPO Development Agenda process aims to ensure all WIPO activities adequately take into account development concerns. WIPO has now acknowledged the need to guide its work in light of the international development objectives established by the UN, including the Millennium Development Goals and the Johannesburg Declaration on Sustainable Development. The conservation and sustainable use of biodiversity, which plays a critical role in overall sustainable development and poverty eradication, is essential in achieving these development goals. The Johannesburg Declaration, for example, acknowledged the importance of biodiversity to human wellbeing and the livelihoods and cultural integrity of people, and stated that the loss of biodiversity can only be reversed if local people benefit from the conservation and sustainable use of biological diversity, in particular in countries of origin of genetic resources, in accordance with the CBD. Moreover, it called for actions at all levels to integrate the objectives of the CBD into global, regional and national programmes and policies, in particular in those of the economic sectors of countries (WSSD, 2002). The Conference of the Parties of the CBD, moreover, has noted that the achievement of the Millennium Development Goals is dependent on the effective conservation of biological diversity, the sustainable use of its components, and the fair and equitable sharing of the benefits arising out of the utilization of genetic resources. It thus urged parties, governments and relevant intergovernmental organizations, as a contribution towards the Millennium Development Goals, to implement their activities in ways that are consistent with, and do not

compromise, the achievement of the objectives of the CBD (CBD, 2004).

In addition, several of the specific Member State proposals have a direct link with biodiversity issues, particularly those of the African Group and the Group of Friends of Development in WIPO. For example, the African Group called on WIPO to examine the flexibilities under the TRIPS Agreement with a view to enabling developing and least developed countries to gain access to essential medicines and food. The African Group proposal states that:

> *[developing country] populations should also be enabled to have access to adequate food and nutrition in order to survive and live decently. Protection of the environment, biodiversity, genetic resources, access to benefit sharing, etc, should also be considered within this context* (African Group, 2005).

The guidelines for norm-setting activities envisioned by the Group of Friends of Development, moreover, would require that all initiatives discussed at WIPO are compatible and supportive of other international agreements, including the CBD and the International Treaty on Plant Genetic Resources for Food and Agriculture (ITPGRFA). Similarly, the assessment of the potential impacts of any norm-setting initiative would consider the effect on core development indicators such as access to essential products (seeds, for example), poverty alleviation, equity and protection of biodiversity.

In June 2007, the Provisional Committee on Proposals Related to a WIPO Development Agenda (PCDA), which is where discussions on the WIPO Development Agenda had been taking place, in what was called a 'major achievement' for sustainable development issues at WIPO, agreed on a number of the proposals that had been put forth by various Member States. It thus recommended specific actions to the September 2007 WIPO General Assembly on issues such as technical assistance, norm setting, transfer of technology, studies on the impact of IP and institutional governance. In addition, the PCDA recommended the creation of a Committee on Development and Intellectual Property, which would develop a work programme relating to the approved recommendations and monitor, discuss and report on its implementation. This Committee would also be able to address other IP and development issues, agreed by members of the Committee itself or of the General Assembly.

In spite of several internal controversies that caused a deadlock on the approval of a new budget, the 2007 General Assembly did move forward on the WIPO Development Agenda. As recommended by the PCDA, it approved the creation of the new Committee on Development and Intellectual Property, which will meet twice during the following year. The main task of the new Committee will be the implementation of the PCDA consensus proposals, which were adopted. In particular, the General Assembly instructed the immediate implementation of a list of 19 proposals, based not on their higher priority but simpler execution in terms of financial and human resources.

Other WIPO Activities, Including Technical Assistance

Even if international provisions establish minimum requirements for national IP systems, sometimes limiting the room for countries to construct their IP system according to their particular needs and conditions, these provisions may provide facultative exceptions, allowing countries to opt between diverse approaches, or otherwise maintain 'flexibilities' for national policies. As discussed in Chapter 3, the TRIPS Agreement, for instance, allows WTO Members to define certain fundamental concepts in a manner they deem adequate. Article 27.3(b) of the TRIPS Agreement, moreover, obliges WTO Members to provide protection for plant varieties, but allows them to choose between providing patent or *sui generis* protection. The use of the flexibilities provided by certain international agreements, therefore, becomes essential to 'claw back' some of the policy space lost to minimum or harmonized standards.

WIPO, as one of the main providers of technical assistance to developing countries in the design and implementation of their national IP regimes, plays a fundamental role in the extent to which these countries become aware of the existence and importance of flexibilities in international IP agreements. Between 1996 and 2000, WIPO assisted 119 developing countries and regional organizations in the preparation of 214 draft IP laws. During that period, WIPO also prepared draft provisions to amend and modernize existing laws and made comments and suggestions on 235 draft laws received from 134 developing countries and regional organizations in developing countries (Pengelly, 2005). However, its approach to technical assistance, which it also provides for the WTO, has come under considerable criticism (Box 4.3).

In its proposals on the WIPO Development Agenda, the Group of Friends of Development recognized the central importance of WIPO in the provision of IP-related technical assistance and capacity building, not only by virtue of its own mandate, but also in light of its agreement with the WTO. While acknowledging that WIPO has made significant strides in providing developing countries with technical assistance, the Group of Friends of Development emphasized that more needs to be done to ensure that such assistance is useful to development objectives, particularly by ensuring the technical assistance programmes focus not only on the implementation and enforcement of obligations, but also on the use

Box 4.3 Technical assistance and WIPO

*Chris May**

Article 67 of the TRIPS agreement sets out the needs for technical assistance to enable signatories to accede to their obligations under the Agreement. This Article forms the basis for an agreement between the WTO and WIPO for the provision of such support. Although not the only agency offering this type of support, WIPO's 'Cooperation for Development Programme' (CDP) is a major element in the support available to countries struggling to implement the TRIPS Agreement. The CDP aims to provide a library of documentation and enacted laws (representing best practice) as well as offering assistance to policymakers, legislators, enforcement agencies and legal firms. This training is extensive and takes place both in home countries and at WIPO's own academy.

WIPO's capacity-building programmes aim to help countries reorient national legal regimes in line with TRIPS when they have no tradition and expertise in the field of IPRs, or if their legislative experience is different from the TRIPS model. Although the TRIPS Agreement does not actually mandate the forms of law that any member may adopt, it has (pretty strongly) given the benefit of the doubt to a certain set of established standards. Indeed, technical assistance and capacity-building programmes do not support novel or different solutions to the problems of IPR protection. Rather, as a statement from WIPO suggests, advice may 'to the extent possible ... take into account the specific needs of the country concerned' (WIPO, 2002c), but only where this does not conflict with the TRIPS Agreement's invocation of required legal effect, and the 'best practice' acknowledged by the various agencies involved in capacity-building programmes.

Thus, these activities are actually a key element in WIPO's ongoing programme of the (re)production of a specific set of norms of IPR recognition and enforcement. While giving lip service to flexibility and national interests, they effectively socialize policymakers, legislators and other students into the dominant TRIPS mindset, whatever its applicability or otherwise to specific national conditions and needs. By promoting the TRIPS model as the standard for all countries, WIPO and its associated training providers establish a situation where any alternative or different methods or practices for managing knowledge and information are rendered as abnormal and suspect. Thus, while presented as a neutral exercise in 'technical assistance', WIPO's training programmes are intended to effectively constrain international political deliberation around the protection of IPRs.

Note: * Professor of Political Economy, University of Lancaster; see also May (2007) and papers from the workshop 'Reflecting on IPR Technical Assistance' available at www.iprsonline.org/resources/Reflecting%20on%20IPR%20Technical%20Assistance%20Burnham%20Beeches.pdf.

of in-built rights and flexibilities in international treaties. Civil society organizations, however, have been more critical of the type of technical assistance provided by WIPO (MSF, 2003).

Conclusion

The launch of the WIPO Development Agenda was considered a milestone in the IP and development debate. It was the first time WIPO was called upon to expressly address its role with respect to internationally agreed development goals. Its Member States voiced agreement on the need to view IPRs as a means, not an end in themselves, and to ensure the work of WIPO contributes to the use of such a means in a manner coherent with development and other public policy concerns. The links between IP and genetic resources and TK make such an approach particularly significant.

IP and genetic resources and TK issues are relevant and important, and have been raised and discussed in a range of WIPO bodies. Many developing countries and civil society organizations consider, however, that more tangible measures are still required to ensure that IP rules and activities in WIPO advance relevant international objectives and principles. As discussions continue in the IGC – whose mandate will once again need to be considered in 2007 – the challenge for the organization and its Member States will be to agree on concrete steps towards the international recognition and protection of TK and folklore. Similarly, as consideration continues regarding the changes needed in both the role and attitude of WIPO to truly serve its goal – the promotion of innovation for the public interest (Boyle, 2004) – a critical undertaking will be to modify WIPO's vision, work programme and activities to adequately recognize its responsibility on issues related to the protection of biodiversity and the promotion of food security. The next two chapters discuss the international agreements on biodiversity in general and for food and agriculture in particular and the role IP plays in them.

Resources

There is a range of resources for following up on various aspects of the issues covered by WIPO, including, on WIPO generally: Musungu and Dutfield (2003), Boyle (2004) and the WIPO website, www.wipo.int. See also:

- *South Centre and CIEL Intellectual Property Quarterly Update, available at www.southcentre.org and www.ciel.org.*
- *IP-Watch website – www.ip-watch.org.*
- *Consumers' Project on Technology WIPO webpage – www.cptech.org/ip/wipo.*
- *Third World Network website - www.twnside.org.sg/.*
- *Bridges Weekly Digest, available at www.ictsd.org/weekly/index.htm.*

On SCP and SPLT: Correa and Musungu (2002), GRAIN (2003) and Correa (2004a).
On the IGC: Lettington and Nnadozie (2003), CIEL and South Centre (2005) and the WIPO IGC Accredited Observers' webpage, www.wipo.int/tk/en/igc/ngo/ngopapers.html.

Safeguarding Biodiversity: The Convention on Biological Diversity (CBD)

Susan Bragdon, Kathryn Garforth and John E. Haapala Jr

Biodiversity encompasses the whole of life on this planet. Today's biodiversity has developed from over four billion years of evolution. Yet the actions and development of one species, ours, is now the biggest threat to the immense biodiversity on the planet – something of irreplaceable value in itself as well as vital for our wellbeing, whether for our food, health or climate. Moves to safeguard all aspects of biodiversity do not take place in a vacuum nor are they uninfluenced by social and economic developments. Indeed, as this and the next chapter show, and earlier chapters have indicated, the expansion of intellectual property (IP) into the biological sphere and the reactions to that have overshadowed at times and helped shape the types of international agreements affecting IP and biodiversity. This chapter gives a background to the negotiation of the Convention on Biological Diversity and its Cartagena Protocol on Biosafety, their key aims, and issues arising in their implementation.

Introduction and background

A growing appreciation of the monetary and non-monetary value of genetic resources – catalysed by enormous strides in molecular biology and genetic engineering – provided the backdrop to the negotiations of the Convention on Biological Diversity (CBD, signed May 1992, entered into force 1993). An understanding of the dynamics behind increasing conflict over rights and responsibilities for these resources is necessary before discussing the CBD itself. It is also relevant to the discussion of the International Treaty on Plant Genetic Resources for Food and Agriculture (ITPGRFA or the Treaty) in Chapter 6.

The current international debate on legal regimes for genetic resources has its origins in the late 1970s and early 1980s, when developing countries became concerned by moves in industrialized countries to extend IP protection to living organisms. New legislation, court rulings and international agreements such as UPOV (see Chapter 2) had made it possible to obtain plant breeders' rights and patent protection over living organisms in the US and many European countries. Prior to this time, economic and political interest had rested at the species level, as the species was the relevant unit at which economic value could be recognized. The ability to gain IP protection over genetic resources gave them economic value and resulted in increased political interest at both the national and international levels. Initially, however, this expanding scope of IP protection only addressed one side of the value chain – biotechnology and plant breeding – without addressing the other side – conservation and traditional development (Bragdon et al, 2005; Bragdon, 2004).

While IP protection expanded in scope most quickly in developed countries, the majority of biodiversity is located in developing countries, although it is not evenly distributed. Traditionally, genetic resources have been considered common resources or common heritage and were freely moved around the world (Brockway, 1979; Crosby, 1986). Politically, this was not a problem while the sources of germplasm were under colonial rule or while genetic resources appeared to belong to no one. But with the dismantling of the colonial system after World War II and the expansion of intellectual property law in Northern countries, genetic resources – and plant genetic resources in particular – became 'politically salient' (Stenson and Gray, 1999, p15).

The concern of developing countries focused on the free flow of genetic resources along a predominantly developing country to industrialized country pathway, with no flow of benefits back to developing countries when research on those resources led to commercial products protected by patents or plant breeders' rights. The focus was on genetic resources collected for pharmaceutical research, since when this research resulted in a commercialized product it tended to generate much more value for the developer than would genetic resources

used in agricultural research. Furthermore, collections of plant genetic resources for food and agriculture had also been of great benefit to developing countries (Bragdon, 2004, pp58–59; see also Chapter 6). Nonetheless, developing countries felt that their contributions to the conservation and development of these genetic resources were not being recognized.

When developing countries debated the ownership and control of plant genetic resources at the UN Food and Agriculture Organization (FAO) (Chapter 6), the debate was highly politicized, with concerns about intellectual property rights (IPRs) and national germplasm embargoes (Mooney, 1983). At the FAO Conference in 1983, developing countries succeeded in forcing through a resolution creating the International Undertaking on Plant Genetic Resources (IU – see Chapter 6). The IU declared plant genetic resources to be the common heritage of mankind, meaning they should be free and open to everybody. It made it clear that this open availability was to apply to all plant genetic resources, including 'special genetic stocks', which was interpreted to include the proprietary lines of breeders (Article 2). Furthermore, in the resolution by which the IU was adopted, Member States recognized that 'plant genetic resources are a heritage of mankind to be preserved, and to be freely available for use, for the benefit of present and future generations'. The aim, then, was to ensure that it was not just genetic resources from the South that could be freely accessed but that all plant genetic resources were subject to free access. The acrimonious debate on access to and the ownership and control of plant genetic resources during the adoption of the IU and its further refinement was dubbed the 'seed wars' by the *Wall Street Journal* (Kloppenburg and Kleinman, 1988).

While the IU was not a legally binding instrument, it represented an effort by developing countries to prevent access to plant genetic resources from being restricted by different forms of IP protection. Because of its rejection

CBD

of IPRs, eight developed countries[1] refused to adhere to the IU, perceiving it to be contrary to their economic interests. The rejection of the IU by these countries meant that the free flow of genetic resources from South to North continued largely unabated, and developing countries continued to feel that access to products for research based on genetic resources would remain encumbered. Another approach was needed.

In an effort to resolve the conflict between the IU and IPRs on genetic resources, three interpretations of the IU were made during the late 1980s and early 1990s. The revisions included calling for farmers' rights, an acknowledgment of plant breeders' rights and a statement that nations have sovereign rights over their plant genetic resources.

CBD origins

The CBD's origins fall roughly into categories corresponding to what became its three objectives. One major source was conservationist concerns that existing international law for the protection of wildlife was a patchwork that covered only selected issues, areas and species (Bragdon, 2004, p15). While the idea of negotiating an umbrella convention that would harmonize existing international conservation treaties was quickly dropped due to the 'numerous practical, political and legal obstacles' it posed (McGraw, 2002, p12), proponents of a conservation rationale did succeed in creating an agreement that embraces an ecosystem approach to conservation (see also Chapters 6 and 8). The ecosystem approach embodies a broader concept of nature and its value, including the full diversity of life at the level of genes, species and ecosystems. For this reason, it should result in the protection of many elements of biodiversity not covered by pre-existing international or national laws. The US, an initial supporter and instigator of the call for an international treaty, was motivated primarily

by such conservation concerns (McGraw, 2002, p11; McConnell, 1996, p5; Bragdon, 1992).

Conservation of biological diversity may have provided the impetus for the initiation of negotiations, but the purpose and scope of the Convention changed as discussions got underway. Notably, developing countries were able to secure concessions that they had been unable to secure in other fora (McGraw, 2002, p7). This included consideration of the economic aspects of conservation, which take two broad forms in the Convention: sustainable use and access issues.

The second origin of the CBD, therefore, was a move to incorporate the goal of sustainable use of biological resources into conservation policy, recognizing the need of local people living amid biodiversity for sustainable development, and hence the need to mobilize support for conservation by providing local benefits. Distinguishing sustainable use from conservation emphasizes the desire of developing countries to use their biodiversity in their economic development (Glowka et al, 1994, pp1 and 4; Bragdon, 2004, p15; Bragdon, 1996).

Finally, many developing countries insisted that the negotiations on the Convention include:

> ... obligations and measures on three types of access: access to genetic resources, which they wished to have recognized as subject to national authority; access to relevant technology, stressing that it includes biotechnology; and access for the providing States to benefits ultimately gained from the use of genetic material in the development of biotechnology. (Glowka et al, 1994, p5).

These access issues resulted in some of the most contentious aspects of the negotiations. They also resulted in significant shifts in international law (Bragdon, 1992). As will be discussed in more detail below, Article 3 of the

Convention provides that states have sovereignty over their resources. When read in conjunction with Article 15(1), this includes state sovereignty over genetic resources. Furthermore, Article 15(3) requires Parties to 'facilitate access to genetic resources for environmentally sound uses', another change in international law. After failing with the common heritage approach in the IU, developing countries changed tactics, seeking and obtaining the right to control access to genetic resources.

In contrast to the IU negotiations that took place under the FAO, and that were normally led by ministries of agriculture, negotiations for an international convention on biological diversity were conducted under the aegis of the United Nations Environment Programme (UNEP), beginning in May 1989 and were generally led by ministries of the environment. An ad hoc Group of Legal and Technical Experts and an Intergovernmental Negotiating Committee together met seven times to conduct the negotiations that resulted in the CBD. Controversial issues during the negotiations included biotechnology, IPRs and financing (McConnell, 1996). The negotiations ran through the United Nations Conference on Environment and Development (commonly known as the Earth Summit) in Rio de Janeiro in June 1992, but in the end the Convention was concluded on time and an astonishing 156 countries signed the CBD during the Earth Summit (McConnell, 1996, p111). The Convention entered into force 18 months later, having received the necessary 30 ratifications, and, as of mid-2007, the CBD has achieved near-universal ratification, with 190 Parties.

A notable non-Party to the Convention is the US. Despite having been an initial proponent of the negotiations, the US was indicating its displeasure with the direction of the negotiations prior to the final text being concluded. Early opposition focused on the inclusion of biotechnology within the scope of the Convention, a move which the US opposed with increasing vehemence (McConnell, 1996). Subsequent opposition included concerns about the provisions on IPRs. Initially, the US declined to sign the CBD, citing concerns with Article 16 and its provisions on IPRs in particular, but in 1993 President Clinton did sign the Convention and sent it to the Senate for ratification, where it is still pending in the Senate Committee on Foreign Relations. The US does attend CBD meetings as a non-Party and is able to exert its influence on CBD processes through other CBD Parties and discussions taking place in other fora such as the WTO.

The Convention

The scope of the CBD includes all aspects of biological diversity, which it defines as meaning the 'variability among living organisms from all sources including, inter alia, terrestrial, marine and other aquatic ecosystems and the ecological complexes of which they are part; this includes diversity within species, between species and of ecosystems' (Article 2). The Convention contains three objectives:

the conservation of biological diversity, the sustainable use of its components, and the fair and equitable sharing of the benefits arising out of the utilization of genetic resources, including by appropriate access to genetic resources and by appropriate transfer of relevant technologies, taking into account all rights over those resources and to technologies, and by appropriate funding. (Article 1)

The CBD is generally considered to be a framework convention that 'creates a global structure to promote continued international cooperation and to support national implementation'; that allows for its further development through the negotiation of annexes and protocols; and that builds upon existing agreements rather than absorbing them (McGraw, 2002, pp20–22). It emphasizes the development of national biodiversity strategies and action plans as the basis for each country's obligations (Article 6(a)): 'A national strategy will reflect how the country intends to fulfil the objectives of the Convention in light of specific national circumstances, and the related action plans will constitute the sequence of steps to be taken to meet these goals.'[2] This approach was advocated initially by the British delegation during the Convention's negotiations, in contrast to the strong desire of France for a more supra-national, top–down approach of global lists of priority areas and species in need of protection (McConnell, 1996).

The text of the Convention consists of a preamble, 42 articles and two annexes (Box 5.1). Since 2000, there has also been a subsidiary instrument – the Cartagena Protocol on Biosafety. The work of implementing the CBD is carried out by the Conference of the Parties (COP) and its subsidiary bodies (Box 5.2), as well as by the domestic implementation of the Convention by states. The CBD is legally binding for the countries that have ratified it. However, for the Convention to be implemented domestically, ratifying countries must adopt appropriate legislation and regulations or bring existing ones into harmony with it.

Key provisions of the CBD

The broad scope of the Convention means that it is impossible to explore all its provisions in detail. Instead, we shall focus on five areas: access to genetic resources and benefit sharing (ABS); traditional knowledge (TK), innovations and practices; technology transfer; agricultural biodiversity; and implementation, compliance and enforcement. This section concludes with a brief consideration of some other provisions in the Convention and their links to IPRs.

Access to genetic resources and benefit sharing

Article 15 of the Convention addresses 'Access to genetic resources'. Paragraph 1 of the article reaffirms the principle from Article 3 of the Convention of state sovereignty over resources. Importantly, however, these sovereign rights now extend to genetic resources (although one could argue that such rights were already implicit in international law prior to the creation of the Convention). The paragraph explicitly vests the authority to determine access to genetic resources with national governments, subject to national legislation. This paragraph helps to explain the rationale behind granting states sovereignty over their genetic resources:

> *Countries could now set the terms for access to these resources, thus allowing them to profit from their biodiversity, further encouraging conservation. The CBD was thus based on both a premise – that developing countries had an equitable right to their own resources – and a promise – that these resources could be used to generate financing for development and conservation.* (Garforth and Cabrera, 2004, p7)

Article 15 is important, therefore, not just for its economic aspects related to benefit sharing but also for how these are intended to also support the conservation and sustainable use of biodiversity.

Paragraph 2 of the article states that each Party is to endeavour 'to create conditions to facilitate access to genetic resources'. As

Box 5.1 Overview of the CBD provisions

Unlike other international agreements such as TRIPS or the ITPGRFA, the articles in the CBD are not grouped into different sections or parts. What follows below, then, is a rough grouping of the articles to provide a concise overview of the Convention, although the articles do still need to be understood together.

- Preamble
- Article 1 – Objectives
- Article 2 – Use of terms
- Article 3 – Principle
- Article 4 – Jurisdictional scope

The Convention's preamble and first four articles are its introduction. They lay the groundwork for understanding and interpreting the rest of the articles to come. They define the limits of the Convention and what falls within and without its scope.

- Article 5 – Cooperation
- Article 6 – General measures for conservation and sustainable use
- Article 7 – Identification and monitoring
- Article 8 – *in-situ* conservation
- Article 9 – *ex-situ* conservation
- Article 10 – Sustainable use of components of biological diversity
- Article 11 – Incentive measures
- Annex I – Identification and monitoring

These seven articles and one annex concern the conservation and sustainable use objectives of the Convention in particular. They illustrate how the Convention is designed to require national actions to achieve its objectives. These articles set out the measures and activities that each Party is to undertake in the different areas addressed by each article.

- Article 12 – Research and training
- Article 13 – Public education and awareness
- Article 17 – Exchange of information
- Article 18 – Technical and scientific cooperation

These four articles address some of the informational aspects of biodiversity. They require the Parties to undertake things like research, training, public education and raising awareness towards achieving the conservation and sustainable use of biodiversity.

- Article 15 – Access to genetic resources
- Article 16 – Access to and transfer of technology
- Article 19 – Handling of biotechnology and distribution of its benefits

Articles 15, 16 and 19 speak to the 'access issues' addressed by the Convention in its third objective. They contain some of the provisions that address the economic aspects of the conservation and sustainable use of biodiversity.

CBD

- Article 20 – Financial resources
- Article 21 – Financial mechanism
- Article 39 – Financial interim arrangements

Article 20 addresses the financial resources that will be needed to achieve the objectives of the Convention. Essentially, it represents the view that if developed countries want to conserve biodiversity in developing countries, they will to have to pay for it (McConnell, 1996, p76). Article 21 describes the financial mechanism that will direct the resources from Article 20 to developing countries. The Global Environment Facility (GEF, described in Box 5.2) was named as the interim financial mechanism in Article 39. The Parties at their third Conference adopted a memorandum of understanding between the COP and the GEF Council providing for the relationship between the two in order to give effect to Article 21(1) (decision III/8).

- Article 22 – Relationship with other international conventions
- Article 23 – Conference of the Parties
- Article 24 – Secretariat
- Article 25 – Subsidiary Body on Scientific, Technical and Technological Advice
- Article 26 – Reports
- Article 27 – Settlement of disputes
- Article 28 – Adoption of protocols
- Article 29 – Amendment of the Convention or protocols
- Article 30 – Adoption and amendment of annexes
- Article 31 – Right to vote
- Article 32 – Relationship between this Convention and its protocols
- Article 33 – Signature
- Article 34 – Ratification, acceptance or approval
- Article 35 – Accession
- Article 36 – Entry into force
- Article 37 – Reservations
- Article 38 – Withdrawals
- Article 40 – Secretariat interim arrangements
- Article 41 – Depository
- Article 42 – Authentic texts
- Annex II

This large group contains the institutional provisions and final dispositive articles. Many other international agreements contain similar sorts of articles. Among other things, they cover how the CBD will be governed and administered (the Conference of the Parties, its subsidiary bodies and the Secretariat) as well as the actions states can and cannot take in joining or leaving the Convention (for example signature, accession, reservations and withdrawals).

mentioned above, this can also be seen as a major shift in international law as no such obligation to facilitate access existed previously. While perhaps somewhat unclear in its wording, paragraph 3 of the article means that the provisions of Articles 15, 16 and 19 do not apply to genetic resources accessed prior to the entry into force of the Convention. Essentially, it incorporates the principle of non-retroactivity, in other words that new legal rules and international agreements do not apply to past actions (Glowka et al, 1994, p79). As will be

Box 5.2 The operations of the CBD in brief

The Secretariat of the CBD is located in Montreal, Canada, with a staff of about 90 people. The Conference of the Parties (COP) is the governing body of the Convention and advances implementation of the Convention through the decisions it takes at its periodic meetings, which are generally held biennially.

The COP establishes different subsidiary bodies as necessary for the implementation of the Convention (Article 23(g)). These include:

- The Ad Hoc Open-Ended Working Group on Access and Benefit Sharing (ABS). This group developed the Bonn Guidelines (discussed below) and is also negotiating an international regime on ABS; and
- The Ad Hoc Open-Ended Inter-Sessional Working Group on Article 8(j) and Related Provisions. This group developed the 'Akwé: Kon Voluntary Guidelines for the Conduct of Cultural, Environmental and Social Impact Assessment regarding Developments Proposed to Take Place on, or which are Likely to Impact on, Sacred Sites and Lands and Waters Traditionally Occupied or Used by Indigenous and Local Communities'. It is also collaborating with the ABS Working Group in the negotiation of an international regime on ABS.

Article 25 of the Convention establishes the Subsidiary Body on Scientific, Technical and Technological Advice (SBSTTA). Among other things, this body provides assessments of the status of biological diversity, assesses the types of measures taken in accordance with the provisions of the Convention, and responds to questions put to it by the COP (Article 25(2)). Recommendations of the SBSTTA are sent to the Conference of the Parties, where they may be incorporated into decisions.

The Clearing-House Mechanism for Scientific and Technical Cooperation. Under Article 18(3), the Parties have also established a clearing-house mechanism (CHM) in order to support technical and scientific cooperation. The CHM includes documents from CBD meetings, case studies, national reports and strategies, contact information for different focal points, and Secretariat publications, among other things.

The Global Environment Facility (GEF) serves as the Convention's financial mechanism. The GEF was established in 1991 by donor countries to provide grants and concessional funds to developing countries for programmes aimed at protecting the global environment. The GEF also serves as the financial mechanism for three other conventions.[a] GEF projects are managed by three implementing agencies: UNEP, the United Nations Development Programme and the World Bank. The GEF, in operating the financial mechanism under the CBD, acts under the guidance given to it by the Conference of the Parties.

Note: [a] These are the UN Framework Convention on Climate Change, the UN Convention to Combat Desertification and the Stockholm Convention on Persistent Organic Pollutants.

discussed below, Article 15(3) left open the question of what ABS rules should apply to *ex-situ* collections of genetic resources accessed prior to the creation of the Convention.

Article 15 also states the general principles on which access must be granted, namely mutually agreed terms and prior informed consent (paragraphs 4 and 5). Paragraph 7 requires the Parties to the Convention to take measures for sharing the benefits from the use of genetic resources with the Party providing access to such resources. The Convention implies that the specific bargain between access to the resources and the sharing of benefits will be open for negotiation between the individual user and provider. For this reason, the Convention is said to favour the negotiation of bilateral ABS contracts between resource provider and resource user. Finally, under paragraph 6, research based on genetic resources provided by Parties to the Convention should involve the full participation of such Parties and, where possible, be conducted in these Parties.

Access to genetic resources and benefit sharing is intimately connected to agriculture and food issues, although most of the CBD negotiators came from ministries of environment rather than ministries of agriculture. They had little knowledge of the characteristics of genetic resources for food and agriculture and all countries' interdependence on one another for these resources (Bragdon, 2004, p15; see also Chapter 6). For these negotiators, the classic ABS scenario involved scientists searching the rainforest for an organism that may contain the next cure for cancer or AIDS. Yet genetic resources and genetic diversity are also of critical importance in agriculture. That said, however, the ABS principles in the CBD are not the only ones that address access to genetic resources for food and agriculture and consequent benefit sharing.

When the negotiators of the CBD agreed in Nairobi in May 1992 on the text of the Convention to be advanced to the Earth Summit, they also adopted a resolution on 'The Interrelationship between the Convention on Biological Diversity and the Promotion of Sustainable Agriculture'. This resolution recognized:

> ... the need to seek solutions to outstanding matters concerning plant genetic resources within the Global System for the Conservation and Sustainable Use of Plant Genetic Resources for Food and Sustainable Agriculture, in particular: (a) access to ex-situ collections not acquired in accordance

with this Convention; and (b) the question of farmers' rights (paragraph 4).

To this end, the FAO began negotiations in the mid-1990s to turn the IU into a binding treaty that is in harmony with the CBD. The result was the International Treaty on Plant Genetic Resources for Food and Agriculture. The Treaty is discussed in more detail in Chapter 6, but it is important here to note its relationship to the ABS provisions of the CBD. The Treaty creates a Multilateral System of Access and benefit sharing that covers the 35 food crop species and 29 forage species listed in Annex I to the Treaty. While ABS under the Treaty is still founded on the principle of state sovereignty over genetic resources (Article 10), access to the genetic resources in the Treaty's Multilateral System is done in accordance with a standard Material Transfer Agreement that also sets the terms for benefit sharing. Individual contract negotiations for each instance of access and benefit sharing are thus no longer required for the species listed in Annex I. This responds to the concern that the transaction costs for bilateral negotiations between providers and users of genetic resources would be so high under the CBD that they would inhibit plant breeding, inadvertently jeopardizing food security. Instead, the Treaty, rather than the CBD, now sets the rules for access to and benefit sharing from these specific crops and forages (see also Chapter 6; Moore and Tymowski, 2005; Garforth and Frison, 2007; Bragdon, 2004).

That said, there are any number of genetic resources that are relevant to food and agriculture that are not covered by the Treaty's Multilateral System. This includes plant genetic resources not listed in Annex I to the Treaty as well as animal genetic resources and aquatic genetic resources, among others (Box 5.3).

Box 5.3 Access and benefit sharing, the CBD and agriculture: The teff agreement

In December 2004, the Ethiopian Agricultural Research Organization (EARO) and the Institute of Biodiversity Conservation (IBC, also in Ethiopia) signed an agreement with Health and Performance Food International (HPFI), a Dutch company. In the agreement, the IBC provides access to teff to HPFI 'for the purpose of developing non-traditional teff-based food and beverage products' listed in an annex to the agreement (paragraph 3.2). The company is not allowed to use teff for other purposes such as chemical or pharmaceutical applications without acquiring the consent of the IBC and is not allowed to access Ethiopian TK on the conservation, cultivation or use of teff. For its part, the IBC cannot grant access to teff genetic resources to other parties to produce the products listed in the annex without obtaining the consent of HPFI (part 3 of the agreement).

On intellectual property, HPFI is not allowed to claim or obtain IP protection over teff genetic resources or any component thereof, although plant variety protection (PVP) over teff varieties is permissible. Any such PVP that is obtained is co-owned by the company and EARO. HPFI is also not allowed to transfer teff seed samples or any component of the genetic resources of teff to third parties without the express written consent of the IBC (see parts 4 and 5 of the agreement).

The agreement contains quite extensive benefit sharing provisions. These include monetary benefits such as lump sum payments, annual royalties, licensing fees and 5 per cent of the company's annual net profit contributed to something called the 'Financial Resource Support for Teff' (FiRST), as well as non-monetary benefits such as the sharing of research results, knowledge and technologies, involving Ethiopian scientists in the research and acknowledging Ethiopia as the country of origin of teff in publications and applications for IP rights. According to the agreement, FiRST is to be 'used for improving the living condi-tions of local farming communities and for developing teff business in Ethiopia' (paragraph 7.4).

The access agreement is to be in effect for 10 years. It also includes provisions on penalties, monitoring and follow-up, and dispute settlement.

Note: The text of the agreement is included as Annex 3 to Feyissa (2006). Parts of this analysis are drawn from Garforth (2007).

CBD

TK, innovations and practices

Another key provision in the CBD is Article 8(j), which obliges the Parties to the Convention, subject to their national legislation, to:

... respect, preserve and maintain knowledge, innovations and practices of indigenous and local communities embodying traditional lifestyles relevant for the conservation and sustainable use of biological diversity, promote their wider application with the approval and involvement of the holders of such knowledge, innovations and practices, and encourage the equitable sharing of the benefits arising from the utilization of such knowledge, innovations and practices.

This provision is included in the article on '*in-situ* conservation' and is frequently summarized as addressing TK, innovations and practices of indigenous and local communities.

The implementation of Article 8(j) has covered a number of different areas including links to Article 15 on ABS. The TK of indigenous peoples and local communities can be very valuable in helping to identify genetic resources of potential interest for research programmes and product development. Furthermore, because of their long-term association with, as well as sustainable use and management of, their local environment, indigenous peoples and local communities may themselves have contributed to the development of the genetic resources. The CBD recognizes state sovereignty over genetic resources; however, this state authority does not extend to TK. Parties are required to respect, preserve and maintain TK with the approval and involvement of the knowledge holders, which are the indigenous peoples and/or local communities themselves. In implementing this provision, Parties such as Peru and the Philippines have required those seeking access to TK to do so on similar terms to those for accessing genetic resources, in other words requiring the prior informed consent of and the negotiation of mutually agreed terms with the knowledge holder.

At their fifth meeting in 2000, the Parties to the Convention adopted a programme of work for Article 8(j) (decision V/16). The programme of work contains a number of elements and tasks concerning participatory mechanisms for indigenous and local communities; the equitable sharing of benefits; monitoring; legal elements; traditional cultural practices for conservation and sustainable use; and exchange and dissemination of information.

At their seventh Conference in 2004, the Parties adopted 'Elements of a Plan of Action for the Retention of Traditional Knowledge, Innovations and Practices Embodying Traditional Lifestyles Relevant for the Conservation and Sustainable Use of Biological Diversity' (part E of decision VII/16). Work is focused on developing technical guidelines for documenting TK; developing indicators for the retention and use of TK; methods and measures to address the underlying causes of the loss of TK; and the development of a Code of Ethical Conduct to ensure respect for the cultural and intellectual heritage of indigenous and local communities. The Plan of Action includes the further development of *sui generis* systems to protect TK based on customary laws of indigenous peoples (SCBD, 2007, p2).

The Working Group on Article 8(j) is mandated to collaborate with the ABS Working Group in the negotiation of an international regime on access and benefit sharing (see below). The form of and process for this collaboration is yet to be determined (Box 5.4 and Chapter 8, Box 8.4). Finally, the Working Group on Article 8(j) has also contributed to the consideration of genetic use restriction technologies (GURTs), which is also covered in more depth below.

Access to and transfer of technology

Article 16 addresses access to and transfer of technologies that are relevant to the conservation and sustainable use of biodiversity or that make use of genetic resources and do not cause significant damage to the environment (Article 16(1)). This article contains the only explicit reference in the Convention to IP rights. The article aims to strike a balance between the need to secure access to and transfer of technology on the one hand, and to respect IPRs on the other.

Article 16(2) begins by stating that access to and transfer of technology 'to developing countries shall be provided and/or facilitated under fair and most favourable terms, including on concessional and preferential terms where mutually agreed, and, where necessary, in accordance with the financial mechanism established by Articles 20 and 21'. This or similar language has become something of a norm in international law. Similar commitments to technology transfer can be found in the UN Convention on Climate Change (Article 4(5)), the Montreal

Box 5.4 Indigenous peoples' views on an international regime on access and benefit sharing

This proposed regime will establish the international rules by which states and corporations will commercialize genetic resources and TK. Indigenous peoples know that means that our traditional medicines and our foods are at risk of theft and exploitation. While States claim national sovereignty over natural resources, they have been unwilling to recognize our rights to the genetic resources that originate within our territories, lands and waters in their negotiations thus far.

At this point, it is unclear whether any future ABS regime will be binding or non-binding. … To date, Indigenous peoples' nations and organizations participating in the CBD processes, through the International Indigenous Forum on Biodiversity (IIFB), have reserved commitment to support either a binding or non-binding regime because it is premature given the unclear status of recognition and protection of our rights within the proposed regime. Parties to the CBD need to recognize our rights to genetic resources and Indigenous knowledge based on the minimum standards set forth in the Declaration on the Rights of Indigenous Peoples.

Indigenous peoples have consistently advocated for the protection of our human rights within the proposed regime. …

[I]t must be made clear that Indigenous peoples' rights with regards to an international regime on ABS are not limited to Indigenous knowledge. Rather our rights include rights over genetic resources, both those that are associated with our Indigenous knowledge and more broadly to all genetic resources that originate in our territories, lands and waters whether or not associated directly with Indigenous knowledge.

This legal analysis must also make clear that Indigenous peoples' rights in this context are not just economic in nature or limited to benefit sharing. Indeed, without recognition of Indigenous peoples' rights to control access to both their genetic resources and Indigenous knowledge, no benefit sharing process will be fair and equitable.

For Indigenous peoples, who are often the most marginalized and impoverished peoples of the world, the promises of benefit sharing agreements may be alluring. By virtue of their right of self-determination, it is, of course, the prerogative of Indigenous peoples to make their own decisions about benefit sharing agreements. Before entering into a benefit sharing agreement, Indigenous peoples must understand that by entering such an agreement, they are submitting to a legal jurisdiction entirely foreign to their own systems of management and protection of natural resources and knowledge. Those who agree to benefit sharing must accept that patent laws will govern the ownership of the products derived from their genetic resources. A patent is a necessary step in securing commercial control over a product derived from a genetic resource.

At the 'Workshop on Biodiversity, Traditional Knowledge and Rights of Indigenous Peoples' held in Geneva in July 2003, the Indigenous experts concluded that 'patenting and commodification of life is against our fundamental values and beliefs regarding the sacredness of life and life processes and the reciprocal relationship which we maintain with all creation'. Those words remembered, it becomes important for Indigenous peoples to evaluate whether the patenting of life, which will necessarily occur in a benefit sharing arrangement concerning genetic resources, is consistent with our fundamental Indigenous cultural values, principles, and laws.

Note: Text excertped from a collective statement by 23 Indigenous peoples' organizations regardng their concerns about the CBD negotiations on an international ABS regime. The statement was made at the sixth session of the UN Permanent Forum on Indigenous Issues held in New York, May 2007. The full text of the statement, including the names of the indigenous organizations who agreed to it, is available on the website of the Indigenous Peoples Council on Biocolonialism: www.ipcb.org/issues/agriculture/htmls/2007/unpfii6_ABS.html.

CBD

Protocol on Substances that Deplete the Ozone Layer (Article 10A), the UN Convention to Combat Desertification (Article 18(1)), and the Johannesburg Plan of Implementation from the World Summit on Sustainable Development (paragraph 105).

Paragraph 2 of Article 16 goes on to provide that for technology subject to patents or other IPRs, such access and transfer must be provided 'on terms which recognize and are consistent with the adequate and effective protection of IPRs'. The inclusion of the phrase 'adequate and effective' makes a direct link to the TRIPS Agreement, which was being concluded at the same time the CBD was finalized:[3]

> *According to the preamble of the TRIPS Agreement … the agreement was inspired by the need for new rules and disciplines in a number of areas relevant to IP, including* adequate *standards concerning the availability, scope and use of IPRs, as well as* effective *means to enforce them.* (Glowka et al, 1994, p89; see also the first recital of the preamble to TRIPS as well as paragraphs (b), (c) and (d) of the second recital).

The terms 'adequate' and 'effective' are not defined in either the TRIPS Agreement or the CBD. One interpretation of 'adequate' is that it reflects the intention of the drafters 'not to create the system of IPR protection that would be considered "optimum" by particular right holders groups, but one that is adequate to protect the basic integrity of the trading system' (UNCTAD-ICTSD, 2005, p10). The lack of clarity over these terms has created tension between developed and developing countries, with the former group wishing to maintain its competitive technological edge and the latter group desiring to gain access to technology and also asserting that the level of IP protection 'should be tailored to a country's economic and technological development', the rationale being

that standards of protection that are too high will hinder a country's development (Glowka et al, 1994, pp89 and 91). The situation has evolved since the negotiation of the Convention, however, and developed and developing countries should not be regarded as discrete blocs with homogeneous positions. Alliances between North and South can and do occur.

Paragraph 4 of Article 16 of the CBD requires each Party to take measures with the objective that the private sector will facilitate 'access to, joint development and transfer of technology … for the benefit of both governmental institutions and the private sector of developing countries and in this regard shall abide by the obligations included in paragraphs 1, 2 and 3 above'.

The final paragraph of Article 16 attempts to provide a counterbalance to paragraph 2. It states that the Parties shall cooperate over IPRs, subject to national legislation and international law, 'in order to ensure that such rights are supportive of and do not run counter to [the Convention's] objectives'. The article as a whole attempts to reconcile two very different perspectives on IPRs and in the process creates rather ambiguous language. Perhaps as a testimony to its ambiguity, the biotechnology industry has worried that the protection is too weak (Rhein, 1992)[4], while some civil society organizations claim the language is too strong. Many developing countries argue that the application of existing IP systems hinders the transfer of technology to the developing world and unfairly disregards the contributions of generations of farmers and indigenous peoples to the world's plant genetic resources, which underpin global food security. These countries have objected to the expansion of IPRs over new crop varieties and other products based on genetic resources, and they proposed that the Convention provide for, or authorize, restrictions on IPRs. Some developed countries, on the other hand, argue that strong universal protection of IPRs would stimulate technology and investment in research and development in developing countries, indirectly increasing the incentives to conserve biological diversity (Fowler et al, 2001, p479). The language on which negotiators eventually agreed does not entirely resolve these differing perspectives on the role of IPRs in achieving the Convention's objectives (UNESCO, 2002).

At their seventh meeting in 2004, the Conference of the Parties adopted a programme of work on technology transfer and technological and scientific cooperation (annex to decision VII/29) with four elements: technology assessments, information systems, creating enabling environments, and capacity building and enhancement. Each element has a number of objectives, operational targets and activities. Activities include such things as preparing transparent impact assessments and risk analysis of the potential benefits, risks and associated costs of the introduction of technologies (paragraph 1.2.1); implementing proposals to enhance the Clearing-House Mechanism as a central mechanism in technology transfer (paragraph 2.1.4); preparing technical studies on the role of IPRs in technology transfer (paragraph 3.1.1); and providing financial and technical support as well as training to enable the conduct of national technology assessments (paragraph 4.1.1). Implementation of this programme of work is still in its early stages, although the Secretariat has prepared a draft technical study responding to paragraph 3.1.1 (CBD, 2006c).

Agricultural biodiversity

The CBD's scope is all types of biodiversity and there is no one article in the Convention that relates specifically to agricultural biodiversity. Countries recognized the interrelationship between the Convention and the promotion of sustainable agriculture in Resolution 3 of the Nairobi Final Act by which the final text of the

CBD was adopted (see above). Consideration of agricultural biodiversity by the Conference of the Parties has covered a broad range of topics, including pollinators, soil biodiversity, animal genetic resources, trade liberalization and GURTs. Much of the work on agricultural biodiversity under the Convention has been carried out in collaboration with the FAO. Furthermore, with the conclusion at the FAO of the International Treaty on Plant Genetic Resources for Food and Agriculture, the Parties to the CBD recognized the important role the IT will play, in harmony with the CBD:

> ... *for the conservation and sustainable utilization of this important component of agricultural biological diversity, for facilitated access to plant genetic resources for food and agriculture, and for the fair and equitable sharing of the benefits arising out of their utilization.* (decision VI/6, paragraph 2)

In decision V/5, the Parties adopted a multi-year programme of work on agricultural biodiversity. The decision describes the scope of agricultural biodiversity as including:

> ... *all components of biological diversity of relevance to food and agriculture, and all components of biological diversity that constitute the agro-ecosystem: the variety and variability of animals, plants and micro-organisms, at the genetic, species and ecosystem levels, which are necessary to sustain key functions of the agro-ecosystem, its structure and processes.* (paragraph 1 of the Appendix to Annex 5 to decision V/5)

The objectives of the programme of work are:

- to promote the positive effects and mitigate the negative impacts of agricultural systems and practices on biological diversity in agro-ecosystems and their interface with other ecosystems;

CBD

- to promote the conservation and sustainable use of genetic resources of actual and potential value for food and agriculture; and
- to promote the fair and equitable sharing of benefits arising out of the use of genetic resources (paragraph 2 of Annex 5).

The programme of work includes four elements: assessments, adaptive management, capacity building and mainstreaming, although it is scheduled for an in-depth review at the ninth Conference of the Parties in 2008. While it is impossible to consider all aspects of agricultural biodiversity addressed by the Convention, a few are particularly relevant in the context of this book, notably GURTs.

Genetic use restriction technologies

GURTs (Box 5.5) first came to public attention in the late 1990s with a US patent on genetically modified plants that produced sterile seeds.

GURTs are not commercially available, perhaps in part because of decisions taken by the Parties to the CBD. In the decision of the Fifth COP (COP-5), the Parties adopted what is frequently considered to be a de facto moratorium on the use of GURTs. The Parties recommended that:

> ... *in the current absence of reliable data on GURTs, without which there is an inadequate basis on which to assess their potential risks, and in accordance with the precautionary approach, products incorporating such technologies should not be approved by Parties for field testing until appropriate scientific data can justify such testing, and for commercial use until appropriate, authorized and strictly controlled scientific assessments with regard to, inter alia, their ecological and socioeconomic impacts and any adverse effects for biological diversity, food security and human health have*

Box 5.5 Genetic use restriction technologies

GURTs are generally divided into two categories: variety-related (V-GURTs) and trait-related (T-GURTs). V-GURTs refer to plants engineered to produce sterile seeds. The technology places restrictions on the plant at the plant variety level, hence the name. V-GURTs are also popularly referred to as 'terminator technology'. T-GURTs, on the other hand, are modifications made to a plant such that a particular trait or characteristic in the plant is not active unless the plant is treated with a chemical. For example, if a plant has been modified to be resistant to a particular pesticide, this resistance may not be 'turned on' until and unless the plant is actually sprayed with the pesticide. The technology places restrictions on the plant at the trait level, ergo T-GURTs. The consequence of both types of GURTs is the same: they require farmers to purchase inputs – be they seeds or chemicals – from the company in order to grow these plants and produce a crop. As described by Kloppenburg, 'The lack of any agronomic utility to terminator technology clearly revealed it as a naked attempt by companies to advantage themselves by limiting the opportunities available to farmers and so highlighted the predatory dimension of concentrating corporate power' (Kloppenburg, 2004, p320).

GURTs are somewhat analogous to digital rights management technologies in the copyright field; they provide a technological means for a company to control who uses its seeds and how these seeds are to be used instead of relying on different forms of IPRs to effect this same goal (see Chapter 1). In essence, GURTs can allow a company to *prevent* uses of seeds of which it does not approve rather than having to rely on IP law to provide a remedy *after* a disapproved use has occurred. Unlike patents or plant breeders' rights, which expire after a set period of time, GURTs can be perpetual, resulting in much stronger protection than might be provided by different forms of IPRs.

CBD

been carried out in a transparent manner and the conditions for their safe and beneficial use validated. (decision V/5, paragraph 23)

Since this decision, there has been an ongoing tug of war between civil society groups who seek to maintain the moratorium and who call for a complete and outright ban on GURTs and certain governments, such as those of Australia, Canada, New Zealand and the US, which have advocated allowing case-by-case assessments of whether plants incorporating GURTs could be used. At COP-8 in 2006, the Parties reaffirmed the COP-5 decision on GURTs (decision VIII/23, part C, paragraph 1). It seems unlikely, however, that this is the end of the debate, particularly as the COP-8 decision calls for further research on the potential impacts of GURTs.

Implementation, compliance and enforcement

As a framework for international cooperation on biodiversity, the CBD relies on its Parties (national governments) to adopt or change legislation to give effect to the Convention. The terms of the CBD are legally binding on its country Parties, but the Convention's provisions do not generally set specific requirements to be undertaken by them. This is unlike other international agreements, such as the Convention on International Trade in Endangered Species of Fauna and Flora (CITES), which has specific trade restrictions and requirements for specific lists of species. The CBD sets general requirements to meet its three objectives and then largely leaves it to individual states to determine how best to implement these provisions in their respective jurisdictions (McGraw, 2002, pp20–21). A number of these requirements are qualified by phrases such as 'as far as possible and appropriate' and 'subject to its national legislation', and

some ascribe the near-universal ratification of the Convention to its lack of effective means of monitoring or enforcing compliance with its provisions (McGraw, 2002, p24).

The CBD does not include a specific compliance mechanism akin to the Compliance Committee under the Biosafety Protocol (discussed in more detail below). That said, there are mechanisms for dispute settlement as well as a provision on liability and redress. Article 27 addresses the settlement of disputes. It creates a graduated response to resolving disputes, first requiring the parties concerned to seek a solution by negotiation, then allowing a third party to mediate or provide good offices if negotiation has not been successful. Paragraph 3 allows the Parties to agree to submit disputes to arbitration in accordance with Part 1 of Annex II to the Convention and/or to the jurisdiction of the International Court of Justice. If the parties to a dispute have not submitted to either of these procedures, the dispute is to be submitted to conciliation in accordance with Part 2 of Annex II unless the parties agree otherwise. None of these dispute settlement mechanisms has been used to date, perhaps because the Convention leaves much of the specifics of its implementation to be determined by each country in light of its own domestic circumstances.

If a dispute under the CBD were ever to be decided by the International Court of Justice, the losing party to the dispute would not necessarily face economic sanctions for not complying with the Court's ruling. This lack of economic consequences for non-compliance with the CBD (and many other multilateral environmental agreements, with notable exceptions such as CITES) is frequently said to give the Convention less 'bite' than the dispute settlement mechanism under the WTO, which allows for compensation and the suspension of concessions in cases of non-compliance with a ruling of one of its dispute settlement bodies (Article 22 of the Dispute Settlement Understanding). There are a number of disad-

CBD

vantages to the dispute settlement mechanism of the WTO, however, and it should not necessarily be regarded as a model to be followed elsewhere (Charnovitz, 2001). Rather than rely on coercive measures as does the WTO, the CBD and other environmental agreements tend to use positive incentives and transparency or 'sunshine' methods to encourage compliance (Weiss, 2000, p463).

Article 14(2) of the CBD requires the COP to examine, 'on the basis of studies to be carried out, the issue of liability and redress, including restoration and compensation, for damage to biological diversity, except where such liability is a purely internal matter'. To date, the Parties have largely engaged in an information gathering exercise on legislation, measures, agreements and case studies relating to liability and redress for damage to biological diversity and have held two meetings of experts to discuss the issue and review information. It seems unlikely that any sort of more formal liability and redress mechanism will be negotiated for the Convention itself, although important liability and redress negotiations are ongoing under the Biosafety Protocol (see below).

Leaving states to implement measures to achieve the Convention's three objectives also places the onus on these states to ensure compliance with their domestic measures. This has created a great deal of frustration for developing countries which face difficulties in monitoring and enforcing the terms of ABS agreements negotiated under their national laws. As agreements in private international law, ABS contracts are not generally subject to the dispute settlement provisions of the CBD.[5]

Technology, research and benefit sharing

A number of other provisions in the Convention involve technology, research and the sharing of benefits and could also relate to IPRs. These include Article 12(c), which deals with research and training and promotion and cooperation 'in the use of scientific advances in biological diversity research in developing methods for conservation and sustainable use of biological resources'; Article 17, which deals with exchange of information; and Article 18, which covers technical and scientific cooperation.

In their decision on 'Scientific and Technical Cooperation and the Clearing-house Mechanism', the Parties at their eighth Conference in 2006 invited 'Parties and other Governments, as appropriate, to provide free and open access to all past, present and future public-good research results, assessments, maps and databases on biodiversity, in accordance with national and international legislation' (decision VIII/11, paragraph 3). This decision points to the growing links being made between copyright, open access to research and publications, and biodiversity (Box 5.6 and Chapter 8).

Article 19 on the 'handling of biotechnology and distribution of its benefits' also contains provisions with links to IPRs. Article 19(1) provides that Parties shall take appropriate measures to provide for the effective participation in biotechnological research by Parties, especially developing countries, that provide the genetic resources for such research, in such Parties where feasible. Article 19(2) requires Parties to 'take all practicable measures to promote and advance priority access on a fair and equitable basis' for Parties providing genetic resources, especially developing countries, to 'the results and benefits arising from biotechnologies based upon [those] genetic resources ... on mutually agreed terms'.

IPRs are also relevant to the implementation of Article 10, which requires Parties, as far as possible and as appropriate, to integrate consideration of the conservation and sustainable use of biological resources into national decision making and to adopt measures relating to the use of biological resources to avoid or minimize effects on biological diversity (Article 10(a) and (b)). The article also requires Parties

Box 5.6 Copyright, open access and biodiversity

In January 2006, the journal *Nature* published a letter to the editor from Donat Agosti of the American Museum of Natural History. In the letter, Agosti makes a link between copyright and biopiracy:

The number of online publications with taxonomic content is increasing, and online tools are becoming available to mash up taxonomic with other information, for example at ispecies.org. ... But copyright and high costs put this information beyond the reach of many in the developing world – which is home to more than 95 per cent of species whose descriptions have been published. More than half the 1600 descriptions of new ant species published in the past ten years are copyrighted, for example, but none are in journals published in the developing world (see www.antbase.org). This seems little better than biopiracy: taking biodiversity material from the developing world for profit, without sharing benefit or providing the people who live there with access to this crucial information.[a]

Since Agosti's letter, there have been a number of developments that recognize the important links between access to information and biodiversity, including initiatives to provide access to information as part of ABS projects. Also in January 2006, the Fogarty International Center of the US National Institutes of Health announced new funding for International Cooperative Biodiversity Groups (ICBGs). One of the ICBGs is a collaboration between American-based researchers and Costa Rica's National Biodiversity Institute (INBio). Under the project, information on Costa Rican biodiversity that is collected will be made publicly available in the ChemBank database.[b]

In March 2007, the open-access journal *Public Library of Science Biology* published a number of articles presenting the initial findings of the J. Craig Venter Institute's Global Ocean Sampling expedition. The expedition included the sampling of microbial sea life from the waters off the coasts of a number of different countries as well as in the high seas.

There was also the COP-8 decision on public-good research results outlined above, which Agosti himself described as a 'breakthrough'.[c] Beyond the ABS field, there are many initiatives on access to information and biodiversity. These include Conservation Commons (including its Conservation Geoportal), the online *Encyclopedia of Life*, the Biodiversity Heritage Library and the Global Biodiversity Information Facility (see also Chapter 8).

Notes: [a] Agosti (2006, p392); [b] Dalton (2006, p568); [c] Shanahan and Massarani (2006).

to 'as far as possible and as appropriate ... [p]rotect and encourage customary use of biological resources in accordance with traditional cultural practices that are compatible with conservation or sustainable use requirements' (Article 10(c)).

Ongoing processes

It may appear as though an international agreement such as the CBD is set in stone once countries have agreed to it but, in fact, it continues to evolve as countries undertake domestic implementation, the Parties adopt new decisions, developments transpire in other related fora and more information about biodiversity is acquired. One such major evolutionary development in the history of the

CBD is the negotiation and adoption of the Biosafety Protocol, discussed below. A current ongoing process is the negotiation of an international regime on ABS.

An international regime on ABS?

As described above, the ABS provisions in the CBD are very general, largely leaving it to Parties to develop and implement more specific rules on ABS domestically and also leaving the terms of ABS contracts to negotiation between the providers and users. In the mid-1990s, as some developing countries, such as the Philippines and Costa Rica, began to try to create national ABS systems, they found it to be an exceedingly complex exercise, requiring the collaboration of experts in science, law and business. Many developing countries lacked the capacity to bring these experts together and so were unable to implement the ABS provisions of the CBD. Furthermore, countries that were able to create domestic regimes faced challenges in their implementation. One such challenge is where access to a genetic resource was granted but the resource was removed from the country's jurisdiction. Most developing countries had little ability to track how such resources were subsequently used or to monitor whether the terms of any negotiated ABS contract were being complied with by the user of the genetic resources. Developing countries also faced a lack of capacity and experience in negotiating access contracts and were vulnerable to agreeing to terms that were not 'fair and equitable'. With much genetic diversity being shared among countries, bioprospectors seeking access might also be able to pit developing countries against each other in a race to the bottom to offer the best terms and gain at least some benefits (see Chapter 7 for a discussion of biopiracy, a related but controversial term). Developed countries, where most of the commercial users of genetic resources are located, had little interest in creating rules that would place obligations on these users to address the concerns of developing countries. They preferred ABS to be purely based on contractual terms negotiated between the providers and the users.

At the CBD, early work on the implementation of ABS provisions focused on information gathering. The Parties began to move beyond this stage at their fifth conference in 2000 when they created the Ad Hoc Open-Ended Working Group on ABS 'to develop guidelines and other approaches' on ABS to help the Parties and stakeholders. At its first meeting in 2001, the Working Group drafted the 'Bonn Guidelines on Access to Genetic Resources and the Fair and Equitable Sharing of the Benefits arising from their Utilization', which were finalized and adopted at COP-6 in 2002. The voluntary guidelines expand upon the concepts of prior informed consent and mutually agreed terms as contained in the CBD. They also provide a list of suggested elements for inclusion in material transfer agreements and list monetary and non-monetary options for benefit sharing. The Bonn Guidelines aimed, among other things, to contribute to the conservation and sustainable use of biodiversity, promote technology transfer, contribute to 'the development by Parties of mechanisms and ABS regimes that recognize the protection of TK, innovations and practices of indigenous and local communities, in accordance with domestic laws and relevant international instruments', and contribute to poverty alleviation and supporting the realization of human food security, health and cultural integrity (paragraphs 11(a), (g), (j) and (k)).

The Bonn Guidelines have proven useful for countries developing national systems to govern ABS and have been explicitly used by Australia and Kenya in the creation of their legislative frameworks. The Bonn Guidelines make little to no mention, however, of obligations on users of genetic resources or issues of enforcement. Growing frustration with the lack of obligations on users of genetic resources led to the formation in February 2002 of the Like-Minded Megadiverse Countries (LMMC), a coalition of developing countries that represents more than 70 per cent of global biodiversity and 45 per cent of the world's population, spanning a number of geographical regions.[6] The initial member countries were Brazil, China, Colombia, Costa Rica, Ecuador, India, Indonesia, Kenya, Mexico, Peru, South Africa and Venezuela. Since then, Bolivia, the Democratic Republic of the Congo, Madagascar, Malaysia and the Philippines have also joined. One of the objectives of the LMMC is the creation of binding international rules on ABS.[7] The group was instrumental in obtaining two commitments on ABS in the Johannesburg Plan of Implementation from the World Summit on Sustainable Development held in September 2002. Chapter IV of the Plan addresses the protection and management of the natural resource base of economic and social development. Paragraph 44 of that chapter focuses on biodiversity, and subsection (n) encourages the implementation and further development of the Bonn Guidelines. Subsection (o) calls for action to '[n]egotiate within the framework of the Convention on Biological Diversity, bearing in mind the Bonn Guidelines, an international regime to promote and safeguard the fair and equitable sharing of benefits arising out of the utilization of genetic resources'.

At COP-7 to the CBD, in February 2004, the Parties agreed to launch the negotiations and also set the terms of reference on which the negotiations are to be based (decision VII/19, part D). There is a list of over 20 elements to be considered in the terms of reference for the negotiations including '(xiv) Disclosure of origin/source/legal provenance of genetic resources and associated TK in applications for intellectual property rights'.

The negotiations on the international regime began at the third and fourth meetings of the ABS Working Group which were held in Bangkok in 2005 and Grenada in 2006 respectively. Negotiations in Grenada were particularly acrimonious, with the African Group tabling a draft protocol on ABS that it sought to be used as the basis of negotiations and the Spanish chair of the meeting tabling a Chair's text. A number of developed countries – such as Australia, New Zealand, Japan, Canada, the EU and Switzerland – felt that the Chair's text and revised versions thereof did not adequately address their views and moved too quickly towards a legally binding regime (IISD, 2006b). A text full of square brackets marking the areas of disagreement was forwarded to COP-8 in Curitiba, Brazil, in March 2006.

In addition to government positions in the ABS negotiations, industry has also begun to take an increasingly vocal role. The International Chamber of Commerce (ICC) has been following ABS negotiations for a number of years and now has a task force on ABS that includes three major industries that use genetic resources: the agricultural sector, the industrial use of microbial resources and the pharmaceutical industry. At the Grenada meeting of the ABS Working Group, the ICC expressed the view that a 'one size fits all' approach to genetic resources would not work given the different interests and needs of different sectors (CBD, 2006b, paragraph 28). While there may be some merit to this view, taking a sector-by-sector approach to regulating genetic resources could also create a number of problems. It could result in a confusing web of rules that would be impractical to apply given that it is difficult if not impossible to predict at the time of access the different fields in which a genetic resource might be used. The sector-by-sector approach may also be a negotiating tactic to divide the discussions into many small parts, diluting the energy and capacity of developing countries to participate. (See Chapter 6 for a discussion of the IT and its ABS rules specific to plant genetic resources for food and agriculture.)

At COP-8, the Parties instructed the ABS Working Group 'to complete its work at the earliest possible time before the tenth meeting of the Parties' in Nagoya, Japan, in 2010 (decision VIII/4, paragraph 6). What exactly is meant by the ABS Working Group 'completing its work' is left open to interpretation. The Parties named two permanent co-chairs – Tim Hodges of Canada and Fernando Casas of Colombia – to lead the ABS Working Group through the negotiations. They also agreed to forward the text from Grenada to the next meeting of the ABS Working Group, but the controversy that surrounds the text and the lack of 'ownership' vested in it by the two co-chairs suggests that it is unlikely to remain an option.

More broadly, these negotiations can be understood as the latest salvo by some developing countries in their attempts to bring balance to the world economic system. Precursors to the ABS negotiations can be found in the debates over revisions to the Paris Convention for the Protection of Industrial Property at WIPO (see Chapters 3 and 4), the negotiation of an International Code of Conduct on the Transfer of Technology at UNCTAD, and the General Assembly Resolution on the Declaration for the Establishment of a New International Economic Order (Sell, 1998). It remains to be seen whether developing countries will be more successful in extracting concessions from developed countries in the ABS negotiations than they were in these previous, largely unsuccessful undertakings.

Monitoring, enforcement and compliance: Certificates and disclosure

The tools and mechanisms to enforce the Convention – an instrument of public international law – discussed above do not necessarily apply to the enforcement of contracts, which are instruments of private international law. Developing countries with national ABS systems cannot easily monitor the use of genetic resources once they leave their jurisdiction and ensure compliance with the terms agreed to in a contract. The lack of user measures in the Bonn Guidelines, the lack of

binding obligations on users of genetic resources and the unwillingness of countries that are home to commercial users of genetic resources to place obligations on these users has created a great deal of frustration among developing countries. At the CBD, this frustration has manifested itself in the push to negotiate an international regime on ABS, while in WIPO and the WTO it has led to calls for mandatory requirements for disclosure in patent applications (see Chapters 3, 4 and 7).

While these debates continue, the Parties to the CBD are considering a measure that could support disclosure requirements: an international certificates scheme. The general idea is that an access provider would also provide the user with a certificate attesting to the fact that the user gained access in accordance with the provider's rules on prior informed consent and on mutually agreed terms. Users could then use these certificates to meet any disclosure requirements in the patent system or product approval process, or in the requirements of funding agencies or publishers, and so forth. While disclosure and certificates are not the same thing – each could exist without the other – many of the debates about disclosure are echoed in the discussion of certificates (Box 5.7). Should a certificate attest to the origin, the source or the legal provenance of the genetic resource in question? Should it also cover TK? Should it be required in patent applications?

In January 2007, the CBD convened a meeting of a Group of Technical Experts on an Internationally Recognized Certificate of Origin/Source/Legal Provenance. The Group explored and elaborated possible options for the form, intent and functioning of such a certificate and analysed its practicality, feasibility, costs and benefits (CBD, 2007b, paragraph 13). The Group 'recognized that the basic role of the certificate is to provide evidence of compliance with national ABS regimes. Thus it found it practical to refer to the certificate as a certificate of compliance with national law, in accordance with the Convention' (CBD, 2007b,

Box 5.7 Implementation of disclosure and certificates: First steps

Some countries have already begun to incorporate certificates schemes into their ABS systems and disclosure requirements into their IP law. Both Brazil and Costa Rica have requirements for disclosure of origin in their patent laws, although neither country has enforced these requirements.[a]

In Norway, the Norwegian Patent Law was amended in 2003, introducing a requirement for disclosure of origin of the providing country of biological materials. If the providing country requires access to be based on prior informed consent, the patent application is also to include information on whether this consent has been obtained. Furthermore, if the providing country and the country of origin are not the same and the country of origin requires prior informed consent in order to gain access, the Patent Law also requires the applicant to include information on whether this consent has been obtained or information relating to the lack of knowledge about this consent. Contravention of these provisions is punishable by fines or imprisonment under the country's Penal Code, rather than affecting the validity of a patent.[b] One limitation to the Norwegian rules is that they do not apply to patent applications submitted through the Patent Cooperation Treaty (PCT), as this would be contrary to the provisions of that treaty. In Norway, 70 per cent of all patent applications come through the PCT and, of the remaining 30 per cent, very few concern biotechnological inventions. For this reason, Norway is supporting a Swiss proposal at WIPO to amend the PCT to allow contracting states to require patent applications coming through the treaty to provide information on the origin of genetic resources (this is related to Norway's support for amending TRIPS, see Chapter 3). The Norwegian Plant Breeders' Rights Law will also be amended to include a disclosure of origin requirement as well.[c]

Norway is also proposing to go a step further and require information on the origin of genetic material imported into the country. More specifically, the draft Act on the Protection of the Natural Environment, Landscape and Biological Diversity includes a provision that would only permit the import of genetic material for use in Norway if the importer has complied with the requirements for consent for the collection and export of the material in the country of origin.[c]

Australia has launched a system of virtual certificates of origin. The system is an online, publicly accessible search tool that allows verification of prior informed consent and the terms on which access was granted by the government: 'The aim is to enable an inquirer, at no cost and at his or her convenience, to obtain key information about the provenance of a sample and terms and conditions under which it was collected'.[d] The system is intended to serve as a good first step for conducting due diligence by those who need to verify the provenance of genetic resources. The Costa Rican Biodiversity Law provides that a certificate of origin will be clearly stipulated in an access permit (Article 71). The Technical Office of the National Commission for the Management of Biodiversity has interpreted this as meaning that the applicant must request the certificate. To date, no certificates have been granted, perhaps due to lack of knowledge about the instrument.

Notes: [a] Rodrigues Jr (2005); [b] Ivars (2004), pp305–306; [c] Ivars and Schneider (2005); [d] Burton and Phillips (2005); the virtual system is available at www.environment.gov.au/biodiversity/science/access/permits.html, accessed 31 May 2007.

paragraph 7 of annex). This change in terminology circumvents the question of origin/source/legal provenance without actually resolving which of these would be certified under a certification system. While the Group explored and elaborated options, the decisions on which options should be pursued are left for the ABS Working Group, which, at the time of writing, has not yet considered the outcomes from the meeting of the Group of Technical Experts.

Industry has also weighed in on both the issues of disclosure and certificates. Most industry organizations are generally opposed to mandatory requirements for the disclosure of origin in patent applications. In September 2005, the US biotechnology industry formed a new lobby group – the American Bioindustry Alliance (ABIA) – under the leadership of Jacques Gorlin, one of a handful of key architects of the TRIPS Agreement. The ABIA has described its activities as 'developing industry positions and programmes to counter the unprecedented global threat to biotechnology patents at the WTO Hong Kong Ministerial Meeting ... and beyond' (Garforth, 2006; see also New, 2006).[8] The group is opposed to mandatory requirements for the disclosure of origin in patent applications and is active at the WTO, the CBD and WIPO in advocating this perspective. Industry views on certificates appear to be less hard-line, as illustrated by the submissions to the CBD's Group of Technical Experts (CBD, 2006a). Industry organizations have a great many questions about how a certificates system may function but may be willing to support some sort of certificates mechanism if it results in legal certainty and does not create undue administrative burdens.

The Cartagena Protocol on Biosafety[9]

One development in the evolution of the CBD was the creation of the Cartagena Protocol on Biosafety. The Protocol is a subsidiary instrument of the CBD and is also an evolving instrument with important links to food security and IP rights as well as biodiversity. Most fundamentally, the commercial development of genetically modified organisms (GMOs) owes much to the extension of patentability and companies' aggressive enforcement of these patent rights (see Chapter 1). What follows is an overview of the negotiations that led to the creation of the Protocol and a discussion of key provisions and ongoing processes therein.

The negotiations

The negotiation of the CBD began at a time when the potential of biotechnology was just beginning to be recognized. From the start, developing countries insisted that biotechnology be one of the key issues addressed in the Convention (McGraw, 2002, p34). This insistence was successful and led to the inclusion in the Convention of Article 19 on the 'handling of biotechnology and distribution of its benefits'. In general, the article provides that Parties to the CBD are to take measures to include countries that provide genetic resources in biotechnology research activities, to share access to the results and benefits of biotechnology, and to provide information about living modified organisms to Parties where they are to be introduced. Paragraph 3 of Article 19 obliges the Parties to the Convention to:

> *... consider the need for and modalities of a protocol setting out appropriate procedures, including, in particular, advance informed agreement, in the field of the safe transfer, handling and use of any living modified organism resulting from biotechnology that may have adverse effect on the conservation and sustainable use of biological diversity.*

This paragraph was somewhat controversial during the negotiations as some countries wanted to make the development of a protocol mandatory (Mackenzie et al, 2003, paragraph 11).

Box 5.8 Precaution and the Protocol

Precaution became an explicit point of contention at the Montreal meeting, where the final text of the Protocol was adopted, and continues to be a key issue in the implementation of the Protocol and its evolution. During the negotiations, the Like-Minded Group of developing countries[a] advocated the incorporation of the precautionary principle throughout the Protocol on the basis that '[t]he very necessity of adopting a protocol stemmed precisely from the need for parties to take precautionary measures'.[b] The Miami Group, on the other hand, perceived the whole Protocol to be a precautionary instrument as no harm from living modified organisms (LMOs) had been demonstrated[c] and so no operative provisions on precaution were necessary.

In the end, the negotiators compromised on language in the statement of the Protocol's objective in Article 1, referencing the precautionary 'approach' rather than 'principle', reflecting disagreement over whether the precautionary principle is a principle of customary international law. The article also makes reference to Principle 15 of the Rio Declaration, which contains perhaps the most frequently cited definition of the precautionary principle: 'Where there are threats of serious or irreversible damage, lack of full scientific certainty shall not be used as a reason for postponing cost-effective measures to prevent environmental degradation.' Articles 10(6) and 11(8) of the Protocol allow precautionary decision making by Parties, although the provisions for precaution are phrased differently from Principle 15 of the Rio Declaration.

Caution and precaution persist as undertones in the debates over the labelling of shipments of LMOs for use as food or feed or for processing as the labelling of shipments affects the ability to label food sold to consumers and in the liability and redress negotiations.

Notes: [a] The Like-Minded Group in the Protocol negotiations emerged from the Group of 77 developing countries and China in order to distinguish themselves from the three developing countries in the Miami Group. The Like-Minded Group supported a strong Protocol. They should not be confused with the Like-Minded Megadiverse Countries, discussed above in the context of the ABS negotiations, as they are not the same; [b] Graff (2002), p412; [c] Mackenzie et al (2003), paragraph 64.

CBD

At COP-1 to the CBD, the Parties authorized two meetings to discuss the need for a protocol. The second of these meetings, by the Ad Hoc Open-Ended Group of Experts, included support by a large majority of the delegations present for the negotiation of a biosafety protocol. At COP-2 in 1995, the Parties agreed to establish the Ad Hoc Working Group on Biosafety to elaborate a protocol on biosafety and for it to endeavour to complete its work sometime in 1998.

In the end, it took until 2000 for the negotiating countries to reach agreement on the text of a protocol. The negotiations were rocky and reached the brink of failure when there was no agreement at a February 1999 meeting in Cartagena, Colombia. In particular, the negotiating bloc of the Miami Group of countries – Canada, the US, Australia, Uruguay, Chile and Argentina, the leading agricultural exporters with the most to lose from strict regulation of GMOs – pressed for the weakest and narrowest protocol possible, nearly scuttling the negotiations at the February 1999 meeting. An extraordinary Conference of the Parties was called for January 2000 in Montreal and consensus was finally achieved. Three and a half years later, in September 2003, the Cartagena Protocol on Biosafety ('Biosafety Protocol' or 'the Protocol') entered into force.

Some of the most contentious issues during the negotiations included the scope of the advance informed agreement procedure under the Protocol and the types of organisms it would cover; inclusion of the precautionary principle in the operational text of the Protocol (Box 5.8); the allowance for socioeconomic considerations in decision making under the Protocol; and the relationship between the Protocol and other international agreements, particularly those of the WTO. In this regard, the CBD has requested but has not yet been granted observer status in both the Sanitary and Phytosanitary and Technical Barriers to Trade Committees of the WTO.

The Protocol

The term biosafety is not defined in either the Protocol or the CBD. According to the CBD Secretariat, 'Biosafety is a term used to describe efforts to reduce and eliminate the potential risks resulting from biotechnology and its products.'[10] Potential risks include the possibility that a genetically modified organism may out-compete other organisms once introduced into the environment, becoming a pest, and that genes introduced into one organism may spread to other organisms, causing environmental, economic and/or social damage.

The Protocol focuses its efforts on reducing the potential risks of LMOs resulting from modern biotechnology. The term LMO stands in contrast to the more frequently used 'genetically modified organism' and it is carefully defined in the Protocol as 'any living organism that possesses a novel combination of genetic material obtained through the use of modern biotechnology'. The Protocol is a subsidiary instrument of the CBD and so only Parties to the Convention may become Parties to the Protocol (Box 5.9). There are 143 Parties to the Protocol as of late 2007.

The Protocol is a complex and intricate instrument and our focus is on two of its decision-making procedures for LMOs. The

scope and terms of these procedures are intimately linked with the economics that were at stake during the negotiations.

The Protocol divides LMOs into several categories. The two main groups of concern are LMOs that are intended for intentional introduction into the environment of an importing Party and LMOs for use as food, feed or for processing (LMOs-FFP):

> *[LMOs-FFP include] such widely traded commodities as genetically modified corn, soy, wheat, canola and tomatoes. Those opposed to including commodities in the Protocol had argued that commodities, since they are not intended for introduction into the environment, pose no threat to biodiversity and should not be the subject of a protocol to the CBD. LMOs intended for introduction into the environment, on the other hand – such as seeds and micro-organisms – can mutate, migrate and multiply, and therefore may pose unexpected threats to native species. Others argued that it was impossible to ensure that LMO-FFPs would not be introduced to the environment, whatever the intent.* (Cosbey and Burgiel, 2000, p4).

By the time the negotiators met in Cartagena in 1999, they had agreed that LMOs-FFP would be included in the scope of the Protocol. The remaining question was whether they would be subject to the Protocol's advance informed agreement (AIA) procedure.

The Miami Group's aim in Cartagena was to keep LMOs-FFP outside the AIA procedure, whereas the Like-Minded Group (see Box 5.8) was similarly insistent that LMOs-FFP should be subject to it or a similarly robust procedure (SCBD, no date, p42). The final text represents a compromise but was essentially a 'win' for the Miami Group as the Protocol creates a separate procedure for LMOs-FFP, a procedure that is less onerous for exporters than the AIA procedure.

Box 5.9 The operations of the Biosafety Protocol in brief

As a subsidiary instrument to the CBD, the Biosafety Protocol shares a number of operational mechanisms and processes with the Convention. The Protocol is administered by the same Montreal-based Secretariat. The Conference of the Parties to the Convention also serves as the meeting of the Parties to the Protocol, but decisions under the Protocol can only be taken by the countries that are party to it (Article 29). The Conference of the Parties serving as the meeting of the Parties (COP/MOP or, more informally, MOP) generally meets biennially and in conjunction with the COP.

Article 27 on liability and redress and Article 34 on compliance foresee the creation of processes and mechanisms by the MOP. The results to date are:

- the Ad Hoc Open-Ended Working Group of Legal and Technical Experts on Liability and Redress, which is mandated to review information relating to liability and redress for damage resulting from transboundary movements of LMOs, analyse issues relevant to liability and redress with a view to building understanding and consensus, and elaborate options for elements of rules and procedures referred to in Article 27 of the Protocol; and
- the Compliance Committee, which has various functions aimed at promoting compliance and addressing cases of non-compliance with the Protocol (decision BS-1/7).

Under the terms of Article 28 of the Protocol, the GEF also serves as the financial mechanism of the Protocol. The COP/MOP develops guidance to be provided to the GEF. This is then forwarded to the COP, which incorporates it into its decision on guidance to the financial mechanism.

Article 20 of the Protocol establishes the Biosafety Clearing-House (BCH) as part of the Convention's clearing-house mechanism. The Protocol was the first instrument of international law to require an internet-based exchange of information. Among other things, Parties taking decisions under the advance informed agreement (AIA) procedure in Article 10 and the procedure for LMOs for food, feed or processing in Article 11 must make these decisions available via the BCH.

Certain provisions of the Convention also apply to the Protocol, including Article 27 on the settlement of disputes.

CBD

The distinction between LMOs that *are* for intentional introduction into the environment and those that *are not* is somewhat of a legal fiction as LMOs in the latter category can easily wind up being released into the environment, regardless of intention (Box 5.10) The introduction of genetically modified commodities into an environment where they are not intended to be introduced raises a number of IP concerns. If a company has a patent on the gene that is spreading through the countryside, will the company be able to sue farmers for patent infringement and stop them from growing any crop that contains the gene? This scenario is not at all far-fetched given the case of *Monsanto v. Schmeiser* (discussed below) and Monsanto's actions over Argentinean exports of Roundup Ready soya (GRAIN, 2006a; see also Chapter 8, Box 8.8). The impacts that this sort of action could have on the livelihoods of subsistence farmers and the biodiversity they cultivate are potentially catastrophic. It can also mean that the introduction and spread of LMOs in the environment becomes a fait accomplish without the organism going through the necessary regulatory process.

LMOs that are intended for intentional introduction into the environment of an importing Party are subject to the AIA procedure (Articles 7–10). The aim of this procedure is to ensure that importing countries have the opportunity to assess 'the possible adverse effects of LMOs on the conservation and sustainable use of biological diversity, taking also into account risks to human health' (Article 15(1)). The procedure requires the Party that intends to export LMOs to notify, or to require the exporter to notify, the Party that is destined to be the importer (Article 8(1)). The notification must include, as a minimum, the information in Annex I to the Protocol, which includes descriptions of the organism in question, intended use of the organism and the regulatory status of the LMO in the country of export. The importing Party is then required to acknowledge receipt of the notification, including '[w]hether to proceed according to the domestic regulatory framework of the Party of import or according to the procedure specified in Article 10' (Article 9(2)(c)). Article 10, in turn, sets out a decision-making procedure that Parties can (but are not obliged to) use to determine whether to approve or prohibit the import, or request additional information. The procedure includes a risk assessment and allows the Party of import to use precaution to avoid or minimize the potential adverse effects of the LMO where there is scientific uncertainty. According to the information available on the BCH, the AIA procedure has been little used.[11]

The procedure for LMOs-FFP is contained in Article 11 of the Protocol. The article requires a Party that makes a decision concerning domestic use of an LMO-FFP that may be subject to transboundary movement to notify the other Parties of the decision via the Biosafety Clearing-House. The procedure still allows countries to make their own decisions about the import of LMOs-FFP and these decisions can be based on precaution.

Key issues in the Protocol

As with the Convention, the final agreed text of the Protocol is not a static instrument. On two issues in particular (labelling plus liability and redress), negotiators were unable to reach agreement on substantive provisions and so included enabling clauses in the Protocol that called for further negotiation on these once the Protocol entered into force. These issues can be seen as part of the balancing requirements and risk sharing for those who benefit from IP-protected products and processes deriving from modern biotechnologies which they promote.

Labelling of shipments

Article 18 of the Protocol concerns 'handling, transport, packaging and identification'. Paragraph 2 of the article sets out the documentation requirements that must accompany shipments of different categories of LMOs. Most controversial is sub-paragraph (a), which, with its chapeau, reads:

> *Each Party shall take measures to require that documentation accompanying … LMOs that are intended for direct use as food or feed, or for processing, clearly identifies that they 'may contain' LMOs and are not intended for intentional introduction into the environment, as well as a contact point for further information. The Conference of the Parties serving as the meeting of the Parties to this Protocol shall take a decision on the detailed requirements for this purpose, including specification of their identity and any unique identification, no later than two years after the date of entry into force of this Protocol.*

This sub-paragraph was the last issue to be agreed by the Extraordinary Conference of the Parties in Montreal in 2000 (SCBD, no date,

Box 5.10 Trade in commodities and the risk of their release into the environment

During the negotiation of the Protocol, the Miami Group of countries insisted that genetically modified commodities – or what came to be known as LMOs intended for direct use as food or feed or for processing – should not be subject to an AIA procedure because these commodities posed a lower risk as they were not intended to be introduced into the environment. Developing countries, on the other hand, 'supported the inclusion of commodities in the scope of the AIA by referring to their domestic situation, in which grains imported for food were often used as seeds by farmers, especially during a crisis'.[a] Thus, just because organisms were *intended* to be used as food or feed or for processing did not mean that they would *actually* be used for any of these purposes and was no guarantee that they would not be introduced into the environment.

Subsequent experience has borne out this position. For example, in 2001, researchers in Mexico reported finding genetically modified corn in the remote region of Oaxaca. The corn had not been approved for planting in Mexico, leading to speculation about the source of the transgenes. A study by the Commission for Environmental Cooperation concluded that a probable pathway for the introduction of the transgenes was that:

> ... *imported transgenic grain that is shipped to rural communities through a government agency (for example Diconsa SA de CV) may be experimentally planted by small-scale farmers. Indeed, small-scale farmers are known to plant Diconsa seeds occasionally, adjacent to their local landraces. Cross-pollination can occur between modern cultivars and landraces that flower at the same time and grow near each other. Farmers save and trade seed, some of which may be transgenic, and thus the cycle of gene flow can be repeated and transgenes can spread further.*[b]

It would be impossible to tell from simply looking at the corn kernels that they were intended to be used as a commodity rather than planted in the ground, so farmers would have no reason not to experiment with the seeds to see how they would grow.

The discovery of the transgenes raised concerns about the impact the introduced genes could have on the native maize landraces of Mexico, the centre of origin for corn, and the great wealth of corn biodiversity that is found in the country. There are also concerns about the sociocultural impacts of the introduced genes in a context where corn is considered sacred.[c]

Notes: [a] Pythoud (2002), p324; [b] CEC (2004), paragraph 10; [c] CEC (2004) and Ribeiro (2004).

CBD

p60). The controversy surrounds the meaning of the words 'may contain' and the extent to which they will enable countries to label LMOs or GMOs that are sold to consumers.

In the event the Parties were unable to reach agreement about Article 18.2(a) during the second meeting of the Parties to the Protocol held in Montreal in May–June 2005,

due in large part to New Zealand and Brazil. This increased the pressure on the Parties at MOP-3 in Curitiba, Brazil, in 2006 to reach agreement, as another failure might seriously compromise the Protocol.

Long negotiating sessions among a few key players, including Ethiopia, Malaysia, Brazil, New Zealand, Mexico and the EU, resulted in decision BS-III/10. Paragraph 4 of the decision sets the 'detailed requirements' requested by Article 18.2(a). It requires Parties to the Protocol to ensure that documentation accompanying LMOs-FFP states, in cases where the identity of the LMOs is known, that the shipment *contains* such LMOs, and, in cases where the identity of the LMOs is not known, that the shipment *may contain* such LMOs. In paragraph 6 of the decision, the Parties acknowledge that the expression 'may contain' does not require a listing of LMOs other than those that constitute the shipment. Overall, the decision tries to balance the concerns and obligations of countries that are likely to be importing bulk shipments of commodities that could contain LMOs with the concerns and obligations of those likely to be exporting such shipments, some of whom are not Parties to the Protocol and so are not bound to comply by its provisions. It seems ironic, then, that New Zealand, which has one of the strictest domestic systems for the regulation of GMOs, was arguing for extremely weak rules at the international level. This illustrates the complexity of international processes and how a country's position may be influenced by a number of different interests, in this case New Zealand's high economic dependence on agricultural exports and its relationship with its trading partners, particularly the US.

Despite the text in decision BS-III/10, all is not what it seems, and the decision largely delays the issue yet again. It requires the Parties at their fifth meeting (in 2010) to review and assess experience gained with the implementation of paragraph 4, with a view to considering a decision at their sixth meeting to ensure that documentation accompanying LMOs-FFP covered by paragraph 4 clearly states that the shipment contains such LMOs (paragraph 7). So, while a decision has been adopted that ostensibly satisfies the demands of Article 18.2(a), the issue is by no means resolved and will continue to be debated by the Parties.

Liability and redress

According to the CBD Secretariat:

> *The term 'liability' is normally associated with the obligation under the applicable law to provide for compensation for damage resulting from an action for which that person is deemed responsible. Liability and redress in the context of the Protocol concerns the question of what would happen if the transboundary movement of living modified organisms ... has caused damage.*[12]

The Like-Minded Group insisted on the inclusion in the Protocol of provisions on liability and redress:

> *The motto 'no liability, no Protocol', displayed on blue-green badges, was adopted during the negotiations by delegates arguing for the inclusion in the protocol of some provision for liability and redress. It was intended to reinforce the message that if this subject were to be left out, the prospects for successfully finalizing a protocol would be minimal. Some of those less well disposed towards the ultimate success of the protocol negotiations also muttered the phrase to themselves, in hope rather than defiance, and at times the words looked like a forlorn prophecy rather than a clarion call to address this knotty issue.* (Cook, 2002, p372)

As it became clear that negotiating substantive provisions on liability and redress would be time-consuming and delay the adoption of the Protocol as a whole, an enabling provision was included in the Protocol mandating MOP-1 to 'adopt a process with respect to the appropriate elaboration of international rules and procedures in the field of liability and redress for damage resulting from transboundary movements of living modified organisms'

(Article 27). At MOP-1, the Parties agreed to establish an Ad Hoc Open-Ended Working Group of Legal and Technical Experts on Liability and Redress. This enabling provision is somewhat analogous to Article 27.3(b) of TRIPS and its requirement for its own review four years after the entry into force of the WTO Agreement (see Chapter 3). Both provisions delay consideration of complicated issues and allow all sides in the negotiations to claim to have achieved something. These perceived achievements might well be contradictory, however, meaning that the US may claim that the Article 27.3(b) review provides for the elimination of any *restrictions* on patentability while developing countries might claim that it provides for the elimination of any *requirements* for the patentability of living organisms. Under the Protocol, developing countries can claim that Article 27 requires the negotiation of legally binding rules on liability and redress, while the main exporters of LMOs can claim that no such rules are mandated, feasible or desirable.

The Protocol's Working Group on Liability and Redress has a mandate to meet five times over four years. However, it is not specifically mandated to negotiate rules on liability and redress; rather it is, among other things, to elaborate options for elements of the rules and procedures referred to in Article 27 of the Protocol (decision BS-I/ 8, Annex).

To date, the Working Group has engaged in an exercise of compiling approaches, options and issues on rules and procedures for liability and redress. However, the difficult compromises have yet to be made and negotiations will truly take place during the final meetings of the Working Group and, in all likelihood, at MOP-4. It is even conceivable that the Parties will need to renew the mandate of the Working Group if it is unable to finalize its deliberations.

Perhaps the most fundamental point to be decided is the nature of the rules and procedures being discussed. The third meeting of the Working Group ended with an impassioned intervention from Malaysia, calling for a legally binding instrument. Anything less, it was stated, would be a betrayal of the trust of the developing countries who agreed to the compromise of the enabling provision in Article 27. Norway also spoke in favour of a legally binding regime in order to ensure consistent and predictable rules across jurisdictions. This could signal the emergence of an important North–South coalition. At the same time, however, while Principle 13 of the Rio Declaration urges the development of international liability rules, past experience with negotiating binding rules on liability has been less than positive. A number of instruments have taken many years to negotiate and to enter into force or have failed to enter into force altogether.[13]

Other key issues in the liability and redress negotiations include:

- The definition of damage. Will it be restricted to damage to biodiversity or the conservation and sustainable use of biodiversity (and if so, what does this mean)? Or will it encompass more traditional grounds, such as damage to the person or property, economic damage, or damage to the environment?

- The functional scope of the rules and procedures. Will the rules and procedures apply to damage resulting from the intentional transboundary movement of LMOs, unintentional transboundary movements, and/or illegal transboundary movements? Will they apply to damage within a Party, within a non-Party and/or beyond national jurisdiction?

- The standard of liability. Will liability be strict or will it require some proof of fault? It might be noted that patent law is a strict liability regime – simple infringement of a patent is sufficient to give rise to liability, with no fault being required (see Chapter 1, Box 1.6, and the discussion of *Monsanto v. Schmeiser*, below).

- Channelling of liability. Who can potentially be held liable? The developer, the producer, the notifier, the exporter, the importer, the carrier, the supplier?

Balancing IPRs with responsibility for damage from LMOs

While the issue has not been considered in any detail during the deliberations of the Working Group, there is a connection to be made between liability for damage caused by LMOs and IPRs over these same organisms. More specifically, it is not the IPRs per se but the control they give to their owner that ties them to the question of liability (de Beer, 2007). The juxtaposition of two Canadian cases illustrates the point quite clearly.

In the first case, the Supreme Court of Canada's decision in *Monsanto v. Schmeiser* granted Monsanto expansive patent protection over the genetically modified gene and cell in its Roundup Ready canola. The Court's interpretation of the patent was expansive because while the patent only claimed the genetically modified gene and the cells containing the gene, the effect of the Court's decision was to give Monsanto patent protection over the entire plant. This was in spite of the fact that higher life forms such as plants are not patentable in Canada.[14] A further outcome of Schmeiser was that it placed all of the burdens on the farmer to avoid infringement of the patent. Canadian patent law, like patent laws in many other countries, does not require a person to intend to infringe or even knowingly infringe a patent in order to be found liable. With Monsanto's patented genes spreading by natural means throughout the Canadian prairies, this rule places the onus on the farmer to monitor his fields for volunteer GM canola plants or the spread of the introduced genes. If and when the patented genes appear, the farmer must call the company to come and remove the plants. In Monsanto's case, at least, in order for the company to remove the plants, the farmer is required to sign a waiver that releases the company from any lawsuits 'associated with the products and forbids the grower

from disclosing the terms of the settlement' (Pratt, 2005).[15] Wilful blindness is not an option – if the farmer does not monitor his fields or call the company after having detected the genes, he faces the threat of patent infringement litigation. And if sued, it is the farmer who must rebut the presumption of use through an innocent bystander defence that the Supreme Court has said exists but has not defined (Garforth and Ainslie, 2006, pp470–471).

In the second case, *Hoffman v. Monsanto*, a group of organic farmers from Saskatchewan are attempting to launch a class action suit against Monsanto and Bayer for damages caused by the spread of the companies' genetically modified varieties of canola. Among other things, the farmers have grounded some of their allegations in the fact that Monsanto, in particular, continues to exercise control over the offending genes and cells through its IPRs and active assertion thereof. In essence, through their lawsuit the farmers are attempting to place some of the burdens for the consequences of GM plants back on the companies that developed them and profit from them.

To date, however, the farmers have been unsuccessful. The courts have refused to certify their class action, finding, among other things, that their causes of action would fail at trial. The combined effect of the Schmeiser and Hoffman decisions is somewhat paradoxical: 'Monsanto can exert unprecedented levels of control over things it could not patent, whilst simultaneously being able to deny that it has any control *over the same product* in the context of the common law or statute. This is an unacceptable incongruity' (Phillipson, 2005, p372). Rather than balancing the IPRs of the companies with a corresponding responsibility, the courts have added to the already heavy burden placed on Canadian farmers in the wake of Schmeiser. In addition to the burden of avoiding patent infringement, the farmer must now also bear the burden of damage (see also Box 1.6).

How has it come to pass that biotechnology companies can enjoy all the benefits of expansive patent protection without any obligations? Through the language of property: 'Patentees are quick to invoke the power of property rhetoric to expand and protect their rights, but when it comes to the liabilities ordinarily associated with ownership, the tune suddenly changes' (de Beer, 2007). Not all countries have the same history of case law as does Canada, however, so this disequilibrium between rights and responsibilities should not be regarded as the norm. It remains to be seen if and how these considerations might be incorporated into the activities of the Biosafety Protocol's Working Group on Liability and Redress.

Compliance

The Protocol addresses compliance (Article 34) and the Parties have set up a Compliance Committee (see Box 5.9). The Committee has 15 members, who are selected on the basis of regional representation and who serve in a personal capacity. The Committee is mandated to meet twice a year and can choose whether its meetings are open to observers. Its functions include identifying the specific circumstances and possible causes of individual cases of non-compliance referred to it; considering information submitted to it regarding compliance and non-compliance; providing advice and/or assistance to a Party 'on matters relating to compliance with a view to assisting it to comply with its obligations under the Protocol'; reviewing general issues of compliance; and taking measures or making recommendations to the MOP. While the Protocol has a more specific compliance mechanism than does the Convention, it still largely relies on the same strategies of transparency and positive incentives to try to effect compliance, as shown by the measures it and the MOP can take. The measures include providing advice, assistance and/or various capacity-building measures to the Party concerned and publishing cases of non-compliance in the Biosafety Clearing-House.[16]

To date, the Compliance Committee has not received any submissions about the compliance or non-compliance of a specific Party. It is even possible that the Committee will never receive a submission as the dictates of diplomacy would suggest that countries may prefer to seek more private solutions to any problems that arise between or among them. In this regard, there is no obligation on Parties requiring them to make submissions on instances of non-compliance if and when they are aware of them. Furthermore, with certain key exporters of LMOs (such as the US, Canada and Argentina) not being Parties to the Protocol, their actions are beyond the mandate of the Committee. In its meetings to date, the Committee has developed its rules of procedure and adopted a work plan, developed recommendations for consideration by the MOP, reviewed general issues of compliance, and reviewed information on measures concerning cases of repeated non-compliance.[17]

CBD

Conclusion

The Biosafety Protocol has already reached some key milestones. It has entered into force and the Parties have agreed to a decision on the detailed identification requirements for implementing Article 18.2(a) on documentation to accompany LMOs. It is still relatively early days for the Protocol, however, and key issues such as the rules and procedures on liability and redress remain to be resolved. The connection between IPRs and biosafety may be less obvious but is certainly present. Biosafety regulation is intended to address concerns about gene flow, but as introduced genes continue to spread through the environments where they have been released and also to spread from country to country, the IPRs over these genes give the proprietor companies increasing control over who can grow what, where and how. This has potentially serious consequences for farmers, food security and biodiversity, but these consequences have, to date, largely remained outside the deliberations under the Protocol.

Neither the Convention nor the Protocol are static instruments. Both are evolving.

Furthermore, the way they evolve is not necessarily logical or rational but is highly dependent on politics. It is difficult to capture in writing the importance of the personalities involved in the negotiations. Meetings led by competent chairs will generally produce better results; when negotiators get along with one another – whether or not their positions on an issue are similar – they will more easily reach a compromise. Personality conflicts and power struggles over process can spell disaster. These are just some of the intangibles that feed into the eventual outcomes of negotiations.

The Convention on Biological Diversity and the Cartagena Protocol on Biosafety are pieces in a larger puzzle of international rules and negotiations on these issues. They should not and cannot be fully understood in isolation and so must be interpreted in light of the other chapters in this book. To this end, the next chapter turns to one of the newest agreements and its role in the IPRs, biodiversity and food security nexus.

Resources

The website of the Secretariat to the Convention can be found at www.cbd.int.

IUCN (The World Conservation Union) has produced two valuable guides, one to the Convention (Glowka et al, 1994) and the other to the Biosafety Protocol (Mackenzie et al, 2003).

6

Giving Priority to the Commons: The International Treaty on Plant Genetic Resources for Food and Agriculture

Michael Halewood and Kent Nnadozie

Intensive human activity over thousands of years created today's agricultural biodiversity. Attempts to create market-based incentives for its conservation and innovative uses, through the application of intellectual property (IP) and CBD-inspired access and benefit sharing (ABS) laws have not benefited large numbers of smallholder farmers, often living in marginal agricultural environments, who are the most active present-day users of agricultural biodiversity. Evidence is also growing that restricted access and use of plant genetic resources for food and agriculture (PGRFA) as a result of the application of these same laws (or political uncertainties surrounding them) can have a deleterious impact on scientific research and breeding. The International Treaty on Plant Genetic Resources for Food and Agriculture provides a general framework for conservation and sustainable use of PGRFA. Most dramatically, it also establishes a plant genetic resources commons to lower transaction costs for conservation, research, breeding and training, and to redistribute back to the commons some of the financial benefits derived from the commercial exploitation of those resources (under certain circumstances). The Treaty is unlike laws analysed in previous chapters because it concentrates on defining and maintaining a commons, instead of means by which to fence portions of it off.

Introduction

The International Treaty on Plant Genetic Resources for Food and Agriculture (the Treaty) represents a spirited reaction to the rising tide of measures that extend private or sovereign control over genetic resources, which is inappropriate for food and agriculture. It recognizes that ABS for agricultural biodiver- sity must be treated differently from the way it is generally treated under the Convention on Biological Diversity (CBD). The Treaty creates an international genetic resources commons – the 'multilateral system of access and benefit sharing' – within which members, in exercise of their sovereignty, provide free (or almost free) access to each other's plant genetic resources for research, breeding, conservation and training. It does not matter how many accessions of different species members bring with them into the club; as long as they agree to share what they have, they can get access to all the other members' materials for their own use. Access to materials within the commons comes largely without strings attached, and the strings that do exist are there to maintain the spirit of the commons. For example, recipients cannot take out intellectual property rights (IPRs) that prohibit others receiving them in the same form from the multilateral system. And if recipients choose to prohibit others from using, for their own research and breeding, any product they develop using materials they got from the commons, they must share a percentage of their sales of that product with the international community through a conservation fund.

The commons does not in any way restrict the sovereignty of countries over their resources; quite the opposite, in fact. The preamble to the Treaty explicitly recognizes that 'in the exercise of their sovereign rights over their plant genetic resources for food and agriculture, states may mutually benefit from the creation of an effective multilateral system for facilitated access to a negotiated selection of these resources and for the fair and equitable sharing of the benefits arising from their use'. Parties first exercised their sovereignty by participating in the negotiations of the Treaty and the creation of the commons, and then by choosing to become a member of it. Furthermore, they can, of course, withdraw from membership in the Treaty if they wish.

The commons created by the Treaty is not yet fully global, but it appears to be well on its way. So far, 113 countries have ratified the Treaty, and a number of others are on the verge of doing so, with each new country adding to the overall number of accessions within the commons. In addition, the eleven International Agricultural Research Centres of the Consultative Group on International Agricultural Research (the CGIAR Centres) holding *ex-situ* collections of plant genetic resources for food and agriculture (PGRFA), the Centro Agronómico Tropical de Investigación y Enseñanza (CATIE) and two of the four organizations hosting collections as part of the International Coconut Genetic Resources Network have placed the collections they host under the framework of the Treaty, to be distributed according to the same rules. At present, it is impossible to say how many accessions of PGRFA are in the Treaty's commons (but it is in the millions), or how many times samples will actually be accessed or provided each year (but it will be in the hundreds of thousands).

Of course, the Treaty is not perfect. It is the product of seven and a half years of often highly polarized negotiations, and a number of compromises were necessary – with some contentious issues left hanging – for the countries involved to be able to agree on the final text in November 2001. Considerable progress has been made since then, but some challenges remain to be addressed before the Treaty, and the commons it creates, can be fully operational.

In this chapter, we briefly review why the Treaty was needed, focusing on the 'international' nature and uses of plant genetic resources for food and agriculture. Then we describe the mechanics of the Treaty, with particular emphasis on the multilateral system of ABS and its intersection with IP laws. We highlight the most innovative aspects of the Treaty, as well as challenges associated with its implementation. We also include accounts of how some of its elements evolved during the negotiations. Finally, we consider the potential implications of the Treaty – both its achievements and its limitations – for ongoing policymaking processes affecting how genetic resources for food and agriculture are conserved (or lost) and used (or ignored).

Why Create a PGRFA Commons?

The history of the development and use of PGRFA has been characterized by relatively rapid movements of domesticated materials – often in the form of a combination of domesticated crops and animals (and associated pests) – across and among continents, with ultimately a relatively small number of species representing a very high percentage of the daily diets of people around the world (Diamond, 2005). A FAO study on national and regional interdependence revealed that 'four crops – rice, wheat, sugar (beet and cane) and maize account for over 60 per cent of human calorie intake from plants' (Palacios, 1998). All countries are interdependent in their reliance on PGRFA. No region or country is self-sufficient. In examining the contribution of major food crops to peoples' daily caloric consumption around the world, the study concluded that all regions were dependent on PGRFA from other regions to a high degree, with the degree of dependence for most regions being over 50 per cent. No country in the study was ranked as even close to

self-sufficient. This interdependency is graphically illustrated in a number of studies of the international flows of PGRFA and in the pedigrees of crop varieties of major food crops (SGRP, 2006a). For example, the wheat cultivar Sonalika, which was planted on over 6 million hectares in developing countries in 1990, has a pedigree drawing on materials acquired from 15 countries. Sonalika is far from being unique. Major spring bread wheats (planted on more than 0.25 million hectares in the developing world in 1997) on average had 50 farmers' varieties parental combinations (Cassaday et al, 2001). Table 6.1 demonstrates the international nature of the pedigrees of a number of rice varieties.

PGRFA differ from other plant genetic resources (and genetic resources of all wild flora and fauna) because human intervention has played a critical role in the domestication of crops and in the human, gene and environmental interactions that have led, over thousands of years, to the genetic diversity within and across

Table 6.1 *Summary of international flows of rice ancestors in selected countries*

Country	Total landrace progenitors in all released varieties	Own landraces	Borrowed landraces
Bangladesh	233	4	229
Brazil	460	80	380
Burma	442	31	411
China	888	157	731
India	3917	1559	2358
Indonesia	463	43	420
Nepal	142	2	140
Nigeria	195	15	180
Pakistan	195	0	195
Philippines	518	34	484
Sri Lanka	386	64	322
Taiwan	20	3	17
Thailand	154	27	127
United States	325	219	106
Vietnam	517	20	497

Source: Fowler and Hodgkin (2004), based on a table originally included in Evenson et al (1998)

species that currently exists. In the absence of active and continuous human management, most crop varieties would cease to exist (Darwin, 1859). Over the millennia, farmers have domesticated wild plants and, through a process of selection and breeding, made them suitable for agriculture. This they have done by breeding out the natural traits, such as shattering of seed-heads prior to maturity or seed dormancy, that allow those plants to survive in the wild. They have also bred in new traits, such as higher yields and drought or disease resistance. Any individual plant variety is thus the product of the breeding work of thousands of farmers over many generations.

Plant genetic resources are the foundation for all agriculture – providing the basis for developing new and improved varieties, and thus essential for achieving food security. Within the weedy and wild relatives, among the farmers' varieties developed on the farm or stored carefully in a seed bank, lie the genetic traits of resistance to plant viruses, diseases and even insects. It is by screening thousands of varieties that critical traits are found that can save an entire crop and perhaps stave off a national or regional hunger crisis. The value of this variety is difficult to estimate, though the benefits from wheat breeding for spring bread wheat alone in the developing world were approximately US$2.5 billion annually by the late 1980s (Byerlee and Traxler, 1995). PGRFA are clearly important as an immediate resource. They provide particular characteristics such as pest resistance, drought tolerance, plant architecture, taste, nutrition and colour essential for market success and adaptation in agricultural systems. PGRFA are also important as insurance against unknown future needs. Maintaining plant genetic diversity both within seed banks and in farmers' fields in the centres of origin is essential for responding to future challenges such as developing resistance to new diseases. As a result of their interdependence on PGRFA, countries must constantly access and use (for breeding, other forms of research and direct

Box 6.1 Global germplasm flows facilitated by the CGIAR Centres' gene banks

Despite the early history of domestication of crops, in more recent times the flow of germplasm, as facilitated by international and some national gene banks, is mostly between developing countries. A study of approximately 1 million samples distributed from *ex-situ* collections of the CGIAR Centres from 1973 to 2001 revealed that 73 per cent of the samples originally collected from developing countries were distributed to developing countries. Transfers to developed countries of materials that were obtained from developing countries accounted for only 16 per cent of the total. Flows from developed to developing countries accounted for some 8 per cent. Only 3 per cent of the transfers carried out by the CGIAR Centres were from developed countries back to other developed countries. Through such transfers, countries are able to enjoy a multiplier effect, gaining access to a much wider range of diverse materials than exists within their own borders, and because of this virtually all countries are net recipients of plant genetic resources.

Maximizing these multiplier effects was one of the original intentions of creating the International Network for the Genetic Evaluation of Rice (INGER). Between 1975 and 2004, over 23,000 unique entries were contributed to the network from all regions of the world, and each region has benefited by being able to evaluate between 2 and 20 times as many varieties as it contributed.

Source: SGRP (2006b)

use) PGRFA from other countries. Analysis of acquisitions and distributions of PGRFA by the gene banks hosted by the CGIAR Centres illustrates this phenomenon (Box 6.1). Another study showed that 88 per cent of the unique accessions of seven crops accessed by Uganda and Kenya between 1980 and 2004 were originally collected in other countries and continents (Halewood et al, 2005).

Scientific hurdles and complex transaction costs

The creation of this commons for PGRFA avoids the problem inherent in the approach to ABS in the CBD, which is predicated upon being able to identify the 'origin' of material as a 'trigger' for benefit sharing. The CBD (Article 2) defines the 'country of origin of genetic resources' as 'the country which possesses those genetic resources in *in-situ* conditions.' In turn, the CBD defines '*in-situ* conditions' as those 'conditions where genetic resources exist within ecosystems and natural habitats and, in the case of domesticated or cultivated species, in the surroundings where they have developed their distinctive properties'. Pursuant to this definition, the CBD requires more than simply identifying the country of origin of a crop – it requires the identification of the country of origin of the distinctive properties of the crop. Much of the literature addressing the international flows and pedigrees of PGRFA suggests, directly or indirectly, that it is difficult or impossible to determine the country of origin of crop varieties, and even more so their distinctive traits, given the long histories of human intervention and cooperation involved in their development (SGRP, 2006a). The Treaty avoids this problem by creating a multilateral system for ABS that builds upon and complements the international historical development of PGRFA. The two specifically listed criteria in the Treaty for identification/inclusion of crops and forages in the multilateral system of ABS are interdependence and importance to food security.

From Recognition of Threats, to the International Undertaking

The interdependence among nations for PGRFA and the common challenge of genetic erosion served as catalysts for the creation of an internationally cooperative system for germplasm collection and conservation through the Plant Genetic Resources and Crop Ecology Unit, established in the FAO in 1968. In 1972, the CGIAR followed recommendations of the UN Conference on the Human Environment and created the International Board for Plant Genetic Resources (IBPGR). The IBPGR was integrated into the CGIAR and had its own budget, and its secretariat was funded by the FAO's Plant Genetic Resources Unit; it was located in the FAO in Rome. Its responsibility was to coordinate (and undertake) collection, conservation, evaluation, documentation and use of germplasm (Esquinas-Alcázar and Hilmi, 2007).

In 1983, as discussed in the introduction to Chapter 5, the 22nd FAO Conference approved, without consensus, and with eight countries registering objections, the International Undertaking on Plant Genetic Resources for Food and Agriculture (IU). It also created, at the same time, the Commission on Genetic Resources for Food and Agriculture (CGRFA) to oversee the IU. The IU was the first comprehensive international agreement dealing with PGRFA. It sought to promote international harmony in matters regarding PGRFA and explicitly declared 'the universally accepted principle that plant genetic resources are a heritage of mankind and consequently

ITPGRFA

should be available without restriction'.

The basis of the reservation on the IU expressed by the eight countries was that it did not recognize plant breeders' rights (PBRs), which were enshrined at that time in the UPOV Conventions of 1961 and 1978 (see Chapter 2). In 1989, Resolution 4/89 – through which all countries finally recognized the primacy of those rights – was adopted by the FAO Conference to appease the 'hold-out' countries and to bring them unto the IU by recognizing their right to 'impose only such minimum restrictions on the free exchange of materials covered by [the IU] as are necessary for [them] to comply with [their] international obligations' under the UPOV Conventions. Another resolution (5/89), with its vaguely formulated recognition of the contribution and rights of farmers, was designed to appease those that had compromised by recognizing plant breeders' rights. The influence of the ongoing negotiations of the CBD was later felt in 1991 with the adoption of Resolution 3/91 by the FAO Conference, which recognized that 'the concept of mankind's heritage, as applied in the International Undertaking on Plant Genetic Resources, is subject to the sovereignty of the states over their plant genetic resources'.

From IU to Treaty

As discussed in Chapter 5, while adopting the text of the CBD as an appendix to the Nairobi Final Act, governments also resolved that there were outstanding issues on 'the interrelationship between the Convention on Biological Diversity and the promotion of sustainable agriculture'. In 1993, the FAO Conference requested the FAO to provide a forum in the Commission on Genetic Resources for Food and Agriculture for negotiation among governments for:

- the adaptation of the IU, in harmony with the CBD;
- consideration of the issue of access on mutually agreed terms to plant genetic resources, including *ex-situ* collections not addressed by the CBD; and
- the issue of the realization of farmers' rights.

Also in November 1993, the FAO Conference adopted the International Code of Conduct for Plant Germplasm Collecting and Transfer (Box 6.2).

Tough negotiations

The negotiations of the Treaty text took six and a half arduous years, from the First Extraordinary Session of the Commission, in November 1994, to its Sixth Extraordinary Session, in June 2001. The negotiations were long and tough, with highly polarized debates between developed and developing countries. Some of the most contentious issues concerned the scope of crops and forages to be included within the multilateral system of ABS (MLS), the actual terms of benefit sharing, and IPRs (Box 6.3). The scope of materials to be included in the MLS was one of the most contentious negotiating issues and it shifted considerably over the course of the negotiations of the Treaty. In the end, negotiators agreed upon a list of 35 crops and 29 forage genera to be included in the MLS. These are popularly referred to as 'Annex I' crops or materials since they are included in Annex I to the Treaty (see Appendix 3, page 249, for a brief history of the list and the crops included).

As is the case in most, if not all, international negotiations, developed countries enjoyed substantially more financial and human resource support during the negotiations of the Treaty and, later, the Standard Material Transfer Agreement (SMTA). Developed country

ITPGRFA

Box 6.2 The International Code of Conduct for Plant Germplasm Collecting and Transfer

The International Code of Conduct for Plant Germplasm Collecting and Transfer (the Code) is based on the principles that 'the conservation and continued availability of plant genetic resources is a common concern of mankind' and that 'nations have sovereign rights over their plant genetic resources in their territories'. This marked a reconciliation between the principles of the 1983 IU and those of the CBD. The Code is voluntary. It provides a set of general principles that governments may wish to use in developing national regulations or formulating bilateral agreements on germplasm exploration and collection, conservation, exchange and utilization. The Code also aims to involve farmers, scientists and organizations in conservation programmes in countries where collecting is taking place. It also aims to promote the 'sharing of benefits' and increase recognition of the rights and needs of local communities and farmers so that they may be compensated for their contribution to the conservation and development of plant genetic resources.

Although voluntary in nature, the Code has, in practice, established both moral and professional standards and is currently being used as a guide by many countries and several institutions, especially the CGIAR Centres, in seeking and granting permits for the exploration and collection of germplasm. In addition to undertaking, under Article 15 of the Treaty, to provide facilitated access to PGRFA in Annex I to the CGIAR Centres, Parties are encouraged to provide similar access, on mutually agreed terms, to non-Annex I PGRFA that are important to the programmes and activities of the CGIAR Centres. It is expected that any access and the collection activity will take into account or may be carried out in accordance with the stipulations of the Code.

delegates therefore came to Treaty negotiating sessions with more thoroughly annotated briefing books, and as part of substantially larger delegations that included experts from a diversity of departments to provide support on technical issues. During the negotiations all regional groups of countries are allowed the opportunity to meet together for a day or two immediately prior to the negotiating sessions, and the stipend from the FAO covers these extra days' expenses. However, regional meetings in preparation for the negotiating sessions in Rome were very important, given that delegations were meant to speak through regional representatives. Not surprisingly, the Europeans (though the coordination mechanism of the European Union) and North America were able to arrange regional meetings and/or communications between a number of the negotiating sessions. The African Group, at the other extreme, did not enjoy the benefit of

any dedicated intersessional regional meetings in Africa until sometime after the Treaty text was actually adopted, and negotiations on the SMTA were underway. These intersessional meetings within regions can make a big difference to groups' effectiveness.[1]

Apart from government negotiators, the private sector (biotechnology, seed and breeding companies), the CGIAR Centres and civil society organizations all played roles in the negotiation of the Treaty. The CGIAR Centres followed the negotiations closely, providing technical inputs on a number of subjects, including crop taxonomies, international flows of PGRFA and global information systems.

The private sector also participated actively in the international negotiations of the Treaty and, subsequently, the SMTA, mostly through the International Seed Federation (ISF), which represents, directly or indirectly, more than 10,000 seed companies around the world. The

Box 6.3 Negotiating dynamics and IPRs

Kent Nnadozie

Much of the utility of genetic resources in agriculture depends upon access to the greatest diversity of germplasm possible. The creation of monopoly rights over elements of this diversity through IPRs limits access and is thus often considered detrimental. Furthermore, there is increasingly frequent broad interpretation of the new and non-obvious conditions for the grant of patent rights. This leads to a blurring of the distinction between invention and discovery and thus potentially allows for the privatization of naturally occurring plants and other organisms. One concern about patents and plant variety protection (PVP) in agriculture is misappropriation. The knowledge and innovations of farmers often form the basis of patented or PVP-protected innovations but are neither acknowledged nor considered eligible for protection in their own right. This is one of the main rationales for seeking to protect farmers' rights under the Treaty.

The parties in the negotiations were broadly divided on IP, although by no means strictly, into the developed countries, with a highly advanced breeding industry, and the developing countries, with a less advanced breeding sector but constituting the predominant sources of the genetic resources. The developed countries, being generally better resourced and, therefore, better prepared for the negotiations, were generally dominant during the negotiations.

Led by the US, developed countries pushed for the recognition of IPRs over genetic resources and strongly opposed any provisions that might take away or otherwise moderate those rights during the Treaty negotiations. With far fewer resources and less capacity, the developing countries' participation and influence over the final outcomes was necessarily limited, although delegations from specific developing countries were remarkably dynamic in pushing their own issues throughout the negotiations. Some level of coordination with other developing countries, especially through regional blocs, also helped bolster their effectiveness. By and large, though, the participation of most developing countries was fragmented and largely uncoordinated. Their delegations were often composed only of officials from the focal points – which are based in specific ministries or departments – even when the issues were cross-sectorial or multidisciplinary and of critical importance to their national interests.

Unfortunately, in the course of multilateral transactions that shape international policy and law, nations do not necessarily get what they desire or deserve, but mostly what they negotiate. Treaty making is not necessarily rational or logical but a largely political process involving impositions, compromises and trade-offs, which accounts for some of the contradictions and ambiguities found in the text of the instruments, notably in part of the Treaty dealing with IPRs:

> *recipients shall not claim any IP or other rights that limit the facilitated access to the PGRFA, or their genetic parts or components, in the form received from the multilateral system.* (Article 12.3(d))

Whether this provision means that no IPRs of any sort can be claimed or that IPRs could be obtained *as long as those rights do not limit the facilitated access* is still uncertain – an uncertainty that has carried over into the SMTA (Box 6.4). There is further uncertainty as to what 'parts and components' mean in practice and the extent to which IPRs may be claimed over them. Different parties have differing takes on what this provision means. Most developed countries interpret it as meaning that IPRs can be taken out on a product if some improvement or modification has been made, in other words if it is not 'in the form received' from the Multilateral System. However, most developing countries take the view that 'parts and components' implies that products containing parts and components of resources received from the Multilateral System, as well as derivatives, are covered by this provision and that it therefore prohibits IPRs over them. Parties fully recognize and admit these differences in interpretation and, it is hoped that the Governing Body of the Treaty will at some point in the future address the issue and give a definitive interpretation consistent with the spirit of the Treaty.

ISF was a keen and active observer throughout the negotiations of the Treaty and related processes, frequently publishing their positions – usually very clearly stated – on the ISF website. Companies, of course, were also consulted by their representative governments, and their influence was, naturally enough, pretty important for some developed countries' delegations and their positions. Some delegations included representatives from the private sector of the countries concerned.

In contrast to both the CGIAR and the private sector, civil society organizations' participation in the Treaty process – while very active at first – declined precipitously over the years. During the First Session of the Governing Body in 2006 (see below), civil society organizations themselves made impassioned pleas for more civil society organizations – farmers' organizations in particular – to be involved in future meetings of the Governing Body, pleas that were supported by most delegations. The Governing Body requested the Secretary to facilitate the participation of civil society organizations in the work of the Treaty, especially in the implementation of its Article 6 on the sustainable use of plant genetic resources.

The text of the Treaty was finally adopted in November 2001 by the FAO Conference (Table 6.2). The Treaty entered into force in June 2004, 90 days after the deposit of the 40th instrument of ratification. As of June 2007, 113 Parties had ratified (approved or acceded to) the Treaty.[2]

However, the entry into force of the Treaty was not enough, in itself, for the genetic resources commons – the MLS – to be operational. In addition, the Parties had to negotiate further to develop the Standard Material Transfer Agreement (SMTA) to be used for all transfers of materials under the multilateral system. The SMTA sets out the legal conditions that apply to both suppliers and recipients and establishes procedures for dispute resolution. The Treaty specified that Parties to the Treaty would have to adopt the SMTA at the First Session of the Governing Body (whenever that might be held). The Governing Body of the Treaty consists of all Parties thereto. Its main function is 'to promote the full implementation of this Treaty, keeping in view its objectives' (Article 19). It may also establish such subsidiary bodies as may be necessary, along with their respective mandates and composition.

The process for the development of the SMTA was spread out over almost four years. In October 2002, the First Meeting of the Commission on Genetic Resources for Food and Agriculture, acting as the Interim Governing Body for the International Treaty, developed terms of reference for an Expert Group to start work on the SMTA. The Expert Group met in October 2004 and set out a basic framework, which was used as the basis for negotiations in the two meetings of a Contact Group for the Drafting of the SMTA and later at the First Session of the Governing Body in June 2006, which adopted the final text of the SMTA. Before that time, the multilateral system could not operate (Lim, 2007).

ITPGRFA

The Treaty's Nuts and Bolts

The main provisions of the Treaty are outlined in Table 6.2. We discuss below some of the key points from the Treaty and some issues arising from its negotiation and implementation.

Table 6.2 *Summary of the main components of the International Treaty on Plant Genetic Resources for Food and Agriculture*

Part	Main provisions
Part 1 – Introduction	• Article 1 establishes that the objectives are the conservation and sustainable use of PGRFA and fair and equitable sharing of benefits arising from their use, in harmony with the CBD, for sustainable agriculture and food security. • Article 2 defines some key terms. • Article 3 establishes the scope of the Treaty *to apply to all PGRFA*, and not just those listed in Annex I to the Treaty.
Part II – General provisions on conservation and sustainable utilization of PGRFA	• Article 4 requires Parties to make sure their laws conform to their Treaty obligations. • Article 5 lists the main tasks for Contracting Parties on the conservation, exploration, collection, characterization, evaluation and documentation of PGRFA and calls for the promotion of an integrated approach to the exploration, conservation and sustainable use of PGRFA. • Article 6 requires the Contracting Parties to develop and maintain appropriate policy and legal measures that promote the sustainable use of PGRFA and gives a non-exhaustive list of the types of measure that may be included. • Articles 7 and 8 deal with national commitments, international cooperation and technical assistance.
Part III – Farmers' rights	• Article 9 deals with farmers' rights, in recognition of the contribution of local and indigenous communities and farmers to the conservation and development of plant genetic resources, and places the responsibility for realizing those rights on national governments. Elements include the protection and promotion of (i) traditional knowledge relevant to PGRFA; (ii) rights of farmers to participate equitably in the sharing of benefits arising from the utilization of PGRFA; and (iii) the right to participate in making decisions at the national level with respect to the conservation and sustainable use of PGRFA.
Part IV – Multilateral System of Access and Benefit Sharing	• Article 10 recognizes the 'sovereign rights of States over their own PGRFA, including that the authority to determine access to those resources rests with national governments and is subject to national legislation'. It further recognizes that 'in the exercise of their sovereign rights, the Contracting Parties agree to establish' the MLS to facilitate access to PGRFA and to share, in a fair and equitable way, the benefits arising from the utilization of these resources.

Part	Main provisions
	• Article 11 deals with the coverage of the MLS. Based on the criteria of their importance for food security and interdependence, the MLS covers a list of crops set out in Annex I to the Treaty (see Appendix 3 of this book).
	• The MLS also includes PGRFA listed in Annex I and held by the CGIAR Centres or by other entities that have voluntarily included them in the MLS.
	• Under Article 12, the Contracting Parties agree to take the necessary legal or other appropriate measures to provide facilitated access through the MLS to other Contracting Parties and to legal and natural persons under their jurisdiction.
	• Recipients of material through the MLS must not claim IP or other rights that limit facilitated access to PGRFA, or their genetic parts or components, in the form received from the MLS. Facilitated access is to be accorded through the Standard Material Transfer Agreement (SMTA) adopted by the Governing Body of the Treaty.
	• Article 13 sets out the agreed terms for benefit sharing within the MLS, recognizing that facilitated access to PGRFA itself constitutes a major benefit of the MLS. Other mechanisms for benefit sharing include the exchange of information, access to and transfer of technology, capacity building, and the sharing of benefits arising from commercialization.
Part V – Supporting components	• These are activities outside the institutional structure of the Treaty itself, but which provide support essential to achieving its objectives. They include promoting the effective implementation of the rolling Global Plan of Action (Article 14), the encouragement of international plant genetic resources networks, and the development and strengthening of a global information system on PGRFA, including a periodic assessment of the state of the world's PGRFA.
	• Article 15 deals with *ex-situ* collections of PGRFA held by the CGIAR Centres and other international institutions. The Treaty includes a provision calling on the CGIAR Centres to sign agreements with the Governing Body to bring their collections under the Treaty. PGRFA listed in Annex I that are held by the CGIAR Centres are to be made available as part of the MLS. Non-Annex I materials will be made available according to a material transfer agreement (MTA) adopted by the Governing Body at its second session in October/November 2007. The Treaty states that this amended MTA must be 'in accordance with the relevant sections of this Treaty, especially Articles 12 and 13'. Article 12 includes the purposes for which access must be granted; charging administrative costs, including passport and other information; restrictions on claims for IPRs, including the phrases 'parts and components' and 'in the form received'; PGRFA under development; access to *in-situ* materials; dispute resolution; and emergency situations. Article 13 includes mandatory financial benefit sharing and voluntary financial benefit sharing. The Governing Body will also seek to establish similar agreements with other relevant international institutions.

ITPGRFA

Part	Main provisions
	• Article 16 deals with cooperation with international plant genetic resource networks. • In Article 17, Parties agree to establish a global information system to facilitate exchange of information. A truly globally harmonized information system is critical for the operation of the MLS; without it, no one will know what is available through the MLS and thus no one will be able to make targeted requests.
Part VI – Financial provisions	• In Article 18, Parties agree to implement a funding strategy to assist in the implementation of the Treaty's activities. The strategy aims to enhance the availability, transparency, efficiency and effectiveness of the provision of financial resources for the Treaty. It will include the financial benefits arising from the commercialization of plant genetic resources under the MLS, and also funds made available through other international mechanisms, funds and bodies.
Part VII – Institutional provisions	• Article 19 establishes a Governing Body composed of all Contracting Parties. This Governing Body acts as the supreme body for the Treaty and provides policy direction and guidance for the implementation of the Treaty and in particular the MLS. All decisions of the Governing Body are to be taken by consensus, although it is empowered to agree by consensus on another method of decision making for all matters other than amendments to the Treaty and to its Annexes. The Governing Body is expected to maintain regular communication with other international organizations, especially the CBD, to reinforce institutional cooperation over genetic resources issues. • The Treaty also provides for the appointment of a Secretary of the Governing Body (Article 20). • Article 21 deals with compliance and requires the Governing Body to deal with this at its first meeting. • Settlement of disputes is covered by Article 22, which also contains provision for a third party to mediate. • Articles 23–35 deal with amendments, annexes, signature, ratification, acceptance or approval, accession to and entry into force of the Treaty, relations with others, and provision for withdrawals from or termination of the Treaty.
Annexes	• Annex I lists the crops covered under the MLS, while Annex II deals with arbitration and conciliation.

ITPGRFA

The MLS

As the introduction already highlighted, the Treaty creates a genetic resources commons – the multilateral system of access and benefit sharing (MLS). The terminology here is very important, as the commons created by the Treaty is not equivalent to the public domain. The MLS is bounded in ways that distinguish it from the public domain. For example, parties have agreed that they will make materials available through the MLS 'solely for the purpose of utilization and conservation for research, breeding and training for food and agriculture, provided that such purpose does not include chemical, pharmaceutical and/or other non-food/feed industrial uses' (Article 12.3 (a)). Of course, they can make materials available for these other purposes if they choose to, but they are not obliged to under the Treaty.

The MLS does not include all PGRFA. Furthermore, not all instances of Annex I crops in a country are automatically included in the MLS, though those which 'are under the management and control of the Contracting Parties and in the public domain' (Article 11.2) certainly are. Contracting Parties do not have to make a list of what satisfies those conditions for it to be included in the MLS – since it is by definition – but it helps if they do, so that potential users know they are there. Beyond those materials, governments, individuals and organizations are encouraged to voluntarily include additional materials. Furthermore, international organizations are also encouraged to place their collections under the Treaty by signing agreements with the Governing Body (Article 15). Since the Treaty is open to membership only by States, the CGIAR Centres and other international institutions holding genetic resources collections needed to have a different way of expressing their consent to be bound by the provisions regarding their collections set out in the Treaty. As stated above, 11 CGIAR Centres, CATIE and Coconut Genetic Resources Network (COGENT) have already signed such agreements, and other international organizations/networks are considering doing so.

As stated above, all materials in the MLS will be distributed under the SMTA. The Treaty makes clear that materials for use for food and agriculture will be made available for free, or for the minimal costs involved (Article 15). If recipients use the materials for something else, they will be in violation of the SMTA. They are, however, allowed to use materials received to develop improved materials. In such cases, if they commercialize a final product that is itself a PGRFA and restrict others from using it for research and breeding, they must pay 1.1 per cent of sales of the product, minus 30 per cent, into a common fund created under the Treaty. If the PGRFA product is available for further research and breeding, no payment is necessary, although it is still encouraged. Recipients may opt for a second mandatory benefit sharing scheme whereby they agree to pay a royalty rate – 0.5 per cent of sales – over a 10-year period on all PGRFA products they commercialize of the same crop, whether or not they are available without restriction for research and breeding. Whatever they choose, the funds generated will be used to support conservation and sustainable use in developing countries; the Governing Body of the Treaty has oversight over such expenditures.

The monetary benefits go back to the MLS, not to any particular supplier (unless one characterizes the MLS as the supplier or source). This is where the MLS departs radically from the kind of bilateral regulatory arrangements that many countries have created (or are creating) pursuant to the CBD. It is also how it addresses the inherent difficulties associated with the CBD's definition of 'country of origin' for PGRFA discussed above. The fact that monetary benefits go to an international fund, and not to the supplier, however, raises questions about enforcement. Stated bluntly, if suppliers do not receive direct benefits back in the form of royalty payments, they will not have an incentive – other than good global citizenship – to pursue recipients who violate the terms of the SMTA, for example by taking out IPRs that prevent others from obtaining the same materials in the form received, using MLS materials for pharmaceutical research or not making due payments to the international fund.

Third party beneficiary interests

Some of the most innovative law-making in the negotiations of the Treaty and SMTA took place in response to this issue. In short, it was agreed that to address the gap in enforcement incentives, the third party beneficiary interests of the MLS as a whole should be given some form of legal recognition and representation. Discussion on this issue stretched over four international meetings (Moore, 2007), and the manner of its resolution is potentially enormously significant for future international law-making; however, it is dealt with in just a few short paragraphs in the SMTA. The SMTA states that the parties agree that:

> *[The entity] representing the Governing Body and the MLS has the right, as a third party beneficiary, to initiate dispute settlement procedures regarding rights and obligations of the Provider and the Recipient under the Agreement.* (Article 8.2)

To empower the entity representing the system's third party beneficiary interests, the SMTA provides that the entity has the right to request information from providers or recipients that are relevant to their obligations under the SMTA. Subsequent to the adoption of the SMTA, the FAO in principle accepted the invitation of the Governing Body to represent the third party interests of the Governing Body and the MLS (Moore, 2007). The procedures to be followed to bring alleged violations of the SMTA to the attention of the FAO as the representative of the MLS's third party beneficiary interests, and the role of the Governing Body in such instances, still have to be clarified, however. Whatever procedures are eventually adopted, it is quite likely they will entail considerably more systematic consideration of alleged wrong-doings at much higher levels within the international community than have ever existed before.

Dispute resolution

Pursuant to the SMTA, recipients and providers agree to a three-stage process for dispute resolution. The first stage is that the parties will attempt to resolve a dispute through negotiation. If negotiations fail, then the parties may choose mediation. If mediation fails, the matter can be referred to binding international arbitration. Furthermore, the SMTA states that the 'applicable law shall be the General Principles of Law, including the UNIDROIT Principles of International Commercial Contracts 2004, the objectives and relevant provisions of the Treaty and, when necessary for interpretation, the decisions of the Governing Body' (Article 7). The combined provisions regarding dispute settlement and applicable law are significant: they provide the foundation for the development of a universally relevant body of law as disputes are resolved. In the absence of these clauses, disputes would often have been settled according to the national laws of either the providers or recipients (or both, since they could both be from the same country). Such decisions would have had less value as precedents, given the differences between countries' laws, and an uneven patchwork of uneven case decisions would have developed. Having binding international arbitration following general principles of law should lead to the gradual build-up of a useful body of consistently applicable precedents, in the form of binding arbitration-panel decisions, to provide guidance on otherwise unclear or unresolved issues, such as those on IPRs (Box 6.4).

Farmers' rights

Article 9 of the Treaty urges parties to take measures to protect and promote farmers' rights, and provides that 'responsibility for realizing farmers' rights ... rests with national governments', including:

Box 6.4 Clarity through arbitration: Resolving outstanding questions about IPRs?

Michael Halewood

One issue that could end up being addressed through binding international arbitration is whether or not genes isolated from MLS materials can be patented. Article 6.2 of the SMTA states that '[t]he Recipient shall not claim any IP or other rights that limit the facilitated access to the Material provided under this Agreement, or their genetic parts or components, in the form received from the MLS'. This article of the SMTA is copied almost directly from Article 12.3(d) of the Treaty (Box 6.3). Some experts say the article allows patenting of isolated genes; others say it does not.

The article is not, however, the product of sloppy drafting during late-night negotiations. It represents a careful compromise among the delegations, which had very different opinions about how the issue should be resolved, but who realized that they would not be able to close negotiations of the Treaty if any side insisted on achieving clarity. So it was left cloudy or ambiguous. One possibility was that it would be further negotiated during the meetings to develop the SMTA. But there too the issue was quickly reconfirmed to be too divisive to address 'head on' and footnotes to negotiating texts offering opposite interpretations were quietly dropped between the Contact Group's two meetings. So the text remains the same.

One possibility is that a recipient will seek to patent a gene isolated from MLS material, and the supplier will end up referring the matter to binding arbitration. In this event the resulting decision would clarify the rules of the game for everyone. Another possibility, in the absence of an actual case of conflict, would be for the Governing Body to refer the question to an arbitration panel for an opinion. This too would promote clarity. A third possibility is that the issue simply will not arise. Would-be patentors may prefer to obtain materials from sources other than the MLS as long as this uncertainty exists.

ITPGRFA

- protection of traditional knowledge relevant to PGRFA;
- the right to equitably participate in sharing benefits arising from the utilization of PGRFA; and
- the right to participate in making decisions, at the national level, on matters related to the conservation and sustainable use of PGRFA.

The concept of farmers' rights was seen as a means to reward farmers and their communities for their contributions in the past, to encourage them to continue in their efforts to conserve and improve PGRFA, and to allow them to participate in the benefits derived, at present and in the future, from the improved use of plant genetic resources, through plant breeding and other scientific methods.

Farmers' rights were primarily canvassed and negotiated, under both the IU and the Treaty, as a counterbalance to the expansion of plant breeders' rights, and later patents, which were seen as major threats to the rights and long-established practices of farmers of saving, exchanging and reusing seeds. Another concern was the failure of plant breeders' rights to acknowledge the contributions of farmers in breeding and developing foundation varieties used in advanced breeding programmes, thereby not requiring the sharing of benefits derived from such use with farmers. The emergence of the concept of farmers' rights was motivated more as part of a political effort to redress the perceived imbalance created by the growing use and expansion of plant breeders' rights and patents than as legal rights, per se, in real property, IP or anything else. In practical terms, countries had intended that farmers' rights would be recognized through an international fund, a fund that was never established. However, unlike breeders' rights, which enjoy internationally recognized standards and application as well as enforcement through UPOV, and with some form of plant variety protection being required under TRIPS, farmers' rights as set out in the Treaty are to be implemented at the national level in accordance with national legislation (Table 6.3). There is also no international forum discussing or promoting farmers' rights akin to UPOV, which exclusively promotes and seeks to protect plant breeders' rights (though some of the ongoing work concerning misappropriation of traditional knowledge under the aegis of WIPO's Intergovernmental Committee on Intellectual Property and Genetic Resources, Traditional Knowledge and Folklore overlaps to some degree).

The inclusion of farmers' rights in the IU and, subsequently, in the Treaty marked the first time that such rights were formally recognized in an international instrument. The primary focus of farmers' rights is not on some form of *sui generis* IPRs, per se, although some literature mentions this as a desirable goal. Indeed the farmers' and peasants' movements supporting the food sovereignty approach specifically reject IPRs in agriculture (see Chapter 8, Box 8.2). Probably a more fruitful emphasis with regard to strategies to promote farmers' rights would be measures to facilitate farmers' stewardship of biodiversity (Andersen, 2006), including preserving their freedom to operate – in other words not being prevented, for instance, from saving, exchanging or reusing harvested seeds, and being allowed access to commercial markets for their varieties and products. Furthermore, although several elements of these rights are outlined in the

Treaty, their conceptual scope is yet to be fully articulated and their application or enforcement in practice still presents major challenges. All these issues are left by the Treaty to national governments to address in their laws. However, only a few countries have, so far, attempted to address the complex conceptual and operational problems that are involved, for instance, with indigenous knowledge, even in the CBD context. India has included the protection of farmers' rights in its recent legislation on biodiversity (Chapter 2, Box 2.1), yet even here, despite their inclusion in the law, there is not a clear definition of the nature and scope of these rights.

Despite the Treaty being ostensibly oriented to their interests, the level of participation of farmers and farmers' groups in the negotiations has been minimal, and their absence was particularly significant during the negotiation of the SMTA. If the Treaty is to be effectively implemented and its objectives realized, it is essential that the Contracting Parties find ways to proactively encourage the effective participation of civil society and farmers' organizations in the work of the Governing Body.

Compliance

Beyond the MLS, where obligations between suppliers and recipients of materials are bound by the terms and conditions of the legally binding SMTA, the Treaty is largely silent on the issue of enforcement, although it does provide for the normal gamut of dispute settlement procedures, including optional acceptance of international arbitration or reference to the International Court of Justice. The Treaty provides for the adoption of procedures and mechanisms on compliance which are simple, facilitative, non-adversarial, non-punitive and cooperative in nature. Such mechanisms will, for instance, involve the provision of advice or assistance, including financial and technical

Table 6.3 *Main differences between plant breeders' rights and farmers' rights*

Breeders' Rights	Farmers' Rights
Internationalized in conception and enforcement through TRIPs Article 27.3(b) (which requires PVP but does not specify UPOV's PBRs or any other particular form) and UPOV, although granted on a national basis through national law.	Can only be elaborated and implemented at the national level, although recognized in the Treaty – the only international agreement to do so.
Strictly IPRs, with more-or-less clear subject matter and legally defined scope or 'boundaries', including territorial limits and time limitation of, usually, up to 25 years for trees and vines and 20 years for other plants.	A bundle of rights, which may include elements of, but extend far beyond, IPRs per se. The scope and contents are yet to be fully elaborated (the Treaty has an indicative list of elements). Perceived as not subject to time or territorial limitations as such.
Private monopoly rights restricting others' actions without the permission of the 'owner' of the property concerned.	Conceived as largely collective/communal in nature and tend to be non-exclusive, since they promote sharing and exchange of materials and knowledge. Carry a certain connotation of freedom from restriction, i.e. rights not to be restricted in carrying out certain actions, especially to save, use, exchange and sell farm-saved seed/propagating material.
Relates to commercial activities and commercially oriented breeding.	Cover much more than commercially oriented activities and issues and include social/policy/political issues, e.g. right to participate in decision making.
Granted upon the satisfaction of a definite set of criteria: • (commercial) novelty; • distinctness; • uniformity; • stability; and • appropriate denomination.	Considered inherent by virtue of past and present contribution in the development of varieties, knowledge and technology.
No requirement or obligation to share benefits even if materials or knowledge are obtained from traditional knowledge or other unprotected sources.	Expectation or right to share benefits when their genetic material or knowledge has been used in the development of a protected variety.

assistance, technology transfer, training, and other capacity-building measures. The Treaty anticipates a mostly cooperative and consensual approach to implementation, to dealing with disputes and outstanding or emerging issues, and to encouraging compliance. This is, in large part, because all countries are interdependent where PGRFA are concerned and all share a common interest in their conservation and sustainable utilization. It is also a reflection of the compromises, or lack of them, on the issue of enforcement during the negotiations. At its First Session, the Governing Body adopted a resolution establishing a compliance committee, though without mandate or terms of reference. It postponed consideration of the procedures and operational mechanisms of the committee to its Second Session, and agreed on provisional procedures and operational mechanisms which would allow parties to raise issues

ITPGRFA

of compliance in advance of the Governing Body's sessions.

Conservation and sustainable use of PGRFA

The MLS received the most attention during the negotiations of the Treaty. Now that the basic rules for the MLS have been established and the SMTA agreed, the Governing Body should be able to shift a larger proportion of its attention to sustainable use under the Treaty. Sustainable use of PGRFA is the ultimate goal. The MLS is not an end itself; it exists to support sustainable use. Moreover, apart from those parts of the Treaty concerning the MLS, the Treaty applies to all PGRFA (in other words well beyond the Annex I list). Article 5, concerning conservation of all PGRFA, encourages countries, subject to national legislation, to survey existing inventories, collect materials under threat, support farmers to conserve on-farm, promote *in-situ* conservation of wild crop relatives and wild plants, and document, characterize, regenerate and evaluate PGRFA. Article 6 obliges member countries to develop policy and legal measures to promote the sustainable use of all PGRFA; it provides an indicative (and mixed) list of the kinds of activities such laws and policies should support, including maintenance of diverse farming systems, research that maximizes variation for farmers' benefit, broadening the genetic base of crops available to farmers, and expanding use of local and locally adapted crops and underutilized species. The two articles provide a framework for future work on sustainable use and conservation. The immediate challenge for the Governing Body will be to develop a programme of work related to these two articles that fully exploits the fact that governments, having just ratified the Treaty, are going to be more willing to invest resources in these areas than they have been in the past.

Looking Forward, Looking Back

Using the MLS and SMTA

Through the Treaty, governments have set up an innovative mechanism to maintain a managed commons for PGRFA. Many issues remain to be ironed out in the course of implementation, however, including how countries are going to approach implementing their participation in the commons, both as suppliers and receivers of materials. To date, there have been very few examples of national implementation to look to as examples, although some regional meetings have been held to tentatively explore possible means to develop harmonized approaches to implementation. There is clearly a need for assistance to be made available, upon request, to assist national policymakers and technicians think through issues such as:

- What materials are in the management and control of the government and in the public domain?
- What information system should they be developing and how can they link it to whatever system is developed as the 'leader' in the global information system envisaged under the Treaty?
- How will they circulate non-Annex I materials?

In addition, on a related issue, countries will have to consider their capacity to ensure the health of samples they supply.

At this point, it is difficult to predict what the role of companies will be in the Treaty's MLS. For the time being, they are under no obligation to make any materials available to others. The Treaty includes provision for a review, within two years of entering into force (that is, say, by June 2006, but the review has not taken place), of whether to discontinue facilitated access to natural and legal persons (in other words companies) that do not themselves include materials in the MLS. On the one hand, pushing forward with such a review now would be premature, potentially raising tensions among a range of actors both inside and outside the MLS at just the time it needs stability and widespread support. On the other hand, the obligation is there, explicitly stated in the Treaty, and the Governing Body will eventually need to make some sort of decision about how to address this issue.

A more immediate question is how frequently private companies will actually request genetic resources from the MLS. In May 2007, the ISF published an opinion piece questioning 'the degree to which the SMTA is acceptable in practice for seed companies to utilize material'. The paper goes on to state that:

> ... *the main concerns of the seed industry are linked to the absence of a threshold for the level of incorporation of accessed material in the final product, and to ambiguity as regards the duration of benefit sharing in case of restrictions for further research and breeding.* (ISF, 2007)

Meanwhile, some companies have indicated independently, to some CGIAR Centres, that they have reservations about receiving materials under the SMTA, citing similar concerns. It is possible, therefore, that the most likely candidates for 'triggering' the mandatory benefit sharing provisions of the Treaty and SMTA may seek PGRFA from other sources, at least for the time being.

It might seem a disappointing start for the operation of the MLS to find that a significant subset of would-be users may choose not to participate in the system. However, representa-

tives of the private sector have said at various meetings that they already had access to (or collections of) the materials they need for the next 5–15 years to support their breeding work. In other words, they did not have pressing needs for access to materials through a global multilateral system, at least not for some time. Only '1.7 [per cent] of samples distributed from the *ex-situ* collections hosted by the CGIAR Centres between 1974 and 2005 inclusive went to commercial companies' (Gaiji, 2006). Evidently most companies already had what they needed (or could get it from other sources). Perhaps then, even if companies did not have these reservations about the SMTA, they would not be accessing much material through the MLS, at least not for a number of years.

The CGIAR Centres themselves will be significant players in the day-to-day operation of the MLS, given their mandate to provide facilitated access to the materials they host in gene banks (and improved materials) and given that these collections represent a significant proportion of the total materials available through the MLS (Box 6.5). In the first nine months of 2007, the CGIAR Centres distributed 97,500 samples (in 833 shipments) under the terms and conditions of the SMTA. During the same period, only 3 would-be recipients refused to take materials under the SMTA (SGRP, 2007).

Although the participation of civil society organizations (CSOs) dropped off over the course of the negotiations of the Treaty and, later, the SMTA, there are potentially very important roles for farmers' and civil society organizations to play in monitoring the proper functioning of the MLS. Civil society organizations have been very effective in raising the alarm concerning allegations of improper actions by a range of actors vis-à-vis genetic resources, and their participation in raising awareness about the MLS and promoting compliance with its spirit will be important. The launching of the MLS provides a poten-

ITPGRFA

Box 6.5 The CGIAR Centres under the Treaty

A significant portion of public agricultural research has traditionally been carried out by the CGIAR Centres. The CGIAR is an informal association, founded in 1971, whose mission is to contribute to food security and poverty eradication in developing countries through research, partnerships, capacity building and policy support, promoting sustainable agricultural development based on the environmentally sound management of natural resources. Its membership consists of 47 countries (of which 25 are developing countries), four private foundations, and 13 regional and international organizations. It is sponsored by the FAO, the International Fund for Agricultural Development, the United Nations Development Programme and the World Bank. In 2005, CGIAR members contributed approximately US$450 million to the CGIAR Centres.

The CGIAR supports an international network of 15 Centres, which include Bioversity International, based in Rome; the International Rice Research Institute (IRRI), based in the Philippines; the International Maize and Wheat Improvement Center (CIMMYT), based in Mexico; and the International Center for Tropical Agriculture (CIAT), based in Colombia. Eleven CGIAR Centres collectively hold approximately 13 per cent of the *ex-situ* PGRFA in the world, with over 700,000 accessions of crop, forage and agroforestry species, encompassing farmers' varieties, improved varieties and wild relative species. Of these, 601,323 were designated, under agreements made in 1994 between the CGIAR Centres and the FAO, to be held 'in trust for the benefit of the international community, in particular the developing countries'. These agreements have been supplanted by the Agreements Between the 11 CGIAR Centres Holding *ex-situ* Collections of PGRFA and the Governing Body of the International Treaty signed on 16 October 2006. Under the Treaty, the CGIAR's *ex-situ* collections of Annex I genetic resources have been added to the MLS and will be distributed using the SMTA. Non-Annex I materials are distributed – as directed by the Treaty – using the MTA Centres used pursuant to the In Trust Agreements of 1994 until the MTA is amended by the Governing Body.

Guiding Principles issued in 1996 stated that the CGIAR Centres will not seek IP control over derivatives:

> ... *except in those rare cases when this is needed to facilitate technology transfer or otherwise protect the interests of developing nations. The Centres do not see their protection of IP as a mechanism for securing financial returns for their germplasm research activities, and will not view potential returns as a source of operating funds* (CGIAR, 2003).

In 2000, attempts to introduce further consideration of the Centres' use of IPRs (CGIAR, 2003) met with stiff resistance by civil society organizations (Thornström, 2001), and finally a statement was issued by the Centres' Directors that, pending resolution of a number of issues, no new guiding principles on IPRs would be adopted (CDC, 2003).

In 1998, a case of a recipient seeking plant breeders' rights over materials received from a Centre was widely publicized by the RAFI (now ETC Group) (RAFI/HSCA, 1998). The Centre involved – ICRISAT – demanded that the claim be withdrawn, as in the end it was. More recently, CIAT has been involved in challenging a patent granted in the US over a yellow bean named variety (Enola). CIAT did not actually supply the bean to the patentee, Mr Larry Proctor; however, CIAT holds very similar beans in the international collection it hosts, and, pursuant to the US patent, CIAT should not send its equivalent beans into the US. Objecting to this, CIAT wrote a letter to Proctor stating that CIAT would continue to export the beans into the US. In 2000, CIAT challenged the patent, asking for a re-examination. Finally, in March 2007, the Patent Examiner notified the patent owner that his claims had been rejected. Since then, Proctor has filed an application with the Board of Patent Appeals and Interferences (CGRFA, 2007).

Given the high numbers of MTAs that have been sent around the world by the CGIAR Centres over the years, there have been very few cases of alleged inappropriate use of materials – in other words use in contravention of those MTAs – by recipients seeking IPRs. In 2004, it was reported that:

> *Of approximately 500,000 accessions 'designated' by the CGIAR, fewer than 200 cases of improper IPR applications/protection have been alleged. All but a handful of these allegations have proven baseless. Allegations associated with fewer than one thousandth of one per cent of total distributions have been substantive enough to provoke action, and in all relevant cases the result was the withdrawal of the application or of the grant of protection. The low rate of 'abuse' does not, of course, excuse those situations in which it has taken place, but it does add context and perspective to the magnitude of the problem.* (Fowler et al, 2004)

tially very important opening for them to re-enter the stage in highly proactive, provocative and positive ways. Of course, some CSOs and farmers' organizations will also be recipients, and possibly suppliers, of PGRFA under the MLS.

What to put on the list?

Some of the hardest and longest negotiated components of the Treaty concern the list of crops to be included in the MLS. The inclusion or non-inclusion of many crops was informed as much by political and strategic considerations as by scientific conclusions. During the negotiations that resulted in the current list, many important crops which clearly or apparently satisfy the criteria set out under the Treaty for inclusion were excluded, for example:

- among food crops: soya bean, groundnut, onion, tomato, cucumber, grape, olive and sugar cane;
- among wild relatives: species of *Phaseolus*, *Solanum*, *Musa*, *Zea*, *Aegilops*, cassava included in the genus *Manihot*;
- most tropical forages; and

- among industrial crops: rubber, oil palm, tea, coffee and cocoa.

One of the main drivers of the expanding and contracting size of the Annex I list was the constantly shifting expectations and positions taken by delegates concerning benefit sharing. Many developing countries felt that, in the absence of appropriate and effective mechanisms for benefit sharing, the Treaty would reinforce historic patterns of Northern exploitation and appropriation of Southern genetic resources without any benefits accruing to the South. They withheld consent or opposed inclusion in the hope of compelling the inclusion of stronger or more effective provisions for benefit sharing. The choice to exclude some crops was also informed by the special interests of particular parties, where, for instance, a country was the centre of origin of the particular crop and wished to retain at least some control over it in the hope of benefiting from it under the terms and provisions of the CBD. Others appear to have withheld inclusion on a tit-for-tat basis. It has been suggested that had a particular country been willing to allow inclusion of particular crops, 'this might well have sparked reciprocal concessions from other

ITPGRFA

countries on other crops' (Moore and Tymowski, 2005). We know that the opposite was certainly the case: in the last sessions of the negotiations, a number of species were taken out of Annex I list in a series of reciprocal retaliations (see Appendix 3 of this book).

The Annex I list of crops could be expanded, and the issue is likely to be raised at some point in the future by the Governing Body. On the adoption of the Treaty, the European region issued a statement in effect calling for the list of crops to be extended and diversified as quickly as possible as a way for the Treaty to have maximum impact on world food security. The Center for Genetic Resources, in The Netherlands, has adopted the policy of using the SMTA whenever possible for transfers of non-Annex I materials around the world.[3] This position reflects, to a large extent, the aspirations of many other parties, role-players and stakeholders. Such developments could create precedents that could be followed by parties and other organizations, thereby broadening the de facto scope of the MLS. Such de facto broadening would set the stage for a de jure lengthening of the list by way of future Governing Body decisions.

Clearly, these are early days for the MLS; everyone is waiting to see how it actually performs before pushing for expansion of the list. If it works well, and the benefits – all the benefits, not just the monetary benefits – are clear to see, increasing the scope of the list should be relatively straightforward, or at least as straightforward as things can get when more than 100 countries have to agree.

Balancing IP and the commons

IP and related issues presented by the implementation of the Treaty are all, in large part, a reflection of the controversies in the broader international arena. Undoubtedly, IPRs and associated marketing of products form an important, and often primary, incentive behind most commercial breeding activities. At present, the key challenge at the multilateral level is to forge greater consensus on the means and mechanisms of having IPRs support access to genetic resources and equitable sharing of benefits. However, for the Treaty specifically, the main concern is how to ensure that IPRs do not unduly inhibit the ability of parties and public institutions to access materials and technology required to carry out research and breeding at the national, institutional and local levels to address food security issues.

The Treaty recognizes that IPRs are an important issue that might affect its implementation and tries to address this directly to some extent. The Treaty pretty artfully creates as much horizontally distributed (in other words across national borders) open research space as is possible, given the pre-existing IP laws and obligations of almost all of the negotiating parties. The interface between the open, public space of the research commons and assertions of private control through IPRs or other restrictive approaches which demarcate the boundaries of the 'commons' was, in fact, one of the main preoccupations of the negotiations. Consider, for example, how the mandatory benefit clause is not triggered by standard plant breeders' rights, because the material is still available for research and breeding, but is triggered by most patents, which generally disallow use for research and further breeding. These are not trite or haphazard distinctions; they reflect the end points of highly politicized negotiations over positions negotiators held dear. And not everyone is equally pleased with the final results. The distinction between PBRs and patents in the Treaty has prompted negative reactions from the biggest, biotech-based life sciences/seed companies, which rely proportionately far more on patents than smaller, traditional breeding companies (which generally seek PBRs). The big companies would prefer to have the mandatory benefit sharing provisions triggered by commercialization, regardless of the form of IPRs claimed and

ITPGRFA

whether or not the commercialized products are available for further research or breeding.

Implementation and extension

The creation of the MLS under the Treaty responds to concerns that important uses of PGRFA can and will be frustrated through the spread of laws (and technologies) that facilitate restrictive controls over people's uses of such resources. Bilaterally oriented access and benefit sharing and IP are among the most commonly cited issues in this context. The MLS directly addresses concerns about bilateral ABS laws by offering an alternative model. The MLS does not address IP issues nearly so directly, however. It merely recognizes and accommodates existing (and possible future) IP laws at the peripheries of the system. When the IP law invoked does not infringe upon the basic tenet of the plant genetic resource commons – that the material is available for further research and breeding without restriction – the MLS does not 'layer on' additional obligations. Thus UPOV-inspired PVP laws, which include research and breeding exemptions, do not trigger the benefit sharing clause of the SMTA. But when the IPR sought (or technology developed) prevents further use of PGRFA in ways that are inconsistent with the spirit of the commons, then the MLS (through the SMTA) requires the owner of that IP or technology to pay a surcharge, penalizing them, in a sense, for not keeping their materials in the commons. So while the Treaty does not make, break or alter IP laws, it is not value-neutral, and it does create additional obligations – sharing 1.1 per cent of sales – for some sorts of IPR holders.

National implementation

The MLS is brand new, and to date, very few countries have made fixed plans for its implementation in their domestic laws and/or practices. They need to do so soon, however, and may need technical assistance, upon request, to work out the most appropriate means of implementation in their specific contexts. The CGIAR Centres started using the SMTA in January 2007, but it is too early to make any informed observations about how it is actually functioning. What one can do, and what we have done in this chapter, is reflect upon the texts of the Treaty and the SMTA, the negotiations the led up to their adoption and the brief period of shuffling around the starting line that has passed since the Governing Body adopted the text of the SMTA in June 2006.

Beyond plants to all genetic resources for food and agriculture?

What implications do the Treaty, and the PGRFA commons it creates, have for future international policymaking? The Commission on Genetic Resources for Food and Agriculture is currently working on animal genetic resources for food and agriculture (Box 6.6). These too are also a global resource essential to achieving food security and to ensuring sustainable livelihoods, especially in marginal areas. A global plan of action on animal genetic resources was agreed at the first International Technical Conference on the subject held in September 2007 in Interlaken, Switzerland, 11 years after that on plant genetic resources in Leipzig. The Technical Conference also received the first 'Report on the state of the world's animal genetic resources', which was compiled by the FAO. The report's analysis has been welcomed by a range of social organizations of pastoralists, herders and farmers, since it recognizes that the industrial livestock system is a major cause of biodiversity loss. However, they have criticized the plan of action for failing to 'challenge the policies that cause the loss of diversity' and governments for failing to commit substantial finances to carry through the plan (UKABC, 2007).

ITPGRFA

Box 6.6 Animal genetic resources

Around 20 per cent of animal breeds are at risk of extinction, with one breed lost each month, according to the FAO. Of the more than 7600 breeds in the FAO's global database of farm animal genetic resources, 190 have become extinct in the past 15 years and a further 1500 are considered at risk of extinction.

Some 60 breeds of cattle, goats, pigs, horses and poultry have been lost over the last five years, according to a draft 'Report on the state of the world's animal genetic resources'.[a] The report is the first ever global assessment of the status of animal genetic resources and the capacity of countries to manage them in a sustainable manner.

Globalization

Keeping livestock contributes to the livelihoods of one billion people worldwide, and approximately 70 per cent of the world's rural poor depend on livestock as an important component of their livelihoods. Livestock currently accounts for about 30 per cent of agricultural gross domestic product in developing countries, a figure projected to increase to nearly 40 per cent by 2030.

According to the FAO, the globalization of livestock markets is the biggest single factor affecting farm animal diversity. Traditional production systems require multi-purpose animals, which provide a range of goods and services. Modern agriculture, on the other hand, has developed specialized breeds, optimizing specific production traits, which have achieved striking productivity increases but depend on high external input.

Just 14 of the more than 30 domesticated mammalian and bird species provide 90 per cent of human food supply from animals. 'Five species: cattle, sheep, goats, pigs and chickens, provide the majority of food production,' says Irene Hoffmann, Chief of the FAO's Animal Production Service:

Selection in high-output breeds is focused on production traits and tends to underrate functional and adaptive traits. This process leads to a narrowing genetic base both within the commercially successful breeds and as other breeds, and indeed species, are discarded in response to market forces.

Maintaining diversity

The existing animal gene pool contains valuable resources for future food security and agricultural development, particularly in harsh environments. 'Maintaining animal genetic diversity will allow future generations to select stocks or develop new breeds to cope with emerging issues, such as climate change, diseases and changing socioeconomic factors,' said José Esquinas-Alcázar as Secretary of the FAO's Commission on Genetic Resources for Food and Agriculture.

Because of countries' interdependence on animal genetic resources, there is a need to facilitate the continued exchange and further development of these resources, without unnecessary barriers, and to ensure that benefits reach farmers, pastoralists, breeders, consumers and society as a whole, adds Esquinas-Alcázar.

Note: [a] Final report available as document CGRFA-11/07/Inf.6 at www.fao.org/ag/cgrfa/cgrfa11.htm.
Source: FAO news release 06/147 E, 15 December 2006

ITPGRFA

The outcome of the 11th Session of the Commission on Genetic Resources for Food and Agriculture (CGRFA) in June 2007 confirmed that the Commission will take an even broader approach in the years to come. Among other things, the Commission agreed to include consideration of policies and arrangements for ABS for genetic resources for food and agriculture at the 12th meeting of the Commission, probably in 2009. Aquatic genetic resources, forest genetic resources, animal genetic resources and microbial genetic resources for food and agriculture all appear to be included in the scope of that work. In addition, the Commission highlighted repeatedly the importance of taking an ecosytem approach to agricultural biodiversity (see Chapter 8).

It is too early to say how work done on ABS for genetic resources for food and agriculture will relate to or affect the ongoing negotiations to develop a new ABS regime or regimes under the CBD (see Chapter 5). But the willingness of all countries to include ABS in the Commission's mandate reflects a growing common concern that progress on ABS issues under the CBD is taking too long, and that, ultimately, the CBD may not be sufficiently well placed to fully appreciate the nuances of the issues surrounding genetic resources for food and agriculture where ABS is concerned. It also reflects a newly confirmed trust, based on the successful conclusion of the Treaty negotiations, that the Commission has the capacity to constructively address ABS issues in ways that are tailored to the realities of food and agricultural uses. The Treaty and the MLS can therefore take some credit for having provided the international community with the confidence to address directly the particularities of genetic resources for food and agriculture as a whole in the context of ABS and to shift, at least partially, work on that subject away from a body whose focus is all biological diversity to one whose raison d'être is food and agriculture.

Proliferating commons?

The creation of the MLS may be one of the early globally endorsed signs of disillusion with exclusive forms of control accreting to public goods. Through its embrace of the MLS, the global community is saying pretty clearly that attempts to create and exploit market incentives to address conservation and development concerns, at least where PGRFA are concerned, are not getting us where we need to be. IPRs and strict controls over genetic resources through bilaterally oriented access regulations are not providing the kinds of results we expected – at least not for the large numbers of people who exist outside functioning markets and without the means to gain meaningful entry into them. The MLS supports other approaches to exploiting the value of PGRFA, approaches based on what can be gained from the exploitation of those resources through cooperative research, sharing and passing on benefits. A similar expression of global interest in more open systems of innovation and gaining value through sharing, albeit at more informal levels, is reflected in the rapidity with which 'copy left' and creative commons ideas have been seized on in the area of software development (see also Chapters 5 and 8).

The recognition of the MLS's third party beneficiary interests in the proper conduct of suppliers and recipients of germplasm in the MLS provides a precedent for how to protect the public interest in other international public goods, or, more accurately, international common interests in international common goods. In so doing, at least in the context of PGRFA under the Treaty's multilateral system, it provides a means of addressing the 'free rider' problem – a problem that plagues so many realms of activity wherein public interests and public goods end up being ignored, overridden or undermined.

The recognition of the third party beneficiary interests of the MLS will not, on its own, fix the tragedy of the commons (or the anti-commons). But it will go some distance to addressing the problem. The model can potentially be adapted and included in other international systems involving a wider range of genetic resources. The existence of such a mechanism should encourage states to see the proliferation of such commons-based systems as a real possibility.

Conclusion

The issues raised in the implementation of the Treaty are part of a broader international context linking with more general concerns about biodiversity, innovation and the role of IPRs in both. It is to the linkages and interactions between the various agreements discussed in this and earlier chapters that we now turn.

Resources

For a detailed guide to the Treaty see Moore and Tymowski (2005).

The Earth Negotiations Bulletin *covers most international negotiations and its report of the First Meeting of the Governing Body of the International Treaty on Plant Genetic Resources for Food and Agriculture is available at www.iisd.ca/biodiv/itpgrgb1/ and www.iisd.ca/vol09/enb09369e.html.*

The FAO Global System on Plant Genetic Resources for Food and Agriculture is found at www.fao.org/ag/AGP/AGPS/pgrfa/gpaeng.htm and the FAO pages on the International Treaty on Plant Genetic Resources for Food and Agriculture at www.fao.org/ag/cgrfa/itpgr.htm.

For links to websites concerned with genetic resources intellectual property rights websites see http://dmoz.org/Society/Issues/Intellectual_Property/Genetic_Resources/ and for details of the System-wide Genetic Resources Programme of the CGIAR see http://sgrp.cgiar.org/.

ITPGRFA

The Negotiations Web: Complex Connections

Tasmin Rajotte

This chapter examines the increasingly complex linkages between the various international negotiations in trade, environment, agriculture and intellectual property (IP) that govern the ownership and control of genetic resources discussed in Chapters 2–6. The diversity of negotiating constituencies and lack of policy coherence at all levels, in addition to the forum management strategies used by some countries, has resulted in an array of agreements that can have inconsistent or overlapping objectives. The various authors of the previous chapters identified what they saw as important linkages; those comments are drawn together, along with other linkages, in this chapter.

Introduction

Chapters 2–6 described how the scope of IP has expanded, through different multilateral agreements, to include genetic resources and associated knowledge for agriculture and food. Forum proliferation and the increasing complexity of the various international treaties create and contribute to controversies, conflicts, grey areas and other problems.

This chapter discusses the strategies being pursued to deepen global IP expansion and harmonization, such as forum management and bilateral and regional free-trade agreements, enforcement mechanisms, World Trade Organization (WTO) accessions and the impli-

cations for genetic resources. Next, it discusses the linkages around the harmonization of IP and the access and benefit sharing (ABS) of genetic resources and the way this is shaping how international instruments such as those discussed in Chapters 2–6 relate to each other. It then moves on to some of the broad problems identified with the approach of balancing the exchange of genetic resources with IP protection within an increasingly patent-dominated system. Finally, it briefly examines other linkages, such as some of the development and emerging human rights issues.

LINKAGES

Strategies to Deepen IP Expansion and Harmonization

This section explores several strategies being pursued to expand and harmonize IP protection and their implications for genetic resources for food and agriculture.

Forum management and bilateral and regional trade agreements[1]

Powerful countries and interests that are unable to get the level of IP protection they want in one forum shift to other fora to achieve their aims (Vivas-Eugui, 2003). This type of forum management is often referred to as 'forum shifting' or 'forum shopping'. As mentioned in Chapter 3, the shortcomings and paralysis of the World Intellectual Property Organization (WIPO), together with an active movement of industrial groups, led to the push to incorporate IP in the trade arena during the Uruguay Round in 1986, resulting in the Agreement on Trade-Related Aspects of Intellectual Property Rights (TRIPS) at the WTO, which came into force in 1995. When these countries and industrial groups were no longer able to get what they wanted at the WTO, they shifted back to certain treaties within WIPO (see Chapter 4) and started directly pressuring developing countries to raise their IP standards through bilateral and regional trade and investment agreements.

The number of bilateral and regional free trade agreements (FTAs) has increased dramatically, from 60 agreements in 1995 to almost 200 in early 2006 (WTO, 2006). In particular, the agreements being negotiated by the US and the EU with developing countries have raised serious concerns among civil society representatives, policymakers and developing country negotiators about a number of so-called 'TRIPS-plus' provisions in these agreements that go beyond countries' obligations under the TRIPS Agreement (Abbott, 2004). These provisions, they argue, will force ever more onerous IP systems on developing (and indeed developed) countries, thereby further limiting their space to implement systems that are supportive of their food security and livelihood objectives. A number of provisions are of particular relevance for agriculture (see also Table 7.1):

- *Requirements to join Union Inernationale pour la Protection des Obtentions Végétales (UPOV):* Many FTAs now include clauses that require the signatories to implement and/or accede to the UPOV Convention as the legal framework to protect plant breeders' rights. This requirement goes beyond the TRIPS Agreement, which allows Members to implement an 'effective *sui generis* system' of plant variety protection, deliberately leaving the nature of such protection undefined. UPOV 1991, in particular, has attracted strong criticism for the limitation it is thought to place on farmers' right to reuse and exchange seed and thereby ensure availability and diversity of seeds. The requirement to join UPOV 1991 has been introduced, for instance, in FTAs between the US and Lebanon, Morocco, Tunisia, Jordan, Central America (under CAFTA) and Peru, while US agreements with other countries, such as Ecuador and Mexico, require them 'to make every effort' to join UPOV 1991.

- *Requirements to introduce patent protection for plants, animals and biotechnological inventions:* Some FTAs, such as those of the US with Jordan, Mongolia, Nicaragua, Sri Lanka and Vietnam, have introduced an obligation to provide patent protection on plants and animals. The TRIPS Agreement, in contrast, explicitly allows for plant and animals to be excluded from patentability as long as patent protection is provided for micro-organisms and some form of IP protection is given to plant varieties. The EU–South Africa agreement requires patent protection for biological inventions, which presumably includes or could be interpreted as including plants and animals in addition to the protection for micro-organisms required by the TRIPS Agreement. Similarly, the scope of the Cotonou Agreement between the EU and the African, Caribbean and Pacific (ACP) countries includes patents for biotechno-logical inventions. The EU has also proposed TRIPS-plus standards of protec-tion in the negotiation of economic partnership agreements (EPAs), notably the obligation to ratify or accede to UPOV 1991. The European Parliament, however, has called on the European Commission 'to ensure that intellectual property rights ... are taken off the negotiating table if ACP countries do not wish to negotiate them.'[2]

- *References to contracts:* Most recently, the US has started to introduce language into FTAs, such as in the agreement reached with Peru and Colombia, recognizing that contracts can adequately address concerns about access to genetic resources or tradi-tional knowledge and the benefit sharing arising from their use. While this provision is not a mandatory requirement, it intro-duces a concept advocated by the US in the WTO negotiations on the TRIPS–CBD relationship to counter proposals on disclosure requirements put forward by developing countries (see below). Since the US has signed but not ratified the CBD, it does not need to observe the Convention's provisions, the Bonn Guidelines on access to genetic resources and the fair and equitable sharing of the benefits arising from their utilization, or any future outcomes from the negotiations on a binding international regime on ABS (Chapter 5).

- *Extension of patent protection period:* Some FTAs have introduced longer patent protection beyond the minimum 20 years provided for in the TRIPS Agreement. For instance, in cases of unreasonable delays in granting a patent the US–Chile Agreement extends patent protection by five years from the date that the patent application was lodged or three years after a request for examination of the application has been made. Such extensions would further restrict access of researchers and farmers to patent-protected seeds (where patenting is allowed) and technologies.

In addition to the provisions in IP chapters of FTAs, these agreements include detailed provi-sions on investment which explicitly include IP rights (IPRs) as protected assets. The acquisi-tion of IPRs over genetic materials obtained by a foreign company will give them, under invest-ment agreements, the status of investor. Government acts affecting IPRs over such materials may raise complaints under applicable investment agreements (Correa, 2004b).

Enforcement

FTAs typically contain a dispute settlement chapter that governs disputes between the parties to the agreement. As the above discus-sion has made clear, the IP chapters of FTAs may in various ways limit choices that were available to states under TRIPS standards. These FTAs may also repeat obligations that the parties to the FTA have already agreed to in the context of TRIPS, meaning that these obligations can be enforced under the FTA between them. There are a large number of FTAs being signed and the dispute resolution chapters vary in their detail, but the following general observations can be made.

Those FTAs that allow for non-violation complaints (discussed below and in Box 3.2) to

LINKAGES

Table 7.1 *Selected North–South agreements with agriculture-related TRIPS-plus provisions*

South counterpart	Type of agreement	Date	Selected TRIPS-plus provisions
UNITED STATES			
Andean countries (ATPA)	trade	1991	trade benefits dependent, inter alia, on extent to which countries protect IPRs
Caribbean countries (CBTP)	trade	2000	trade benefits dependent, inter alia, on extent to which countries protect IPRs
Central America (CAFTA)	trade	2004	must join UPOV 1991 if no patents on plant varieties; make reasonable efforts to provide patents on plants
Cambodia	IPR	1996	must join UPOV
Chile	trade	2003	must join UPOV 1991 by 2009; make reasonable efforts to provide patents on plants within 4 years of entry into force
Colombia	trade	2006	must join UPOV 1991 by 2008; make reasonable efforts to provide patents on plants
Ecuador	IPR	1993	must conform with UPOV if no patents on plant varieties
Laos	trade	2003	must join UPOV 1978 or 1991 without delay; no exclusions for plants and animals from patent law
Jordan	trade	2000	must join UPOV within one year; no exclusions for plants and animals from patent law
Mongolia	trade	1991	no exclusions for plants and animals from patent law
Morocco	trade	2004	must join UPOV 1991; must provide patents on plants and animals.
Nicaragua	IPR	1998	must join UPOV 1991; no exclusion for plants and animals from patent law
Peru	trade	2005	must join UPOV 1991 by 2008; must make efforts to provide patent protection for plants; notes that ABS can be adequately addressed through contracts
Singapore	trade	2003	must join UPOV 1991 within 6 months of entry into force; no exclusion for plants and animals from patent law
Sri Lanka	IPR	1991	no exclusions for plants and animals from patent law
Sub-Saharan Africa (AGOA)	trade	2000	trade benefits dependent, inter alia, on extent to which countries protect IPRs
Trinidad and Tobago	IPR	1994	must implement and make best effort to join UPOV
Vietnam	trade	2000	must implement and make best effort to join UPOV; must provide patent protection on all forms of plants and animals that are not varieties as well as inventions that encompass more than one variety
Mexico (NAFTA)	trade	1994	must join UPOV within 2 years of entry into force
Latin America (FTAA)	trade	under negotiation	US negotiating position is no exclusions for plants and animals from patent law; actual negotiating text contains many proposals to implement UPOV

South counterpart	Type of agreement	Date	Selected TRIPS-plus provisions
EUROPEAN UNION			
ACP (Cotonou Agreement)	trade	2000	recognize need to ensure an adequate and effective level of protection of IPRs (including patents for biotech inventions)
Algeria	trade	2002	must join UPOV 1991 within 5 years of entry into force (or effective *sui generis* system)
Bangladesh	trade	2001	must make best effort to join UPOV 1991 by 2006
Egypt	trade	2001	must join UPOV 1991 within 5 years of entry into force
Jordan	trade	1997	must join UPOV
Korea	trade	2001	must make best effort to join UPOV 1991 as soon as possible
Morocco	trade	2000	must join UPOV 1991 by 2004
South Africa	trade	1999	ensure adequate and effective protection for patents on biotechnological inventions
Syria	trade	2004	must join UPOV 1991 within 5 years of entry into force (or effective *sui generis* system)
Tunisia	trade	1998	must join UPOV 1991 by 2002
SWITZERLAND			
Vietnam	IPR	1999	must join UPOV 1991 by 2002

Sources: GRAIN, 2001; GRAIN 2005c; http://ec.europa.eu/comm./trade/issues/index_en.htm; www.ustr.gov

be brought in respect of the obligations agreed to in the IP chapters (for example the US–Australia FTA) set a dangerous precedent, especially for countries that are importers of patented technology and choose to regulate those patented technologies in some way. Non-violation complaints potentially open the door to arguments that a state's domestic regulation of patented products is inconsistent with its FTA obligations because it is robbing a group of patent owners of market benefits that they would have gained but for the regulation. Obviously this kind of logic, if accepted, could have a sweeping effect on regulation in areas such as pharmaceuticals, agricultural and food products. FTAs that permit non-violation complaints can in a sense be said to be TRIPS-plus since Article 64(2) of TRIPS introduced a five-year moratorium on non-violation complaints, a moratorium that was then extended.

FTAs also constitute alternative fora for disputes over IP. Since so many FTAs are being signed, a global system of many trade courts is rapidly coming into being. The critical issue is whether this system will do much for trade, and in particular whether it will serve the trade interests of weaker players. Typically, developing countries gain little in an FTA on agriculture, but give away a lot on IP. By definition such players cannot resort to power politics to protect their rights under the trade regime. Whatever the criticisms of the WTO, its dispute settlement system is a comparatively transparent system that offers weaker players coalitional possibilities, but the same cannot be said of dispute settlement under an FTA. Given the intensity with which the US and EU have globally pursued their IP trade agenda, developing states may well come to rue the day when they helped to create bilateral enforcement rods for their own backs.

LINKAGES

WTO accessions[3]

The TRIPS Agreement is one of the multilateral trade agreements to which all WTO Members are party. As an ordinary consequence of joining the WTO, a state or autonomous customs territory would be expected to become party to the TRIPS Agreement and take on the obligations applicable to other Members at their respective levels of development. However, the terms of the WTO Agreement do not expressly limit the 'entry fee' imposed on newly acceding Members to an equivalence of concessions with existing Members. As a consequence of this, accession negotiations have been used by certain Members as a mechanism for securing commitment to obligations in the field of IPRs that are more extensive than those established by the TRIPS Agreement (so-called 'TRIPS-plus' commitments) (Abbott and Correa, 2007).

In assessing the public policy implications of TRIPS-related provisions in accession agreements, the different legal mechanisms involved in the process are significant. In most cases, acceding countries do not make specific commitments on TRIPS-plus elements, although there are notable exceptions. However, the national legislation put in place during the accession process and reported or notified to the Members often contains TRIPS-plus elements beyond those identified in specific commitments. An acceding country is 'bound' only with respect to 'commitments' in the context of dispute settlement. However, an acceding country runs the risk of being the subject of a non-violation complaint brought on the basis of its Protocol of Accession, if such complaints are finally deemed applicable in the context of matters related to IP (Chapter 3, Box 3.2). Perhaps more important from a practical standpoint, the acceding country faces the prospect of diplomatic representations from economically important WTO Members about its failure to maintain the legislation adopted or announced during the accession process, even if technically the acceding country is free to change that legislation and to limit the level of protection to what is required by the TRIPS Agreement. The importance of economic diplomacy outside the specific context of WTO dispute settlement should not be discounted. That diplomacy may be combined with threats relating to suspension of trade preferences or economic aid packages.

TRIPS-plus provisions have even been required from least developed countries in the accession process. For example, Cambodia made a commitment to adhere to UPOV. This implies that plant varieties should be protected in Cambodia under breeders' rights in accordance with the 1991 Act of that Convention. Other countries have indicated that they have ratified or intend to ratify UPOV.

Harmonizing Genetic Resource Exchange with IP Protection

Controversies surrounding the role of IP and the misappropriation or 'biopiracy' of genetic resources and associated traditional knowledge (TK) have not only been at the heart of key issues negotiated in the various multilateral agreements discussed in Chapters 2–6, but also in setting the framework from which problems are being addressed. This section explores issues related to biopiracy and, in turn, how they have tended to shape responses to the problem and relationships between international instruments.

Biopiracy[4]

The vast majority of countries formally recognize that cross-border exchange of genetic

LINKAGES

resources and TK should be carried out in compliance with the principles of the Convention on Biological Diversity (CBD). IPRs, particularly patents but also plant variety protection, have become central to discussions on this matter for various reasons:

- the conviction – widely held among developing countries and NGOs – that biodiversity and associated traditional knowledge have tremendous economic potential;
- the fact that patent claims in various countries may incorporate biological and genetic material, including life forms, within their scope;
- the belief, also shared by developing countries and NGOs, that this feature of the patent system enables corporations to misappropriate genetic resources and associated TK or at least to unfairly free-ride on them;
- the ability of modern IP law to protect the innovations produced by industries based mainly in the developed world and its *inability* to protect adequately those in which the developing countries are relatively well-endowed; and
- the perception that, as a consequence of the above reasons, the unequal distribution and concentration of patent ownership and the unequal share of benefits obtained from industrial use of biogenetic resources are closely related.

Biopiracy has emerged as a term to describe the ways that corporations from the developed world free-ride on the genetic resources, TK and technologies of developing countries. While these and other corporations complain about 'intellectual piracy' perpetrated by people in developing countries, the latter group of nations counters that their biological, scientific and cultural assets are being 'pirated' by these same businesses. Intellectual piracy is a political term, which is inaccurate and deliberately so.

The assumption behind it is that the copying and selling of pharmaceuticals, music CDs and films anywhere in the world is wrong irrespective of whether the works in question had patent or copyright protection under domestic laws. After all, if drugs cannot be patented in a certain country, copying them by local companies for the domestic market and/or overseas markets where the drugs in question are also not patented is not piracy in the legal sense of the word.

Similarly, biopiracy is an imprecise term, and there are good reasons to keep it so, at least in the international arena. But such 'strategic vagueness' is not a helpful approach for those working on legal solutions in national laws, regulations or international conventions.

So what does biopiracy mean? It is a compound word consisting of 'bio', which is short for 'biological', and 'piracy'. According to the *Concise Oxford Dictionary*, 'piracy' means (1) the practice or an act of robbery of ships at sea; (2) a similar practice or act in other forms, especially hijacking; and (3) the infringement of copyright. Apart from the use of 'piracy' for rhetorical effect, the word does not seem to be applicable to the kinds of act referred to as biopiracy. But what about the verb 'to pirate'? The two definitions given are (1) appropriate or reproduce (the work or ideas etc of another) without permission for one's own benefit; and (2) plunder.

These definitions seem to be more appropriate since inherent to the biopiracy rhetoric are misappropriation and theft. In essence, 'biopirates' are those individuals and companies accused of one or both of the following acts: (1) the misappropriation of genetic resources and/or TK through the patent system and (2) the unauthorized collection for commercial ends of genetic resources and/or TK. Since biopiracy is not just a matter of law but also one of morality and of fairness, it is not always easy to draw the line between an act of biopiracy and a legitimate practice. This difficulty is compounded by the vagueness in the way the

LINKAGES

term is applied. To illustrate this point, a wide range of acts, listed below, have been considered as acts of biopiracy of TK:

Collection and use:
- the unauthorized use of common TK;
- the unauthorized use of TK only found among one indigenous group;
- the unauthorized use of TK acquired by deception or failure to fully disclosure the commercial motive behind the acquisition;
- the unauthorized use of TK acquired on the basis of a transaction deemed to be exploitative;
- the unauthorized use of TK acquired on the basis of a conviction that all such transactions are inherently exploitative ('all bioprospecting is biopiracy'); and
- the commercial use of TK on the basis of a literature search.

Patenting:
- the patent claims TK in the form in which it was acquired;
- the patent covers a refinement of the TK; and
- the patent covers an invention based on TK *and* other modern/traditional knowledge.

It is not clear how much biopiracy actually takes place. Apart from lack of information, the answer depends on how one differentiates between legitimate and unfair exploitation. The distinction is not always obvious. The answer also depends on whether resources are considered to be wild and unowned or domesticated and owned. A common view among critics of conventional business practice is that most companies do not recognize that they may have a moral obligation to compensate communities providing genetic material for their intellectual contribution *even when* such material is assumed to be 'wild'. Often genetic resources considered 'gifts of nature' in fact result from many generations of selective crop breeding and landscape management. Essentially the argument is that failing to recognize and compensate for the past and present intellectual contributions of traditional communities is a form of intellectual piracy.

The likely response from industry is that this is not piracy since the present generation may have done little to develop or conserve these resources. The argument might continue that this is, at worst, a policy failure, and that measures outside the IPR system could be put into place to ensure that traditional communities are rewarded.

As for the patent-related version of biopiracy, there is little doubt that companies are in an advantageous position in the sense that, while a useful characteristic of a plant or animal may be well known to a traditional community, without being able to describe the phenomenon in the language of chemistry or molecular biology, the community cannot obtain a patent even if it could afford to do so. While it is unlikely that a company could then obtain a patent simply by describing the mode of action or the active compound, it could claim a synthetic version of the compound or even a purified extract. In the absence of a contract or specific regulation, the company would have no requirement to compensate the communities concerned.

The aim of this discussion is not to deny the existence of biopiracy, but to show that the lack of clarity is becoming counterproductive. The problem with the biopiracy rhetoric and the strategic vagueness behind its usage is that without agreement on what it is, it cannot be measured. Neither is it possible to decide what should be done about it. One extreme view is that all bioprospecting is biopiracy. If so, the answer is to ban access outright. If biopiracy is merely an irritation, then such a ban need not be enforced too rigorously, since legal enforcement of higher-stakes areas of the law would have to take priority. If biopiracy causes demonstrable economic and/or cultural harm, the country should invest in enforcing the ban. On the other hand, if the problem is that provider countries or communities are unable to negotiate beneficial agreements, the answer may be to improve the provision of legal and technical assistance. If the problem is that the patent system legitimizes or encourages misappropriation, then we may need to improve the standards of examination, ban patents on life forms and natural, or even modified, compounds, or incorporate a disclosure of origin requirement. In short, how you define biopiracy goes a long way towards determining what you should do about it.

Bad patents affect negotiations

Developing countries' governments, negotiators and civil society groups argue that the IP system not only fails to provide sufficient safeguards to prevent biopiracy or misappropriation but also fails to prevent the issuing of 'bad patents', in other words where the invention does not fulfil basic patent requirements, for instance in cases where inventions are based on existing TK or make use of traditional plant varieties developed by farmers. The onus of identifying potentially erroneous patents and proving the existence of 'prior art' is placed on the challenger of a patent – a process that is costly, time-consuming and difficult, in particular in cases where the TK has been kept and transmitted orally rather than in writing. Moreover, overly broad patents threaten to restrict innovation by impeding access to and use of genetic material, including for use by farmers and public research for further breeding.

Controversies surrounding the role of IP and misappropriation have played a key role not only in shaping various multilateral agreements, but also in setting the framework from which problems are being addressed. In responding to biopiracy, the misappropriation of genetic resources and barriers that were placed on the free flow of genetic resources through the

expansion of IP protection (such as plant breeders' rights and patents), much of the focus in the different international negotiations revolved around the *sharing of benefits* from IP on genetic resources and TK. This failed to address the issue of patents that were bad in the first place, or whether IP is appropriate for genetic resources and TK, or alternative systems that would encourage conservation and exchange at the same time. The focus on benefit sharing shaped the way the CBD was developed, in that 'so much of it deals with matters that are not directly related to conservation of biological diversity' (Dutfield, 2002) but concern access and benefit sharing instead. The main approach on how to deal with the 'ABS–IP relationship' by different multilateral agreements has been on how to *harmonize* them. It is this harmonization, or lack of it, that mainly shapes many of the linkages between the different agreements, usually as a relationship between IP and the regulation of access to and the sharing of benefits from the use of genetic resources.

For example, in 2002, the Conference of the Parties of the CBD adopted the first Strategic Plan for the Convention, with the target of significantly reducing the rate of biodiversity loss by 2010. To achieve this target, the CBD must coordinate and harmonize with other international instruments, such as the WTO TRIPS Agreement and the UN Food and Agriculture Organization's (FAO) International Treaty on Plant Genetic Resources for Food and Agriculture (ITPGRFA, or the Treaty) as well as the Law of the Sea Convention (CBD, Article 22). An exception is carved out in the CBD for when 'those rights and obligations would cause a serious damage or threat to biological diversity' (Article 22.1). This raises the grey area, in the case of international agreements such as TRIPS and the CBD with provisions and aims that may be in conflict, of which agreement would have priority.

LINKAGES

Harmonization nexus: Shaping relationships between international instruments

TRIPS and the CBD .

The relationship between the provisions of TRIPS and the CBD has given rise to different opinions, ranging from those who see them as perfectly compatible to those who see them as quite inconsistent. Developing countries contend that TRIPS does not require patent applicants whose inventions incorporate or use genetic material or associated knowledge to comply with the obligations under the CBD (as discussed above and in Chapter 5). Developing countries have repeatedly voiced concern about possible misappropriation of their genetic resources by developed country patent applicants.

Different views on the TRIPS–CBD relationship have been expressed at the WTO during the review of Article 27.3(b) of TRIPS. While a number of developed countries have found no inconsistencies between the two treaties, several developing countries have indicated the need to reconcile them, possibly by means of a revision of TRIPS. The built-in review of Article 27.3(b) (discussed in Chapter 3) has not yet generated consensus and is one of the outstanding negotiating issues of the Doha Development Round, including 'the relationship between the TRIPS Agreement and the Convention on Biological Diversity, the protection of traditional knowledge and folklore' (WTO Doha Ministerial Declaration, paragraph 19). Since the adoption of the WTO Doha Ministerial Declaration, the issue has been included in the agenda of the TRIPS Council.

To address these concerns, developing countries have proposed in the WTO to amend the TRIPS Agreement to require an applicant for a patent relating to biological materials or TK to provide, as a condition for obtaining the patent:

- disclosure of the source and country of origin of the biological resource and of the TK used in the invention;
- evidence of prior informed consent through approval by authorities under the relevant national regime; and
- evidence of fair and equitable benefit sharing under the relevant national regime.

The approach to enforce CBD obligations through the TRIPS patent system is opposed, however, by a number of developed countries that see no conflict between the TRIPS Agreement and the CBD. For example, in the view of the US the proposed disclosure requirement is not an appropriate solution, and Members should focus on remedies such as the use of organized databases, information material to patentability, and the use of post-grant opposition or re-examination systems as an alternative to litigation.[5] Moreover, despite repeated requests by several WTO Members, the CBD does not have permanent observer status in the TRIPS Council.

UPOV and the CBD

The Council of UPOV has adopted a position on ABS 'in order to provide some guidance on UPOV's views on the "process, nature, scope, elements and modalities of an international regime on access to genetic resources and benefit sharing"' (UPOV, 2003, paragraph 5). This position is based on the principles of the 1991 UPOV Convention. As part of the position, UPOV expresses its opposition to mandatory disclosure of origin as a condition for obtaining plant variety protection as this would be contrary to the terms of the UPOV Convention (paragraph 8). Similarly, UPOV is opposed to any certification requirements that would be a mandatory precondition to obtaining plant variety protection (paragraph 10). Finally, UPOV is also opposed to any revenue-

LINKAGES

sharing mechanism that would 'impose an additional administrative burden on the authority entrusted with the grant of breeders' rights and an additional financial obligation on the breeder when varieties are used for further breeding' (paragraph 12). UPOV believes that such a mechanism would run counter to the breeders' exemption in the UPOV Convention (see Chapter 2).

CBD and the ITPGRFA

The ITPGRFA has very strong institutional and historical links with the CBD, as discussed in Chapters 5 and 6. The Treaty is largely based on the premise that bilateral, private sector and market forces approaches do not function well for agriculture, and since agriculture has always been based on continued access and exchange of materials, a more 'communal access' approach is needed. The CBD provides for 'national sovereignty', which is frequently interpreted to mean various forms of exclusive ownership and control (sometimes state, sometimes private, sometimes hybrid). The Treaty is also based on the concept of national sovereignty, but exercised in such a way as to maintain a relatively open system. While allowing for the possibility of private ownership (through IPRs) at the periphery of the commons it creates, the Treaty focuses on maximizing the public goods aspects of plant genetic resources for food and agriculture (PGRFA). Its multilateral system of access and benefit sharing (MLS) 'pools' these crucial plant genetic resources in a managed commons and makes them available under the Standard Material Transfer Agreement (SMTA) – a single legal instrument that cannot be altered for all movements of materials within the MLS. Because these genetic resources are pooled, there is no need for individual negotiations for ABS as found in the kinds of bilaterally oriented access laws that countries are putting in place as

they implement the CBD. Under the Treaty, decisions are also expected to be made collectively and the benefits must be shared in a pooled, multilateral manner, under the direction of the Governing Body (which is composed of all countries that have ratified the Treaty).

Although the Treaty was negotiated to bring the earlier International Undertaking on PGRFA (IU) into harmony with the CBD, it is neither subsidiary nor subject to the CBD. However, mutual supportiveness, including joint work programmes between the CBD and the Treaty, is very high on the agenda in both processes, and the FAO has concluded a Memorandum of Cooperation with the CBD.

The CBD provisions of prior informed consent and mutually agreed terms are 'built into' the MLS: all members mutually agree 'up front' to the terms set out in the Treaty and the SMTA. Annex I crops – for the purposes set out in the Treaty – now fall under a commons regime of facilitated access, without the transaction costs associated with the CBD. However, the CBD remains in force for all non-Annex I crops (for example soya), acquired after the entry into force of the CBD.

One of the most controversial parts of the Treaty is Article 12.3(d), which states that 'recipients shall not claim any IP or other rights that limit the facilitated access to the plant genetic resources for food and agriculture, or their genetic parts and components, in the form received from the MLS'. Such an undertaking is also included in the SMTA adopted to regulate the facilitated access.

The issue here is that in some legal jurisdictions, it is possible to patent DNA sequences and chemical substances that have been isolated from plant material without any structural modification. Therefore a patent holder could restrict – subject to possible research exemptions – use of the protected sequence or compound by others, and even access if the patent covered the method of isolation. It is not clear, however, whether this isolated material is still considered to be 'in the form received'

LINKAGES

from the MLS and so whether the prohibition against IP rights as contained in Article 12.3(d) would apply (Moore and Tymowski, 2005). To some developed countries, allowing such patents is necessary to encourage innovation and disclosure of the 'invention'. But to many developing countries (and perhaps some developed countries too), they legitimize misappropriation of resources to which they have sovereign rights and are contrary to the spirit of an international agreement that emphasizes exchange rather than appropriation. For others it is a fundamental mistake to allow the patent system to be extended to living organisms or parts thereof.

Garforth and Frison (2007) point out that the existence of these two instruments and their differing rules creates the potential for a number of debatable grey areas where it is not clear which obligations apply. For example:

- Countries that have ratified both the CBD and the Treaty will apply the rules of the MLS to those seeking to access the PGRFA listed in Annex I to the Treaty and the rules of the CBD to all other genetic resources. Countries that have only ratified the CBD, however, have no obligation to make the Annex I PGRFA available under the MLS and so can continue to apply the CBD rules for those seeking access to these resources. Presumably, someone seeking access to a specific PGRFA under the MLS would try to go to a country that has ratified the Treaty in order to take advantage of the presumably more facilitative access mechanism of the MLS. It is possible, therefore, to have the same genetic resource subject to a different approach to ABS (multilateral versus bilateral) depending on the country in which it is located.
- The distinction between what constitutes the use of a PGRFA and what constitutes the use of a plant genetic resource for other purposes is not always clear. A good example would be the case of Golden Rice. Golden Rice is rice that has been genetically engineered to produce extra vitamin A in order combat vitamin A deficiencies in children, which can lead to blindness. Golden Rice was obviously intended to be grown and eaten so it can be considered as a use related to food and agriculture. It was also intended, however, to combat a health problem, which would not make it a PGRFA. Food, nutrition and health are aptly conceived as a continuum rather than as distinct categories, so it can be unclear where the application of CBD rules should end and where the Treaty rules should begin. Determining which system of ABS should apply may become more complicated as the fields of nutraceuticals and biofortification develop and more crops are engineered to deliver specific health benefits. A further complication arises if the plant genetic resources have been accessed through the MLS with the original intention of using them for food and agriculture. If the intention subsequently changes, must the researcher trace the country of origin of the genetic resources in order to negotiate ABS terms?

- A final grey area concerns PGRFA not listed in Annex I to the Treaty. The obligations under the Treaty apply to all PGRFA, but the MLS only applies to the PGRFA listed in Annex I. Which ABS rules are countries to apply to non-Annex I PGRFA? Should they apply the CBD model or unilaterally treat them like part of the MLS? The presumption would probably be that the CBD rules (or a national ABS system implementing the CBD) would apply, particularly given the desire of some countries to specifically keep some species out of the MLS (see Chapter 6). However, The Netherlands is setting an example by already opting to use the SMTA for non-Annex I crops. The Ouadadougou Declaration[6] recommended that some form of the SMTA should be used for non-Annex I crops. Finally, it is quite possible that the Treaty's Governing Body will decide that the CGIAR Centres should use the SMTA for non-Annex I crops. This last precedent, if it comes to pass, would not be 'unilateral' but an expression by the global community that using the SMTA for non-Annex I crops – in other words extending the same terms and conditions for ABS as in the MLS – is the most appropriate way forward. It is realistic to hope that these are precedents that will be followed, as suggested in Chapter 6. If the Governing Body of the Treaty agrees to expand the list of Annex I crops and forages at some point in the future, however, this grey area could become all the more murky.

ITPGRFA and UPOV

Article 13(d) of the ITPGRFA requires that:

> ... *a recipient who commercializes a product that is a plant genetic resource for food and agriculture and that incorporates material accessed from the Multilateral System, shall pay to [a financial mechanism to be established] an equitable share of the benefits arising from the commercialization of that product, except whenever such a product is available without restriction to others for further research and breeding, in which case the recipient who commercializes shall be encouraged to make such payment.*

In effect, this means that a recipient that sells a PGRFA product incorporating material from the multilateral system *must* pay monetary benefits from commercialization under the following circumstances: either he/she owns a patent on the product and – as is normally the case – there is no exemption in the patent law

of the relevant jurisdiction that would freely allow others to use it for further research and breeding, or if access to using the new PGRFA product for research or breeding is blocked through technological means and/or by restrictive contractual provisions.

However, PGRFA products protected under UPOV Convention-compliant laws (or more flexible *sui generis* models) which include research and breeding exemptions would not trigger the benefit sharing mechanism. This reflects the political nature of the balance that was struck during negotiations (see Chapter 6) – (i.e. what kind of protection would trigger mandatory benefit sharing and what would not; the dissatisfaction of companies that depend on patents) – and to a large degree the bargaining power (or savvy) of the players at that point in history. Definitions in international fora about where the public domain starts and stops will be a key point to watch in the future. For example, it is known that big industry wants to interject a five-year 'grace period' during which time the research exemption would not operate under UPOV. If they are successful, that would remove a great deal of the current flexibility available to researchers and breeders under UPOV. This issue of 'what's left in the public domain' or 'what room is left to construct a commons' is one of the key issues to watch in the future.

The ITPGRFA and TRIPS

The interaction between the Treaty and the TRIPS Agreement has not yet been discussed in detail in the Treaty's Governing Body, although it is fully recognized that a strong relationship exists, not least because of the likely impact of IPRs on the ability to easily access or freely exchange genetic resources for food and agriculture and related technologies. However, as noted, the issues arising here largely reflect the ongoing global debates on the

LINKAGES

153

relationship between genetic resources and IPRs.

Articles 12.3(f) and 13.2(b)(iii) of the Treaty acknowledge that access to genetic resources shall be consistent with the *adequate and effective* protection of IPRs and relevant international agreements. However, unlike the CBD, which sees the possibility of actively using IPRs to further its objectives, the Treaty is more wary of their effects on its own objectives – prohibiting their use in the case of materials from the MLS to the extent that they would prohibit access to the materials in the form received, tolerating them where they will not constitute obstacles to access, and layering on an obligation to share financial benefits when they do. If countries sign agreements that oblige them to do away with breeders and research exemptions, the financial benefit sharing clause of the Treaty will be triggered more frequently. That is the most immediate nexus between TRIPS and possible future UPOV amendments. Although the interactions may be somewhat different, it is expected that the IPRs–genetic resources nexus in the context of the Treaty will evolve along similar paths as in the CBD, with the highly polarized positions (loosely along North–South lines) manifesting themselves once more.

Harmonization Versus Differentiation: The Relationship between WIPO and Other Intergovernmental Organizations

This section briefly explores some general issues and concerns being raised about WIPO's activities in relation to other intergovernmental organizations and some of the current relationships between WIPO and TRIPS, the CBD, the FAO and UPOV.

WIPO's role and mandate

IP is not like health, education, food or agriculture. It is a form of business regulation not a fundamental aspect of human needs. As such it is a subordinate activity that should be modified, reviewed and restructured according to how it helps or hinders meeting human needs. ... Deciding on the shape and structure of the [IP] regime, the detailed rules that shape it, the balance of interests to be met and the measures by which it is judged requires a far wider range of inputs than those from legal and technical groups that make up the IP community and which dominate the practice of WIPO. (Musungu, 2005, p23)

Given the cross-cutting impact of IP rules on international objectives, norms and policies, and the breadth of WIPO activities in relation to IP rules, WIPO is often considered, by default, a lead UN agency dealing with IP matters.

Moreover, the Convention establishing WIPO stated that the organization should, where appropriate, establish working relations and cooperate with other intergovernmental organizations – over 60 intergovernmental organizations have observer status in WIPO, including the FAO, the United Nations Educational, Scientific and Cultural Organization (UNESCO), the World Health Organization (WHO), UPOV and the WTO. For example, WIPO has signed a number of agreements or memoranda of understanding that establish specific topics or activities for cooperation. As the UN specialized agency on IP, WIPO also provides support on IP-related issues that surface in a range of discussions and processes.

Certainly, the establishment of agreements between WIPO and other agencies is an important means of cooperating and pooling resources. Nevertheless, WIPO's collaboration with other intergovernmental agencies has not always been viewed positively. Fundamental questions have been raised about whose interests WIPO has in mind when it approaches the IP-related issues of other agencies. These questions arise given that the nature and orientation of WIPO, as seen by many developing countries and civil society organizations, is to promote protection of IP and to extend its coverage, no matter what. WIPO has also been heavily criticized for ignoring crucial development-oriented elements of its mission statement (Chapter 4, Box 4.1).

A key concern being raised about WIPO's collaboration with other UN agencies is that, under the guise of making the UN system more effective and efficient, WIPO's influence could end up reducing individual UN agencies' capacity to take a robust approach to ensuring IPRs do not undermine the environmental, food, farming, health and educational concerns that the UN promotes. UN agencies dealing with agriculture, health and the environment need to understand where and how IP is useful and where it is not. For this, though, agencies such as the FAO and the CBD need to have their own legal and technical expertise so they can analyse IP from the point of view of their mandates and determine how IP affects those objectives and how it needs to be dealt with to achieve them. For example, the FAO should be able to make the case for changes in the IP regime as and when necessary in the interest of people's access to food, seeds or other genetic resources.

The relationship between WIPO and other international instruments

WIPO and the CBD

Despite developing country concerns – or perhaps because of them – WIPO contributions to the ABS discussions at the CBD have been technical documents that generally avoid supporting a particular outcome for IP-related issues. To date, two technical studies have been requested by the Conference of the Parties of the CBD and approved by the WIPO General Assembly. The first study (CBD, 2003) was presented in 2004 and addressed 'methods consistent with obligations in treaties administered by WIPO for requiring the disclosure within patent applications, as per the CBD request'. The study found there is a range of disclosure requirements that are consistent with the essential elements of patent law and key aspects of WIPO treaties. However, the request itself seemed to imply that an international regime under the CBD should adequately consider and support IP rules, rather than vice versa, as foreseen by the CBD.

The second study derived from an invitation by the Seventh Meeting of the CBD Conference of the Parties for WIPO 'to examine, and where appropriate address, taking into account the need to ensure that this work is supportive of and does not run counter to the objectives of the CBD, issues regarding the interrelation of access to genetic resources and disclosure requirements in intellectual property rights applications' (CBD, 2004). Owing to concerns about such WIPO input precluding adequate consideration of the role of disclosure requirements in the CBD negotiations for an international regime on ABS, developing countries and civil society organizations aimed to ensure the 2005 WIPO response to the CBD request was balanced and recognized the leading role of the CBD on biodiversity-related issues. For instance, developing countries and civil society organizations called for the inclusion of a disclaimer that explicitly framed the document as only a technical input to facilitate discussions. They also urged for the WIPO response to include a clearer recognition that, while WIPO as an institution has a significant role in terms of addressing these issues within its own IP rules, it is only able to provide peripheral input into the CBD process. A five-stage process, with the possibility for WIPO Member States and observers to provide comments, was established to prepare the

LINKAGES

response, which thus – and as requested by many developing countries – provides an overview of the different positions on these issues rather than taking a particular stance in terms of the way forward (CBD, 2006d).

There seems to be almost a schizophrenic relationship between WIPO and the CBD. On the one hand, it could be beneficial for these institutions, as well as others dealing with genetic and biological resources, to cooperate and for the different negotiators at each to be more aware and understanding of the pertinent issues at the other. There is obviously some willingness for collaboration, judging by the CBD invitations to WIPO. On the other hand, though, there is a fear that inviting WIPO into the CBD will result in inappropriate influence on CBD discussions, particularly given the strength of certain countries in WIPO, notably the US, which are not Parties to the CBD.

WIPO and the WTO

Although the focus seemed to switch to the WTO with the advent of the TRIPS Agreement, WIPO did not diminish in its importance with the introduction of IP into the multilateral trading system. As discussed in Chapter 3, the Preamble to the TRIPS Agreement recognizes a desire to establish a mutually supportive relationship with WIPO, and two WIPO-administered treaties were incorporated into the TRIPS Agreement. WIPO found an important niche in providing technical assistance to support the implementation of the new international standards of IP protection.

The 1995 agreement on cooperation between WIPO and the WTO aims to facilitate the implementation of the TRIPS Agreement and provides for cooperation in three areas:

1   the notification of, access to, and translation of national laws and regulations;

2   the implementation of procedures for the protection of national emblems; and

3   technical cooperation.

As part of this cooperation, two joint technical cooperation agreements have also been launched. For example, in 1998 WTO and WIPO joined forces to assist developing country WTO Members in meeting the January 2000 deadline for implementing the TRIPS Agreement. Other activities include a range of national and regional seminars and colloquia for teachers of IP from developing countries and countries with economies in transition. In all these activities, WIPO's technical assistance has been heavily criticized for not considering both the costs and benefits of IP protection (Chapter 4, Box 4.3). Developing countries have called for a more balanced approach to technical assistance, focusing not only on the need to comply with the protection of IPRs, but also on the importance of IP rules contributing to:

> ... *the promotion of technological innovation and to the transfer and dissemination of technology, to the mutual advantage of producers and users of technological knowledge and in a manner conducive to social and economic welfare, and to a balance of rights and obligations.* (TRIPS Agreement, Article 7).

In addition, the role of WIPO vis-à-vis the WTO in IP discussions has also come up expressly in discussions on IP and biodiversity. As developing countries seek to introduce disclosure requirements into the TRIPS Agreement (see Chapter 3), one of the recurring arguments used by some developed countries is that priority on these issues should be given to the WIPO Intergovernmental Committee on Intellectual Property and Genetic Resources, Traditional Knowledge and Folklore (IGC) (see Chapter 4). Although the WIPO IGC has done useful work on IP and biodiversity issues, there is significant concern that, rather than aiming to addressing IP and biodiversity issues, the emphasis on the IGC is primarily aimed at sidelining the WTO, considered as fundamental by developing countries given the potential conflicts between the CBD and TRIPS discussed above.

WIPO and the FAO

In 2005, an agreement between the FAO and WIPO was discussed by the Committee on Constitutional and Legal Matters at the FAO. This first version of the text included a preamble framing the draft agreement under the general premise that access to food may be more important than the protection of IP per se (Tansey, 2007). In 2005, the FAO Conference, the supreme governing body of the FAO, approved the memorandum of understanding between the FAO and WIPO devoid of the preamble and forwarded it to WIPO. The FAO–WIPO agreement aims to 'establish a mutually supportive relationship' between the FAO and WIPO and to establish 'appropriate arrangements for cooperation between them' (FAO, 2005). Provisions of the agreement encourage exchange of information; joint activities such as studies, seminars and workshops; and technical assistance or cooperation. The text of the agreement also contains a list of issues in which the organizations' work may intersect, including farmers' rights and TK; agricultural biotechnology; genetic resources for food and agriculture; promotion of innovation and the effective capture of benefits from public investment in research; use of distinctive signs in the food and agriculture sector; and ethical issues in food and agriculture. All these issues are essential from a public policy and sustainable development perspective. Concerns thus quickly arose regarding the potentially negative impact of the often limited WIPO perspective informing the FAO mission and role on these issues.

In 2006, Brazil, supported by other countries, opposed the approval of the agreement by the WIPO General Assembly. Their reasons focused on the potential negative impact of WIPO, which would counsel the FAO on major IP issues and on the FAO mission and role. They also objected to the fact that, under the agreement, the WIPO Secretariat, through the director general, would be able to establish and carry out work programmes with no involvement of Member States. The approval of the agreement was thus suspended.

Nevertheless, WIPO has already been actively contributing to FAO activities and discussions, particularly in relation to the Treaty. Because some of the most important elements in the MLS of the Treaty are directly related to IP, WIPO has participated both formally and informally in their elaboration. For example, WIPO was invited to send a representative to provide technical advice to both the Expert Group and Contact Group on the terms of the SMTA, the terms for access to all genetic resources covered by Annex I to the Treaty. WIPO is also preparing a report assessing patent data relevant to availability and use of material from *ex-situ* collections under the auspices of the FAO and the Treaty, undertaken at the request of the Commission on Genetic Resources for Food and Agriculture (CGRFA)

WIPO and UPOV

UPOV is an organization wholly independent of WIPO. However, under a 1982 Agreement, UPOV headquarters are located within WIPO buildings and the UPOV Council is obliged to appoint the director general of WIPO as the secretary general of UPOV. In addition to such administrative collaboration and support, WIPO also works closely with UPOV on a variety of issues.

LINKAGES

In its 2004 annual report, UPOV describes a range of cooperation activities with WIPO. For example, UPOV participated in a meeting organized by WIPO towards the implementation of the Cooperation Agreement between WIPO and the governments of the Caribbean countries and gave a lecture about plant breeders' rights and small and medium-sized enterprises at a special programme organized by WIPO and the World Association for Small and Medium-sized Enterprises.

For many developing countries and civil society organizations, these activities raise concerns about the pressure for developing countries to adopt the UPOV Convention despite broad recognition that its provisions are suited for industrialized agriculture, rather than the agricultural systems that prevail in the developing world. As a result, there are increasing calls for any participation of UPOV in WIPO technical assistance activities to be balanced with information about other *sui generis* options for implementing the WTO requirement to protect plant varieties. Nevertheless, even though the TRIPS Agreement makes no mention of UPOV, UPOV is often the sole expert advice provider in technical assistance activities on the implementation of plant variety protection, with a view to complying with the TRIPS Agreement.

Implications for Genetic Resources for Food and Agriculture

Part of the problem in all of the various negotiations is that different constituencies have been negotiating them – primarily trade officials at the WTO, patent lawyers at WIPO, environment ministries at the CBD and agricultural ministries at the FAO – often without much domestic coordination. As a result, the same issue is being dealt with differently depending on the negotiating context. It is IP and trade constituents, in particular, that are driving the agenda: defining the strategies, issues and solutions and thus creating all kinds of implications for the conservation and biodiversity of genetic resources crucial for food and agriculture.

Interdependence versus sovereign rights[7]

As discussed in Chapter 5, the CBD clarified the inapplicability of 'common heritage' for plant genetic resources, affirming 'state sovereignty' of natural resources. Article 15 of the CBD on access to genetic resources assigns to national governments the authority to determine such access, which is subject to the prior informed consent of the provider country and the fair and equitable sharing of benefits. Presumably, the expectation here is that the exercise of such authority will enable countries to capture more of the benefits from industrial use of their biogenetic resources, which in turn will encourage them to invest in conserving and sustainably utilizing biodiversity.

However, there are five reasons to question whether the bargaining position of individual developing countries in plant genetic resource transactions is all that strong:

1 They tend to lack the scientific and technological capacity to capture the benefits from agro-biodiversity themselves.

2 Apportioning the benefits fairly may be impossible or unfeasible. For example, new plant varieties are often the product of generations of breeding and cross-breeding, which in turn are the result of selection and breeding by farmers throughout the world and of the evolution of non-domesticated varieties. Depending on the crop, plant breeders commonly work with up to 60 or so different landraces originating from 20 to 30 different countries (Chapter 6).

3 Countries are interdependent and not even

biodiversity-rich tropical developing countries are self-sufficient. Every country is ultimately dependent upon exotic (non-indigenous) genetic resources essential for food and agriculture in such forms as wild crop progenitors, semi-domesticated crop relatives, landraces and cultivated varieties (cultivars), and therefore benefits from free access to genetic resources collected previously in other countries. To give just one example, when Brazil started to breed soya beans, the country imported genetic resources from the US. Interestingly, the origin of the soy bean is not North America at all, but East Asia. Despite this interdependence, it is ironic that during the 1990s, the extent of plant genetic resource collecting activities was reduced due, in no small part apparently, to concerns by some countries about 'biopiracy'.

4   A great deal of crop genetic resources are stored in *ex-situ* collections, such as those at universities, botanic gardens and gene banks held at the various CGIAR Centres. It is to the professional plant breeder's advantage to acquire genetic material from these sources for three reasons: first, because the collections are extensive and freely accessible; second, because basic information on accessions (material acquired) is usually available; and third because, in many cases, CGIAR breeding programmes have already selected some of the material for its desirable characteristics (see also Box 6.1).

5   Temperate zone countries may lack the species richness of tropical countries, yet may still be well endowed in terms of crop genetic diversity. The concentration of the world's biodiversity richness in the tropical zone may not necessarily coincide with the geography of agro-biodiversity-richness, especially of the major food crops. Temperate developed countries that have cultivated certain crops for centuries may be well endowed in balanced genetic struc-

tures, genes and traits that are desirable for crop breeders, and developing countries often need to import crop genetic resources from these countries for this reason. Strong evidence suggests, then, that if a developing country establishes a strong regulatory regime for access to crop genetic resources, industrialized world crop breeders would be affected far less than breeders in the South that might wish to exchange genetic resources with countries sharing the same agro-climatic conditions.

Country of origin, source or legal provenance[8]

Fights between countries are likely to arise as they quarrel over which gene 'originated' where and which nation should rightfully capture any benefits arising from its use. (Safrin, 2004)

Disclosure of origin is used as a general term that refers to different proposals concerning the disclosure of information on genetic resources and/or TK in patent applications. Certificates of origin are proposed as one tool for implementing potential disclosure of origin requirements. In essence, the idea entails requiring a person (natural or legal) who is applying for a patent on a biological or genetic resource to include as part of the patent application a certificate from the relevant authority attesting that the resource and any associated TK have been obtained in full compliance with the law of the country of origin. The purpose of disclosure and certificates of origin is to try to prevent instances of biopiracy where biological and genetic resources are acquired and patented without the patentee complying with the ABS requirements of the country from which the resources were obtained. Others have suggested refinements to the certificates concept. These include creating certificates of source or certificates of legal provenance. These concepts would not necessarily require

LINKAGES

tracking back a genetic resource all the way to its country of origin (in other words where the resource is found *in-situ*) but just to the place where the patent applicant obtained it (for example gene bank or botanical garden) or illustrating that the resource was obtained from a provider entitled to grant access.

Given the wide geographical dissemination of PGRFA over the centuries, it is in many cases impossible to establish where certain traits of agricultural value have developed (Chapter 6). This is one of the reasons why the Treaty opted for the MLS, under which benefits are shared multilaterally and there is no tracking of the 'country of origin' for Annex I materials. This only applies when the plant genetic resources are used for food or feed; for other uses, such as the development of a medicinal product, countries supplying materials may enforce CBD rules.

The absence in the Treaty of the concept of 'country of origin' or similar concepts of 'source' or 'legal provenance' is crucial for the facilitated access to and exchange of PGRFA. It does not mean, however, that sovereign rights are ignored. It is in the exercise of such rights (as recognized in Article 10.2 of the Treaty) that the Contracting Parties agreed to establish a system delinked from the determination of the origin or source.

Within the Treaty, the MLS is considered to be the origin of any accessed material as it secures appropriate benefit sharing. Therefore, the debate over whether to create international requirements for disclosure or certificates of origin is not as relevant. However, it is an issue to be considered given the centrality of certificate/disclosure of origin discussions in the CBD, the WTO and WIPO.

The CBD convened a meeting of a Group of Technical Experts on certificates in January 2007. During the meeting, the experts recognized that PGRFA fall within the scope of the ITPGRFA and that duplications with the Treaty should be avoided (CBD, 2007). There has thus been recognition of the fact that the creation of

a certificates system at the CBD must also involve consideration of the modalities of the Treaty. As discussed in Chapter 5, another outcome from the meeting was a potential shift in terminology. The Group 'recognized that the basic role of the certificate is to provide evidence of compliance with national ABS regimes. Thus, it found it practical to refer to the certificate as a certificate of compliance with national law, in accordance with the Convention'. This avoids the debate over the different proposals for certificates of origin, source or legal provenance, at least as far as what to call it.

Farmers' rights

The Treaty does not define farmers' rights and leaves it up to national governments to give effect to these rights as they see fit (see Chapter 6). The last paragraph of Article 9, however, points out that 'Nothing in this Article shall be interpreted to limit any rights that farmers have to save, use, exchange and sell farm-saved seed/propagating material, subject to national law and as appropriate.' Since the 1991 UPOV Convention does not permit the sale of protected seed without the authorization of the right holder, parties to the FAO Treaty that are not also parties to the UPOV Convention are free to adopt PVP legislation that upholds farmers' rights to the full extent allowable under the Treaty, which includes sale of protected seed. Otherwise, they must limit farmers' rights.

New enclosures

Some resources benefit from being shared. ... The more the resources are shared, the more they are preserved. Genetic resources are this type of good. In contrast to engendering a tragedy of the commons, where a common resource is used to depletion, the sharing of genetic material under an open system increases the global genetic pool, as it ensures the maintenance of genetic material in multiple locations. The open system that predated the expansion of IP rights and sovereign rights over genetic material accounts for the widespread distribution and preservation of crops and crop varieties away from their places of origin. The maintenance of genetic material in multiple countries and locations has benefited all. For example, under the open system, grape seedlings from France were brought to the US. Later a blight destroyed many French vineyards and the US sent grape seedlings back to France. (Safrin, 2004)

The shift from the concept of 'common heritage' to sovereign rights over genetic resources risks creating an anti-commons or new enclosure systems in raw genetic material (Safrin, 2004; see also Chapter 1). In response to biopiracy and other concerns discussed above, developing countries are asserting their sovereign ownership over genetic materials by passing laws that restrict access to genetic materials within their countries. Whether it is from restricting access to genetic resources via IPRs or laws that restrict access 'an anti-commons can occur when too many individuals or entities have rights of exclusion to a given resource' (Safrin, 2004). Given the interdependence of all countries on PGRFA (see Chapter 6), an anti-commons or new enclosure systems in genetic resources poses many problems for the conservation, breeding and improvement of genetic resources crucial for food security.

Some critics have decried the CBD as an 'absolute disaster' for scientists seeking access (IFCNR, 2003). They point out that the Convention does not distinguish among scientists 'bioprospecting' for new drugs and pharmaceuticals, scientists conducting academic research, and scientists collecting samples for agricultural research and plant breeding, although others point out that many national rules implementing the CBD do make

this distinction. The core problem, it is argued, is that the Convention is very narrowly fixated on the retention of rights and royalties on indigenous genetic resources. Resource-rich but economically depressed developing countries are loath to 'give away' any biological material that might prove lucrative. That emphasis has all but dried up sample collecting for gene banks that could well be the last chance to prevent biological extinction, an unintended consequence that undermines the entire purpose of CBD. For example, Dr Ricardo Callejas, a professor at the University of Antioquia in Medellín, Colombia, specializes in the 2000 species in the black pepper family (Revkin, 2002). His discipline is taxonomy, and he expressed the concern that the CBD had made the effort of collection and surveying impossible. 'If you request a permit,' Dr Callejas said, 'you have to provide coordinates for all sites to be visited and have to have the approval from all the communities that live in those areas.' After 14 months he was still waiting for a permit for collecting in Choco, Columbia (Revkin, 2002).

In some cases, scientists have been detained and their collections destroyed. In the Brazilian Amazon in 1998, an American geographer studying the forest for hints of ancient cultivation methods was placed under house arrest by the federal police in Santarem, and his boat, equipment and samples were seized. The scientist, Joseph McCann, had all the appropriate permits and visas. His gear and the title to his old riverboat were eventually returned, but most of the collection of pressed plants rotted because the police had stored it outside. The plants were destined for a Brazilian herbarium, not a pharmaceutical laboratory.

Safrin (2004) also argues that pushing the boundaries of sovereignty to achieve remuneration for accessed genetic materials also risks 'infringing on the autonomy and interests of individuals and indigenous communities whose land or property contains the genetic material' when states use pressure or force.

LINKAGES

Other Linkages

There are a whole range of other international goals and agreements that are related to the linkages between IP, biodiversity, TK and food; this section provides a brief guide to some of them.

Human rights, access to seeds and the right to food [9]

International rules on both trade, formerly through the General Agreement on Tariffs and Trade (GATT), and human rights were developed in the 1940s in response to the same set of circumstances following the Second World War (Harrison, 2007). Despite this, both evolved separately, leading to the risk of inconsistencies, difficulties and conflicts between human rights and trade law and policy (de Schutter, 2007). The introduction of minimum global IPRs standards into the trade arena, through the TRIPS Agreement (Chapter 3), drew the attention of human rights advocates to the possibility of clashes between trade and human rights policy.

International human rights law applies – in some degree at least – to all countries. However, the relationship between IPRs and human rights has been a controversial issue since the beginning. Some argue that IPRs are implicit in the right to the protection of the moral and material interests of authors and the right to property in the Universal Declaration of Human Rights (UDHR) and the International Covenant on Economic, Social and Cultural Rights (ICESCR). Others argue that IPRs 'cannot be equated with the fundamental and inalienable entitlements of the human person', that they 'lack the fundamental characteristics of human rights as [they] are ... limited in time and can be bought, sold or revoked'(3D→ THREE, 2006), and that the language used to describe IPRs should be changed to more accurately reflect what they are – 'intellectually-based monopoly privileges (IMPs) granted by society to a few to exclude the rest' (FEC, 2002).

Many human rights can be affected by the types of monopoly privileges that are granted by IPRs. The rights at stake include the right to health (and the related obligation to ensure access to affordable medicines), the right to education (and the related access to educational materials), the right to food, the right to an effective remedy and the rights of indigenous peoples. For reasons of brevity, only the right to food and the mechanisms available to assist in its implementation are discussed here.

The right to food

The right to food is enshrined in many international human rights instruments, including the UDHR, ICESCR and the Convention on the Rights of the Child (CRC). Moreover, it is also protected through regional instruments such as the San Salvador Protocol to the American Convention on Human Rights and the African Charter on the Rights and Welfare of the Child.

IPRs can adversely affect the right to food in many different ways. For example, patents and plant variety protection on seeds can prevent farmers from breeding, saving and reusing seeds to feed themselves and their communities. Furthermore, patents can increase the cost of seeds, thereby making them inaccessible for small farmers – as they need to be bought each year and often require additional inputs such as herbicides and pesticides. Moreover, patents on microbiological processes, plants and animals may be culturally unacceptable for communities and traditional societies that are based on principles of free exchange of knowledge and seeds.

IPRs can affect the right to food, not only in terms of limiting access to food itself, but because the right extends beyond nutrition to encompass the notion of 'adequacy and sustainability of food'.[10] The UN Committee on Economic, Social and Cultural Rights (CESCR), which oversees implementation of the ICESCR in the 156 countries that have agreed to be bound by the Covenant, have provided the most authoritative and detailed analysis of the scope of the right to food. This specifies that in order for the right to food to be realized, every individual alone or in a community must have physical and economic access at all times to adequate food or a means for its procurement. This requires cultural and consumer *acceptability*, *availability* of food by feeding oneself directly from productive land, natural resources or a well-functioning distribution system, and economic and physical *accessibility*.

States have an obligation to take measures to *respect, protect and fulfil* the right to food and move expeditiously towards this goal. The obligation to respect requires the state not to impede access to adequate food. This could include refraining from adhering to IPRs or plant variety protection systems that reduce access to seeds. The obligation to protect requires the state to take measures to ensure that individuals or enterprises do not deprive people of their access to adequate food. This could involve prohibiting biotech companies from patenting micro-organisms, plants and animals that obstruct the right to food, such as terminator seeds (terminator technology, also called genetic use restriction technology; see Chapter 5, Box 5.5). Finally, the obligation to fulfil requires the state to strengthen people's access to resources, in order to ensure their means to a livelihood and food security. This could be fulfilled by passing *sui generis* plant variety protection in a manner that is consistent with sustainable development and human rights.

The Voluntary Guidelines to Support the Progressive Realization of the Right to Adequate Food in the Context of National Food Security were adopted at the FAO Council in 2004. The aim was to provide practical guidance to states on the implementation of the right to adequate food in the context of national food security and to achieve the goal of the World Food Summit. Without very strong political commitment to implementing the guidelines, however, it is debated whether the guidelines achieved 'a breakthrough in setting standards' of interpretation of the right to food developed in the human rights system of the UN (Windfuhr and Jonsén, 2005) or actually weakened it.

Human rights mechanisms

Human rights mechanisms can be used to hold states and private actors accountable for any adverse effects of IPRs on the right to food. Human rights treaty bodies have held states accountable for IPRs by recommending that governments systematically consider human rights norms when negotiating IPRs and implementing them into national law, in addition to undertaking impact assessments before negotiating such agreements.[11] Moreover, a number of mechanisms have stressed that corporate actors must respect the right to food. For example, the UN Commission on Human Rights in 2005 requested 'all states and private actors, as well as international organizations … to take fully into account the need to promote the effective realization of the right to food for all, including in the ongoing negotiations in different fields'.[12] Finally, the UN Special Rapporteur on the right to food has called on states to put greater emphasis on the responsibility of private actors and international organizations – such as the IMF, World Bank and WTO – in ensuring that their activities do not violate enjoyment of the right to food.[13]

LINKAGES

TK

In a sense, international IP agreements like TRIPS are a form of 'globalized localism', in which European and North American norms concerning the regulation of knowledge have become universal. If TK were to be protected in the form of a widened applicability of the customary norms of the TK holders, it would be a manifestation of the same phenomenon. The problem is that while TRIPS was foisted on the world by big business and powerful governments, TK protection cannot depend on such support, meaning that a truly effective and culturally appropriate international regime is unlikely to be achieved. Moreover, TK tends to be discussed in fora like the WTO Council for TRIPS and WIPO. Important as the debates in these fora are, TK is inevitably treated narrowly in such places as an IP issue, and governments like to keep it that way. To treat TK in a more holistic fashion might require some serious reflection on national governance, including the possibility of providing legal pluralism and ceding power from central government to the regions. It is hardly surprising, then, that many governments are unwilling to broaden the discussion. Moreover, the motives of some developing country governments in pursuing a TK 'solution' appear to be based on questionable assumptions about the commercial potential of TK. TK is of value primarily to local people. The idea that local high-tech industries could use TK to discover lots of blockbuster drugs and help significantly to increase a country's gross national product and trade balance is probably illusory. Sooner or later governments will realize this. And when they do, there is a real concern that they will quietly drop the TK issue, especially if they are granted concessions on other IP or trade-related concerns in return for doing so.

Internationally, TK protection is a very fragmented issue. TK relating to biodiversity is covered by the CBD, WIPO and the WTO. TK and health is a WHO matter, except when the emphasis is on plant-related knowledge, in which case the former three institutions are relevant. The WHO is not involved in norm setting in this area, however. As for agricultural knowledge, the FAO also has an interest. UNESCO provides a forum for discussion of expressions of folklore and culture, along with WIPO. How much of the deliberations in these fora have affected international law? Perhaps not as much as they should. WIPO has drafted two sets of provisions for the protection of TK and of traditional cultural expressions (WIPO, 2006a and b). Potentially these could form the basis for international treaties, but only time will tell if they will. In 2003, UNESCO adopted its Convention for the Safeguarding of the Intangible Cultural Heritage. Important as this treaty may turn out to be, it is somewhat soft in the extent of its binding obligations on governments. The 2005 UNESCO Convention on the Protection and Promotion of the Diversity of Cultural Expressions reaffirms in Article 1 'the sovereign rights of states to maintain, adopt and implement policies and measures that they deem appropriate for the protection and promotion of the diversity of cultural expressions on their territory'. Unfortunately, one can envisage this top–down principle being used to legitimize paternalistic and ineffective policies that run counter to the wishes of those peoples possessing the cultural expressions to be protected and promoted.

One demand of developing countries that has cut across several of these fora (WIPO, the WTO and the CBD) is disclosure of origin (see above). As we have seen, the proposal is that countries amend their patent laws to require that inventions claiming or using genetic resources and associated TK disclose the source of such resources and knowledge in their patent applications, otherwise the patent may not be granted or may be revoked if already granted. While such a measure may provide some additional transparency in terms of international movements of genetic resources and TK, some are less certain that it will do much to prevent misappropriation of TK. Moreover, the US is completely opposed to the idea of amending its patent law to require disclosure of origin and is unlikely to shift its position.

Millennium Development Goals, IPRs and food security

The Millennium Development Goals (MDGs) are non-binding international targets on reducing global poverty to be achieved by 2015. They are drawn from the actions and targets contained in the Millennium Declaration that was adopted by 189 nations and signed by 147 heads of state and governments during the UN Millennium Summit in September 2000. Of the eight goals, three goals are of particular interest to the intersection between IPRs and food security:

MDG 1: Eradicate extreme hunger and poverty

Indicators:

- Reduce by half the proportion of people living on less than a dollar a day.
- Reduce by half the proportion of people who suffer from hunger (incorporated from the 1996 World Food Summit at the FAO but changed from numbers to proportion of hungry people; see Chapter 1).

Countries' poverty reduction strategies may include supporting their small-scale farming sector to increase income levels, enhance food supply and reduce poverty. Farmers' free access to improved seeds and the right to reuse and exchange seeds can provide one of the tools towards this goal by ensuring sustained input into the farming sector. At the same time, investments in public research – unimpeded by onerous IP requirements – may be required to improve agricultural productivity and nutritional content for crops of particular interest to local farmers. In addition, incentives, including within the IP system, might need to be put in place to stimulate private sector innovation that addresses the needs of the poor.

MDG 7: Ensure environmental sustainability

Indicator:

- Integrate the principles of sustainable development into country policies and programmes; reverse loss of environmental resources.

Efforts to achieve this goal might require addressing concerns that the existing IP system and associated private monopoly privileges encourage a shift towards large-scale monoculture production that threatens to erode agricultural biodiversity while negatively impacting on environmental sustainability (through water pollution or habitat loss, for example). This goal is directly related to MDG 1, given that sustainable agricultural production – which is necessary to reduce hunger and poverty – relies on genetic seed diversity for future breeding and on the continued viability of the land.

MDG 8: Develop a global partnership for development

Indicators:

- Develop further an open trading and financial system that is rule-based, predictable and non-discriminatory and includes a commitment to good governance, development and poverty reduction – nationally and internationally.

LINKAGES

- In cooperation with the private sector, make available the benefits of new technologies – especially information and communications technologies.

As an integral part of the MLS, the TRIPS Agreement might need to be rebalanced to provide sufficient flexibilities for countries to implement policies necessary to achieve their specific objectives under the MDGs and include provisions that actively support these objectives. In line with MDG 8, this would include access to relevant technologies necessary to meet development priorities, including in the agriculture sector.

Trade and development

UNCTAD

Food security is one important facet of the 'development dimension' of IPRs, which also includes issues such as poverty reduction, environmental protection, innovation, technology transfer and public health. As the main international body charged with examining trade issues from a development perspective, the UN Conference on Trade and Development (UNCTAD) undertakes policy analysis, technical assistance and consensus building activities designed to ensure that the development dimension of IPRs is fully addressed by both domestic policies and international action. UNCTAD has three main areas of work connected with IPRs and food security:

1 supporting the protection, preservation and promotion of the TK and genetic resources of developing countries;
2 promoting organic agriculture as a trade and sustainable development opportunity for developing countries; and
3 building the capacity of developing countries to analyse and negotiate trade-related IPRs.

UNCTAD's approach to TK and genetic resources focuses on providing in-depth analytical support to inform the debate on national and international measures related to TK and genetic resources. This research considers both IPR- and non-IPR-based policy options and deals with food security as one aspect of sustainable development. UNCTAD aims to develop policy options that respect the rights and interests of the holders of TK and that ensure that any exploitation of genetic resources is carried out according to principles of prior informed consent and fair and equitable benefit sharing. Recent research by UNCTAD has identified practical measures that developing countries can take at the national level to protect, preserve and promote TK, such as legal recognition of the customary practices and knowledge ownership of local communities and acting to preserve TK in living diverse communities through securing land rights and enhancing livelihoods. In response to a request by the CBD, UNCTAD has also provided a thorough analysis of policy options for implementing disclosure of origin requirements in IP applications (Sarnoff and Correa, 2006). Such measures could help to improve the IP system and aid food security goals by ensuring that developing countries have control over their knowledge and genetic resources and receive a fair share of any benefits derived from them.

One policy response to food security concerns is the promotion of organic agriculture. The results of UNCTAD's research and capacity-building activities in this area indicate that organic agriculture can deliver a number of trade and sustainable development opportunities for developing countries, including enhanced food security, improved public health, decreased pollution and increased incomes for smallholder farmers. These benefits provide a further rationale for protecting TK, as organic agriculture builds on a foundation of traditional agricultural practices, varieties and knowledge to adapt organic

LINKAGES

techniques to local conditions. Under the Capacity-Building Task Force on Trade and Environment, UNCTAD is working with the United Nations Environment Programme (UNEP) to identify and develop opportunities for organic agriculture in East Africa. UNCTAD is also working with the FAO and the International Federation of Organic Agriculture Movements in an International Task Force aimed at harmonizing the multiplicity of standards and regulations faced by organic exporters.

UNCTAD also collaborates with the International Centre for Trade and Sustainable Development (ICTSD) on the Capacity Building Project on IPRs and Sustainable Development. This aims to improve understanding of the development implications of the TRIPS Agreement and to strengthen the analytical and negotiating capacity of developing countries so that they are better able to participate in IPR-related negotiations. To this end, UNCTAD and ICTSD have published a *Resource Book on TRIPS and Development* and several research papers and organized a series of seminars and dialogues that brought together negotiators, experts in the field and representatives from intergovernmental organizations and NGOs to discuss IP-related policies and negotiations.

UNCTAD also pays particular attention to the needs of the least developed countries. It has recommended that they should not be subject to any arbitrary deadline for complying with TRIPS obligations and that neither should those undertaking WTO accession (discussed above) be subject to 'TRIPS-plus' requirements (UNCTAD, 2007). In general, it suggests IP regimes should be adapted to enable least developed countries improve their ability to produce and market competitive products, that TRIPS flexibilities should be enhanced and not eroded via bilateral agreements.

Finally, the UNCTAD BioTrade Initiative promotes trade and investment in biological resources in line with the objectives of the CBD. It works on legal and policy issues linked to IP, including the role of geographical indications in distinguishing BioTrade products. It also collaborates with Bioversity International (formerly the International Plant Genetic Resources Institute, or IPGRI) on these issues. UNCTAD BioTrade also heads a working group of biodiversity-related multilateral environmental agreements looking at issues such as trade, private sector engagement and incentive measures. The UNCTAD BioTrade Initiative is also developing guidelines for benefit sharing in BioTrade activities, including issues such as TK and IP.

UNCTAD's future work on this subject, as on others, will be decided by its member states. Therefore, if the relationship between IP and food security is recognized as an issue that is central to development efforts, further emphasis can be expected to be placed on the provision by UNCTAD of research, consensus building and technical assistance in this area.

Conclusion

As IPRs have expanded and the number of agreements has grown, so too has the level of complexity of problems – and the creation of new ones – as they intersect with an ever-widening range of issues. Chapter 8 will explore how more and more groups are becoming involved and responding to some of these issues in different ways.

Part III

Responses, Observations and Prospects

The creation of new global rules and the higher profile given to intellectual property (IP) has led to growing attention being paid to these than before. The impact of IP on many aspects of life – from food to health, from education to artistic endeavours – has led to a growing concern about whether the new rules strike the right balance between private and public interest and between countries with very different levels of wealth, power, agricultural practices and technological capacities.

Chapter 8 draws together some of the responses from civil society to the changing rules and concerns arising from them, particularly how the IP rules are shaping the direction of research and development. Chapter 9 reflects on the earlier chapters and makes some observations based on those reflections. Finally, Chapter 10 discusses the nature of global negotiations and various alternative futures and the roles the rules will play in influencing them.

Responding to Change

Heike Baumüller and Geoff Tansey

Most changes have unintended consequences, and changing global rules on intellectual property (IP) are no exception. Those promoting greater IP protection face growing resistance as civil society groups learn about its implications and campaign for changes. Many civil society responses so far have focused on the effects on farming and biodiversity rather than the processing and distribution side of the food system. They have raised concerns that these changes facilitate corporate control over the world's seed supply and agrifood production at the expense of small-holder farmers and that they favour commercial interests over the public interest in food security and sustainable livelihoods. Other concerns focus on the impact on research and development (R&D) on avoiding restrictions on access to scientific knowledge and IP protected materials, and on alternative approaches to R&D to benefit poor people farming more marginal lands.

Introduction

The growing mix of global rules affecting food and agriculture has made life more complicated for governments, researchers, industry and civil society groups. The various international agreements, treaties, conventions and protocols discussed in Part II of this book are not the end point – they are part of a process of framing and reframing rules to address changing concerns, and inevitably they suit certain interests. Once the agreements are reached and treaties signed, negotiations do not stop. Further pressures arise in interpreting and implementing what was agreed or to amend rules if they do not produce desired outcomes.

The increasing complexity of rule-making and the growing web of agreements requiring follow-up is a problem in itself for civil society and governments. For many poorer countries and groups – from farmers' and peasants' organizations, to small and medium-sized enterprises, to officials and negotiators – the capacity to deal with the global negotiations and rules, or influence them so that they reflect their interests, is very limited. For many, the application of new global rules to their area of activity came as a surprise; this was particularly the case with those on IP – even some governments signing up to the World Trade Organization (WTO) in 1994 were unaware of the far-reaching implications of the Trade-Related Aspects of Intellectual Property Rights (TRIPS) regime.

RESPONSES

For those who wanted stronger global IP rules through the TRIPS Agreement, there have been unintended consequences. One of these has been raising the profile of what were esoteric, complex legal issues in the public consciousness and on the front pages of newspapers – initially most notably in developing countries over the question of the impact of the IP regime on access to medicines. As mentioned in Chapter 3, TRIPS itself is partly an unintended consequence of an earlier struggle by developing countries to seek a new international economic order, in which developing countries failed to have various IP rules adjusted to fit more closely with their needs. A few global industries subsequently succeeded in creating global rules that suited them. Part II of the book showed that the consequences of that failure fed into negotiations on other issues.

The Convention on Biological Diversity (CBD), in the way it is structured, is, perhaps, also a consequence of the anger felt in developing countries that biological and genetic resources originating and taken from them were used in creating products netting billions of dollars, no share of which accrued to them. The Convention has produced a complex regime, still far from being implemented, with much uncertainty about how far it is able to achieve its goals and with continuing pressures for stronger provisions on access and benefit sharing (ABS), labelling of living modified organisms (LMOs), and liability and redress. The tension and anger over broader economic injustices and the conflicts between those able to use the privileges granted through patents and other forms of IP and those who have developed and sustained agricultural biodiversity also spilled over into the negotiations of the International Treaty on Plant Genetic Resources for Food and Agriculture (the Treaty) at the UN Food and Agriculture Organization (FAO), with battles over access, farmers' rights and IP running through the negotiations. All this has resulted in a very unbalanced set of international institutions, with only the WTO having a strong dispute settlement mechanism backed by cross-sectoral sanctions.

Those who promoted the IP rules are still seeking to expand and strengthen them further and increasingly to criminalize infringement of these private rights. Criminalization shifts the costs of enforcement from those private parties who benefit from the privileges to states and therefore taxpayers. Currently, this expansive approach is holding sway through many bilateral free trade and investment agreements (see Chapter 7). But as awareness has grown, so too have the reactions and responses. This chapter focuses on civil society responses and then looks at how the new rules impact on R&D for food and farming. Responses vary according to which group is involved. Some are trying to accommodate to the new rules in the least damaging way, others to inform those affected and to empower them to challenge or resist, remake or rebalance them. A few seek to rethink the rules entirely.

The capacity of different groups to engage with and respond to the changes in the international regulatory regime is very varied. So too is the ability of different groups to deal, in particular, with IP matters, where having deep pockets to pay for expensive lawyers and lobbyists is a major advantage. Competing in the patent game, for example, requires considerable resources – both to take out and maintain patents – and legal expertise to defend them. Unless patent holders are able to defend them, at least in the major markets, they are useless. According to Blakeney (2001, Note 60), 'a single patent application, carried to completion in key markets, costs an estimated US$200,000. Defending a patent application costs at least this amount again'. Most small players look for larger companies to license their inventions or buy them out and acquire the rights to use the patent portfolios they hold.

In the area of food, many of the responses so far have focused on the effects on farming and biodiversity rather than the processing and

Box 8.1 Trademark 'TM' power

While most attention has focused on the patent and plant variety protection regimes, other forms of IP are important in the food system. One form, which is relatively poorly studied, is trademarks. These are of vital importance for firms dealing with consumers and also for marketing products to farmers as they underpin brand-based marketing strategies.

As Bill Kingston has pointed out in raising concerns about tobacco advertising, given its health impact there are no grounds for refusing trademark applications, such as the product being trade-marked being injurious to health, and a very lax approach to what is being allowed to be trademarked is developing (Kingston, 2006).

An example of their power and this laxity arose in the UK in May 2007. As various British media reported, a small, family-run pub (a bar serving food) in Northern England was told by Kentucky Fried Chicken (KFC) to remove the words 'family feast' from its menu. The American fast food company's lawyers said that the pub landlords were using a term the company had registered as a trademark and so were infringing it.

The pub serves their 'family feast' at Christmas and uses the term to describe their Christmas menu, which includes Guinness and Stilton pâté, roast turkey and Christmas pudding. KFC uses the term to describe a cardboard bucket of fried chicken and chips, coleslaw, potato and gravy, with a 1.25-litre bottle of a fizzy drink.

A company spokesman reportedly said:

'Family Feast' is a registered trademark of Kentucky Fried Chicken (Great Britain) Limited. KFC devotes significant resources to promoting and protecting its trademarks. This particular instance is being dealt with by our solicitors.

The pub's managers at first thought it was a joke and then received offers of help to fight the case once it got a lot of national publicity in the UK. Subsequently, the company decided it would not take the case any further.

While there was much comment on the case, very few questioned what is and is not allowed to be trademarked. Stricter trademarking criteria would prevent trivial or obvious wording being given a trademark in the first place and avoid this kind of problem. Additionally, for Kingston, a key issue is to change trademark registration rules to curb the worst excesses by not giving the privilege of registration where this is for harmful products. Denying registration would not prevent anybody from making and selling cigarettes or drink or junk foods, or from advertising them, but the power of this advertising and other marketing ploys to shape culture would be much reduced. Compulsory arbitration, which he also advocates, would also eliminate intimidation of small businesses by larger ones.

Sources: http://news.bbc.co.uk/1/hi/england/north_yorkshire/6641819.stm; http://business.timesonline.co.uk/tol/business/law/article1769516.ece; www.thepublican.com/story.asp?storyCode=55352 – all accessed 17 May 2007.

RESPONSES

distribution side of the food system, although other forms of IP play a major role there too (Box 8.1).

Civil Society Critiques

The changing international regimes have brought about several levels of response. Some, by international non-governmental organizations (NGOs) and activist groups have focused on a critique of the changes, highlighting their implications, producing information materials and working to support developing country negotiators dealing with the international regimes. Some grew up from or focused more on grass roots level work with farmers', peasants' and consumers' organizations, while others have focused on monitoring effects in the field and working with national governments to strengthen their capacity to deal with IP, biodiversity and food, and related issues.

Many criticisms directed at the IP system basically revolve around the limitations it places on access to knowledge and knowledge products, thereby tipping the balance increasingly in favour of private (commercial) interests to the detriment of public policy objectives. Civil society movements have sprung up around this theme, targeting diverse sectors such as software, medicines, seeds, research, music and the media. What unites these movements are concerns that the IP system curtails the freedom to:

- access information and the products that embody the information;
- use the information for private purposes or further development; and
- share the knowledge and the products derived from it.

Civil society groups have argued that the implications of the IP system on public policy objectives related to food security, livelihoods and biodiversity conservation include:

- intellectual property rights (IPRs), especially in agricultural biotechnology, facilitating corporate control over the

world's seed supply and agrifood production at the expense of traditional farmers;
- the TRIPS Agreement and other IP rules favouring commercial interests over public research efforts that address food security concerns and ensure sustainable livelihoods;
- IPRs providing an incentive for the misappropriation of genetic resources and associated TK, an issue that has been picked up by governments, as discussed in Chapter 7; and
- bilateral and regional trade agreements imposing TRIPS-plus requirements on developing countries that further limit flexibilities in implementing measures to address public policy objectives (also discussed in Chapter 7).

These concerns are clearly interlinked, and many civil society groups often focus on several aspects of the issue with differing degrees of emphasis depending on their institutional goals, focus and constituencies. Underlying many of the concerns are fundamental differences in opinion over who owns or should own genetic resources and associated TK – individuals, communities, nation states or humankind – and how knowledge and innovation have been or should be generated – collectively or through rewarding individual efforts. While the different systems of ownership and knowledge generation might feasibly be able to exist in parallel, the expanding scope and reach of the IP system is seen increasingly to reduce that possibility.

The debates are further coloured by concerns over the changes in social and cultural dynamics and structures that a strong IP system is feared to bring. The concerns are particularly acute for food security and agricultural production and the livelihoods that depend on it. Small-scale, informal agricultural production systems in developing countries – developed by farmers and public research institutions and made possible through the sharing of knowledge and seeds – are seen to clash with formal systems in developed countries dominated by large-scale agricultural production and significant commercial interests that rely on IPRs to protect their market position. Thus it is ultimately the vision of the world that we see ourselves living in that is driving many of these concerns and related debates (see Chapter 10).

Corporate control

Today control over agricultural biotechnology is effectively limited to a few multinational corporations who integrate seeds, agrichemicals and biotechnology. This disturbing consolidation of power is matched with a trend towards 'me-too', big-ticket 'innovations' of remarkable dullness. How many herbicide-tolerant big acreage crops are enough? (Jefferson, 2007)

The corporate sector has seen a remarkable consolidation over the past few years. Just ten multinational companies – dubbed 'genes giants' by the Action Group on Erosion, Technology and Concentration (ETC Group) – are estimated to account for half of the world's commercial seed sales (ETC Group, 2005). This trend is particularly apparent in the agricultural biotechnology sector, where six companies – Aventis, Dow, Du Pont, Mitsui, Monsanto and Syngenta – control 98 per cent of the global market for patented biotech crops (ActionAid, 2003).

Patents and plant variety protection are widely seen as one of the key driving forces behind this trend. Compared to many other goods, seeds do not easily lend themselves to commodification as they are easily reproduced and may not require repeat purchase (FEC, 2002). IPRs have provided the legal mechanism to control the use of seeds in an effort to

protect ever-growing investments. In the US, for instance, over half of the private-sector-held agricultural biotech patents granted between 1982 and 2001 are owned by five companies, namely Monsanto, Dupont, Syngenta, Bayer and Dow (Graff et al, 2003).

With control over the seeds – as the first link in the food chain – comes growing control over the world's agricultural production, which is seen as increasingly subjected to the commercial interests and market manoeuvres of the corporate sector (ETC Group, 2005). Much of the focus has been on the need to protect farmers' rights to save, use, exchange and sell farm-saved seed – as reflected in the International Treaty on Plant Genetic Resources for Food and Agriculture (Chapter 6). In many developing countries, where small-scale farmers continue to provide for the bulk of agricultural food production and livelihoods, such farmers' rights are seen as a prerequisite for survival. Restrictions on seed use from a mixture of plant variety protection, patents and seed laws threaten to force farmers into dependency on purchased seeds while driving up the price of seeds. In addition to IP, contracts with farmers are also used that effectively mean that the seller is licensing a technology embodied in the seed so that farmers cannot do whatever they want with it, since they do not actually own the seed when they buy it (see Chapter 1, Box 1.6).

Related to these concerns are potential impacts on agricultural biodiversity and consequently the long-term sustainability of food production (FEC, 2002). The expansion of patents and plant variety protection, with their various requirements for uniformity and industrial applicability (or 'utility' in the US), is feared to encourage agricultural systems that are further dominated by large-scale monoculture cropping, often primarily for export and are genetically vulnerable to pest, pathogen or environmental changes. The genetic erosion resulting from the replacement of local plant varieties by uniform modern varieties could lead to the loss of varieties that are adapted to

RESPONSES

local conditions along with valuable genes for further breeding. Such varieties are being replaced by a narrow selection of uniform varieties, thereby increasing crops' susceptibility to single pathogens and thus requiring the use of pesticides and other inputs. As the FAO has reported:

> *One of the main causes of genetic vulnerability is the widespread replacement of genetically diverse traditional or farmers' varieties by homogeneous varieties. … The main cause of genetic erosion in crops, as reported by almost all countries, is the replacement of local varieties by improved varieties or exotic varieties and species.* (FAO, 1998)

This is one reason why many civil society organizations want to see more emphasis on *in-situ* conservation through sustainable use of these local farmers' varieties. Similar concerns are being raised by those focusing on animals. In commercial poultry, for example, 'Between 1989 and 2006, the number of companies supplying poultry genetics at a global scale has reduced from 10 to 2 in layers and from 11 to 4 in broilers' (Gura, 2007).

Proposals for specific amendments to the IP system are also driven by civil society movements that draw on fundamental human rights and the Millennium Development Goals to back their case (see Chapter 7). Moreover, a campaign for greater 'food sovereignty' has emerged out of broader concerns over the globalization of the world's food system (GRAIN, 2005a). Launched by the peasants' movement Via Campesina at the 1996 World Food Summit, the concept of food sovereignty has emphasized, among other things, prioritizing local agricultural production, safeguarding the right of farmers to produce foods and ensuring populations' right to make agricultural policy choices (Box 8.2). It has also become a focus for resistance to the expansion of IP in agriculture.

The TRIPS Agreement and the International Union for the Protection of New Varieties of Plants (UPOV) have come in for particular criticism. The TRIPS Agreement's requirement for WTO Members to provide minimum standards of IP protection, including the patenting of life in the form of micro-organisms and some form of IP protection for plant varieties – either through patents or *sui generis* systems – is seen to limit countries' flexibility to decide for themselves what level of protection they deem necessary for their particular agricultural context. It also does not explicitly provide for a farmers' exemption, leaving it open to what extent such an exemption could be legally integrated in a *sui generis* system.

Similarly, the UPOV Convention is thought to provide excessive rights for plant breeders without any benefit sharing requirements. Its plant variety protection (PVP) criteria, in particular the requirement for uniformity, have been criticized for being adapted to the needs of commercial, professional plant breeders rather than farmers who rely on diversity to cope with agricultural and climatic complexities. In particular, the 1991 revision – which any country acceding after 1999 is required to sign up to – has been attacked for further undermining farmers' rights (GRAIN, 1998), since it only provides an option to allow farmers to reuse seeds on their own holdings.

While the CBD and the International Treaty aim to address some of these concerns at the multilateral level, many feel that these efforts have not been able to keep pace with the continuously expanding IP system. Countries have been slow to implement the Convention's provisions, which provide for fair and equitable benefit sharing based on mutually agreed terms, and the US – the world's key player in the biotech field – has yet to ratify it.

While many welcome the International Treaty's valiant attempt to redress the balance by incorporating farmers' rights and provide for the sharing of benefits derived from plant

Box 8.2 Six pillars of food sovereignty

In February 2007, a gathering of over 500 representatives, from more than 80 countries, of peasants/family farmers, artisanal fisherfolk, indigenous peoples, landless peoples, rural workers, migrants, pastoralists, forest communities, women, youth, consumers, and environmental and urban movements met in the village of Nyéléni in Sélingué, Mali, to strengthen a global movement for food sovereignty. They identified six key pillars of food sovereignty, namely that it:

1   ***Focuses on food for people:*** *Food sovereignty puts the right to sufficient, healthy and culturally appropriate food for all individuals, peoples and communities, including those who are hungry, under occupation, in conflict zones and marginalized, at the centre of food, agriculture, livestock and fisheries policies; it rejects the proposition that food is just another commodity or component for international agribusiness.*

2   ***Values food providers:*** *Food sovereignty values and supports the contributions, and respects the rights, of women and men, peasants and small-scale family farmers, pastoralists, artisanal fisherfolk, forest dwellers, indigenous peoples, and agricultural and fisheries workers, including migrants, who cultivate, grow, harvest and process food; it rejects those policies, actions and programmes that undervalue them, threaten their livelihoods and eliminate them.*

3   ***Localizes food systems:*** *Food sovereignty brings food providers and consumers closer together; puts providers and consumers at the centre of decision making on food issues; protects food providers from the dumping of food and food aid in local markets; protects consumers from poor quality and unhealthy food, inappropriate food aid and food tainted with genetically modified organisms; and resists governance structures, agreements and practices that depend on and promote unsustainable and inequitable international trade and give power to remote and unaccountable corporations.*

4   ***Puts control locally:*** *Food sovereignty places control over territory, land, grazing, water, seeds, livestock and fish populations on local food providers and respects their rights. They can use and share these resources in socially and environmentally sustainable ways which conserve diversity. It recognizes that local territories often cross geopolitical borders and ensures the right of local communities to inhabit and use their territories; it promotes positive interaction between food providers in different regions and territories and from different sectors that helps resolve internal conflicts or conflicts with local and national authorities; and it rejects the privatization of natural resources through laws, commercial contracts and IPR regimes.*

5   ***Builds knowledge and skills:*** *Food sovereignty builds on the skills and local knowledge of food providers and their local organizations that conserve, develop and manage localized food production and harvesting systems, developing appropriate research systems to support this and passing on this wisdom to future generations; it rejects technologies that undermine, threaten or contaminate these, for example genetic engineering.*

RESPONSES

6   **Works with nature:** *Food sovereignty uses the contributions of nature in diverse, low external input agro-ecological production and harvesting methods that maximize the contribution of ecosystems and improve resilience and adaptation, especially in the face of climate change; it seeks to heal the planet so that the planet may heal us. It rejects methods that harm beneficial ecosystem functions and that depend on energy-intensive monocultures and livestock factories, destructive fishing practices and other industrialized production methods which damage the environment and contribute to global warming.*

These six pillars embrace most of the elements of food sovereignty and all six need to be incorporated into any sets of policies or practices that aim to realize food sovereignty.

Source: Taken from the synthesis report of the Nyéléni meeting. Full documents can be found on the forum website, www.nyeleni2007.org

genetics resources for food and agriculture accessible under the Treaty primarily to farmers, some are concerned about its practical implications (GRAIN, 2005b). The implementation of farmers' rights, for instance, is left to the discretion of national governments rather than enshrining them as universally applicable rights. Moreover, benefit sharing is only manda-tory in cases where the commercialization of the product restricts its availability for use in further research and breeding (for example through patenting).

For many national and regional civil society organizations, too numerous to mention here, the focus is on empowering farmers' and peasants' movements to enable them to resist

Box 8.3 SEARICE – Southeast Asia Regional Initiatives for Community Empowerment

SEARICE works primarily to strengthen farmers' seed systems and to advocate for farmers' rights to plant genetic resources as essential components of sustainable agricultural systems in Southeast Asia. SEARICE believes that farmers' rights emanate from basic human rights to life and to development and are essential to promoting the general welfare and interests of farmers.

It recognizes the need to build and support a farmer-led advocacy to enhance the capacity of farmers themselves to protect and promote their rights to plant genetic resources amid current threats and challenges. It aims to help facilitate farmers' access to, and to broaden and create political spaces for their engagement in, plant genetic resources conservation, development and use in various arenas at the local, national, regional and international levels. In the process, SEARICE intends to enable farmers to assert their rights in addressing issues of access to and control of plant genetic resources in light of political, economic and technological trends.

Its policy and information unit is involved in lobbying, advocacy and networking mainly oriented at policy impacts and actions around the issues of IPRs, new technologies (in seeds and agriculture) and farmers' rights in general. SEARICE implements community-based plant genetic resources conservation, development and use projects in Vietnam, Lao PDR, Thailand, Bhutan and the Philippines.

Source: Adapted from www.searice.org.ph

RESPONSES

corporate control. They often lack the resources to work internationally and may focus policy work in helping national policymakers understand the implications of global rules. One example of a regional group working at various levels is the Southeast Asia Regional Initiatives for Community Empowerment (SEARICE – Box 8.3).

Traditional and indigenous knowledge

The rights of indigenous peoples and the role of traditional and indigenous knowledge have been controversial and complex issues in most of the negotiating fora, as discussed in Chapter 7, and have not been addressed to indigenous people's satisfaction in the new agreements (Box 8.4). There is an enormous diversity of peoples and situations involved, and most groups lack resources. Moreover, there is often a lack of political will on the part of governments of states in which these groups live to recognize all their concerns and involve them in negotiations at national and international levels. Unsurprisingly, as the results of what has often been agreed with little or no involvement on their part become known, more and more groups want to be involved in shaping these decisions and in some cases in resisting proposed changes. Some international and national NGOs, as well as governments and international institutions, support work to inform and assist these groups to engage them with what is going on. Others, however, fear indigenous peoples being drawn into accommodating individual IP-based approaches to dealing with their concerns rather than building on communal- and customary-law-based approaches that do not rely on IP.

Patenting life

[T]he scientific community will need to rethink some long-held views about what genes are and what they do, as well as how the genome's functional elements have evolved. (Francis S. Collins, Director, National Human Genome Research Institute)[1]

Conflict over the patent system and its application to living organisms lies at the heart of many concerns about IP in agriculture, which deals with biological systems rather than the mechanical systems for which patents were designed. For many critics a system developed for inanimate objects should never have been extended to living organisms or their parts, especially as the functions of genes, for example, are far from understood, as more research is showing (Egziabher, 2002; Caruso, 2007). Such critics want to see new methods for balancing public and private interests dealing with innovation involving biological systems, rather than the extension of the patent system to them, and see this extensions as the core issue from which many of the problems arise. For others, the distinction is meaningless and anything people do in any sphere that involves invention and innovation should be patentable. Moreover, as the patent system has come to be increasingly about protecting investment rather than promoting innovation, they see this as a necessary thing if the private sector is to continue investing in these areas.

Balancing private and public interests

For many civil society organizations and academics, the balance between public and private interest has swung too far away from the public to the private in the current global regime. In the UK, following concerns raised by civil society organizations and feedback

RESPONSES

Box 8.4 Indigenous peoples want rights but question patents and an ABS regime

In May 2007, 44 indigenous people's groups meeting in New York issued the following declaration:

Declaration on Indigenous Peoples' Rights to Genetic Resources and Indigenous Knowledge

We, the undersigned indigenous peoples and organizations, having convened during the Sixth Session of the United Nations Permanent Forum on Indigenous Issues, from 14 to 25 May 2007, upon the traditional territory of the Onondaga Nation, present the following declaration regarding our rights to genetic resources and indigenous knowledge –

- *Reaffirming our spiritual and cultural relationship with all life forms existing in our traditional territories;*
- *Reaffirming our fundamental role and responsibility as the guardians of our territories, lands and natural resources;*
- *Recognizing that we are the guardians of the indigenous knowledge passed down from our ancestors from generation to generation and reaffirming our responsibility to protect and perpetuate this knowledge for the benefit of our peoples and our future generations;*
- *Strongly reaffirming our right to self-determination, which is fundamental to our ability to carry out our responsibilities in accordance with our cultural values and our customary laws;*
- *Strongly reaffirming our commitment to the United Nations Declaration on the Rights of Indigenous Peoples as adopted by the Human Rights Council, including Article 31, which establishes that:*
  1. *Indigenous peoples have the right to maintain, control, protect and develop their cultural heritage, TK and traditional cultural expressions, as well as the manifestations of their sciences, technologies and cultures, including human and genetic resources, seeds, medicines, knowledge of the properties of fauna and flora, oral traditions, literatures, designs, sports and traditional games and visual and performing arts. They also have the right to maintain, control, protect and develop their IP over such cultural heritage, TK and traditional cultural expressions;*
  2. *In conjunction with indigenous peoples, states shall take effective measures to recognize and protect the exercise of these rights;*
- *Recalling the Declaration of Indigenous Organizations of the Western Hemisphere of Phoenix, Arizona, in February 1995, which asserted, 'Our responsibility as indigenous peoples is to ensure the continuity of the natural order of all life is maintained for generations to come. ... We have a responsibility to speak for all life forms and to defend the integrity of the natural order. ... We oppose the patenting of all natural genetic materials. We hold that life cannot be bought, owned, sold, discovered or patented, even in its smallest form;*

- *Recalling the Beijing Declaration of Indigenous Women, issued at the United Nations Fourth World Conference on Women in Beijing, which stated that, 'We demand that our inalienable rights to our intellectual and cultural heritage be recognized and respected. We will continue to freely use our biodiversity for meeting our local needs, while ensuring that the biodiversity base of our local economies will not be eroded. We will revitalize and rejuvenate our biological and cultural heritage and continue to be the guardians and custodians of our knowledge and biodiversity';*
- *Recalling the Ukupseni Declaration at Kuna Yala, Panama, of 12–13 November 1997, which declared that, 'We reject the use of existing mechanisms in the legalization of intellectual property and patent systems use of existing mechanisms including intellectual property rights and patents to legalize the appropriation of knowledge and genetic material, whatever their source, and especially that which comes from our communities';*
- *Recalling the International Cancun Declaration of Indigenous Peoples at the 5th WTO Ministerial Conference in Cancun, Quintana Roo, Mexico on 12 September 2003, which stated, 'Stop patenting of life forms and other IPRs over biological resources and indigenous knowledge. Ensure that we, indigenous peoples, retain our rights to have control over our seeds, medicinal plants and indigenous knowledge';*
- *Concerned by the accelerated elaboration and negotiation of an international regime on ABS under the auspices of the Convention on Biological Diversity and the nation-states who are Parties to the Convention's failure, to date, to recognize the rights of indigenous peoples to control access to, and utilization of, the genetic resources that originate in our territories, lands and waters –*

Urge the United Nations Permanent Forum on Indigenous Issues to:

1. *Prepare a legal analysis on states, peoples and sovereignty and their relationship, scope and application, to assist the parties to the Convention on Biological Diversity in understanding sovereignty in the context of the Convention and the role of sovereignty in developing an international regime on ABS;*
2. *Recommend to the Convention on Biological Diversity that, consistent with international human rights law, states have an obligation to recognize and protect the rights of indigenous peoples to control access to the genetic resources that originate in their lands and waters and associated TK. Such recognition must be a key element of the proposed international regime on ABS.*
3. *Prepare a report on the social, cultural and economic impacts of commercialization of genetic resources and indigenous knowledge on indigenous peoples.*
4. *Disseminate this Declaration and the above recommended reports to all relevant UN fora.*

Note: See also United Nations Permanent Forum on Indigenous Issues (UNPFII) at www.un.org/esa/socdev/unpfii.

from developing countries about the impact of IP on development, in 2001 the government set up a Commission on Intellectual Property Rights, which reported in 2002 (IPRs Commission, 2002; see also Chapter 3). The six members of the Commission came from Argentina, India, the US and the UK. In a widely praised report it made a number of recommendations for agriculture and genetic resources, including that developing countries:

- do not allow patenting of plants and animals;
- develop different forms of *sui generis* PVP;
- Strengthen public research focused on poor farmers and ensure that public sector varieties are available to provide competition for private sector varieties; and
- rapidly ratify the ITPGRFA and implement its provisions on farmers' rights and not allowing IPRs on materials transferred under the multilateral system.

The strengthened patent regime is not going unchallenged even in the industrialized countries driving the process forward. As Keith Maskus noted in his study of the economics of IP in 2000:

> *There are legitimate reasons to be concerned about the highly protective standards that have emerged recently in the US and the EU. These laws and judicial interpretations provide broad patent protection for software and biotechnological inventions. They also promote extensive rights in the formulation of databases, which could have a negative effect on scientific research. It remains to be seen whether such standards tilt the balance within those jurisdictions towards the private rights of inventors and away from the needs of competitors and users. It is not too early to claim that they are inappropriate for developing economies and net technology importers.* (Maskus, 2000, pp 237–8)

Patenting practice in the US – and the pressures for others to adopt similar approaches – is a major concern. The granting of biotechnology patents on fragments of DNA, the loosening of the definition of 'utility', the way inventive step and novelty are applied in patent applications, and an apparent willingness to leave it to the courts to decide the validity of patents are bringing the system into disrepute. Some see a risk of the US system turning into a patent application registration system, as opposed to a patent granting one. US practice is fuelling concern and resentment globally about the acquisitive tactics of US firms. It also prompts industry elsewhere to drive European, Japanese and other industrialized countries to follow suit. Biotechnology is seen largely as an industrial competition issue, with the US, EU and Japan each determined to be a major player.

Maskus has also argued that the US has misguidedly strengthened the IP system for over 20 years to the detriment of the innovation it is supposed to deliver and is forcing inappropriate standards on developing countries through its bilateral trade agreements (Maskus, 2006). He argues this has resulted in:

- mushrooming litigation costs to defend against infringement lawsuits;
- patents that are overly broad or unclear about the breadth of protection; and
- a laissez-faire antitrust policy that allows firms to use patents to actively exclude potential competitors.

These recent trends have worked against the cross-fertilization of ideas and the ability to build on the work of predecessors – both essential elements in innovation.

Such concerns are not restricted to the US, however. Questions about the appropriateness of the system led the European Patent Office (EPO) to engage in a major exercise to examine possible future scenarios (Box 8.5). The aim was to examine possible uncertainties that might arise in a complex and turbulent environment. To their surprise:

> *What had started as a small institutional exercise rapidly grew into a larger more comprehensive overview of the whole IP system. It became clear that the system of IP required*

Box 8.5 Patent scenarios for 2025

The European Patent Office project ended up with four scenarios to help think about the future:

1 Market rules: A world where business is the dominant driver

This is a story of the consolidation of a system so successful that it is collapsing under its own weight. New forms of subject matter – inevitably including further types of services – become patentable and more players enter the system. The balance of power is held by multinational corporations with the resources to build powerful patent portfolios, enforce their rights in an increasingly litigious world and drive the patent agenda. A key goal is the growth of shareholder value. Patents are widely used as a financial tool to achieve that end. In the face of ever-increasing volumes of patent applications, various forms of rationalization of the system occur and it moves to mutual recognition of harmonized patent rights. The market decides the fate of the system, with minor regulation of visible excesses. Patent trolling, anti-competitive behaviour and standards issues all come under scrutiny.

2 Whose game? A world where geopolitics is the dominant driver

This is the story of a boomerang effect which strikes today's dominant players in the patent world as a result of changing geopolitical balances and competing ambitions. The developed world increasingly fails to use IP to maintain technological superiority; new entrants try to catch up so they can improve their citizens' living standards. But many developing world countries are excluded from the process and work instead within a 'communal knowledge' paradigm. Nations and cultures compete, with IP as a powerful weapon in this battle. The new entrants become increasingly successful at shaping the evolution of the system, using it to establish economic advantage, adapting the existing rules as their geopolitical influence grows. Enforcement becomes increasingly difficult and the IP world becomes more fragmented. Attempts are made to address the issues of development and technology transfer.

3 Trees of knowledge: A world where society is the dominant driver

In this story, diminishing societal trust and growing criticism of the IP system result in its gradual erosion. The key players are popular movements – often coalitions of civil society, businesses, concerned governments and individuals – seeking to challenge existing norms. This 'kaleidoscope society' is fragmented yet united – issue by issue, crisis by crisis – against real and perceived threats to human needs: access to health, knowledge, food and entertainment. Multiple voices and multiple world-views feed popular attention and interest, with the media playing an active role in encouraging debate. This loose 'knowledge movement' echoes the environmental movement of the 1980s, initially sparked by small, established special interest groups but slowly gaining momentum and raising wider awareness through alliances such as the A2K (Access to Knowledge) movement. The main issue is how to ensure that knowledge remains a common good, while acknowledging the legitimacy of reward for innovation.

RESPONSES

4 Blue skies: A world where technology is the dominant driver

The final story revolves around a split in the patent system. Societal reliance on technology and growing systemic risks force this change; the key players are technocrats and politicians responding to global crises. Complex new technologies based on a highly cumulative innovation process are seen as the key to solving systemic problems such as climate change, and diffusion of technology in these fields is of paramount importance. The IP needs of these new technologies come increasingly into conflict with the needs of classic, discrete technologies. In the end, the patent system responds to the speed, interdisciplinarity and complex nature of the new technologies by abandoning the one-size-fits-all model: the former patent regime still applies to classic technologies while new ones use other forms of IP protection, such as the licence of rights. The patent system increasingly relies on technology, and new forms of knowledge search and classification emerge.

The point of the scenarios is not to suggest that any one is specifically going to happen but that by looking at possible scenarios from different perspectives they 'aim to provide the right questions for input into the policymaking process'.

Source: EPO (2007)

comprehensive examination, at multiple levels, ranging from the global to the regional (European), national and institutional. (EPO, 2007)

For those looking at the future of food and farming this kind of exercise should give much food for thought.

For the larger players in industry, however, the IP regime has become central to their way of doing business. Both individually and through various lobby groups – some newly set up to defend their interests in the CBD and WTO against implementation of disclosure of origin and other requirements in patent applications – they are lobbying to maintain and strengthen the system and see it enforced globally. While firms are, in some cases, willing to make concessions for food crops with no significant commercial markets in poor countries, questioning the system itself and seeking new business models is not on the agenda.

At the EPO discussions of the scenarios, it seems the most strident proponents of the IP system were the lawyers – and the more IP there is, the more lawyers there are – and the industry associations. Internationally, industry lobbyists have focused on the negotiations where their interests might be most threatened, such as in the creation of the Biosafety Protocol to the CBD and subsequently over biosafety labelling, liability and redress elements, and more recently on the ABS regime and disclosure of origin issues at both the CBD and the WTO.

Some legal and academic experts are also keen to redress the imbalance between large countries and firms promoting and able to use IP, on the one hand, and small countries and small and medium-sized enterprises, public bodies and civil society organizations with very limited capacity to do so, on the other. This has led to various initiatives, including one to provide a global IP resource (Box 8.6).

Box 8.6 Public Interest Intellectual Property Advisors, Inc.: A US patent attorney's response

IP laws are neither inevitable nor immutable ... there must be a balance between the freedom of an IP owner to exclude others and the freedom of others to access the innovation. (Gollin, 2008)

Michael Gollin is a patent attorney and partner at Venable, a major US law firm. He has many years' experience with both the US system and developing countries. He sees IP as a driving force affecting innovation but he also sees a constant need to rebalance the system, and he is far from sure the current balance is right. His concern about the lack of capacity of developing countries and those promoting access to medicines and agricultural innovations led him to propose a new approach to make sure legal expertise was available to all.

For Gollin, one of the biggest problems is complexity itself. The topics of IP, food and biodiversity involve complicated legal, technical and economic issues. No one is expert in all three topics, though a few people may be in two. It therefore necessarily requires the combined expertise of several experienced people to analyse the problems and formulate and advance a policy or legal position at the international or national level. The same is true in forming a strategy and implementing it within an individual organization, whether non-profit or for-profit. Experienced people are easier to find in wealthier countries, and by people with money to pay them. Gollin believes that one way to help balance the problem of access to expertise is to mobilize volunteers who will help developing country organizations deal with IP issues at the international and national level and with individual organizations. That is the business model for Public Interest Intellectual Property Advisors, Inc. (PIIPA), which seeks to be a global non-profit resource for developing countries and public interest organizations needing expertise in IP matters to promote health, agriculture, biodiversity, science, culture and the environment. PIIPA provides worldwide access to IP professionals who can advise and represent such clients *pro bono publico* (as a public service). PIIPA volunteers have worked in many projects involving food and agriculture, including freedom to operate analysis for Public Intellectual Property Resource for Agriculture (PIPRA), defining trademark rights for local growers in developing countries, invalidating patents that were improperly awarded, negotiating ABS agreements and counselling Haiti, the Philippines, Vietnam and Sierra Leone on national IP legislation. PIIPA is working to build an international network of hubs that will bring together developing country organizations with IP professionals knowledgeable about both local and global issues to help shape innovation in a way that benefits developing countries.

Sources: Interview with Michael Gollin and www.piipa.org

Changing Face of R&D

Farmers using and sharing knowledge – and seeds – gained from experience and trial and error experimentation have been behind innovation and development in agriculture for millennia. That experience has been supplemented and expanded by an organized, state-supported, science-based research effort for about 150 years. Agricultural research has

Box 8.7 China's hybrid rice

In the 1970s, Professor Yuan Longping developed the first hybrid rice varieties, now widely grown in China and other countries. This work was funded by the government, which also promoted widespread use of the rice by farmers, with IP playing no part. Farmers have to get new seed to plant each year, and this has created a potentially huge hybrid rice seed market, since hybrid seed is planted on about half of China's rice growing area.

With decreasing agricultural land area in China, rapid urbanization and growing rural unrest, officials expect a need for greater use of science and technology to increase production from the remaining land. Now that China is a member of the WTO and subject to its minimum IP standards, however, there is concern about the impact of IPRs on future patterns of agricultural development and the rural population. There are therefore ongoing discussions in China about the future of agricultural R&D and whether to give more public good R&D or private IPRs-based incentives. The results of these discussions will be very important to small farmers. There is also growing concern about the impact on farmers that an opening up to private seed businesses under the new IP regime might have.

Sources: Personal communications; Longping (2004); www.worldfoodprize.org/laureates/Past/2004.htm; www.chinaculture.org/gb/en_aboutchina/2003-09/24/content_26399.htm; www.grain.org/research/hybridrice.cfm?lid=159

been carried out by public bodies – and freely spread to farmers – largely for the public good, since those needing its results are too small to do scientific research themselves, and the benefits flowing from improved agriculture go to society as a whole through improved food security. It was this approach that lay behind the 'green revolution', which was largely made possible through public research efforts to improve varieties in wheat and rice and agricultural techniques, as was the introduction of hybrid rice in China (Box 8.7).

In recent decades, there has been a change in the nature of research (RAFI, 2000; Pardey and Beintema, 2001). The private sector has played a growing role in R&D in the industrialized countries, with their small farming populations and wholly commercial farming systems, but focuses on areas where it can ensure returns on its investment. The public sector has traditionally focused more on farm-level technologies to increase agricultural productivity, often made freely available; more recently it has also increasingly focused on post-harvest and food safety. There has also

been a move away from public funding for applied agricultural research of direct use to farmers in some industrialized countries, notably the US, the UK and The Netherlands, with that being left to the private sector, and a greater focus on basic research. In the US, the focus of private agricultural R&D has changed from agricultural machinery and post-harvest food-processing research (about 80 per cent of the total in 1960) towards plant breeding and veterinary and pharmaceutical research. Some 70 per cent of the chemical research related to agriculture is done in just three countries – the US, Japan and Germany. Private research priorities are also being driven by the need to compete in the oversaturated food markets in industrial countries, for instance by expanding production of 'functional' foods with health-promoting and/or disease-preventing properties.

Several factors lie behind these changes, including a major scientific revolution in biology and legal changes, initially in the US, permitting the patenting of living organisms (see Chapter 1). These attracted new firms,

RESPONSES

many formerly in agrochemicals, into plant breeding R&D, as they saw opportunities to enter and dominate markets. Technological innovation has long been a way of entering an industry, and genetic engineering in particular has allowed new firms to enter the seed industry and promote innovations in agricultural production. Patent-protected innovation has been used as a means of gaining legal quasi-monopolistic control of certain products and sectors since the 19th century: even at that time, by institutionalizing innovation in R&D labs, 'large corporations sought to control technological change as a means of protecting and fortifying their positions in the industry' (Jenkins, 1975).

Concerns over IP and R&D

Ironically, one of the problems to arise has come from the public sector in the US, as Gary Toenniessen and Deborah Delmer (2005) from the Rockefeller Foundation argue:

... a major IPR change that is threatening the operations of the international agricultural research system comes from public, not private sector, research institutions. To promote technology transfer and product development in the US, the 1980 Bayh-Dole Act gave universities and other public-funded research institutions the right to obtain patents on and commercialize inventions made under government research grants. Similar arrangements have emerged in most other industrialized countries. The result is that while many biotechnology discoveries (for example knowledge of gene function and gene regulation) and enabling technologies (for example agrobacterium and biolistic transformation methods) are generated with public funding in research institutions and agricultural universities, these discoveries are no longer being treated as 'public goods'. Rather, they are being patented

and licensed, often exclusively, to the for-profit sector (Graff et al, 2003). Such discoveries now primarily flow from the public sector to the for-profit sector. If they flow back out, it is usually under material transfer agreements (MTAs) that significantly restrict their use (usually for research purposes only), limit further sharing and often include reach-through provisions to capture results of future research.

Since crop genetic improvement is a derivative process, each incremental improvement made through biotechnology now comes with a number of IP constraints, with new IP added with each transfer or further improvement (Barton and Berger, 2001). IP is used to protect biotechnology tools and reagents; genes and gene sequences; regulatory sequences; processes of transformation, regeneration and diagnosis; and the resulting modified plants. It is in part to deal with this thicket of patents, and to gain 'freedom to operate' (FTO), that the private sector is becoming greatly centralized through a large number of mergers, acquisitions and cross-licensing agreements.

Many civil society groups, researchers and foundations are concerned that the extension and strengthening of IPRs could inhibit the use of R&D processes and products, including biotechnological, which would benefit people in developing countries. Another concern is that the current focus on biotechnology, which is partly driven by IP, is skewing the overall research effort away from other approaches to improve farming, especially for poor and marginalized farmers, such as better water management, more appropriate equipment and integrated pest management techniques.

The need for agriculture R&D to benefit the poor and marginalized has not gone away. Research by the International Food Policy Research Institute (IFPRI) and Indian and Chinese researchers has highlighted the importance of public investment in rural areas,

RESPONSES

especially low-potential lands in Asia, and the fact that R&D is one of the three key areas for investment, along with education and roads. While the better-favoured areas need existing levels of investment, additional investment is needed in the less-developed areas. In many poorer countries, especially in Africa, there has not been sufficient investment in the high-potential lands either. Moreover, the researchers argue:

> *These investments will provide a long-term solution to the problem of food security and poverty. ... Contrary to conventional wisdom, investments in low-potential lands generally produced higher returns for agricultural productivity growth than those in high-potential lands.* (IFPRI, 2002)

Most developments in agriculture have happened in a very different environment from today's IP-dominated and increasingly private-sector-led world. As Joseph Stiglitz pointed out when he was chief economist at the World Bank, when there is a shift in R&D to the private sector, 'relying on the private sector for agricultural research is likely to result in under investment from the point of view of society'. Basically, it will not work on things for poor farmers, who have no money, nor on things that can be freely copied and given away. Moreover, this applied research in industry relies on continued publicly funded basic research and has greatly benefited from past university and other public-sector research (Pinstrup-Andersen, 2000). In other words the public has subsidized, and continues to subsidize, private R&D. Moreover, private companies are not likely to work on those technologies, crops and traits that are of limited commercial value, but which are important to protect food security and livelihoods in developing countries. Commercialized biotech crops, for instance, have been targeted primarily at developed country producers, focusing on a limited

number of commodities (soya beans, maize and cotton) and traits (insect resistance and herbicide tolerance) with a sufficiently large market to ensure financial returns on investments.

For those wanting to use the science in other ways, their concern is their freedom to do so.

Freedom to operate

> *Private research will not and cannot assume the burden of ensuring the food supply of the world's poor. Even in the developed countries, the now-dominant private-sector research efforts are concentrated on a small number of traits in crops with high commercial value. ... [I]n agricultural biotechnology, the very IPRs associated with the surge of private biotechnology research now threaten to block public and non-profit researchers. ... Plant breeders in developed countries increasingly find their access to essential innovative inputs uncertain, unduly expensive or, in some reported cases, blocked altogether. ... Unlicensed production in the South of a crop only protected in the North is both legal and moral per se.* (Binenbaum et al, 2003)

> *For the future, how the World Trade Organization's TRIPS Agreement is implemented with respect to plant-breeding technology, domestically and in important export markets, is a crucial issue for developing-country policymakers. Where patenting of plant and other life forms is allowed, the patenting of key biotechnologies in the South will grow, threatening developing-country researchers' freedom to operate and freedom to trade in developing-country agricultural products, both South–North and South–South. This issue ranks with implementation of farmers' rights as an important policy concern for plant breeders, farmers, and*

the food consumers of the South. But domestic *freedom to operate is generally the relevant IPR issue; exports of food staples that dominate agriculture are not important growth drivers in most developing countries.* (Pardey et al, 2003)

Apart from the effects of publicly funded researchers patenting and licensing technologies, agricultural research companies are increasingly patenting basic research tools and processes, thereby limiting their use for other researchers (Jaszi, 2004). Furthermore, companies have employed so-called patent clustering (obtaining several interlocking patents on different components of a product) and bracketing (patenting information around a competitor's patent so that the competitor's patent cannot be commercialized without cross-licensing) (Dutfield, 2003a). These trends are feared to further limit public researchers' freedom to operate (in other words their ability to research, commercially produce, market and use their new product, process or service without infringing the IPRs of others). While this is probably true in the OECD countries, however, most international institutes and developing countries have more legal freedom than they think, although they may still lack know-how and/or resources.

Countries do have flexibility in how they interpret and use the existing agreements. Under TRIPS, for example, countries can exclude plants and animals from patentability and define the meaning of terms such as novelty, inventive step and utility. Indeed, some things that may be patented in the US may not in the EU. Patents are national and only valid in countries where they have been applied for. Many things subject to patent in richer countries are simply not patented in poorer countries and may be freely used there. Researchers, however, should be aware that contractual arrangements can impose more rigorous IP requirements on them than

required by their national laws or licensing terms that restrict commercial use of what is developed from their research. Given the different standards of examination and approaches to patenting requirements, it may also be the case that many patents would be found invalid if challenged, as has happened on various occasions.

So countries and research institutions are free to use technologies and processes that may be patented in other jurisdictions but which are not patentable in theirs. They may also see them used in the field in producing crops. A problem may arise, however, when those crops, or products derived from them, are exported to places where the technology used in their production is patented and is detectable in the product. Then the patent owner can seek to block their import – as has happened over the export of GM soya from Argentina, where it is not patented, to Europe, where it is (Box 8.8). This would not apply, of course, to staple food crops that are not traded widely or to trade between developing countries with similar, minimal IP regimes. The three crops most likely to be involved are soya beans, bananas and rice. However, soya is not a staple food crop and the type of bananas that are staple food crops are generally not exported, but there have been problems with the Enola bean (Chapter 6, Box 6.7).

Increasingly complex IP protection has also led to high transaction costs in assessing researchers' freedom to operate, negotiating access to technologies and licence fees. This can be particularly problematic in the case of agricultural biotechnology, which relies on multiple and often interdependent technology components and processes that may be owned by several institutions. An assessment of the patents involved in producing 'Golden Rice' – a rice variety genetically modified to contain higher levels of beta-carotene – for example, found some 30 patents and 40 technical property rights in the form of material transfer agreements. This required extensive negotia-

RESPONSES

Box 8.8 *Monsanto v. Argentina* over soyameal imports into the EU

Carlos Correa[a]

One illustrative case of how patenting in different jurisdictions may be used is provided by the detainment (on the basis of an expansive interpretation of European Regulation 1383/2003) of shipments of soyameal exported from Argentina by customs authorities of The Netherlands, Denmark, the UK and Spain, and the litigation in course in those countries against soyameal importers.

Soya beans account for around 50 per cent of the total seeded area of oily cereals in Argentina, and is one of its main export items (over US$2 billion annually). Most soyameal is exported to Europe, which obtains around 50 per cent of its soyameal consumption (mainly for animal feed) from Argentina.

Monsanto did not obtain a patent on its herbicide resistant Roundup Ready (RR) technology in Argentina, as it filed the respective application after the expiry of the applicable legal terms. The RR gene in soya beans was first commercialized in 1996 and, thanks to the lack of patent protection, rapidly disseminated in the country. An estimated 95 per cent of soya beans produced in Argentina are derived from varieties incorporating the RR gene. Almost 200 varieties containing it have been developed since 1996 (only a fraction by Monsanto itself); these varieties were subject to plant variety protection in Argentina, without Monsanto's opposition.

The introduction of transgenic soya beans in Argentina without patent protection permitted Monsanto to rapidly disseminate them not only throughout Argentina but also to Brazil and other South American countries. Sales of RR seed also boosted sales of Monsanto's glyphosate herbicide Roundup.

In choosing to transfer its technology to Argentine seed producers, Monsanto voluntarily stimulated the production of transgenic soya beans there. Although Monsanto obtained royalties for the RR technology under private contracts with seed companies, it aimed at getting an additional payment from Argentine farmers, who refused to pay an additional charge for a technology that was in the public domain. Monsanto then targeted the importation of Argentine soyameal into Europe, on the basis of two patents (EP0218571 and EP546090) that protect the gene and gene constructs as such as well the transformed cells in a soya bean plant. Thus Monsanto attempted to use patents covering herbicide-resistant genes to prevent trade in industrially processed products where such genes cannot perform their function.

On 9 August 2006, the Directorate-General Internal Market and Services of the European Commission provided an interpretation of Article 9 of the Directive on Biotechnological Inventions (98/44/EC).[b] It confirmed that derivative products, such as soyameal, are not covered by patent claims relating to genetic information which do not perform their function in such products. Although it may be reasonably predicted that this paradigmatic case of 'strategic litigation' will end up with Monsanto's legal defeat, the resources invested by the Argentine government (which requested the status of affected third party in legal proceedings) and importers are very substantial.

This case illustrates a significant attempt to expand the legal powers conferred by patents covering genes. If these attempts were successful, they could have a major adverse effect on the transfer to developing countries of materials with genes patent-protected in developed countries. Any derivative products (for example shirts made out of Bt cotton) would be potentially targeted by patent holders and imports encumbered or prevented in the developed countries where the genes are patented.

Notes: [a] Director of the Center for Interdisciplinary Studies on Industrial Property Law and Economics (CEIDIE) and of the Post-graduate Course on IP of the University of Buenos Aires. [b] In accordance with Article 9 of the Directive, the protection given by patents on a product containing or consisting of genetic information extends 'to all material, save as provided in Article 5(1), in which the product is incorporated and in which the genetic information is contained *and performs its function*' (emphasis added).

tions between the developer of the variety – researchers from the Swiss Federal Institute of Technology in Zurich and the University of Freiburg – and the patent holders, including Syngenta and Monsanto, who in the end agreed to make the technologies freely available for humanitarian use (Kryder et al, 2000). Many of these technologies, however, were not in fact patented in developing countries (Binenbaum et al, 2003). Anecdotal evidence also suggests subsidiaries in developing countries will not copy the inventions of the parent firms (and perhaps other firms too), even when they are not subject to patent in the developing country concerned (Dutfield, personal communication).

The TRIPS Agreement allows for limited exceptions for the use of patent-protected technologies and products without the authorization of the rights holder in some circumstances, for example in cases of national emergency or for non-commercial purposes (Articles 30 and 31). Such provisions have not yet been used for agricultural research, although compulsory licensing is now being used in some countries to ensure access to medicines.

Unlike a patented plant, a plant variety protected by plant breeders' rights under UPOV is not excluded from being used by others for further research and breeding. Plant breeders' rights may also be restricted for reasons of 'public interest', provided that 'all necessary measures' are taken to ensure

equitable remuneration. However, the 1991 revision of the Convention has been criticized for limiting research rights by extending PVPs to include essentially derived varieties, in other words varieties that retain the essential characteristics of the parent varieties (GRAIN, 1998). As a result, some varieties that were previously considered new would now be treated as essentially derived and could not be exploited commercially without consent, although this change was aimed at preventing firms genetically engineering an existing variety to introduce a particular trait, such as herbicide resistance, and then gaining control of the variety through patents without the original breeder gaining any reward.

Broken bargains, sharing knowledge

The expansion of IPRs in plant breeding has fuelled a strong sense in developing countries and in some of those in the Consultative Group on International Agricultural Research (CGIAR) system that an implicit bargain has been broken – with germplasm used in breeding programmes largely provided by the South for free – being still in the public domain – but science becoming increasingly proprietary (Serageldin, 2000). It is a feeling echoed in many civil society critiques of changes taking place.

RESPONSES

Access to genetic resources

> *The maintenance of present-day yield levels for major food crops will depend on combining many genetic traits, found in materials of a wide variety of origins, that must be placed into a wide range of varieties and used in many different locations. Future food security depends on it and international public goods deliver it.* (Petit et al, 2001)

The bilateralist approach in the CBD and the sense of unfulfilled promises the developing countries have about commitments made both in the CBD and TRIPS to transfer technology to them are fuelling development of national access laws that could seriously hinder the collection and dissemination of both the materials from germplasm collections and the materials being developed by the CGIAR Centres. The new International Treaty and its rules on the use of plant genetic resources for food and agriculture may help alleviate these problems. For the considerable number of food crops not included in the Treaty's multilateral system, there may be much greater transaction costs in using germplasm, which could adversely affect their development (Stannard, 2000). A study commissioned for the Global Forum on Agricultural Research (GFAR) in 2000 concluded that a 'scenario in which all germplasm exchange falls under bilateral agreements entails excessively high transaction costs' and felt that only for very few crops, such as industrial crops, might a bilateral approach to germplasm exchange have acceptable transaction costs (Visser et al, 2000).

The extension of IPRs in agriculture – both PVP and patents – is already having some effects on the exchange and use of plant genetic resources. In the US, public sector breeding programmes have found it harder to get materials from companies, which has interfered with their ability to release new lines and train students (Riley, 2000). Tim Reeves, former director of the International Wheat and Maize research Institute (CIMMYT) in Mexico, also said that the expansion of plant breeders' rights led to some collaborators no longer sending their best lines for use in the breeding programmes (Personal communication, at the GFAR-2000 Conference). Since the breeding programmes work by many partners exchanging material, everyone normally gets much more out of them than they put in, but if the quality of what is put in goes down, everyone will suffer.

Technology transfer and dissemination

One of the objectives of the TRIPS Agreement, also included in the CDB and ITPGRFA, is the promotion of the transfer and dissemination of technology to developing countries, and many feel more should be done about this. Various researchers and foundations have been attempting to do so in effect by trying to reinvent the open exchange system for agricultural research or provide developing countries' researchers with resources to overcome the problems created by a more privatized, IP-dominated research environment.

Reinventing open source agricultural R&D

Farming has been built on open exchanges and the copying of techniques that worked between farmers over millennia. Research too used to be much more open, with sharing of techniques, processes and knowledge. There is a certain irony, then, that now some in the research community have responded to the impact of the current trends by following in the footsteps of the 'open source' movement launched in the mid-1980 in software development. This made software freely available for use and adaptation, did not restrict any party from selling or giving

RESPONSES

Box 8.9 The BiOS Initiative

The BiOS (Biological Open Source) Initiative aims to build a 'protected commons' of biological IP. To this end, the Initiative makes patented and non-patented technologies freely available under the terms of the BiOS licence, which stipulates that licensees must agree not to prevent other licensees from using the technology or improvements made to it. While the licences are free, for-profit licensees are asked to contribute to the cost of the supporting information technology.

BiOS is one of four tools CAMBIA (which means 'change' in Spanish and Italian) has been creating. These tools are aimed at fostering innovation and a spirit of collaboration in the life sciences and enabling people in disadvantaged communities and developing countries to choose their own methods to help themselves meet their own challenges in food security, health, and natural resource management. The other three are:

1 Patent Lens, which provides tools to make the world of patents and patent landscapes more transparent and to help focus paths leading to freedom to (co)operate;
2 BioForge, a prototype portal to a dynamic protected commons of enabling technologies, available to everyone who agrees to keep them available for sharing for improvement and use in innovations; and
3 CAMBIA's Materials, molecular enabling technologies designed, developed and delivered by CAMBIA with a focus on their use by disadvantaged communities in, for example, international agriculture and public health.

Source: Jefferson (2007)

away the software and required that the source codes were provided. An open source approach in agriculture is found in the Biological Open Source (BiOS) Initiative, set up by the Australia-based independent non-profit research institute CAMBIA (Box 8.9 and Jefferson, 2007). Others are also exploring 'open source biotechnology', which extends the principles of commerce-friendly, commons-based peer production exemplified by open source software development to the development of research tools in biomedical and agricultural biotechnology (Hope, 2008).

The Rockefeller Foundation has supported various groups trying to combat the trend to restrict access to technology by use of IP, including the Public Intellectual Property Resource for Agriculture (PIPRA) and the African Agricultural Technology Foundation (AATF). PIPRA began as a consortium of primarily US agricultural universities and plant research institutes, hosted by the University of California Davis, committed to strategically managing IP on behalf of its members, to enable the broadest commercial and humanitarian applications of existing and emerging agricultural technologies. In mid-2007, it had 45 members in 13 countries. The universities and institutes associated with PIPRA have generated much of the IP in crop biotechnology, but they have also entered into exclusive licensing agreements for this IP with the private sector. These agreements often eliminate their ability to share their technologies with each other or with other public-sector institutions such as national and international research centres that are working on new crop varieties for poor farmers in developing countries. The AATF, for example, is an Africa-based and -led organization, with an office in Nairobi, Kenya, that aims

RESPONSES

to promote public–private partnerships to use, usually under royalty-free licences, new technologies otherwise protected by IP for agricultural development in Africa (Toenniessen and Delmer, 2005).

Rethinking R&D and IP

For some civil society organizations these partnerships and licences are simply creating the way for large biotech-based transnational corporations to come in and take over any profitable areas of farming and introduced biotechnology and make farmers dependent. They and others want more radical rethinking and reorientation of R&D and the IP system that has been introduced into agriculture. A wider public movement among civil society groups promoting access to knowledge (A2K) has grown up and has been supported by librarians, who are concerned about the impact of changing copyright rules for people in developing countries. Here the concern is that developing country researchers will simply find it too difficult or expensive to access scientific and technical information being held in databases and journals. One response by some scientists to this has been the Public Library of Science – a non-profit organization of scientists and physicians committed to making the world's scientific and medical literature a freely available public resource. Others, such as Jamie Love of KEI/CPTech, are promoting a R&D treaty to make sure scientific knowledge and tools for medicine are available globally – something equally applicable to food and agriculture.

Some groups have been calling for the terms and conditions of patentability to be amended so as to facilitate agricultural research for development, such as limiting the patent period on research processes to five to six years or introducing a flat fee for use of patented processes (Tansey, 2002). Jerry Reichmann has developed this last idea for plant breeding,

which usually involves relatively small-scale innovation and has to draw on the public domain for much of what lies behind each innovation. He calls for the creation of a compensatory liability regime. This would take away the monopoly from the privilege a patent holder has by denying the first inventor the right to exclude people from using the invention. Instead, it would involve an automatic licence for use of the protected item by someone else. If it was used within the first few years, there would be a set compensation fee payable, but this would be waived if the follow-on developer waited a set time. By that time, the knowledge would be considered freely available in the public domain as by then the inventor should have recouped any R&D cost either through his exclusive use of the innovation or from payments from others using it through the set fee arrangements (Reichmann, 2000).

Another approach to R&D

Ecosystem approaches applied to food and agriculture tend to place humans more explicitly at the centre of the management strategy and give greater emphasis to goals related directly to human wellbeing, and on the social and economic advantages that result from their application. (FAO, 2007)

For many NGOs and civil society groups, such as those in the food sovereignty movement, the above approaches are fundamentally flawed. These groups see farmers themselves as innovators and the challenge being to support *them*. This is something the market-based approaches will not do as the poor and marginal have no income to spend. Moreover, following the patterns of innovation in the industrialized countries will rapidly push small farmers out of farming, whether they like it or not. Thus the nature of publicly funded R&D, especially in developing countries, and its linkages to local

Box 8.10 Ethiopia's farmers and scientists pioneering *in-situ* conservation and use

Today, in some of Ethiopia's diverse rain-fed environments, a partnership has developed between farmers and researchers from the national gene bank, a local NGO, Ethio-Organic Seed Action, and a Candian NGO, USC-Canada, in its Seeds of Survival (SoS) programme. Since the 1980s, as a result of both loss of sorghum seed in the drier lowlands during the famine, when people had to eat them to survive, and locally bred and adapted varieties of durum wheat being replaced in the wetter highlands by uniform 'high-yielding' (high input) bread wheats, many farmers' varieties (sometimes called landraces) have been lost.

The then head and founder of the national gene bank, Dr Melaku Worede, recognized that farmers knew more about the range and characteristics of varieties than he did. Farmers also had bred varieties well adapted to local environments using multiple selection criteria. These could stand the stresses from climate fluctuations and pests better than the more uniform modern varieties that were replacing them and which, with their increasingly expensive inputs, led farmers into debt and did not perform as well when conditions were poor.

When Dr Melaku met farmers who had been unhappy with the newly introduced bread wheat and wanted to reintroduce the heterogeneous farmers' varieties of durum wheats, he made some improvements to the farmers' varieties so that they yielded better but with little loss of biodiversity. This work, developed through a local farmers' association, now involves the establishment of community seed banks, seed multiplication and farmers' trials comparing compost-fed plots of the same farmers' variety with fertilizer-fed ones. Early results are showing greater yields at lower costs for the compost-fed wheats. The SoS programme has spread not just around the country but around the world. It links the breeding skills and capacity of farmers with researchers who can join with them to develop better products suited to local environments.

Ethiopia has a better chance than most countries to safeguard and develop its agriculture biodiversity because, according to Dr Tewolde Berhan Gebre Egziabher, director of Ethiopia's Environmental Protection Authority, 'the seed supply from research that tends to erode genetic diversity very fast is still very small so genetic diversity is fairly intact'. He feels that what makes Ethiopia so important today for genetic diversity is that, unlike in many other places, 'farmers themselves still continue generating and regenerating their seed'.

Sources: Research by Geoff Tansey during a visit to Ethiopia, November 2006; see also www.africanfarmdiversity.net/Case_Study_EOSA.html and www.usc-canada.org/?page_id=21

private or community-based innovation will greatly affect the options farmers have. Alternative products and practices geared to the real needs of small farmers, especially in marginal areas, could provide competitive, freely available and socially desirable products and practices that would enable them to increase their agricultural production in a sustainable manner, avoid debt traps and produce a surplus that could be used to generate income (Box 8.10).

Some emphasize the need for participatory processes with small farmers and an agro-ecological approach to agricultural development in keeping with rural development needs. In this approach, biodiversity is viewed broadly, the importance of *in-situ* conservation and use stressed, and natural resource management

RESPONSES

strategies used to develop technologies with resource-poor farmers that support the agro-ecological conditions (Altieri and von der Weid, 2000). Genetically re-engineering plants is seen as a biologically dangerous and socially simplistic way of dealing with the 'complex realities facing small farmers' who have few resources other than knowledge of how to farm in difficult conditions. That knowledge needs to be nurtured and supported, rather than replaced. Many civil society groups would agree that the problems facing small farmers, especially in marginal areas, are not going to be solved first and foremost with technology. Where technology can contribute, alongside investments in infrastructure, healthcare, education and so forth, it may not be that the technology of most immediate importance is that of improved varieties.

This view also questions the ability of the existing international and national research systems to deliver on this approach. It sees seeds as an integral part of farmers' strategies for managing the land and risks, with farmers in the Andes, for example, using hedgerows as decentralized and farmer-managed *in-situ* gene banks. Agricultural biodiversity is not just about the genetic resources but about the economic and social systems that are essential to its creation, maintenance and further development. One response to this vision in Peru seeks a non-IPR-based way of safeguarding food security by creating a space for local communities to manage and develop their genetic resources – potatoes – within the framework of traditional and indigenous knowledge and practices.

Conclusion

The controversies and conflicts arising from the expansion of global rules on IP and their interactions with biodiversity, food security and rural people's livelihoods are not going to go away. Indeed, they look likely to become more intense in the face of growing uncertainty in the light of climate change and the various measures being promoted to combat it, includ-

ing a rapid expansion of biofuels for vehicles (most people, of course, have relied on biomass as biofuel for centuries – wood, dung and crop residues). What observations may be made from negotiations about IP and from developments in the creation of these regimes to date? That is the question for the next chapter.

9

Postcards from International Negotiations

Peter Drahos and Geoff Tansey

This chapter includes reflection on experiences with international negotiations about issues that arise from biodiversity, food security and intellectual property (IP). It discusses the types of leverage available to countries in negotiations as well as turning negotiating gains into real gains and more evidence-based approaches. The experiences are crystallized as observational postcards, rather than lessons.

Introduction

The negotiations that have led to the current set of treaties, conventions and international institutions dealing with IP, biodiversity and food have a long, interacting history, as discussed in Part II of this book. To individuals involved, negotiations in different fora may appear to be unconnected and episodic activities. Yet as earlier chapter authors have discussed, positions taken by some states, such as developing countries promoting a new international economic order from the 1960s to the early 1980s, led to reactions by others, as in the promotion of IP rules into the trade regime. Competition between industrialized countries underlay pressure for expansion of IP rights (IPRs) into agriculture, with Europe creating plant breeders' rights and UPOV in response to developments in the US. IPRs were becoming an important element in the industrial model of agricultural production

developed in those countries and being exported globally.

Competition between the major OECD trading powers also promoted strengthening of IPRs globally as some industries based in those countries saw the need for global IP rules for their business models to survive in the face of technological innovation and intensified competition. States themselves saw IPRs as a tool to help them gain a greater share of the benefits that flowed from the domination and control of new technologies. Supporting monopolies through the passage of national IP laws became, somewhat paradoxically, a key element in promoting national competitiveness in a globalizing economy. The nature and type of global IP rules we have today emerge not only from concerns about our food and environment but also from the competing interests of states to maintain their economic power and regulate business activity in their interests.

A key concern behind the Quaker programme of work is for fairer processes that reflect the needs of people and the environment. Much could be said about what constitutes fairness, but at the most basic level it involves states, which are committed to representing the needs of their citizens, participating in an informed way in negotiations affecting IP, food and biodiversity. International negotiations should be, as a minimum, procedurally fair, and, in the case of negotiations concerning food and biodiversity, serve the basic needs of citizens everywhere. It was this ideal that lay behind the Quaker work that first focused on supporting sub-Saharan African countries' participation in the negotiations on the International Treaty on Plant Genetic Resources on Food and Agriculture (ITPGRFA – the Treaty) and then subsequently moved to supporting informed participation in the review of Article 27.3(b) of the TRIPS Agreement, begun in 1999, and its impact on food and biodiversity (Tansey, 1999 and Tansey, no date).

One fact, illustrated by some of the chapters in this book, is that many more actors now participate in international negotiations. Many more states, for example, participate in WTO negotiations than did in the GATT rounds of earlier decades. Robert Wolfe (2007) lists more than 30 negotiating clubs that are active in WTO negotiations of one kind or another. More developing countries participate and there are more developing country coalitions than ever before, reflecting their diversity and different interests. Gone are the days when developing countries had few and probably unwieldy coalitions (for example the G-77). Developing countries have shown that they can organize coalitions quickly and effectively, the G20 and its role in the WTO's Cancun Ministerial Meeting being one example. In Chapter 5, Bragdon, Garforth and Haapala draw attention to a number of developing country coalitions in the context of the CBD,

including the formation in 2002 of the Like-Minded Group of Mega-Diverse Countries, a coalition that aims to create more enforceable obligations for users of genetic resources. More striking than the increased participation of developing countries, however, is the involvement and influence of civil society actors in international negotiations (see Chapter 8 in particular). Naturally, civil society groups do not sign treaties as legal agents, but they do influence outcomes. One example of that influence is farmers' rights (see Chapter 6) and another is the de facto moratorium on genetic use restriction technologies (GURTs) mentioned in Chapter 5. As the authors of the latter chapter note, the struggle over the future of that moratorium is a struggle between civil society and pro-GURT countries such as Australia, Canada, New Zealand and the US.

Internationally influential social movements have existed in the past (for the anti-slavery movement, the temperance movement and the women's movement), but information technology in particular has driven down the costs of organizing internationally and there is, in effect, a global pool of capital available from developed country governments, philanthropic organizations and society in general to meet the costs of organizing. The scale of civil society networks is thus unprecedented in historical terms.

One very important consequence of this network scale is that civil society has acquired a global scanning and detection capability. Put simply, lots of people and networks gather and release information about what governments and business are doing when it comes to the regulation of food, biodiversity and IP. Multinational companies have long had this kind of capability; at a collective level civil society now also has it. Business organizations and companies have, of course, always participated in negotiations around food, biodiversity and IPRs (see Graham Dutfield's observations in Chapter 2 about the role of the seed industry in UPOV). They continue to do so and to form new organizations for that purpose, the forma-

Box 9.1 Postcards from an insider: Things are different now – A personal view of WIPO negotiations

Ron Marchant, CB*

A few years ago discussions at WIPO were conducted in the context of the impact of treaty provisions on rights holders, albeit with an eye to balance and impact on third parties. Business-interest NGOs, representing rights holders in the main, made contributions at those meetings, though rights holders' most effective contributions came from work at a national level prior to meetings and with their inclusion as part of national delegations in some instances. That contribution undoubtedly was beneficial to discussions.

Three things have changed the context of discussions. First, the increased importance of businesses built on knowledge and hence a greater role for IP. Second, and in part a consequence of the first, the growth of globalization as the context for today's businesses. And third, the nature of innovation itself, with increasing activity within information technology and biotechnology (including crops, foods and pharmaceuticals).

The impact of this has been greater activity within developing countries and a wider range of NGOs with something to contribute. The UK Commission on Intellectual Property Rights set the scene and a number of developing countries came together as the Friends of Development, with a series of demands in WIPO. While the initial discussion seemed negative, this has changed over the last couple of years and there is now common agreement on a set of proposals which will give greater force to development-related work at WIPO. This is to be welcomed and hopefully will be translated into action.

What lessons do I take from this?

- Member states will have to engage with a wider range of NGOs than in the past and this will alter the consultation process.
- Discussion cannot be restricted to WIPO. There is a need for discussion at the international level in a wider political environment.
- The IP system is not by itself able to improve the position of developing countries. IP gives power in the market place and the prime need is to enable innovation, which can then be fostered by improved IP systems.

Note: * Former CEO of the UK Intellectual Property Office (2003–2007) and Director of Patents (1992–2003).

tion of the American Bioindustry Alliance by Jacques Gorlin, a key player in TRIPS, being an example (see Chapter 5).

Summing up, we can say that in the last decade or so we have moved into a period of history where there are more international fora than ever before to negotiate food, biodiversity and IPRs (TRIPS and the CBD, for example, only came into operation in the early 1990s) and there are more actors, coalitions and networks participating and exercising some kind of influence in those negotiations than ever before. What have we learned from this short period of history? Box 9.1 is one personal synthesis of key lessons. We are tempted to say that it has become overwhelmingly complex and leave it at that; however, avoiding the temptation to duck the question, we consider in the next section

OBSERVATIONS

some of the lessons that have been learned from the increased participation of non-state actors in the negotiations over IP, biodiversity and food. Lessons is probably too strong a term since it implies some kind of systematic instruction in negotiation that we cannot offer. Instead, we make observations that suggest themselves from a reading of the earlier chapters of this book. We believe that these observations have some degree of generalizability, but we cannot be sure, for negotiation is closer to art than it is to science. If negotiation

were like a game of draughts, governed by fixed and determinate rules leading to a large but finite number of possibilities, we might be able to program, as has been done for draughts, a computer to cover all the possibilities. However, negotiation, as all the chapters of the book show, keeps on introducing new rules, enabling actors to make new moves. To a large extent, our guide to future negotiations becomes observational experience of varying degrees of generalizability.

Leverage Points: Some Observations

Structural leverage

We can define structural leverage as large-scale institutionalized economic or military power. One clear example of structural leverage that matters in a trade negotiation is how much a country imports (on this point and for figures see Odell, 2007). In 2004 the US's share of world merchandise imports was 21.95 per cent and the EU's was 18.4 per cent. The only developing country to come close to these two was China, with an 8.07 per cent share. India and Brazil had 1.37 per cent and 0.95 per cent respectively. Smaller countries may be willing to give up a lot in order to gain access to these markets, especially if US or EU trade preferences give them an advantage over a competitor nation in an export market. Structural leverage may also have military sources that lead small states to calculate the costs and benefits of free trade agreements (FTAs) in geopolitical terms rather than simply trade terms. Even if, as is usually the case, the economics of an FTA do not favour the weaker state (Freund, 2003), the leaders from that weaker state may see political benefit in having a bilateral relationship with the world's strongest state. Political leaders from a weak state may well be ready to give up hard-won negotiating gains in other fora as part

of the price of securing a 'special' relationship with the US. The gain to a weak state may have little to do with trade and much more to do with its perceptions of security and how to manage the military power of the US, a point that has special salience for the Arab world (El-Said and El-Said, 2005). Robert Keohane's insight about the 'Al Capone alliance' between small and great powers is also relevant here. In this type of alliance:

> ... *remaining a faithful ally protects one not against the mythical outside threat but rather against the great power ally itself, just as, by paying 'protection money' to Capone's gang in Chicago, businessmen protected themselves not against other gangs but against Capone's own thugs.* (Keohane, 1969, p302)

Much more work needs to be done to understand the bigger web of relations and obligations that surround FTA negotiations, a web that often has strong strands of security and aid (including military) running through it, strands that produce dependencies. Perhaps then we will have a better understanding of why FTAs have proven to be a successful forum-shifting strategy for the US and EU (see Chapter 7). In any case, it is worth noting some of the examples of negotiating positions mentioned in the preceding chapters that perhaps are the product of this larger, more complex web of relations:

- Australia is a mega-diverse country, but is not a member of the Mega-Diverse Coalition.
- From the discussion in Chapter 5 of the negotiations concerning the Cartagena Protocol on Biosafety, Australia and New Zealand appear to have sided with the US in pressing for a weaker protocol even though both have domestic systems for the regulation of GMOs that would point to them favouring a stronger one.
- More generally, we have seen that a number of countries that are members of the Mega-Diverse Coalition (see Chapter 5) also have FTAs or are part of regional agreements with the US and EU (for example Peru, Colombia, Ecuador and Mexico; see Table 7.1 for other examples). One can ask to what extent these agreements assist the goals of the Mega-Diverse Coalition (see Box 9.2). Some civil society activists may be tempted to borrow the words of that great tennis philosopher, John McEnroe: 'You can't be serious'.

Floating points of leverage

Chapter 5 identified Ethiopia as a key player in the negotiations over the Cartagena Protocol on Biosafety. Ethiopia imports a minute percentage (less than 0.04 per cent in 2005 according to WTO figures) of the world's goods. For practical purposes it has zero structural power. This suggests that the art of negotiation is itself a rather important residual that helps to explain why an Ethiopia can be a significant player in a major international negotiation and why we end up with rules that do not match what we might predict on the

basis of structural leverage alone. While the CBD is not a trade negotiating forum, the Biosafety Protocol certainly had implications for agricultural exporters, leading to the formation of the Miami Group of countries (members included Australia, Canada and the US), a group that pushed for a weak protocol (see Chapter 5). The fact that Ethiopia became a player in these negotiations suggests that it, along with others, was able to find floating points of leverage by perhaps drawing on its level of technical capacity or its capacity to forge relations and build networks. Floating points of leverage are very context-dependent and essentially fleeting. Ethiopia is, for example, also applying for WTO membership, and it will be telling how far it can ensure it is not pressured during the accession process to sign up to TRIPS or TRIPS-plus measures since, as a least developed country, it is not required to do so until 2013 (2016 for pharmaceuticals) and even then would have the right to seek a further extension. As is pointed out in Chapter 7, the WTO accession process to date has not given acceding countries, even least developed countries, the freedom to use the options and flexibilities within the TRIPS regime. For the time being, the WTO's accession process appears to be a site where structural leverage dominates. Whether the greater attention now being given to the accession terms and the recommendations from UNCTAD for least developed acceding countries 'not to be required to provide accelerated or TRIPS-plus protection' can lead to new floating leverage remains to be seen (Abbott and Correa, 2007; UNCTAD, 2007, px).

Finding floating points of leverage, or perhaps creating them, is what good negotiators do. Explaining how floating points of leverage are obtained is difficult, much more difficult than explaining the outcomes that arise from structural leverage, but in the next few sections we offer some suggestions.

OBSERVATIONS

Box 9.2 IP, genetic resource negotiations and free trade agreements

Despite the progress made by developing countries in articulating their demands for an internationally binding disclosure obligation, bilateral negotiations conducted with the US for FTAs may defeat the very objectives they pursue. Such FTAs include provisions limiting the grounds on which a patent can be revoked, thereby possibly excluding revocation based on breach of such obligation. In addition, for example, the FTA between the US and Peru includes an 'understanding regarding biodiversity and traditional knowledge' according to which:

The Parties recognize the importance of traditional knowledge and biodiversity, as well as the potential contribution of traditional knowledge and biodiversity to cultural, economic and social development.

The Parties recognize the importance of the following: (1) obtaining informed consent from the appropriate authority prior to accessing genetic resources under the control of such an authority; (2) equitably sharing the benefits arising from the use of traditional knowledge and genetic resources; and (3) promoting quality patent examination to ensure the conditions of patentability are satisfied.

The Parties recognize that access to genetic resources or traditional knowledge, as well as the equitable sharing of benefits that may result from use of those resources or that knowledge, can be adequately addressed through contracts that reflect mutually agreed terms between users and providers.

Each Party shall endeavor to seek ways to share information that may have a bearing on the patentability of inventions based on traditional knowledge or genetic resources by providing:

a) publicly accessible databases that contain relevant information; and

b) an opportunity to cite, in writing, to the appropriate examining authority prior art that may have a bearing on patentability'.[a]

Although the legal value of this 'understanding' is unclear, it seems to undermine the Peruvian strong stand in favour of a binding international instrument or provision to deal with misappropriation and benefit sharing, as it suggests that these problems can be 'adequately addressed' by contractual agreements. This, however, is not in reality the case, particularly when resources or traditional knowledge have been fraudulently acquired.

Note: [a] The full text of the FTA is at www.ustr.gov/Trade_Agreements/Bilateral/Peru_TPA/Final_Texts/Section_Index.html; see also GRAIN (2006c).

Choose multilateral arenas rather than bilateral ones

The fact that multilateral fora are better for weaker actors has been said often enough. Here we can only add that one reason for this is that multilateral fora seem to provide more opportunities for floating points of leverage. A skilled negotiator backed by a prepared group (as the Cairns Group was in the Uruguay Round) can take advantage of, say, a temporary split between the US and EU. Chapters 5 and 6 of this book corroborate this basic point about multilateralism. It is hard to see how the concept of farmers' rights, a concept that recognizes the rights of some of the poorest people in the world, could have emerged in anything other than the multilateral arena of the International Undertaking and the Treaty. We do not wish to idealize multilateral fora such as the FAO or the WTO, however, as they are far from perfect. Country members of the WTO are not equal in terms of their capacity to block consensus: blocking a consensus is comparatively easy for power centre countries like the US and EU (and increasingly China and India); it is not easy for Fiji or Papua New Guinea. Nevertheless, it remains true that the multilateral processes described in this book generate more floating points of leverage than bilateral processes and are more transparent to civil society, so it follows that they come closer to the ideal of procedural fairness that we mentioned at the beginning of this chapter.

Stick with winning contests of principles; reframe losing ones

The Sophists understood that what matters in political life is how people perceive the world. Investing in improving one's rhetorical skills mattered because through persuasive speaking one could change perceptions and therefore political outcomes. This insight is important for global negotiations because such negotiations often come down to a contest of principles. TRIPS, for example, was framed as contest between the right to have property protected and piracy. The simple but effective logic behind this contest of principles was that those against protecting the IPRs of innovators were for piracy; it takes some eye-glazing information economics to explain the problems with this argument, and most journalists have lost

interest after the first 30 seconds of explanation. The negotiations that eventually led to the Doha Declaration on the TRIPS Agreement and Public Health in 2001 (the Doha Declaration) saw civil society public health networks reframe the contest of principles in the case of patents and medicines (Box 9.3). One could be for increasing the profits of already wealthy pharmaceutical monopolists or for helping to treat millions of dying and desperately poor people, but not both. The coalition that supported the Doha Declaration lacked structural leverage, at least of the kind that the US and the EU possess; reframing the contest of principles helped to create a floating point of leverage. We are not suggesting that reframing a contest of principles is sufficient to win a negotiation, but it matters. In most fora, from the WIPO Intergovernmental Committee on Genetic Resources, Traditional Knowledge and Folklore (IGC) (Chapter 4) to the CBD on access and benefit sharing (ABS) (Chapter 5), developed countries and business interest argue that one size does not fit all. When it comes to IP they tend to argue that a minimum size fits all, with preferably an ever bigger minimum. This is another example of sophistry.

Contests of principles and reframing have been important in the negotiations surrounding food, biodiversity and IP. We saw, for example, in Chapter 5 that developing countries supported the principle of the common heritage of mankind for plant genetic resources in the context of the International Undertaking. Concerns about the effect of IPRs led to changes in the choice of principles – the adoption of the principle of sovereignty in the context of the CBD and the use of the principle of biopiracy to gain more leverage in the negotiations concerning IPRs in the CBD, the FAO and TRIPS. There is a danger that one can be blinded by one's own rhetoric, a point we will come back to in the next section, but there is little doubt that the principle of biopiracy has been an effective framing tool. It has helped to unite developing country coalitions such as the

OBSERVATIONS

Box 9.3 Access to medicines and WTO rules:
A brief chronology

2001

In 2001, 39 pharmaceutical companies sued the South African government, alleging that a South African law was illegal and contrary to the patent rules in TRIPS. The law allowed for the import of cheaper drugs from other countries, primarily to address the HIV/AIDS crisis. Even though South Africa was abiding by the TRIPS rules, the companies only dropped the suit and withdrew following widespread condemnation nationally and internationally in the media and by public health advocates (Abbott, 2003).

Also in 2001, worldwide public concern and activism led to political pressure and much activity among negotiators in Geneva, prior to the WTO Ministerial Conference in Doha that year, to ensure TRIPS did not impede access to medicines. Developing countries worked on a declaration for the Ministerial Conference to make clear that patent rules should not undermine their health needs.

In November 2001, members of the WTO adopted the Doha Declaration on TRIPS and Public Health, which recognizes that TRIPS 'does not and should not prevent [WTO] Members from taking measures to protect public health'. The Declaration clarifies that governments have the right to override patents using a 'compulsory licence' to produce lower cost drugs and to determine the grounds upon which this can be done. The poorest, least developed countries were also allowed to ignore TRIPS rules on pharmaceutical products until 2016.

2002–2003

The Declaration left one item outstanding (the paragraph 6 issue) – the problem of what countries with insufficient or no manufacturing capacity for medicines can do. Even if they issue a compulsory licence to produce generic drugs, they have no industry to produce them. They thus need to find a country where drugs could be made without interference from the patent holder and then exported to them. But under TRIPS rules this could be challenged. WTO Members were given until the end of 2002 to find a solution.

Instead of helping rapidly craft a workable solution, negotiations were long and difficult and developed countries loaded the draft agreement with administrative conditions. Even then, the US only joined the consensus waiver decision at the end of August 2003, eight months past the deadline and just before the next WTO ministerial meeting in Cancun in September 2003, following the formulation of some rather modest statements to appease the pharmaceutical lobby. The extent to which the WTO decision, and the subsequent amendment adopted in December 2005, will prove helpful in addressing public health needs remains to be tested in practice. In July 2007, Rwanda made the first notification to the WTO of intent to import antiretroviral products under a compulsory licence to be issued in Canada for export by Apotex, a major Canadian generic pharmaceutical producer.

Mega-Diverse Coalition and been important in opening the door to serious dialogue about the need for a disclosure obligation in patent law. It has also forced various actors to re-evaluate their own conduct and examine their normative commitments (see, for example, Box 6.5 describing the conduct of the CGIAR Centres on the issue of IPRs and Box 5.7 describing the introduction of a disclosure obligation in Norway's patent law and Australia's system of virtual certificates of origin). Australia, we might note in passing, has been an opponent of the disclosure obligation and has tended to side with the US on issues related to the regulation of genetic resources in the context of the FAO and the CBD. Overall the principle of biopiracy has been important in pushing public and private actors towards a greater public accountability when it comes to their use of genetic resources.

Network networks to increase points of leverage

Once a point of leverage is created it can be increased and built upon. Perhaps the best example of this comes not from the chapters of this book but from the negotiations surrounding the Doha Declaration. We suggested above that because different principles are linked to different conceptions of the world, reframing a contest of principles in a negotiation can be a good idea. One reason why reframing may work is that it brings other kinds of actors into play in a negotiation. By choosing simple principles (for example patent monopolies versus access to medicines), a wider range of networks can potentially be enrolled in support of a negotiating position because the simplified contest is more readily understood by the wider range of networks. The Africa Group could never have achieved the Doha Declaration alone because they were and remain a weak group. But an Africa Group that joined with a large coalition of developing countries that included Brazil and India, that drew on the power of Northern NGOs to work the Northern mass media, that gained the quiet support of some European states, that drew on independent technical expertise to evaluate draft text, and that gained resources from

Geneva-based NGOs was a group strengthened by many networks (Odell and Sell, 2006). In his comments upon this chapter, Fred Abbott, Edward Ball Eminent Scholar Professor of International Law at Florida State University's College of Law, suggested that in the case of the negotiations over the paragraph 6 issue (Box 9.3) it was difficult for NGOs to rally public support around narrow technical issues (such as NGO preference for the Article 30 over the Article 31 solution to the paragraph 6 issue). (The insider nature of this example illustrates the problem we are talking about, since it requires a great deal of detailed knowledge to understand what it is about.) It was, Professor Abbott suggested, important for non-technical matters to be identified as the basis for debate. The right choice of principles can therefore bring in other networks to increase a point of leverage and perhaps create others. For weaker states the key is to network and then network some more, nationally, regionally and finally globally. We saw this maxim of networking networks in operation in Chapter 6, where, in the negotiations over the Treaty, regional networking served the US and EU well. Once Africa was able to arrange a regional meeting it became much more effective in the negotiations over the Standard Material Transfer Agreement (SMTA).

At the same time, however, there has to be more than just the rhetoric of principles. Those on the inside of the negotiation have to have access to experts who can craft the technical solutions that embody one's chosen principles. Shakespeare's suggestion in Henry VI, 'let's kill all the lawyers', is probably a widely shared sentiment, but in a negotiation one should not do away with them till they have crafted the text that embodies the victory that one seeks and have torn apart the other side's text.

OBSERVATIONS

Box 9.4 Postcards from the periphery: TRIPS in Geneva

Geoff Tansey

After almost 10 years working through a number of projects with IP negotiators in Geneva, mostly in the WTO, four observations in particular seem relevant here:

1   The processes by which rule-making operates are flawed and unfair. Major trading partners often demand concessions from developing country markets while offering strikingly unequal access to their markets and technologies. The sense of injustice this leaves, along with subsequent experience in trying to address developing country concerns, for example over health, biodiversity and food, undermines trust in the ability of multilateral institutions to take the interests of developing countries and their peoples sufficiently into account.

2   There is often little connection between those negotiating rules in different institutions and often little knowledge of those in other places, despite their connections and potential conflicts in implementation. Initiatives to permit dialogue between these groups are necessary if more balanced outcomes are to arise. Informal dialogues are an important way of increasing mutual understanding and helping overcome unfounded or mistaken assumptions.

3   For developing country negotiators having to deal with the unfamiliar territory of IP, small, focused interventions to provide information, access to technical and legal expertise, and access to those with differing positions can help them in both better understanding the issues and developing more appropriate negotiating positions. Even very small NGOs, working in the right place with the right people, can have a disproportionate impact. When they cooperate together, as those in Geneva have done, they can maximize their effectiveness and use of scarce resources.

4   Despite talk of states and their interests, individuals matter. Those who do the negotiating and their personal relationships can have a profound effect on outcomes, especially where few people in a capital or country are familiar with the issues. The development of confidence between those dealing with Article 27.3(b) of the TRIPS review laid the groundwork of trust for a very rapid response to the need to address the access to medicines issue. The short period negotiators spend in places like Geneva, usually three to four years, also means there is a need for constantly informing, educating and exchanging between them and those people developing materials to assist these negotiators.

Be patient and persistent

This is obvious, but its obviousness does not change its truth and we should probably remind ourselves of it from time to time. Halewood and Nnadozie in Chapter 6 remind us of it when they note the precipitous decline of civil society participants in the six and half years of negotiations that it took to produce the Treaty, despite the fact that many delegations supported greater involvement by civil society. Perhaps the explanation is the one suggested by Braithwaite and Drahos (2000, p619): 'Most NGO activists are colourful and charming people with limited tolerance for spending long hours, days and years in Geneva sitting around large tables surrounded by punctilious bureaucrats in grey suits.' Real power, as those who have spent decades in universities know, comes from having sat on the same committee for years and years. Over the years of a negotiation, individual negotiators who become 'fixtures', particularly those who follow an issue across fora (for example the CBD and FAO), acquire an intimate historical knowledge of the issues, countries' positions and, like good swimmers, a knowledge of the currents and what is possible in them. This time and experience often gives them a status of trust that allows them to forge coalitions and coordinate with other coalitions and ultimately to help broker the deals that shape the final treaty. Large country powers do not have a monopoly on these kinds of individuals. For smaller powers and non-state players the key perhaps is, when they have identified such an individual, to let that person stay the course of the negotiation.

The variables we probably need to know more about are career structures for civil society activists and funding mechanisms. For many larger NGOs active in different sectors and working on policy, campaigning and field programmes, it is difficult to maintain an activity over a long period on a specific issue, especially if their supporters keep pressing for new areas of activity or if fundraising requirements or maintaining supporter motivation

mean moving on regularly. For smaller NGOs dependent on donors, the short-term nature of much of that funding can make it difficult to maintain an activity over the long term. Moreover, as with negotiators, skills are short and knowledgeable staff move on, often leaving no-one with the expertise necessary to fill their shoes. A similar problem also arises in donor agencies themselves.

In any case, staying the course in a negotiation is a prerequisite to seizing points of leverage, which do not come along all that often for weaker players. Probably staying the course also involves coalitions of weaker players institutionalizing networks of expertise that can be called upon over the years of a negotiation, as has happened in Geneva (Box 9.4; see also Tansey, 2004). None of the negotiations that gave rise to the multilateral treaties discussed in this book were short affairs. For example, work on the Biosafety Protocol started in 1995, with a text only being produced in 2000 (see Chapter 5), and the text of the Treaty involved 'six and a half arduous years' of negotiation (see Chapter 6).

Negotiating Gains, Real Gains and Evidence-Based Approaches

Negotiating wins or gains may or may not turn into real gains. In trade negotiation, an example of a negotiating gain that is turned into a real gain is where a state wins a tariff concession and the state granting the concession does nothing to frustrate the granting thereof with the result that the first state gains a share of an export market that it did not have before. (In economic terms the state granting the concession also wins, but this is not how it is seen in the world of trade negotiators (Finger, 2005).) Where mutual gains providing for self-enforcement do not exist, or where there is no strong enforcement mechanism, there is a real danger that a negotiating win, especially one by a

weaker actor, will not be realized. Under these conditions it is essential that the negotiating win is accompanied by some strategy of post-negotiation implementation (Drahos, 2007a). Below we offer some examples drawn from earlier chapters of where negotiating gains that can be said to exist in a weakened form need support through implementation.

Compromises, ambiguity – Who really wins?

International negotiations are full of examples of where coalitions end up settling on ambigu-

OBSERVATIONS

ous language that allows both sides to claim some measure of negotiating gain. As Michael Halewood in Box 6.4 points out, Article 6.2 of the SMTA was deliberately left 'cloudy'. Recipients of materials from the MLS will not be able to claim IPRs on those materials in the form they received them. To begin with, not everybody will see this as ambiguous. Patent attorneys specialize in drafting patent specifications that overcome restrictions and prohibitions on patentability, and drafting claims that do not claim the material in the same form will not, one suspects, be seen by them as some sort of mission impossible. Yet if the matter goes to arbitration, a lot will depend on the chosen interpretive approach. The Percy Schmeiser saga recounted in Chapter 5 is a reminder that the technicality of patent jurisprudence does not necessarily serve broader environmental goals. Before developing countries seek the refuge of compromise or ambiguity they should ask whether in reality they are simply opening the door to defeat. The question they should be asking is which party in the end game will be in the best position to resolve the ambiguity in its favour.

Doing away with the lawyers – Develop scientific, evidence-based approaches

If climate change has taught us anything, it is that no amount of political manipulation and investment in technologies of spin will change how physical systems behave. At some point the weight of evidence drives all the parties towards taking a more evidence-based approach. Shakespeare's 'killing all the lawyers' in this context means, for example, not adopting legal distinctions that are scientifically meaningless. We saw in Chapter 5 that a distinction between living modified organisms intended for release in the environment and those that are not is a 'legal fiction'. The example of genetically modified corn being

found in a remote region of Mexico despite not being intended for release that we encountered in that chapter shows how meaningless legal distinctions can compromise scientific risk assessment. Similarly, lawyers who tend to resort to property-based forms of regulation may not understand the limitations of such models for agricultural biodiversity and innovation because they do not understand how systems of innovation in agriculture – where, in essence, breeding works best when many people exchange many materials – actually work. (See Chapter 8 for a discussion of the problems in allowing IPRs to dominate this many-to-many model of agricultural innovation.) There is too much at stake in agricultural biodiversity and biodiversity generally to allow global regulatory standards to rest on legal fictions. Generally, one suspects that all actors will have to move to higher levels of evidence-based negotiation when it comes to food, biodiversity and IPRs. There is no point, for example, in mega-diverse countries creating access regimes of such stringency that they defeat the capacity of their own scientists to understand what is happening to biodiversity (see Chapter 7 on this point). There is a danger, as noted earlier, of being blinded by one's own negotiating rhetoric.

Capturing real gains

We suggested at the beginning of this part of the chapter that negotiating gains have to be turned into real gains. Winning a negotiating gain, however, may bring its own complex implementation costs, especially if it requires a country to do something positive in the form of the creation of a system to capture those gains (doing something negative such as reducing tariffs is usually easier to implement). One clear example of the difficulty of meeting the implementation costs of gains that comes from the chapters of this book is the right, which Members of the WTO have under Article

27.3(b), of creating an effective *sui generis* system of protection of plant varieties. Few countries have been able to design their own system owing to the difficulties involved (as discussed in Chapters 2 and 3). The one example mentioned in this book is the Indian Plant Variety Protection and Farmers' Rights Act passed in 2001 (Chapter 2, Box 2.1). India is one of the world's largest economies, and its capacities of implementation are not representative of developing countries in general. It is true that various bilateral and regional agreements with both the US and EU have seen developing countries accept UPOV as the required standard (as discussed in Chapter 7). One reason is because, without considerable capacity or assistance, as Graham Dutfield noted in Chapter 2, '[i]t is actually very difficult for developing countries to design and implement their own systems of PVP if, as is likely, these would diverge at all from the latest version of the UPOV'.

That said, if a country enters into an FTA negotiation with the US or EU with a *sui generis* system in place, it probably has a better bargaining position than a country which has no system in place. The onus then falls on the US or EU to say that the relevant national system for the protection of plant varieties is not effective. The more general lesson here is that if an international negotiation permits the creation of alternative standards, countries had better act sooner rather than later to generate those alternatives. Otherwise, they will have little choice but to accept the international standard. Obviously this sets a massive challenge for many developing countries as they have to find the resources to implement a regulatory system that will satisfy the critical scrutiny of the US and EU.

Countries should also be sensitive to the strategies that other countries use to capture real gains. Once a negotiation over IP between a developed and developing country is finished, offers of technical assistance often follow. For those countries wanting to make the most of the IP rules in their interests, technical assistance can be dangerous or useful (Chapter 4, Box 4.3). Technical assistance by IP exporters may help create a Trojan horse IP approach and a community in developing countries that sees things through the dominant US–EU–Japanese approach. Assistance based on development values can help those affected in agriculture and environment understand the implications and impact of minimum standard IP rules, use whatever flexibilities there are to safeguard their interests, and better analyse and develop proposals for alternative approaches (Tansey, 2004). The central questions here are from whose perspective and with what objectives the assistance is given and whose capacity to do what does it support? Imagine, for example, you are in a messy divorce in which you need a lawyer. You would not really want to have your spouse's lawyers also representing you – there would be a clear conflict of interest and you would not expect them to see things from your point of view. Too much IP technical assistance is like that – given by those whose entire mindset is based on the dominant US or EU approach to IP, whether in implementation or enforcement, not on what might be most helpful for developing and least developed countries.

Steering global systems

There is another point about the UPOV story that is worth drawing out a little more. UPOV is not just a set of treaty standards. It is also a system of decision making by technical committees (Figure 9.1), which over time make many decisions on things like the interpretation of standards or the kinds of scientific tests and guidelines to apply when examining for distinctness, uniformity and stability (see, for example, UPOV, 2002). It is the many individual decisions of these committees that become collectively important to a shaping of the UPOV regime. These technical committees

OBSERVATIONS

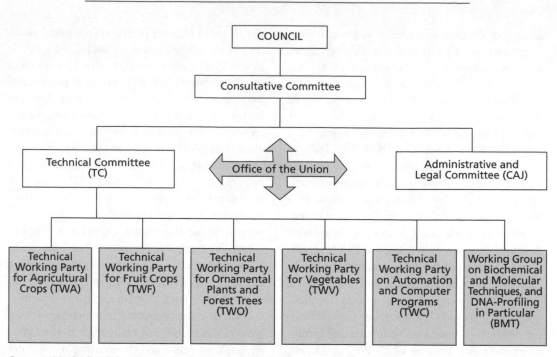

Source: 'UPOV bodies' link on www.upov.int/en/about/mission.html

Figure 9.1 *UPOV's committee structure*

represent yet another level of negotiation that is relevant to the global rules affecting food and agriculture. They will, no doubt, be important to the issue of harmonization identified in Chapter 2 as the big emerging issue for UPOV. If, as seems likely, more and more developing countries end up joining UPOV, they will have to find ways to participate in and influence the incremental processes of decision making that take place on these committees, because these processes shape the evolution of the regime. Encouragingly, Chapter 4's discussion of the Group of Friends of Development's success in pushing the WIPO Development Agenda shows that developing countries can take a holistic view of an international organization and develop an agenda for reform that recognizes the different vertical levels at which negotiations take place in the global system. Chapter 4 also suggested that, increasingly, developing countries will focus on systemic issues when it comes to IP and biodiversity rather than being steered into the negotiating ghetto of a single committee in a single organization (for example WIPO's IGC). Perhaps UPOV will find in the long run that the FTA processes that bring it more members will cause more negotiating diversity to flourish within its walls.

Conclusion

One optimistic conclusion that we can draw is that states in the last decade and a half have been successful in creating two important multilateral fora for the negotiation of food and biodiversity issues – the CBD (along with Biosafety Protocol) and the Commission on Genetic Resources for Food and Agriculture, where the Treaty was negotiated and which is now looking at other areas, beginning with animal genetic resources (Chapter 6). Developing countries have shown that they can organize coalitions that are responsive to their needs in ways that move beyond the coalitions they used to have in the bipolar world of the Cold War – the Like-Minded Group of Mega-Diverse Countries on the use of genetic resources, the Like-Minded Group of developing countries that emerged in the context of the Biosafety Protocol, and the African Group and the Friends of Development Group in the context of WIPO are all examples of this more differentiated approach by developing countries to negotiation. Chapter 7 in particular showed that WIPO, UPOV, the FAO, the WTO and the CBD are slowly but surely being edged into work programmes that treat food, biodiversity and IPRs as integrated issues of regulatory design. The IP system, in particular at the multilateral level, is more open than at any other time in its history. Surely much of the credit for this change can be claimed by developing country coalitions supported by a range of civil society actors.

Less optimistically, the structural leverage of the EU and US remains a problem for developing country coalitions. Hold-out groups in a multilateral negotiation that contains the US or EU can achieve much (for example the Miami Group with the Biosafety Protocol (Chapter 5) or the negotiations in the FAO over the International Undertaking (Chapter 6)). FTAs continue to undermine the goals of developing country coalitions in multilateral negotiations. There is no simple solution to this. Self-interest will do what self-interest will do. But at the same time, civil society groups, farmers and scientists are starting to build their own local systems. The emphasis here is on systems, for that is what is needed to counteract the global administrative systems of an organization like UPOV. Models of administration cannot be replaced by speeches and declarations, but only by counter-models. The example of BiOS, the open source system for biotechnology developed by CAMBIA in Australia, the work of Dr Melaku in Ethiopia with local farmer associations and the work of SEARICE in Southeast Asia are all examples of local systems building (see Chapter 8). It is not necessary for every local system to go global, but it is important that it is part of a linked system. Perhaps the maxim we should practise for food and biodiversity systems is to build locally and link globally.

10

Global Rules, Local Needs

Geoff Tansey

This chapter discusses the democratic deficit that surrounds global rule-making. It then briefly outlines various scenarios for the future development of the food system and questions the roles the global intellectual property (IP) rules will play in this. Next it suggests that the current framework promotes an overemphasis on technological innovation while neglecting the need for social, political and institutional innovation. Finally, it discusses a range of ethical criteria for evaluating developments and changes as a way to bring about more equitable outcomes.

Introduction

This century there will be more people, new climate patterns and seismic political changes as new industrial and economic powers emerge on this planet. The challenge of ensuring everyone can eat sustainably and well, without the double burden of undernutrition and overnutrition, will be considerable. The future role of hundreds of millions of smallholder and marginal farmers in meeting this challenge is unclear and the farming systems best placed to do so are contested. Many factors affect the food system from local to global levels – from environmental change to the direction of technological innovation, market structures and trading arrangements. The rules and ongoing negotiations discussed in earlier chapters will play an increasing role in whether or not we are successful in meeting everyone's food needs in a sustainable way. This book has provided a brief guide to these interconnected negotiations, as discussed in Chapter 7, to enable more people to have a greater understanding of what is happening and so be more able to participate in shaping how these global rules develop and monitor the impact they have. The next sections draw out some important issues.

Global Negotiations – A Democratic Deficit

During my work on the UN Security Council, I had often been struck by a very obvious imbalance – between the diplomatic resources and skills of the powerful countries, and every- *one else. ... The numerous smaller UN missions struggle to cover the enormous and proliferating agendas of the UN General Assembly, Security Council and specialized committees with just one or two horribly overworked and under-equipped diplomats. ...*

Often those with most at stake are not even allowed into the room where their affairs are being discussed. This imbalance of course does not serve those marginalized, but nor, paradoxically, does it serve the powerful. In this complex and interconnected era, agreements that fail to take into account the interests of all concerned parties are not good or sustainable and they often fall apart. The ultimate effect is a less stable world. If people are ignored, they tend to find ways — sometimes violent — to get heard. (Ross, 2007)

As earlier chapters showed, these rules do not emerge from a relatively balanced representative interplay of interests but from unequal and sometimes coercive bargaining relationships in which the strong undermine the weak. Procedural fairness, which should be a key ideal in negotiating the rules around food security and biodiversity (see Chapter 9), has for the most part not been respected. Whether in WIPO, the WTO, the CBD or the FAO, the stronger states are better able to coordinate, participate, draw on expertise and play off weaker states against each other. Something similar happens in business between larger transnational firms and smaller businesses, farmers and consumers. Within states, farmers and indigenous groups are often suspicious, for various reasons, of government claims to be acting in their interests by protecting traditional knowledge (TK) or genetic resources, as the statements and actions of indigenous and farmers' groups indicate (see Boxes 5.4 and 8.4).

Negotiations in Geneva, Rome, Montreal or elsewhere discussed in this book take place a long way from the rural reality of smallholder farmers, indigenous peoples, landless labourers and shanty town dwellers. It can be hard for negotiators to understand and take account of such people's needs when they are part of a global jockeying for power, for trade advantages, and influenced most by the needs of the urban, corporate and diplomatic elites. The question thus arises of whether negotiators have too much power and if the institutions where they operate are appropriate for the challenges facing us.

As the preambles, declarations and objectives related to the various agreements show, fine-sounding language about ending hunger, farmers' rights and the like too easily becomes lost in a *realpolitik* of advantages and interests to be traded between states in different fora and is not acted upon on the ground. The TRIPS Agreement, for example, represents a kind of global regulatory capture in which just four major industries shaped global rules to suit themselves (Chapter 3). They did so partly by having strong states adopt their policies and partly by having those states insert IP into trade negotiations covering different areas, all of which had to be agreed as a single undertaking. A kind of trade poker then occurs, often when last minute trade-offs are made at the highest level on things that should be not be traded off as they are incommensurables, and where the benefits that might be gained will not go to those who bear the costs. In the case of IP, the benefits are largely speculative (developing countries' future innovation capacity) and the costs much more immediate and tangible (royalty payments and licensing fees).

As noted in Chapter 7 on linkages, both IP and trade regimes may need to be subject to other minimum global standards on such things as state and corporate respect for human rights, with a similar level of enforceability backed by sanctions — which should also be applicable to environmental, health and food goals — as is given to trade and IP goals through the WTO. Other elements needed to balance the globalization of minimum IP standards are stronger antitrust, fair competition and user rights rules, along with strict liability regimes for those introducing new technologies that affect biodiversity, ecological functions and environmental wellbeing.

Complexity and Coercion

Higher standards and various forms of business regulation are used by larger players to make their roles in the food system easier, or entry for smaller competitors more difficult, from nutrition labelling to production practices to trademarks. Today, stronger IP rules are seen by some as a way of locking developing countries out of the methods for development used by the richer, more industrialized countries or locking them into new technologies such as genetically engineered plants and animals and pesticide-resistant crops, which will be controlled by large corporations.

Similarly, increasingly complex rules tend to advantage the stronger countries and larger businesses. There are serious concerns that higher IP standards as well as complex access and benefit sharing regimes could disadvantage not only smaller countries and firms but also those working in agriculture, where informal innovation systems and exchange mechanisms underpin the innovation practices of traditional farming.

When weaker countries' negotiators do become more informed and better able to argue for their interests, they may face coercive measures to get them to desist. For example, this may happen to negotiators taking a strong position in the TRIPS Council that is disliked by richer countries. Some may be told by their superiors in the capital to back off following pressures from developed country capitals on ministers or presidents in developing countries suggesting that unless they quieten down the demands of their negotiators then trade prefer-

ences elsewhere may be affected. Or it may happen in free trade negotiations where the IP standards are forced up by the bigger player on a take-it-or-leave-it basis. The emphasis may be on the short-term potential gains to be made from trade concessions, which may bring more immediate, though not necessarily evenly distributed benefits, than the long-term often indeterminate costs imposed by higher IP standards.

To suggest anything else may seem naïve and unrealistic. Yet to tackle the enormous global problems facing humanity, such as extremes of poverty and wealth, climate change through global warming, dealing with diseases that threaten animal and human health, and loss of biodiversity, we need new forms of action, from global to local levels and not built on the old approaches to diplomacy and negotiation. We need action based on cooperation and sharing of best practices to deal with the challenges, not competition that pits peoples and societies against each other. For that, on the basis of performance to date, we need to rethink the way we make global rules and the nature of international negotiating processes. Ensuring food security requires action from local to global levels, but much of the current approach undermines and devalues the enormous capacity that exists for innovation and action at a local level done by those with the most intimate knowledge of the environment in which they live – the farmers, fisherfolk and herders who have managed and maintained agricultural biodiversity.

Alternative Futures

The rules we create shape our future and our future food systems. They encourage or discourage different kinds of roles for small farmers, different approaches to biodiversity,

and different approaches to the distribution of wealth and power. Lang and Heasman (2004) describe two very different visions of our food future. They argue that we are moving away from a productionist paradigm, which has led to the industrialization of food production over the past 200 years and increased production to match population growth, to a conflict between two different, but science-informed, approaches.

One, which they call the 'life sciences integrated paradigm', has 'at its core a mechanistic and fairly medicalized interpretation of human and environmental health'. It envisages a highly technological, highly controlled, broad application, wide adaptation approach to the future of food, with large production units and professionalized supply systems from inputs and seeds to final consumer. This future is more monocultural, industrial, corporate-dominated and dependent on IP. It is also one that sees little or no future for smallholder farmers or semi-subsistence farmers, a view echoed by the OECD: 'The long-term future for most semi-subsistence farming households lies outside agriculture' (OECD, 2007). The rapid displacement of such farmers from farming and migration could cause major social and political upheaval in countries still with large farming populations. The World Bank is re-emphasizing the need to give a much higher priority to investing in agriculture for economic development after a long period of neglect (World Bank, 2007). While the focus on agriculture is welcomed, the appropriateness of Bank's proposals and their effects on poor people and the planet are being questioned by a range of civil society organizations (Actionaid, 2007; Murphy and Santarius, 2007; Oxfam, 2007).

The second approach is what Lang and Heasman call the 'ecologically integrated paradigm': 'Its core assumption recognizes mutual dependencies, symbiotic relationships and more subtle forms of manipulation, and it aims to preserve ecological diversity.' This approach sees biodiversity and diversity in general as a strength and says humans must live within ecological realities and work with them rather then dominate and ignore them. It wants to build on the millennia of experimental

empirical work by farmers in diverse environments that have led to a huge range of agricultural biodiversity and to promote connection between producers and consumers; favours the micro, small and medium-sized enterprises, rather than the transnational; and sees a local to global hierarchy, where the local goes first. It promotes organic, integrated pest management, low external inputs, more skilled, open systems of exchange, family-farm-based biodiverse farming, healthy diets, and keeping cooking and farming skills alive from farm to flat.

There are other possibilities. One is collapse, be it economic, physical or a descent into violent conflict over resources or beliefs (Diamond, 2005). Another is based on extreme genetic engineering, synthetic biology, nanotechnology and the ideas of the transhuman movement, which looks to enhance human beings by genetic engineering and technological augmentation (ETC Group, 2007; Wolbring, 2007). This builds on the 19th-century positivist dream of domination and control of nature and assumes humans can do anything, have no biological constraints and can deal with any problem they create, including destroying the biosphere. Ultimately this vision sees humans – or at least some, wealthier, humans – being liberated from ecological and biological constraints and farming as unnecessary. Eventually, food will be synthesized from any feedstock, for example by producing proteins in fermentors and then spinning, texturing and flavouring them to appear like any form of meat. This is still science fiction, but a fiction some seem to be seeking to make fact. Maintaining biodiversity and developing more ecologically sound approaches, as envisaged by the CBD and the Treaty, are part of the attempts to avoid collapse, while the latter, technologically triumphalist, vision seems to recognize no biological limits, sees no difference between biological and other systems, and treats everything as a resource, able to be owned and patentable.

The one vision of the future that is not being facilitated and encouraged by the way IP rules are developing and affecting the direction of R&D is the ecological approach; yet that is probably the one with the best chance of working in the long term. Ultimately, there is a basic tension between IP and biodiversity that those in favour of global IP standards have failed or refused to discuss. IP owners do best (in terms of profit) if they have a global standard or product (Windows, Viagra, Roundup and so on) that is protected globally by high IP standards. Yet innovation in food and agriculture does best if it can draw on a rich biodiversity, a biodiversity that depends on fragile variables such as TK, local farming systems and free exchange of materials. By building a property rights system that rewards standardization and homogeneity, we almost certainly risk affecting those variables that underpin our systems of biodiversity.

Whose Innovation?

The current IP regime provides incentives for innovation in the formal sector by commercial interests but fails to provide incentives for the sustainable conservation and use of biodiversity by farmers. As Joseph Gari (2001, p23) from the FAO argues:

IP rights over life convey an asymmetric system of conserving, using, transforming, managing and controlling biodiversity. This asymmetry is detrimental to many indigenous and peasant people, who are precisely amongst those most in need of biological innovation and who can best carry it out.

The private rights of innovators or those investing in innovation protectable by IPRs have to be balanced by concern over the public wellbeing of the whole of society and the environment that may be affected by these innovations. As noted in a report by the Food Ethics Council (FEC, 2002), there seems to be an assumption that innovation is intrinsically a good thing, irrespective of what or where it is. But is that the case? To draw an analogy – this is like saying driving from A to B ever faster is a good in itself when in fact society places limits on the speed at which you may drive to reduce risks to other road users and the individual, and nowadays to reduce CO_2 emissions. Perhaps there is a case for guarding against innovation without due care and attention, reckless innovation, and even causing death or damage by innovation. This may be of particular relevance for the impact on traditional and indigenous communities, where inappropriate innovations may damage or even destroy them, rather then support them and their innovation systems. There is a need to nourish and sustain the long-standing local innovation systems, such as varietal selection and soil fertility and risk management methods, of many farming communities, that are ignored by the current approach and to recognize the knowledge, skills and experience of local communities (Dutfield, 2006b; see also Abraham, 2007).

Most discussion about innovation focuses on technological innovation. For national politicians it is part of a mantra linked to competitive national advantage. IP rules are thought of in relation to how far they will help underpin that competitive advantage, which is one reason why many OECD countries are seeking to expand them. Yet what much of the discussion in this book suggests is that the most challenging areas we face call for institutional, social and political innovation to do things differently in the world, for the benefit of both the poor and the environment, if we are to have a sustainable food system and ensure food security from the global to the household level. As discussed in Chapter 8, the way the IP rules are playing out does not encourage sustainability goals but rather tends to focus R&D towards rather narrow approaches. These focus on products and processes that are protectable by different forms of IP, are subject to proprietary interests, fit commercial markets and do so in ways that advantage the bigger players, firms and countries. These ignore the need for R&D for the public good and indigenous and traditional innovation systems and seem unlikely to support the ecological approach to food and farming that is called for in the CBD and more recently by the Commission on Genetic Resources for Food and Agriculture at the FAO (Chapters 5 and 6).

Fortunately, there is some recognition of the wider importance of the IP system and the need for change within the IP community, as shown by the European Patent Office's scenarios project (Box 8.5). Some, noting how the IP system has changed in the past, argue that in the 20th century industrialized countries came to depend excessively on patents to reward innovation and that, with the growth of patent bureaucracy, the patent system has become a self-sustaining enterprise that needs changing (Box 10.1).

We need to go beyond the IP system for real change, however, and look to developing and using incentives and supports for innovation that enhance both livelihoods and environments, without the exclusion and monopoly involved in IP. One such alternative to IP is the use of prizes for innovation (Stiglitz, 2006).

Dealing with Complexity

Indirectly, we all depend on agriculture, but most of the poorest people in the world today still live in rural areas and directly depend on agriculture for their livelihoods. Farming is a site-specific activity, needing different approaches in different environments, and food habits are partly cultural and social expressions of relationships and beliefs. The trend of industrialized farming has been towards more linear agricultural systems – using fossil fuels, fertilizers, pesticides, antibiotics and mechanization as inputs to permit more industrial approaches to farming – bypassing the skilled, local knowledge needed to manage complex local ecologies (Weiss, 2007). At the same time as seeking to simplify the complex ecological requirements of production, the food system has developed increased complexity in processing and distribution. There are ever longer and more complex supply chains to consumers, who are segmented into ever more types. Added to this are legal regimes, also of growing complexity, of which those discussed in the book are perhaps the most recent. But this complex superstructure rests on a fragile ecological base.

In looking at how these varying and increasingly complex rules affect people, the key words to look at are who will bear the *risks* and who will get the *benefits* from changes, who is *empowered* or *disempowered*, and whose capacity to *control* is enhanced or reduced? By asking such questions the effects of changes will become clearer. And these effects need to be considered using various parameters. One tool to help in making clearer the impact of technological changes, and one that could also help in looking at the impact of these rules, is the ethical matrix (Mepham, 2005). This uses a number of basic ethical criteria that people generally use in one way or another when weighing up what to do and examines how an action, technology or policy affects different individuals, groups, environments and animals. The criteria used are how it affects the *wellbeing* of those groups and environments, how it affects their *autonomy* or freedom of action, and

PROSPECTS

Box 10.1 Institutional innovation for innovation

Peter Drahos

To manage climate change, states will want faster innovation and diffusion of alternative energy technologies, plants for food and agriculture, and technologies for efficient water use. The patent system in its present form is a risk factor, rather than a tool of risk management, for handling these kinds of large-scale changes and crises. The system has an appalling track record in producing medicines for tropical diseases, for example.[a] Patent specifications, which are meant to disclose the invention, are drafted by patent attorneys in a species of legalese that mocks the values of open science and communication. Patent systems in their present form represent unhealthy concentrations of power and dominance in which networks of big business, patent attorneys and patent offices cooperate to produce an insider governance of the system.

The way to reshape this insider governance is to use the principle of the separation of powers by:

- Greatly expanding the representation of wider publics and including broader interests on patent offices' policy or advisory committees.
- Introducing external audit mechanisms for patent offices to catalyse different information flows about patents to legislators.
- Establishing transparency registers to deal with the failure of the patent system in practice to disclose invention information and create certainty for downstream innovators. Currently, it is too easy to get large numbers of patents at a comparatively cheap price from the world's patent offices, with the result that there are too many patents for downstream innovators to find, analyse and litigate. Simple rules are needed to remove this complexity,[b] such as for regulatory agencies to establish patent transparency registers in areas of technology where, to borrow the words of Article 27(2) of TRIPS, patent transparency was necessary 'to protect human, animal or plant life or health or to avoid serous prejudice to the environment'.[c] A register could target, for example, research tools in biotechnology, particular classes of drugs, specific plants or genes. Companies would be required to use the register to make a full disclosure of the patents surrounding the targeted technology. Other companies would be able to rely on the register, knowing that there were no other hidden surprises for them. In addition, such registers would require the disclosure of information relating to ownership and licensing.
- Creating a technology platform to search all the world's patents to allow users to organize that information in various ways (around ownership, technologies or countries, for example). Such global patent transparency would be the foundation upon which to build other reforms of the patent system.

Notes: [a] Thirteen of the 1223 new chemical entities between 1975 and 1997 related to tropical diseases; see Mirza (1999). [b] For a philosophical defence of simple rules for dealing with complexity see Epstein (1995). [c] I first put forward the idea of transparency registers in 2004 in debates over the US–Australia FTA.

Source: Drahos (2007b)

whether it is *fair* to the different groups or environments or favours some much more than others – in other words what impact it has on justice and equity (Table 10.1). Changes that promote the wellbeing of a few, or a firm or industry, say, while curtailing the autonomy or freedom of action of others (such as farmers), or that create injustice for many, are likely to be problematic. It might be telling, for example, to look at how IP rules are being used to place IP

Table 10.1 *A generalized example of the ethical matrix*

Respect for	Wellbeing (Health and welfare)	Autonomy (Freedom and choice)	Justice (Fairness)
Industrialized farming model farmers	Income and working conditions	Freedom of action	Fair trade and IP laws and practices
Organic farmers/seed savers	Income and working conditions	Freedom of action	Fair trade and IP laws and practices
Citizens	Food quality and safety	Democratic informed choice	Availability and affordability
Farm animals	Animal welfare	Behavioural freedom	Intrinsic value
The living environment (biodiversity)	Conservation	Maintenance of biodiversity	Sustainability

Source: Taken from www.foodethicscouncil.org.uk

rights over real property rights, as discussed in the case of patent-protected genes in genetically engineered canola in the Canadian court judgement discussed in Chapters 1 and 5.

The approach to developing new kinds of technologies, or making new rules, from a smallholder farmer's or a consumer's or a biodiversity perspective might mean tackling different problems in different ways from those you might adopt from looking at them from a scientist's, IP lawyer's or trade negotiator's point of view.

Conclusion

While much of the public debate about the impact of global rules on IP so far has focused on access to medicines, this is likely to change as their impact on biodiversity and on access to food, knowledge, and the direction of research and development become more apparent. Food security, as briefly discussed in Chapter 1, is a complex matter requiring action from local to global levels (Box 1.1). Although definitions vary and many now adopt the term food sovereignty (Boxes 1.7 and 8.2), our need for food, in every society and in every time and place, past, present and future, will not change. Food connects us all and, apart from providing sustenance, is used in many ways in our various human expressions of culture, social systems and religious beliefs. The global rules discussed in this book will have a significant impact on our food future and on who controls it and for what ends.

The interaction between IP and biodiversity is producing two parallel experiments unheard of before. One introduces a set of minimum, more-or-less global, legal requirements on IP, irrespective of circumstances. These rules in turn are also fuelling the most rapid and biggest ever biological experiment on the planet with the food we eat and raw materials we use, as any living organism of commercial value is liable to be redesigned by private actors for private ends. Yet the IP system was not developed for biological systems, and its global extension has largely been brought about as a conservative, protectionist response to fundamental technical change by a set of industries whose business models may be outdated and outmoded but who want to retain and extend control of the system as it exists today. Moreover, this is proceeding without countervailing responsibilities and brakes being put on commercial firms through such things as antitrust and liability regimes, helped by a public failure to look at other incentives for biological innovation that builds on traditional systems or creates new ones. We are, but should not be, playing a high stakes poker game with the sustainability of agriculture upon which all our lives – directly and indirectly – depend. It would be ironic – and potentially tragic – if just as other sectors are turning to and seeing the value of open source, informally networked means for innovation (Benkler, 2006), farming and food, which has been based on such systems for millennia, moves in the opposite direction.

As with any guide, there is much more that could be said about any of the topics briefly covered here. But also, as with any guide, the aim here has been to elicit an interest in and inform about something that matters. Food matters. Yet it is an area where globally we are failing to meet humanity's current needs and are in danger of not meeting future needs. It is also a complex area, with many different interests. This book is a tool that we hope will help make the discussion and rule-making about IP, biodiversity and food security more informed and lead to fairer outcomes for all.

Notes

Preface

1   Quakers (Members of the Religious Society of Friends) have opposed war, promoted peaceful resolution of conflict, and supported multilateral institutions to deal with global problems as well as practising and promoting simplicity, truth and integrity in daily living: www.quaker.org.uk and www.quaker.ca; see also Tansey (no date) for more information about this programme.

Chapter 1

1   For Coca Cola figures see US Securities and Exchange Commission, Form 10-k, 'Annual report pursuant to section 13 or 15(d) of the Securities Exchange Act of 1934', p50, available at www.thecoca-colacompany.com/investors/form_10K_2006.html; for McDonald's see US SEC report for McDonald's, pp30 and 34, at www.sec.gov/Archives/edgar/data/63908/000119312507039707/d10k.htm. The McDonald's figures included US$689.8m in advertising costs for company-operated restaurants plus a further US$97.4 production costs for radio and television advertising, primarily in the US, to which should be added an unaccounted, but 'significant', set of advertising costs by franchisees. For the fiscal year ended 31 December 2006 WHO's total proposed programme budget for the two years 2006–2007 was just over US$ 3.3 billion (see www.who.int/gb/e/e_pb2006.html) but 'Financing of the organization is increasingly from voluntary contributions, the majority of which are earmarked for specific projects or programmes. This earmarking can distort priority-setting and may threaten the impartiality of WHO, as well increase its administration costs', according to the draft eleventh programme of work 2006–15(revised), p22 (see www.who.int/gb/pbac/pdf_files/Extraordinary/PBAC_EXO1_2-en.pdf).

For 2004–5, total expenditure for the FAO was a little over US$1.5 billion, about half of which was regular core budget (from Programme Implementation Report (PIR) for 2004–05, Table 1 – see www.fao.org/docrep/meeting/011/j8013e/J8013e04.htm).

Chapter 3

1   The General Agreement on Tariffs and Trade (GATT) adopted in 1947 has marginal references to IP but at the same time it includes a number of provisions, which, without specifically mentioning intellectual property rights (IPRs), lay down general rules capable of having a bearing on certain trade-related aspects of IPRs. The GATT 1947 contains basic principles and rules on governmental measures affecting trade of goods, and these rules and principles apply to all such measures, irrespective of the policy area in which they are taken, including such measures when they are in connection with IPRs, particularly the national treatment, the most-favoured nation treatment, general elimination of quantitative restrictions or non-discriminatory application of quantitative restrictions (see GATT document MTN.GNG/NG11/W/6).

2   See GATT document PREP.COM(86)W/41/Rev.1.

3   See Articles 400 and 401 of GATT document MTN.GNG/NG11/W/73.

4   Cf. *State Street Bank and Trust Co. v. Signature Financial Group*, 149 F.3d 1368 (Fed. Cir. 1998) (business methods); *AT&T Corp. v. Excel Communications, Inc.*, 172 F.3d 1352 (Fed. Cir. 1999) (software). In other countries, such creativity may not be considered an invention or industrially applicable, requirements for patentability under a different TRIPS' provision.

5   See Canada – Patent Protection of Pharmaceutical Products, Report of the Panel, WT/DS114/R, paragraphs 7.101–7.105 (17 March 2000) (analysing provisions of Canadian law for de facto, rather than de jure, discrimina-

tory effects or discriminatory purpose; finding no discriminatory purpose and suggesting that in the absence of discriminatory purpose the application of disadvantageous conditions beyond a particular field of technology will preclude a finding of discrimination by field of technology).

6 More explicit language to require data exclusivity was proposed but was not adopted. See Gervais (2003).

7 See Vienna Convention on the Law of Treaties, Article 31(1) (treaties are to be interpreted in good faith and conformity to the ordinary meaning of the terms of the treaty in their context and in light of its object and purpose).

8 See WT/GC/564/Rev.2 (5 July 2006), including a communication from Brazil, China, Colombia, Cuba, India, Pakistan, Peru, Tanzania and Thailand on a new Article 29(b) of TRIPS dealing with the Disclosure of Origin of Biological Resources and/or Associated Traditional Knowledge (WT/GC/W/566, 14 June 2006).

9 See IP/C/W7469 (13 March 2006).

10 See WT/GC/W/566 (14 June 2006).

Chapter 5

1 Denmark, Finland, France, New Zealand, Norway, Sweden, the UK and the US officially indicated their unwillingness to support the IU. In addition, Australia, Canada and Japan were also unwilling to support it but did not issue official statements to this effect (Tilford, 1998, note 251). Canada and the US joined the Commission in 1990 thanks largely to agreed interpretations to the IU, discussed below. They did not, however, sign the IU itself (Tilford 1998, p413). Japan has also joined the Commission but did not sign the IU. The other eight countries have both joined the Commission and signed the IU; see 'Members of the FAO Commission on Genetic Resources for Food and Agriculture' at www.fao.org/ag/cgrfa/memC.htm (accessed 8 June 2007) and Silva Repetto and Cavalcanti (2000).

2 Convention on Biological Diversity, 'Introduction [to national biodiversity strategies and action plans]', online at

www.cbd.int/nbsap/introduction.shtml (accessed 8 June 2007).

3 The preamble to the TRIPS Agreement, which makes reference to adequate protection and effective enforcement, was substantially concluded in 1990, well before the finalization of the CBD (UNCTAD-ICTSD, 2005, p10).

4 The President and CEO of Genetech, G. Kirk Rabe, wrote to President Bush before the latter's departure to Rio, where the CBD would be signed, saying 'the proposed Convention runs a chance of eroding the progress made in protecting American intellectual property rights' (Hamilton, 1993, p623, citing Usdin, 1992). President Clinton signed the treaty the day before it closed for signature with the support of the biotechnology industry and with the promise that it would be sent to the Senate to consider ratification with an interpretive statement alleviating the industry's IP concerns.

5 An exception here would be the teff agreement discussed in Box 5.4, above. Paragraph 12.1 of the agreement requires the parties to the contract, in the event of a dispute, to seek a solution by negotiation. If the dispute cannot be resolved by negotiation, it is to be 'submitted to an arbitration body in accordance with the procedure laid down in part I of Annex II of the Convention on Biological Diversity'.

6 Like-Minded Megadiverse Countries, 'Prologue', online at www.lmmc.nic.in/prologueLmmc_new.php?Section=two (accessed 4 June 2007).

7 Paragraph 1(h) of the Cancun Declaration of Like-Minded Megadiverse Countries (18 February 2002), online at www.lmmc.nic.in/Cancun%20Declaration.pdf (accessed 8 June 2007). Paragraph 1 of the Cancun Declaration states that the LMMC is to serve 'as a mechanism for consultation and cooperation to promote our interests and priorities related to the preservation and sustainable use of biological diversity'.

8 The ABIA appears to have changed its website as this statement no longer appears.

9 Parts of this analysis are drawn from Garforth (2003) and Garforth et al (2005).

10 Convention on Biological Diversity, 'Frequently asked questions on the Biosafety Protocol', online at www.cbd.int/biosafety/faqs.shtml?area=biotechnology&faq=2 (accessed 9 June 2007).

11 At the time of writing, there were only two records in the BCH on LMOs under the advance informed agreement procedure. One record from Ireland contained no information and the other record from Norway concerned a decision taken prior to the entry into force of the Protocol.

12 Convention on Biological Diversity, 'Liability and redress', online at www.cbd.int/biosafety/ issues/liability.shtml (accessed 9 June 2007).

13 The Basel Protocol on Liability and Compensation for Damage Resulting from Transboundary Movements of Hazardous Wastes and Their Disposal took six years to negotiate. It was concluded in December 1999 and has not yet entered into force. The International Maritime Organization (IMO) International Convention on Liability and Compensation in Connection with Carriage of Hazardous and Noxious Substances by Sea took over 10 years to negotiate. It was concluded in May 1996 and has not yet entered into force. Other examples include the Convention on the Liability of Operators of Nuclear Ships (concluded in 1962, not yet in force); the United Nations Economic Commission for Europe (UNECE) Convention on Civil Liability for Damage Caused During Carriage of Dangerous goods by Road, Rail and Inland Navigation Vessels (concluded in 1989, not yet in force); the IMO International Convention on Civil Liability for Bunker Oil Pollution Damage (concluded in 2001, not yet in force); the UNECE Protocol on Civil Liability and Compensation for Damage Caused by the Transboundary Effects of Industrial Accidents on Transboundary Waters (concluded in 2003, not yet in force); see Cook (2002), p376 and CBD (2007a), pp16–17.

14 The Supreme Court of Canada rejected the patentability of higher life forms in an earlier decision: *Harvard College v. Canada* (Commissioner of Patents), [2002] S.C.J. No 77.

15 On this point, Percy Schmeiser has recently initiated an action against Monsanto in the small claims court. The action stems from Monsanto's Roundup Ready canola appearing in his fields once again. He contacted the company to come and remove the plants, which the company agreed to do if Schmeiser would sign the waiver described above. Schmeiser refused saying the document infringed his right to freedom of speech and sent the company an invoice for the costs he incurred in removing the offending plants from his field (Pratt, 2007). Schmeiser characterizes the dispute as involving a liability issue and a court date has been set for January 2008 (see www.percyschmeiser.com).

16 Part VI to the Annex to decision BS-I/7 also potentially provides for some coercive measures to address non-compliance. The MOP may issue a caution to the concerned Party, although the effect of this caution is unclear and it may be more of a 'sunshine' measure to draw attention to the wrongdoing of a Party (Weiss, 2000, p461). Part VI also allows the MOP to take measures in cases of repeated non-compliance, although the range of possible measures that can be taken in such circumstances has yet to be adopted. A decision on this point is slated to be taken at MOP-4 in 2008.

17 Convention on Biological Diversity, 'Compliance', online at www.cbd.int/biosafety/ issues/compliance.shtml (accessed 9 June 2007).

Chapter 6

1 In the lead up to the First Meeting of the Contact Group for the Drafting of the Standard Material Transfer Agreement in Hammamet, Tunisia, in July 2005, the African Group, hosted by the SADC Plant Genetic Resources Centres in Lusaka, Zambia, was able to meet together before a meeting for one of the very few times in Africa. This preparation time greatly facilitated the African Group's ability to take the lead on a number of issues at the subsequent meeting and introduce various options for the global community to discuss.

2 Sixteen countries that signed the Treaty before the date for signature expired have not yet ratified. One such country is the US, which, it appears at the time of writing, may ratify the Treaty sometime soon.

3 See CGN website: www.cgn.wur.nl/UK/ CGN+Plant+Genetic+Resources/Search+ and+order+germplasm/Ordering+seeds/+acc ess+and+benefit+sharing/.

Chapter 7

1 This section is based on material initially drafted by Heike Baumüller.
2 European Parliament Resolution of 20 June 2007 on the Millennium Development Goals, paragraph 94.
3 This section is based on material drafted by Frederick Abbott.
4 This section is based on Dutfield (2006a).
5 See IP/C/W7469 (13 March 2006).
6 www.croptrust.org/documents/web/WCA%20Declaration%20-%2015-10-06-English.pdf.
7 This section is adapted from Dutfield (2004).
8 This section is adapted from Garforth and Frison (2007).
9 Most of this section was written by Davinia Ovett, 3D→THREE, in June 2006.
10 See Committee on Economic, Social and Cultural Rights, General Comment No 12 (1991) 'The right to adequate food?' E/C.12/1999/5, 12 May 1999.
11 See, for example, Committee on the Rights of the Child, Concluding Observations, El Salvador, CRC/C/15/Add.232, 30 June 2004.
12 See Commission on Human Rights, 'The right to food', Human Rights Resolution 2005/18, E/CN.4/RES/2005/18, 15 April 2005.
13 See Report of the Special Rapporteur on the right to food, E/CN.4/2006/44, 16 March 2006.

Chapter 8

1 Quoted in *NIH News*, 13 June 2007, available at www.genome.gov/25521554, accessed 16 July 2007, commenting on The ENCODE Project Consortium (2007) 'Identification and analysis of functional elements in 1% of the human genome by the ENCODE pilot project' *Nature*, vol 447, 14 June 2007, pp800–816.

References

3D→THREE (Trade, Human Rights, Equitable Economy) (2006) 'Intellectual property and human rights: Is the distinction clear now? An assessment of the Committee on Economic, Social and Cultural Rights' General Comment No 17 (2005)', *Policy Brief*, no 3, 3D→THREE, Geneva, available at www.3dthree.org/en/pages.php?IDcat=5

Abbott, F. M. (2004) 'The Doha Declaration on the TRIPS Agreement and public health and the contradictory trend in bilateral and regional free trade agreements', Occasional Paper 14, QUNO, Geneva, www.quno.org/economicissues/intellectual-property/intellectualLinks.htm, accessed 2 August 2007

Abbott, F. M. (2003) 'Trade diplomacy, the rule of law and the problem of asymmetric risks in TRIPS', Occasional Paper 13, QUNO, Geneva, www.quno.org/economicissues/intellectual-property/intellectualLinks.htm, accessed 2 August 2007

Abbott, F. M. and Correa, C. (2007) 'World Trade Organization accession agreements: Intellectual property issues', QUNO, Geneva, available at www.quno.org/economicissues/intellectual-property/intellectualLinks.htm, accessed 2 August 2007

Abraham, C. (2007) 'West knows best', *New Scientist*, 21 July, vol 195, no 2613, pp35–37

ActionAid (2003) *Trade Related Intellectual Property Rights*, Action Aid, London

ActionAid (2007) 'The World Bank and agriculture: A critical review of the World Bank's World Development Report 2008', ActionAid, Johannesburg, available at www.actionaid.org/main.aspx?PageID=947, accessed 20 October 2007

ActionAid International (2005) *Power Hungry – Six Reasons to Regulate Global Food Corporations*, ActionAid International, Johannesburg

Adcock, M. and Llewelyn, M. (2000) 'Micro-organisms – Definition and options under TRIPS', Occasional Paper 2, QUNO, Geneva, www.quno.org/economicissues/intellectual-property/intellectualLinks.htm, accessed 2 August 2007

African Group (2005) 'The African proposal for the establishment of a development agenda for WIPO', Document IIM/3/2, Third Session of the Inter-Sessional Intergovernmental Meeting on a Development Agenda for WIPO, July 18, Geneva

African Group (2001) 'Proposal presented by the African Group to the First Meeting of the Intergovernmental Committee on Intellectual Property and Genetic Resources, Traditional Knowledge and Folklore', Document WIPO/GRTKF/IC/1/10, Annex, WIPO, Geneva

Agosti, D. (2006) 'Biodiversity data are out of local taxonomists' reach', *Nature*, vol 439, p392

Altieri, M. and von der Weid, J. M. (2000) 'Prospects for agro-ecological natural resource management in the 21st century', Global Forum on Agricultural Research (GFAR), Dresden, Germany, available at www.egfar.org

Andersen, R. (2006) 'Realising farmers' rights under the International Treaty on Plant Genetic Resources for Food and Agriculture', summary of findings from the Farmers' Rights Project (Phase 1), FNI Report 11/2006, Fridtjof Nansen Institute, Lysaker, Norway, available at www.fni.no/doc&pdf/FNI-R1106.pdf

Barton, J. (2003) 'Intellectual property, biotechnology, and international trade: Two examples', in T. Cottier and P. C. Mavroidis (eds), M. Panizzon and S. Lacey (associate eds) *Intellectual Property: Trade, Competition, and Sustainable Development, The World Trade Forum*, vol 3, University of Michigan Press, Ann Arbor, MI

Barton, J. (1999) 'Intellectual property management', in Gabrielle J. Persley and John J. Doyle (eds) *Biotechnology for Developing-Country Agriculture: Problems and Opportunities*, 2020 Focus No 02, IFPRI, Washington DC available at www.ifpri.org/2020/focus/focus02.asp

Barton, J. H. (1998) 'The impact of contemporary patent law on plant biotechnology research' in *Intellectual Property Rights III: Global Genetic Resources: Access and Property Rights*, CSSA Miscellaneous Publication, Crop Science Society of America, American Society of Agronomy, Madison, WI, pp85–97

Barton, J. and Berger, P. (2001) 'Patenting agriculture', *Issues in Science and Technology*, vol 17, pp43–50

Baumüller, H. and Apea, Y. (2006) 'A preliminary analysis of the WTO biotech ruling', *Bridges Monthly Review*, year 10, no 7, pp13–14

Benkler, Y. (2006) *The Wealth of Networks: How Social Production Transforms Markets and Freedom*, Yale University Press, New Haven, CT, and London

Binenbaum, E., Nottenburg, C., Pardy, P. G., Wright, B. D. and Zambrano, P. (2003) 'South–North trade, intellectual property jurisdictions, and freedom to operate in agricultural research on staple crops', *Economic Development and Cultural Change*, vol 51, no 2, January, pp309–336

Blakeney, M. (2001) 'Intellectual property rights and food security', *Bio-Science Law Review*, vol 4, no 5, pp1–13

Boyle, J. (2004) 'A manifesto on WIPO and the future of intellectual property', *Duke Law and Technology Review*, 9 September, pp1–12, available at www.law.duke.edu/boylesite, accessed 20 October 2007

Boyle, J. (2001) 'The second enclosure movement and the construction of the public domain', paper presented at Conference on the Public Domain, Duke University School of Law, Durham, NC, 9–11 November, www.law.duke.edu/pd

Boyle, J. (1996) *Shamans, Software & Spleens – Law and the Construction of the Information Society*, Harvard University Press, Cambridge, MA

Bragdon, S. (ed) (2004) 'International law of relevance to plant genetic resources: A practical review for scientists and other professionals working with plant genetic resources', *Issues in Genetic Resources*, no 10, www.bioversityinternational.org/Publications/pubfile.asp?ID_PUB=937

Bragdon, S. H. (1996) 'The evolution and future of law of sustainable development: Lessons from the Convention on Biological Diversity', *Georgetown International Environmental Law Review*, vol VIII, issue 3, pp389–513

Bragdon, S. H. (1992) 'National sovereignty and global environmental responsibility: Can the tension be reconciled for the conservation of biological diversity?', *Harvard International Law Journal*, vol 33, no 2, pp381–392

Bragdon, S., Fowler, C., Franca, Z. and Goldberg, E. (eds) (2005) *Law and Policy of Relevance to the Management of Plant Genetic Resources: Learning Module with Review of Regional Policy Instruments, Developments and Trends*, 2nd edition, IPGRI, Rome

Braithwaite, J. and Drahos, P. (2000) *Global Business Regulation*, Cambridge University Press, Cambridge, UK

Brockway, L. H. (1979) *Science and Colonial Expansion: The Role of the British Royal Botanic Gardens*, Yale University Press, New Haven, CT

Burgmans, A. and Fitzgerald, N. (chairmen of Unilever) (2002) *Unilever Annual Report*, Unilever, UK and The Netherlands

Burton, G. and Phillips, B. (2005) 'Developing a system of virtual certificates of origin and provenance', paper presented to the International Expert Workshop on Access to Genetic Resources and benefit sharing, 20–23 September, Cape Town, South Africa

Byerlee, D. and Traxler, G. (1995) 'National and international wheat improvement research in the post-green revolution period: Evolution and impacts', *American Journal of Agricultural Economics*, vol 77, no 2, pp 268–278

Caruso, D. (2007) 'A challenge to gene theory, a tougher look at biotech', *New York Times*, 1 July

Cassaday, K., Smale, M., Fowler, C and Heisey, P. (2001) 'Benefits from giving and receiving genetic resources: The case of wheat', *Plant Genetic Resources Newsletter*, no 127, pp1–10

CBD (Convention on Biological Diversity) (2007a) 'Recent developments in international law relating to liability and redress, including the status of international environment-related third party liability instruments: Note by the Executive Secretary', Document UNEP/CBD/BS/WG-L&R/3/INF/2, CBD, Montreal, Canada

CBD (2007b) 'Report of the meeting of the Group of Technical Experts on an internationally recognized certificate of origin/source/legal provenance', Document UNEP/CBD/WG-ABS/5/2, CBD, Montreal, Canada

CBD (2006a) 'Compilation of submissions provided by parties, governments, indigenous and local communities, international organizations and relevant stakeholders regarding an internationally recognized certificate of origin/source/legal provenance: Note by the Executive Secretary', document UNEP/CBD/GTE-ABS/1/3, CBD, Montreal, Canada

CBD (2006b) 'Report of the Ad Hoc Open-Ended Working Group on Access and benefit sharing on the work of its fourth meeting', Document

UNEP/CBD/COP/8/6, CBD, Montreal, Canada

CBD (2006c) 'Technology transfer and cooperation: Preparation of technical studies that further explore and analyse the role of intellectual property rights in technology transfer in the context of the convention on biological diversity: Note by the Executive Secretary', Document UNEP/CBD/COP/8/INF/32, CBD, Montreal, Canada

CBD (2006d) 'Interrelation of access to genetic resources and disclosure requirements in applications for intellectual property rights: Report of the World Intellectual Property Organization (WIPO)', Document UNEP/CBD/COP/8/INF/7, available at www.cbd.int/doc/meetings/cop/cop-08/information/cop-08-inf-07-en.pdf

CBD (2004) 'Decisions adopted by the Conference of the Parties to the Convention on Biological Diversity at its seventh meeting', CBD, Montreal, Document UNEP/CBD/COP/7/21/Part 2, p306, available at www.cbd.int/doc/meetings/cop/cop-07/official/cop-07-21-part2-en.pdf

CBD (2003) 'Technical study on disclosure requirements related to genetic resources and traditional knowledge: Submission by the World Intellectual Property Organization (WIPO)', document UNEP/CBD/COP/7/INF/17, available at www.cbd.int/doc/meetings/cop/cop-07/information/cop-07-inf-17-en.pdf

CDC (2003) 'CDC Statement on the guiding principles on intellectual property rights relating to genetic resources', in *Booklet of CGIAR Centre Policy Instruments, Guidelines and Statements on Genetic Resources, Biotechnology and Intellectual Property Rights*, Version II, SGRP, Rome, p33, available at www.bioversityinternational.org/publications/pdf/1178.pdf

CBD (2002) 'Thematic programmes of work – Progress reports on implementation: Agricultural biological diversity: Assessing the impact of trade liberalization on the conservation and sustainable use of agricultural biological diversity: Note by the Executive Secretary', Document UNEP/CBD/COP/6/INF/2, CBD, Montreal, Canada

CEC (Commission of the European Communities) (2002) 'Life sciences and biotechnology – A strategy for Europe', report to the Council, the European Parliament, the Economic and Social Committee, and the Committee of the Regions, full report available at www.europa.eu.int/comm/biotechnology/pdf/policypaper_en.pdf

CEC (2004) *Maize and Biodiversity: The Effects of Transgenic Maize in Mexico*, Commission for Environmental Cooperation, Montreal, Canada

CGIAR (2003) 'Guiding principles for the Consultative Group on International Agricultural Research centres on intellectual property and genetic resources', in *Booklet of CGIAR Centre Policy Instruments, Guidelines and Statements on Genetic Resources, Biotechnology and Intellectual Property Rights*, Version II, SGRP, Rome, p30, available at www.bioversityinternational.org/publications/pdf/1178.pdf

CGRFA (Commission on Genetic Resources for Food and Agriculture) (2007) 'Updated information provided by the International Centre for Tropical Agriculture (CIAT) regarding its request for a re-examination of US Patent No 5,894,079, CGRFA-11/07/Inf.10', 11th Session, CGRFA, Rome

Charnovitz, S. (2001) 'Rethinking WTO trade sanctions', *American Journal of International Law*, vol 95, pp792–832

Chang, H. J. (2002) *Kicking Away the Ladder – Development Strategy in Historical Perspective*, Anthem Press, London

CIEL (Center for International Environmental Law) and South Centre (2005) 'Protecting traditional knowledge: Misappropriation, intellectual property, and the future of the IGC', available at www.ciel.org/Publications/IGC8SC_CIEL_June2005_FINAL.pdf

Cook, K. (2002) 'Liability: "No liability, no protocol"' in C. Bail, R. Falkner and H. Marquand (eds) *The Cartagena Protocol on Biosafety: Reconciling Trade in Biotechnology with Environment and Development?*, Royal Institute of International Affairs, London, pp371–384

Correa, C. (2004a) 'The proposed Substantive Patent Law Treaty: A review of selected provisions', TRADE Working Paper 17, South Centre, Geneva, www.southcentre.org/publications/workingpapers/wp17.pdf

Correa, C. (2004b) 'Bilateral investment agreements: Agents of new global standards for the protection of intellectual property rights?', GRAIN, available at www.grain.org/briefings/?id=186

Correa, C. (2002) 'Protection and promotion of traditional medicines: Implications for public health in developing countries', *South Perspectives*, December, South Centre, Geneva, www.south-centre.org/publications/traditionalmedicine/toc.htm

Correa, C. (2000) 'Options for the implementation of farmers' rights at the national level', TRADE Working Paper 8, South Centre, Geneva, www.southcentre.org/publications/publist_category_WorkingPapers_index.htm

Correa, C. M. and Musungu, S. F. (2002) *The WIPO Patent Agenda: The Risks For Developing Countries*, South Centre, Geneva, November

Correa, C. et al (2007) 'EU in danger of breaking its promise to the poor', *Financial Times*, May 24

Crosby, A.W. (1986) *Ecological Imperialism: The Biological Expansion of Europe, 900–1900*, Cambridge University Press, Cambridge, UK

Cosbey, A. and Burgiel, S. (2000) 'The Cartagena Protocol on Biosafety: An analysis of results', International Institute for Sustainable Development, Winnipeg, Manitoba, Canada

Crucible II Group, The (2001) *Seeding Solutions Volume 2: Options for National Laws and Governing Control over Genetic Resources and Biological Innovations*, IDRC, IPGRI and Dag Hammarskjöld Foundation, Ottawa, Rome and Uppsala

Dalmeny, K., Hanna, E. and Lobstein, T. (2003) 'Broadcasting bad health: Why food marketing to children needs to be controlled', report by the International Association of Consumer Food Organizations for the World Health Organization consultation on a global strategy for diet and health, International Association of Consumer Food Organizations (IACFO), London

Dalton, R. (2006) 'Cashing in on the rich coast', *Nature*, vol 442, pp567–569

Darwin, C. (1859) *On the Origin of Species by Means of Natural Selection, or the Preservation of Favoured Races in the Struggle for Life*, John Murray, London

de Beer, J. (2007) 'The rights and responsibilities of biotech patent owners' *University of British Columbia Law Review*, vol 40, no 1

de Schutter, O. (2007) 'Human rights principles for international trade', paper presented at Conference on Reconciling Trade and Human Rights, Ottawa, 28–29 May

Dhar, B. (2002) '*Sui generis* systems for plant variety protection: Options under TRIPS', Quaker United Nations Office (QUNO), Geneva, www.quno.org/economicissues/intellectual-property/intellectualLinks.htm, accessed 2

August 2007

Diamond, J. (2005) *Collapse: How Societies Choose to Fail or Survive*, Allen Lane, London

Diamond, J. (1997) *Guns, Germs and Steel: The Fates of Human Societies*, W.W. Norton & Company, New York

Drahos, P. (2007a) 'Four lessons for developing countries from the negotiations over access to medicines, *Liverpool Law Review*, vol 28, no 1, April, pp11–39

Drahos, P. (2007b) 'Patent reform for innovation and risk management: A separation of powers approach', *Knowledge Ecology Studies*, Knowledge Ecology International, available at www.kestudies.org/ojs/index.php/kes, accessed 29 July 2007

Drahos, P. (1996) *A Philosophy of Intellectual Property*, Dartmouth, Aldershot, UK

Drahos, P. (1995) 'Global property rights in information: The story of TRIPS at the GATT', *Prometheus*, vol 13, no 1, pp6–19

Drahos, P. and Braithwaite, J. (2002) *Information Feudalism – Who Owns the Knowledge Economy*, Earthscan, London

Dutfield, G. (2007) 'Should we regulate technology through the patent system? The case of terminator technology', in H. Somsen (ed) *The Regulatory Challenge of Biotechnology: Human Genetics, Food and Patents*, Edward Elgar, Cheltenham, pp203–213

Dutfield, G. (2006a) 'Protecting traditional knowledge: Pathways for the future', draft paper, UNCTAD-ICTSD Series, Geneva, available at www.iprsonline.org/resources/tk.htm, accessed 11 September 2007

Dutfield, G. (2006b) 'Promoting local innovation as a development strategy: Innovations case discussion: The honey bee network', *Innovations: Technology, Governance, Globalization*, summer, pp 67–77

Dutfield, G. (2004) *Intellectual Property, Biogenetic Resources and Traditional Knowledge*, Earthscan, London

Dutfield, G. (2003a) *Intellectual Property Rights and the Life Science Industries: A Twentieth Century History*, Ashgate, Aldershot, UK

Dutfield, G. (2003b) 'Protecting traditional knowledge and folklore: A review in diplomacy and policy formulation', Issues Paper no 1, UNCTAD-ICTSD Series, Geneva, available at www.ictsd.org/pubs/ictsd_series/iprs/CS_dutfield.pdf, accessed 11 September 2007

Dutfield, G. (2002) 'Sharing the benefits of biodiversity: Is there a role for the patent system?', *Journal of World Intellectual Property*, vol 5, no 6, pp 899–931

Dutfield, G. (2000) *Intellectual Property Rights, Trade and Biodiversity*, Earthscan, London

Dutfield, G. and Suthersanen, U. (2005) 'Harmonisation or differentiation in intellectual property protection? The lessons of history', *Prometheus*, vol 23, no 2, pp131–147

Egziabher, T. B. G. (2002) 'The human individual and community in the conservation and sustainable use of biological resources', Darwin Lecture, London, available at www.darwin.gov.uk/news/initiative/lecture_2002.html

El-Said, H. and El-Said, M. (2005) 'TRIPS, bilateralism, multilateralism and implications for developing countries: Jordan's drug sector', *Manchester Journal of International Economic Law*, vol 2, p59

EPO (2007) 'Scenarios for the future: How might IP regimes evolve by 2025? What global legitimacy might such regimes have?' EPO, Munich, also available at www.epo.org/

Epstein, R. (1995) *Simple Rules for a Complex World*, Harvard University Press, Cambridge, MA

Esquinas-Alcázar, J. and Hilmi, A. (2007) 'Breve Historia de las Negociaciones del Tratado Internacional sobre los Recursos Fitogeneticos para la Alimentacion y la Agricultura' ['A brief history of the negotiations of the International Treaty on Plant Genetic Resources for Food and Agriculture'], *Revista de CATIE: Recursos Naturales y Ambiente*

ETC Group (2007) 'Extreme genetic engineering: An introduction to synthetic biology', available at www.etcgroup.org

ETC Group (2005) 'Global seed industry concentration – 2005', Communiqué No 90, Action Group on Erosion, Technology and Concentration, Ottawa, available at www.etcgroup.org/en/

ETC Group (2004) 'Down on the farm: The impact of nano-scale technologies on food and agriculture', www.etcgroup.org/en/materials/publications.html?pub_id=80

Evenson, R. E., Gollin, D. and Santaniello, V. (eds) (1998) *Agricultural Values of Plant Genetic Resources*, CAB International, Wallingford, UK

Falcon, W. P. and Fowler, C. (2002) 'Carving up the commons – Emergence of a new international regime for germplasm, development and transfer', *Food Policy*, vol 27, pp197–222

FAO (2007) 'The ecosystem approach applied to food and agriculture: Status and needs', Document CGRFA-11/0715.4 Rev.1, FAO, Rome, www.fao.org/ag/cgrfa/cgrfa11.htm

FAO (2005) 'Agreement between FAO and WIPO (2005)' Document C 2005/LIM/6, FAO, Rome

FAO (2001) *State of Food Insecurity*, FAO, Rome

FAO (1999) 'Issues paper: The multifunctional character of agriculture and land', FAO/Netherlands Conference on the Multifunctional Character of Agriculture and Land, Conference Background Paper no 1, Maastricht, September

FAO (1998) *The State of the World's Plant Genetic Resources for Food and Agriculture*, FAO, Rome

FEC (Food Ethics Council) (2002) 'TRIPS with everything? Intellectual property and the farming world', Food Ethics Council, London, www.foodethicscouncil.org/node/51, accessed 2 August 2007

Feyissa, R. (2006) 'Farmers' rights in Ethiopia: A case study', Background Study 5 for the Farmers' Rights Project, Fridtjof Nansen Institute, www.fni.no/doc&pdf/FNI-R0706.pdf, accessed 24 May 2007

Fikkert, K. A. (2005) 'Judgement on essentially derived varieties (EDVs) in the first instance', *Plant Variety Protection*, vol 99, pp9–10

Finger, J. M. (2005) 'A diplomat's economics: Reciprocity in the Uruguay Round negotiations', *World Trade Review*, vol 4, p27

Fowler, C. (1994) *Unnatural Selection: Technology, Politics and Plant Evolution*, Gordon and Breach, Yverdon, Switzerland

Fowler, C., Engels, J. and Frison, E. (2004) 'The question of derivatives: Promoting use and ensuring availability of non-proprietary plant genetic resources', *Issues in Genetic Resources*, no XII, September, IPGRI, Rome

Fowler, C. and Hodgkin, T. (2004) 'Plant genetic resources for food and agriculture: Assessing global availability', *Annual Review of Environmental Resources*, vol 29, pp10.1–10.37

Fowler, C., Smale, M. and Gaiji, S. (2001) 'Unequal exchange: Recent transfers of agricultural resources and their implications for developing countries', *Development Policy Review*, vol 19, no 2

Freund, C. (2003) 'Reciprocity in free trade agreements', World Bank, April, http://wbln0018.worldbank.org/LAC/LACInfoClient.nsf/5996dfbf9847f67d852567360

05dc67c/5caa488a9e5d4cff85256caa005ba2b5/ $FILE/Freund%20reciprocity%20jan-03.pdf

Friends of Development (2005) 'Proposal to establish a development agenda for WIPO: An elaboration of issues raised in Document WO/GA/31/11', WIPO Document IIM/1/4, WIPO, Geneva, available at www.wipo.int/meetings/en/doc_details.jsp?doc_id=42376, accessed 11 September 2007

Gaiji, S. (2006) 'Through transparency comes trust – Possibilities for monitoring using existing information systems', presentation at the Second Meeting of the Contact Group, Alnarp, Sweden, April, http://singer.cgiar.org/search/summary/transuser.php, accessed 12 July 2007

Gallochat, A. (2002) 'The criteria for patentability: Where are the boundaries?' paper prepared for the WIPO Conference on the International Patent System, 25–27 March, Geneva

Garforth, K. (2007) 'Teff agreement', *Blogging Biodiversity*, http://kathryn.garforthmitchell.net/?p=109, accessed 24 May 2007

Garforth, K. (2006) 'The ABIA and the SCBD', *Blogging Biodiversity*, http://kathryn.garforthmitchell.net/?p=33, accessed 12 June 2007

Garforth, K. (2003) 'When biosafety becomes binding: Marking the entry into force of the UN Cartagena Protocol on Biosafety', Centre for International Sustainable Development Law, Montreal, Canada, www.cisdl.org/pdf/Biosafety_LegalBrief.pdf

Garforth, K. and Frison, C. (2007) 'Key issues in the relationship between the Convention on Biological Diversity and the International Treaty on Plant Genetic Resources for Food and Agriculture', occasional paper, Quaker International Affairs Programme (QIAP), Ottawa, www.qiap.ca/pages/publications.html, accessed 2 Aug 2007

Garforth, K. and Ainslie, P. (2006) 'When worlds collide: Biotechnology meets organic farming in *Hoffman v. Monsanto*', *Journal of Environmental Law*, vol 18, pp459–477

Garforth, K., Manga, S., Frison, C., Cabrera J. M. and Cordonier Segger, M. C. (2005) 'Biosafety scoping study', Centre for International Sustainable Development Law, Montreal, Canada

Garforth, K. and Cabrera, J. M. (2004) 'Sustainable biodiversity law: Global access, local benefits: A scoping study on future research priorities for access to genetic resources and benefit sharing', Centre for International Sustainable Development Law, Montreal, Canada

Gari, J. A. (2001) 'Conservation, use and control of biodiversity: Local regimes of biodiversity versus the global expansion of intellectual property rights', *Perspectives on Intellectual Property*, vol 9, special issue on 'IP in Biodiversity and Agriculture'

Gervais, D. (2003) *The TRIPS Agreement: Drafting History and Analysis*, 2nd edition, Sweet and Maxwell, London

Glowka, L., Burhenne-Guilmin, F. and Synge, H. (1994) *A Guide to the Convention on Biological Diversity*, IUCN, Gland, Switzerland

Gollin, M. A. (2008) *Driving Innovation: Intellectual Property Strategies for a Dynamic World*, Cambridge University Press, Cambridge, UK

Gowers, A. (2006) *Gowers Review of Intellectual Property*, HM Treasury, HMSO, UK, available at www.hm-treasury.gov.uk/independent_reviews/gowers_review_intellectual_property/gowersreview_index.cfm, accessed 12 October 2007

Graff, G. D., Cullen, S. E., Bradford, K. J., Zilberman, D. and Bennett, A. B. (2003) 'The public–private structure of intellectual property ownership in agricultural biotechnology', *Nature Biotechnology*, vol 21, no 9, pp989–995

Graff, L. (2002) 'The precautionary principle' in C. Bail, R. Falkner and H. Marquand (eds) *The Cartagena Protocol on Biosafety: Reconciling Trade in Biotechnology with Environment and Development?*, Royal Institute of International Affairs, London

GRAIN (2006a) 'Argentina: Driven from the GE Garden', www.grain.org/research/contamination.cfm?id=366, accessed 12 June 2007

GRAIN (2006b) 'Economic Partnership Agreement between Eastern and Southern Africa and the European Community – Title VI - Intellectual property rights', 4th Draft EPA/8th RNF/24-8-2006, www.grain.org/bio-ipr/?id=492, accessed 2 August 2007

GRAIN (2006c) 'FTAs: Trading away traditional knowledge', available at www.grain.org/briefings/?id=196

GRAIN (2005a) 'Food sovereignty: Turning the global food system upside down', *Seedling*, GRAIN, April

GRAIN (2005b) 'The FAO seed treaty – From farmers' rights to breeders' privileges', *Seedling*, GRAIN, October

GRAIN (2005c) 'Bilateral agreements imposing TRIPS-plus intellectual property rights on biodiversity in developing countries', *Seedling*, GRAIN, September

GRAIN (2003) 'One global patent system? WIPO's substantive patent law treaty', *Seedling*, GRAIN, October.

GRAIN (2001) 'TRIPS-plus through the back door – How bilateral treaties impose much stronger rules for IPRs on life than the WTO', GRAIN in cooperation with South Asia Network for Food, Ecology and Culture (SANFEC), available at www.grain.org/briefings/?id=6, accessed 11 September 2007

GRAIN (1998) 'Ten reasons not to join UPOV', GRAIN, available at www.grain.org/briefings/?id=1 accessed 11 September 2007

GRULAC (2001) *Traditional Knowledge and the Need to Give it Adequate Intellectual Property Protection*, Group of Countries of Latin America and the Caribbean, Submission to the Intergovernmental Committee on Intellectual Property and Genetic Resources, Traditional Knowledge and Folklore, First Session, Geneva, April 30 to May 3, 2001, WIPO document WIPO/GRTKF/IC/1/5, March 16, 2001

Gura, S. (2007) 'Livestock genetics companies: Concentration and proprietary strategies of an emerging power in the global food economy', League for Pastoral Peoples and Endogenous Livestock Development, Ober-Ramstadt, Germany, www.pastoralpeoples.org

Halewood, M, Gaiji, S. and Upadhyaya, H. (2005) 'Germplasm flows in and out of Kenya and Uganda through the CGIAR: A case study of patterns of exchange and use to consider in developing national policies', IPGRI, Italy and ICRISAT, India

Hamilton, N. (1993) 'Who owns dinner: Evolving legal mechanisms for ownership of plant genetic resources', *Tulsa Law Journal*, vol 28, pp587–646

Harrison, J. (2007) 'Envisioning a multilateral system that prioritizes human rights: Addressing current problems and identifying strategic openings', paper presented at Conference on Reconciling Trade and Human Rights, Ottawa

Heitz, A. (1987) 'The history of plant variety protection', in *The First Twenty-five Years of the International*

Convention for the Protection of New Varieties of Plant*, UPOV, Geneva

Hettinger, E. C. (1989) 'Justifying intellectual property', *Philosophy and Public Affairs*, vol 18, no 1, pp31–52

Hope, J. (2008) *BioBazaar: Biotechnology and the Open Source Revolution*, Harvard University Press, Cambridge, MA; see also http://regnet.anu.edu.au/program/people/link_documents/jhope.php, accessed 20 Oct 2007

ICTSD (International Centre for Trade and Sustainable Development) (2002) 'WIPO Committee: Countries divided on need for and scope of legal system to protect TK', *Bridges Trade BioRes*, vol 2, no 12, www.ictsd.org/biores/02-06-27/story1.htm, accessed 12 June 2007

IFCNR (International Foundation for the Conservation of Natural Resources) (2003) 'CBD Treaty called "disaster" and "nightmare" to science', http://biotech.ifcnr.com/news.cfm?ArticleTypeID=3, accessed 2 August 2003

IFPRI (International Food Policy Research Institute) (2002) 'Sound choices for development, The impact of public investments in rural India And China', IPGRI, Washington, DC, www.ifpri.org/pubs/ib/ib7.pdf

IISD (International Institute for Sustainable Development) (2006a) *Earth Negotiations Bulletin*, vol 9, no 369, June, www.iisd.ca/vol09/enb09369e.html

IISD (2006b) 'Summary of the fourth meeting of the Working Group on Access and benefit sharing of the Convention on Biological Diversity: 30 January–3 February 2006', *Earth Negotiations Bulletin*, vol 9, no 344

IPGRI (International Plant Genetic Resources Institute) (1999) 'Key questions for decision-makers: Protection of plant varieties under the WTO Agreement on Trade-Related Aspects of Intellectual Property Rights', IPGRI, Rome

IPRs Commission (Commission on Intellectual Property Rights) (2002) *Integrating Intellectual Property Rights and Development Policies*, IPRs Commission, London, September, www.iprcommission.org

ISF (International Seed Federation) (2007) 'Position paper on plant genetic resources for food and agriculture', International Seed Federation, Christchurch, May, available at www.worldseed.org/Position_papers/PGRFA.htm, accessed 19 October 2007

Ivars, B. (2004) 'Government user measures –
Incentives for compliance', in M. Bellot-Rojas
and S. Bernier (eds) *International Expert Workshop
on Access to Genetic Resources and Benefit Sharing:
Record of Discussion*, Cuernavaca, Mexico, 24–27
October 2004, CONABIO and Environment
Canada, pp305–308

Ivars, B. and Schneider, G. (2005) 'Norwegian ABS
legislative developments', *Bulletin of the University of
California – Davis ABS Project*, Spring

Jaffé, W. and van Wijk, J. (1995) *The Impact of Plant
Breeders' Rights in Developing Countries: Debate and
Experience in Argentina, Chile, Colombia, Mexico and
Uruguay*, Directorate General for International
Cooperation, Ministry of Foreign Affairs, The
Hague

Jasanoff, S. (2005) *Designs on Nature: Science and
Democracy in Europe and the United States*, Princeton
University Press, Princeton, NJ, and Oxford, UK

Jaszi, P. (2004) 'Rights in basic information: A
general perspective', paper presented at the
UNCTAD-ICTSD Dialogue on 'Moving the Pro-
development IP Agenda Forward: Preserving
Public Goods in Health, Education and
Learning', Bellagio, Italy, 29 November–3
December

Jefferson R. (2007) 'Science as social enterprise: The
CAMBIA BiOS Initiative', *Innovations: Technology,
Governance, Globalization*, 2006, vol 1, no 4, Fall,
pp13–44, available at www.cambia.org

Jenkins, R. V. (1975) *Images and Enterprise: Technology
and the American Photographic Industry 1839 to 1925*,
Johns Hopkins University Press, Baltimore, MD

Jensen, W. and Salisbury F. (1984) *Botany*, Wadsworth
Publishing Company, Belmont, CA

Jördens, R (2002) 'Legal and technological develop-
ments leading to this symposium: UPOV's
perspective', paper presented at WIPO-UPOV
Symposium on the Co-existence of Patents and
Plant Breeders' Rights in the Promotion of
Biotechnological Developments, Geneva, 25
October, www.upov.int/en/documents/
Symposium2002/pdf/wipo-upov_sym_02_
2.pdf#search='J%C3%B6rdens%20upov%
20symposium

Kingston, W. (2006) 'Trademark *registration* is not a
right', *Journal of Macromarketing*, vol 26, no 1, June,
pp17–26

Keohane, R. (1969) 'Lilliputians' dilemma: Small
states in international politics', *International
Organization*, no 23, pp291–310

Kloppenburg, J. R. (2004) *First the Seed: The Political
Economy of Plant Biotechnology, 1492–2000*, 2nd
edition, University of Wisconsin Press, Madison,
WI

Kloppenburg, J. R. Jr (1988) *First the Seed: The Political
Economy of Plant Biotechnology*, Cambridge
University Press, Cambridge, UK

Kloppenburg, J. R. Jr and Kleinman, D. L. (1988)
'Plant genetic resources: The common bowl', in
J. R. Kloppenburg Jr (ed) *Seeds and Sovereignty: The
Use and Control of Plant Genetic Resources*, Duke
University Press, Durham, NC

Kryder, R. D., Kowalski, S. P. and Krattiger, A. F.
(2000) 'The intellectual and technical property
components of pro-vitamin A rice (Golden
Rice^{TM}): A preliminary freedom-to-operate
review', ISAAA Brief 20, Ithaca, NY

Lappé, M. and Bailey, B. (1998) *Against the Grain:
Biotechnology and the Corporate Takeover of Your Food*,
Common Courage Press, Monroe, ME

Lang, T. and Heasman, M. (2004) *Food Wars: The
Global Battle for Mouth, Minds and Markets*,
Earthscan, London

Lesser, W. (1997) 'The role of intellectual property
rights in biotechnology transfer under the
Convention on Biological Diversity', ISAAA
Brief 3, Ithaca, NY, www.isaaa.org/Briefs/
3/briefs.htm

Lettington, R. J. L. and Nnadozie, K. (2003) *A Review
of the Intergovernmental Committee on Genetic Resources,
Traditional Knowledge and Folklore at WIPO*, South
Centre, Geneva

Lewontin, R. C. (1993) *The Doctrine of DNA: Biology as
Ideology*, Penguin Books, London

Lim, E. S. (2007) 'El acuerdo normalizado de trans-
ferencia de material' ['The Standard Material
Transfer Agreement'], *Revista de CATIE: Recursos
Naturales y Ambiente*

Longping, Y. (2004) 'Hybrid rice for food security in
the world', paper presented at FAO Rice
Conference, Rome, 12–13 February, Document
FAO Rice Conference 04/CRS.21

Louwaars, N. P., Tripp, R., Eaton, D., Henson-
Apollonio, V., Hu, R., Mendoza, M., Muhhuku, F.,
Pal, S. and Wekundah, J. (2005) *Impacts of
Strengthened Intellectual Property Rights Regimes on the
Plant Breeding Industry in Developing Countries. A
Synthesis of Five Case Studies*, study commissioned
by the World Bank, Wageningen UR,
Wageningen, The Netherlands, available at
www.iprsonline.org/resources/docs/LouwaarsC

GN_Plants_05.pdf

Macdonald, S. (2001) 'Exploring the hidden costs of patents', Occasional Paper 4, Quaker United Nations Office (QUNO), Geneva, www.quno.org/economicissues/intellectual-property/intellectualLinks.htm, accessed 2 August 2007

Mackenzie, R., Burhenne-Guilmin, F., La Viña, A. G. M. and Werksman, J. D. (2003) *An Explanatory Guide to the Cartagena Protocol on Biosafety*, IUCN, Gland, Switzerland

Mannion, A. M. (1995) *Agriculture and Environmental Change: Temporal and Spatial Dimensions,* John Wiley and Sons Ltd, London

Maskus, K. E. (2006) 'Reforming US patent policy – Getting the incentives right', Council on Foreign Relations, CSR no 19, November, www.cfr.org/publication/12087/reforming_us_patent_policy.html?breadcrumb=%2Fpublication%2Fby_type%2Fspecial_report

Maskus, K. E. (2000) *Intellectual Property Rights in the Global Economy,* Institute for International Economics, Washington, DC

Maskus, K. E. and Reichman, J. (eds) (2005) *International Public Goods and Transfer of Technology Under a Globalized Intellectual Property Regime*, particularly Part III ('Sectoral Issues: Essential Medicines and Traditional Knowledge'), Cambridge University Press, Cambridge, UK

Matthews, D. (2006) 'NGOs, intellectual property rights and multilateral institutions', Report of the IP-NGOs research project, Queen Mary Intellectual Property Research Institute, London, www.ipngos.org

Matthews, D. (2002) *Globalising Intellectual Property Rights: The TRIPS Agreement*, Routledge, London

May, C. (2007) *The World Intellectual Property Organization: Resurgence and the Development Agenda*, Global Institutions Series, Routledge, London

May, C. (2002) 'How intellectual property rights could work better for developing countries and poor people', presentation to the Commission on Intellectual Property Rights Conference, London, 21–22 February

May, C. (2000) *A Global Political Economy of Intellectual Property Rights – The New Enclosures?*, Routledge, London

McConnell, F. (1996) *The Biodiversity Convention: A Negotiating History*, Kluwer Law International, London

McGraw, D. M. (2002) 'The story of the Biodiversity Convention: From negotiation to implementation', in P. G. Le Prestre (ed) *Governing Global Biodiversity: The Evolution and Implementation of the Convention on Biological Diversity*, Ashgate, Burlington, VT

Memorandum of the Director General (2001) 'Agenda for development of the international patent system', Document A/36/14, prepared for the Thirty-Sixth Series of Meetings of the Assemblies of the Member States of WIPO, WIPO, Geneva

Mepham, B. (2005) *Bioethics: An Introduction for the Biosciences*, Oxford University Press, Oxford

Millstone, E. and Lang, T. (2003) *The Atlas of Food – Who Eats What, Where and Why*, Earthscan, London

Mirza, Z. (1999) 'WTO, TRIPS, pharmaceuticals and health: Impacts and strategies', *Development*, vol 42, no 4, pp92–97

Mooney, P. R. (1983) 'The law of the seed: Another development and plant genetic resources', *Development Dialogue*, vol 1, no 2, pp7–172

MSF (Médecins Sans Frontières) (2004) 'Drug patents under the spotlight – Sharing practical knowledge about pharmaceutical patents', www.accessmed-msf.org/prod/publications.asp?scntid=225200385263&contenttype=PARA&

Moore, G. (2007) 'La tercera parte beneficiaria en el acuerdo normalizado de transferencia de material' ['Third party beneficiary under the standard material transfer agreement'], *Revista de CATIE: Recursos Naturales y Ambiente*

Moore, G. and Tymowski, W. (2005) *Explanatory Guide to the International Treaty on Plant Genetic Resources for Food and Agriculture*, IUCN, Gland, Switzerland, www.iucn.org/bookstore/HTML-books/EPLP057-expguide-international-treaty/cover.html

MSF (2003) 'Doha derailed: Technical "assistance" – A case of malpractice?', MSF Reports, available at www.msf.org/msfinternational/invoke.cfm?objectid=2FCD1BDD-94B2-49EB-8EC939E2C87E54C7&component=toolkit.report&method=full_html, accessed 11 September 2007

Mulvany, P. (2006) 'Now is the time for food sovereignty!', *Bulletin of the Food Ethics Council*, vol 1, no 4 (winter), p10

Murphy, S. (2006) 'Concentrated market power and agricultural trade', EcoFair Trade Dialogue

Discussion Papers no 1, www.ecofair-trade.org

Murphy, S. and Santarius, T. (2007) 'The World Bank's WDR 2008: Agriculture for development ñ response from a slow trade – sound farming perspective', EcoFair Trade Dialogue Discussion Papers, No 10, Heinrich Boll Stiftung and Misereor, available at www.ecofair-trade.org/pics/en/EcoFair_Trade_Paper_No_10_Murphy_Santarius.pdf, accessed 20 October 2007

Musungu, S. (2005) 'Rethinking innovation, development and intellectual property in the UN: WIPO and beyond', TRIPS Issues Paper 5, Quaker International Affairs Programme (QIAP), Ottawa, www.qiap.ca/pages/publications.html, accessed 2 August 2007

Musungu, S. and Dutfield, G. (2003) 'Multilateral agreements and a TRIPS-plus world: The World Intellectual Property Organization (WIPO)', TRIPS Issues Paper 3, QIAP and Quaker United Nations Office (QUNO), Ottawa and Geneva, www.qiap.ca/pages/publications.html, accessed 2 August 2007

New, W. (2006) 'Biotech industry fights disclosure in patents on three IP policy fronts', *Intellectual Property Watch*, www.ip-watch.org/weblog/index.php?p=235&res=1280_ff&print=0, accessed 11 June 2007

Odell, J. S. (2007) 'Growing power meets frustration in the Doha Round's first four years', in L. Crump and S. J. Maswood (eds) *Developing Countries and Global Trade Negotiations*, Routledge, London and New York, pp7–40

Odell, J. and Sell, S. (2006) 'Reframing the Issue: The coalition on intellectual property and public health in the WTO, 2001', in John Odell (ed) *Negotiating Trade: Developing Countries in the WTO and NAFTA*, Cambridge University Press, New York

OECD (2007) *Agricultural Policies in non-OECD Countries: Monitoring and Evaluation 2007*, Organisation for Economic Co-operation and Development, Paris

OECD (1981) *Food Policy*, Organisation for Economic Co-operation and Development, Paris

Oxfam International (2007) 'What agenda now for agriculture? A Response to the World development Report 2008', available at www.oxfam.org.uk/resources/policy/trade/bn_wdr2008.html, accessed 20 October 2007

Palacios, X. F. (1998) 'Contribution to the estimation of countries' interdependence in the area of plant genetic resources', Background Study Paper no 7, rev 1, FAO Commission on Genetic Resources for Food and Agriculture, Rome, available at www.fao.org/ag/cgrfa/docs.htm, accessed 11 September 2007

Pardey, P. G., Wright, B. D., Nottenburg, C., Binenbaum, E. and Zambrano, P. (2003) 'Brief 3: Intellectual property and developing countries: Freedom to operate in agricultural biotechnology', in Philip G. Pardey and Bonwoo Koo (eds) *Biotechnology and Genetic Resource Policies*, IFPRI, Washington DC, available at www.ifpri.org/pubs/rag/br1001.htm, accessed 11 September 2007

Pardey, P. G. and Beintema, N. M. (2001) 'Slow magic: Agricultural R&D a century after Mendel', Food Policy Report, IFPRI, Washington, DC, www.ifpri.org/pubs/pubs.htm#fpr

Pauwely, J. (2004) 'Bridging fragmentation and unity: International law as a universe of inter-connected islands', *Michigan Journal of International Law*, vol 25, no 903–916

Pengelly, T. (2005) 'Technical assistance for the formulation and implementation of intellectual property policy in developing countries and transition economies', Issue Paper no 11, ICTSD Programme on IPRs and Sustainable Development, Geneva

Petit, M., Fowler, C., Collins, W., Correa, C. and Thornstrom, C. G. (2001) 'Why governments can't make policy – The case of plant genetic resources in the international arena', International Potato Center (CIP), Lima

Phelps, M. (2005) 'Marshall Phelps: US Senate Testimony on Patent Harmonization and Other Issues', written testimony of Marshall C. Phelps, Jr., Corporate Vice President and Deputy General Counsel for Intellectual Property, Microsoft Corporation, before the Subcommittee on Intellectual Property, Committee on the Judiciary, United States Senate, July 26, available at www.microsoft.com/presspass/exec/mphelps/07-26-05Patent Testimony.mspx, accessed 24 September 2007

Phillipson, M. (2005) 'Giving away the farm? The rights and obligations of biotechnology multinationals: Canadian developments', *The King's College Law Journal*, vol 16, pp362–372

Pinstrup-Andersen, P. (2000) 'Is Research a global public good?', *Entwicklung + L%onderlicher Raum*, no 2

Pistorius, R. and van Wijk, J. (1999) *The Exploitation of Plant Genetic Information: Political Strategies in Crop Development*, CABI Publishing, Wallingford, UK, and New York

Pratt, S. (2007) 'Schmeiser renews Monsanto battle', *The Western Producer*, 31 May

Pratt, S. (2005) 'Roundup back in Schmeiser field', *The Western Producer*, 28 October

Price, S. C. (1999) 'Public and private plant breeding', *Nature Biotechnology*, vol 17, p938

Pythoud, F. (2002) 'Commodities', in C. Bail, R. Falkner and H. Marquand (eds) *The Cartagena Protocol on Biosafety: Reconciling Trade in Biotechnology with Environment and Development?*, Royal Institute of International Affairs, London

RAFI (Rural Advancement Foundation International) (2000) 'In search of higher ground – The intellectual property challenge to public agricultural research and human rights and 28 alternative initiatives', Occasional Paper Series 6(1), Rural Advancement Foundation International (now ETC Group)

RAFI and CBDCP (Community Biodiversity Development and Conservation Program) (1996) *Enclosures of the Mind: Intellectual Monopolies – A Resource Kit on Community Knowledge, Biodiversity and Intellectual Property*, RAFI and the Community Biodiversity Development and Conservation Program, Ottawa

RAFI/HSCA (1998) 'Plant breeders wrongs: An inquiry into potential for plant piracy through international intellectual property conventions', Rural Advancement Foundation International in partnership with Heritage Seed Curators Australia, available at www.etcgroup.org/en/materials/publications.html?id=400

Rangnekar, D. (2002a) 'R&D appropriability and planned obsolescence: Empirical evidence from wheat breeding in the UK (1960–1995)', *Industrial and Corporate Change*, vol 11, no 5, pp1011–1029

Rangnekar, D. (2002b) *Access to Genetic Resources, Gene-based Inventions and Agriculture – Issues Concerning the TRIPS Agreement*, Commission on Intellectual Property Rights, London

Reichman, J. H. (2000) 'Of green tulips and legal kudzu: Repackaging rights in subpatentable innovation', *Vanderbilt Law Review*, vol 53, no 6 (November), pp17–43

Revkin, A. (2002) 'CBD: Biologists sought a treaty; now they fault it', *New York Times*, 7 May, www.nytimes.com/2002/05/07/science/earth/07TREA.html

Rhein, R. (1992) 'Biological diversity convention would limit patent rights, says IBA', *Biotechnology Newswatch*, vol 10, no 12, p1

Ribeiro, S. (2004) 'The day the sun dies: Contamination and resistance in Mexico', *Seedling*, July, pp4–10

Riley, K. (2000) 'Effects of IPR legislation on the exchange and use of plant genetic resources', Global Forum on Agricultural Research (GFAR), Dresden, Germany, available at www.egfar.org

Rivette, K. G. and Kline, D. (2000) *Rembrandts in the Attic: Unlocking the Hidden Value of Patents*, Harvard Business School Press, Boston, MA

Rodrigues, E. B. Jr (2005) 'How indispensable is biodiversity to Brazil? – A brief introduction to the Brazilian biodiversity-related framework', paper presented at the 'Patenting Lives' conference, London, 1–2 December

Roffe, P. (2004) 'Bilateral agreements and a TRIPS-plus world: the Chile–USA Free Trade Agreement', TRIPS Issues Paper 4, Quaker International Affairs Programme (QIAP), Ottawa, www.qiap.ca/pages/publications.html, accessed 2 August 2007

Roffe, P., Tansey, G. and Vivas-Eugui, D. (eds) (2006) *Negotiating Health: Intellectual Property and Access to Medicines*, Earthscan, London

Ross, C. (2007) *Independent Diplomat, Dispatches from an unaccountable elite*, Hurst & Co, London

Safrin, S. (2004) 'Hyperownership in a time of biotechnological promise: The international conflict to control the building blocks of life', *American Journal of International Law*, vol 98, October, pp641–685

Sarnoff, J. and Correa, C. (2006) 'Analysis of options for implementing disclosure of origin requirements in intellectual property applications', Document UNCTAD/DITC/TED/2005/14, Geneva, www.unctad.org/en/docs/ditcted200514_en.pdf

SCBD (Secretariat of the Convention on Biological Diversity) (2007) 'Traditional knowledge and biodiversity: A road to success', *Pachamama*, vol 1, no 1, pp2–3

SCBD (no date) *The Cartagena Protocol on Biosafety: A Record of the Negotiations*, Secretariat of the Convention on Biological Diversity, Montreal,

Canada

Sell, S. K. (2003) *Private Power, Public Law: The Globalization of Intellectual Property Rights*, Cambridge University Press, Cambridge, UK

Sell, S. K. (1998) *Power and Ideas: North–South Politics of Intellectual Property and Antitrust*, State University of New York Press, Albany, NY

Serageldin, I. (2000) 'International cooperation for the public good: Agricultural research in the new century', Global Forum on Agricultural Research (GFAR), Dresden, Germany, www.egfar.org

SGRP (2007) 'Experience of the CGIAR centres with the implementation of the agreements with the governing body, with particular reference to the SMTA', information paper submitted by the SGRP to the Second Session of the Governing Body of the International Treaty, FAO, Rome, Italy, 29 October to November, available at www.planttreaty.org/gbnex_en.htm

SGRP (System-wide Programme on Genetic Resources) (2006a) *Annotated Bibliography Addressing the International Pedigrees and Flows of Plant Genetic Resources for Food and Agriculture*, IPGRI, Rome

SGRP (2006b) *Developing Access and benefit sharing Regimes: Plant Genetic Resources for Food and Agriculture*, Bioversity International, Rome, available at www.bioversityinternational.org/publications/pubfile.asp?ID_PUB=1146, accessed 11 September 2007

SGRP (1996) 'Report of the internally commissioned external review of CGIAR genebank operations', IPGRI, Rome

Shanahan, M. and Massarani, L. (2006) '"Breakthrough" reached on access to biodiversity data', www.scidev.net, accessed 12 June 2007

Shyamkrishna, B., Dev, G., Nikiforova, T. and Piper, T. (2004) 'Report on the draft Broadcasting Treaty', www.public-domain.org/docs/oxreport.htm

Silva Repetto, R. and Cavalcanti, M. (2000) 'Article 27.3(b): Related international agreements (Part II)', in *Multilateral Trade Negotiations on Agriculture: A Resource Manual. IV Agreement on Trade-Related Aspects of Intellectual Property Rights (TRIPS)*, Food and Agriculture Organization, Rome, www.fao.org/docrep/003/x7355e/X7355e06.htm, accessed 12 June 2007

Sperling, L., Remington, T. and Haugen, J. (2006) 'Seed aid for seed security – Advice for practitioners: Ten practice briefs – Using seed aid to give

farmers access to seed of new varieties', Catholic Relief Services, http://crs.org/publications/entry.cfm?category=Agriculture

Stannard, C. (2000) 'The relationship between Article 27.3b of the WTO TRIPS Agreement and the FAO Undertaking on Plant Genetic Resources', paper presented at the Workshop on TRIPS, the Convention on Biological Diversity and Farmers' Rights, organized by the South Centre in collaboration with the Istituto Agronomico Oltremare, Geneva, 23 June

Stenson, A. J. and Gray, T. S. (1999) *The Politics of Genetic Resource Control*, St Martin's Press, Inc., New York

Stiglitz, J. E. (2006) 'Patent, profits and people', chapter 4 in *Making Globalization Work*, Allan Lane, London

Tansey, G. (2007) 'Fear over growing WIPO–FAO links', *Seedling*, GRAIN, pp56–57

Tansey, G. (2004) 'The role and perspectives of "non-traditional" providers of IPR technical assistance', in final report of the workshop 'Reflection on IPR Technical Assistance for Developing Countries and Transition Economies', Burnham Beeches, UK, 15–17 September, www.iprsonline.org/resources/iprs.htm

Tansey, G. (2002) 'Food security, biotechnology and intellectual property: Unpacking some issues around TRIPS', Quaker United Nations Office, Geneva, available at www.quno.org/economicissues/intellectual-property/intellectualLinks.htm

Tansey, G. (1999) 'Trade, intellectual property, food and biodiversity: Key issues and options for the 1999 review of Article 27.3(b) of the TRIPS Agreement', Discussion Paper, Quaker United Nations Office (QUNO), Geneva, www.quno.org/economicissues/intellectual-property/intellectualLinks.htm, accessed 2 August 2007

Tansey, G. (no date) 'Questions about … Patents and Quaker action', Quaker United Nations Office (QUNO) and Quaker International Affairs Programme (QIAP), Geneva and Ottawa, www.qiap.ca/pages/publications.html, accessed 2 August 2007

Tansey, G. and Worsley, T. (1995) *The Food System – A Guide*, Earthscan, London

Thornström, C. G. (2001) 'Makt och tillträde: Offentliga sektorn, biologisk innovation och genetiska resurser' ['Authority and access: Public sector biological innovation and genetic resources'], Report to Parliamentary Commission on Swedish Policy for Global Development, available on the website of the Swedish Biodiversity Centre, www.cbm.slu.se/eng/non_event.pdf

Tilford, D. S. (1998) 'Saving the blueprints: The international legal regime for plant resources', *Case Western Reserve Journal of International Law*, vol 30, pp373–445

Toenniessen, G. and Delmer, D. (2005) 'The role of intermediaries in maintaining the public sector's essential role in crop varietal improvement', report prepared at the request of and submitted to the Science Council of the Consultative Group on International Agricultural Research, The Rockefeller Foundation, New York, March

Trebilcock, M. J. and Howse, R. (1995) 'Trade-related intellectual property (TRIPS)', in M. J. Trebilcock (ed) *The Regulation of International Trade*, Routledge, London, pp307–334

Tripp, R. (2001) 'Agricultural technology policies for rural development', *Development Policy Review*, vol 19, no 4, pp479–489

Tripp, R (ed) (1997) *New Seed and Old Laws: Regulatory Reform and the Diversification of National Seed Systems*, Intermediate Technology Publications and Overseas Development Institute, London

UKABC (2007) 'Wilderswil Declaration on Livestock Diversity', Wilderswil, Switzerland, 6 September, available on website of UK Agricultural Biodiversity Coalition, www.ukabc.org/wilderswil.pdf, accessed 27 September 2007

UNCTAD (2007) *Least Developed Countries Report 2007: Knowledge, Technological Learning and Innovation for Development*, UNCTAD, Geneva, www.unctad.org/Templates/Page.asp?intItemID=3073, accessed 2 August 2007

UNCTAD (1997) *The TRIPS Agreement and Developing Countries*, United Nations publication, Sales No E.96.II.D.10., UN, Geneva

UNCTAD-ICTSD (2005) *Resource Book on TRIPS and Development*, Cambridge University Press, www.iprsonline.org/unctadictsd/Resource BookIndex.htm, accessed 2 August 2007

UNCTAD-ICTSD (2003) 'Intellectual property rights: Implications for development', policy discussion paper, Geneva, August

UNDP (1999) *Globalization with a Human Face – Human Development Report 1999*, Oxford University Press, Oxford, for UNDP, New York

UNESCO (United Nations Educational, Scientific and Cultural Organization) (2002) 'Cultural policy resources: Issues on culture and development', www.unesco.org/culture/industries/trade/html

UPOV (2005a) *UPOV Report on the Impact of Plant Variety Protection*, UPOV, Geneva

UPOV (2005b) 'Annual Report of the Secretary-General for 2004', UPOV Document C/39/2, 39th Ordinary Session of the UPOV Council, Geneva, 27 October

UPOV (2003) 'Access to genetic resources and benefit sharing: Reply of UPOV to the Notification of 26 June 2003 from the Executive Secretary of the Convention on Biological Diversity (CBD)', adopted by the Council of UPOV at its 37th Session, 23 October

UPOV (2002) 'General introduction to the examination of distinctness, uniformity and stability and the development of harmonized descriptions of new varieties of plants', Document TG/1/3, UPOV, Geneva, 19 April

Usdin, S. (1992) 'Biotech industry played key role in US refusal to sign BioConvention', *Diversity*, vol 8, no 2, p8

van Wijk, J., Cohen, J. I. and Komen, J. (1993) 'Intellectual property rights for agricultural biotechnology: Options and implications for developing countries', ISNAR Research Report no 3, International Centre for National Agricultural Research, The Hague

Vernooy, R. (2003) *Seeds that Give: Participatory Plant Breeding*, International Development Research Centre (IDRC), Ottawa

Visser, B., Eaton, D., Louwaars, N. and Engels, J. (2000) 'Transaction costs of germplasm exchange under bilateral agreements', Global Forum on Agricultural Research (GFAR), Dresden, Germany, 21–23 May, available at www.egfar.org

Vivas-Eugui, D. (2003) 'Regional and bilateral agreements and a TRIPS-plus world: The free trade area of the Americas (FTAA)', TRIPS Issues Paper 1, Quaker International Affairs Programme (QIAP) and Quaker United Nations Office (QUNO), Ottawa and Geneva, www.qiap.ca/pages/publications.html, accessed 2 August 2007

Vorley, B. (2003) *Food Inc. Corporate Concentration from Farm to Consumer*, UK Food Group, London.

War on Want (2007) *Growing Pains: The Human Cost of Cut Flowers in British Supermarkets*, War on Want,

London, www.waronwant.org/?lid=14243,
accessed 2 August 2007

Weis, T. (2007) *The Global Food Economy: The Battle for
the Future of Farming*, Zed Books, London

Weiss, E. B. (2000) 'Strengthening national compliance with trade law: Insights from environment',
in M. Bronckers and R. Quick (eds) *New Directions
in International Economic Law: Essays in Honour of
John H. Jackson*, Kluwer Law International, The
Hague, pp457–471

Windfuhr, M. and Jonsén, J. (2005) *Food Sovereignty:
Towards Democracy in Localised Food Systems*, ITDG
publishing, Rugby, UK

WIPO (World Intellectual Property Organization)
(2006a) 'The protection of traditional cultural
expressions/expressions of folklore: Revised
objectives and principles', Document
WIPO/GRTKF/IC/9/4, WIPO, Geneva, available at www.wipo.int/edocs/mdocs/tk/en/
wipo_grtkf_ic_9/wipo_grtkf_ic_9_4.pdf

WIPO (2006b) 'The protection of traditional knowledge: Revised objectives and principles',
Document WIPO/GRTKF/IC/9/5, WIPO,
Geneva, available at www.wipo.int/edocs/
mdocs/tk/en/wipo_grtkf_ic_9/wipo_grtkf_
ic_9_5.pdf

WIPO (2005) 'Overview of the committee's work on
genetic resources', Document
WIPO/GRTKF/IC/8/9, WIPO, Geneva

WIPO (2002a) 'Elements of a *sui generis* system for
the protection of traditional knowledge',
Document WIPO/GRTKF/IC/3/8, WIPO,
Geneva

WIPO (2002b) 'Traditional knowledge – Operational
terms and definitions', Document
WIPO/GRTKF/IC/3/9, WIPO, Geneva

WIPO (2002c) 'Assistance in the field of intellectual
property legislation', WIPO, Geneva

WIPO (2001) *Agenda for the Development of the
International Patent System*, Memorandum of the
Director General, presented to the Assemblies of
the Member States of WIPO, Thirty-Sixth Series

of Meetings, Geneva, 24 September to 3 October
2001, WIPO document A/36/14, August 6

WIPO (no date) 'Traditional cultural expressions
(folklore)', www.wipo.int/tk/en/folklore/,
accessed 27 September 2007

WIPO General Assembly (2003) 'Report of the
Thirtieth (16th Ordinary) Session', Document
WO/GA/30/8, WIPO, Geneva

WIPO Press Release 401 (2005) 'WIPO marks filing
of one millionth PCT application', WIPO,
Geneva, 14 January

Wolbring, G. (2007) weblogs on Innovation Watch
website, www.innovationwatch.com/commen-
tary_choiceisyours.htm, accessed 2 August 2007

Wolfe, R. (2007) 'Adventures in WTO clubland',
BRIDGES, vol 11, no 4, pp21–22

World Bank (2007) *World Development Report 2008:
Agriculture for Development*, World Bank,
Washington, DC; see http://go.worldbank.org/
2IL9T6GO0 for full text of report

World Bank (1998) *Knowledge for Development – World
Development Report 1998/99*, published for the
World Bank by Oxford University Press,
Washington DC and New York

WSSD (World Summit on Sustainable Development)
(2002) 'Plan of implementation', Johannesburg,
26 August–4 September

WTO (2006) *Regional Trade Agreements: Facts and
Figures*, WTO, Geneva, available at
www.wto.org/english/tratop_e/region_e/
regfac_e.htm, accessed 30 May 2006

WTO Secretariat (2006) 'Note by the WTO
Secretariat. The relationship between the TRIPS
Agreement and the Convention on Biological
Diversity: Summary of issues raised and points
made', IP/C/W/369/Rev.1, 9 March, paragraphs
28–29

Wuesthoff, F. and Wuesthoff, F. (1952) 'Protection
of new varieties of cultivated plants', report in the
name of the German Group, Vienna Congress
1952, International Association for the
Protection of Industrial Property

Appendix 1

List of Organizations

Descriptions are taken from the websites of the organizations listed.

3D→Trade, Human Rights, Equitable Economy (3D→THREE)

Maison des Associations
15 rue des Savoises
1205 Geneva
Switzerland
Tel: +41 22 320 21 21
Fax: +41 22 320 69 48
Website: www.3dthree.org/en

3D promotes collaboration amongst trade, development and human rights professionals, to ensure that trade rules are developed and applied in ways that promote an equitable economy.

American Bioindustry Alliance (ABIA)

3514 30th Street NW
Washington, DC 20008
USA
Tel: +1 202 973 2870
Fax: +1 202 296 8407
Website: www.abialliance.com

An alliance of companies representing the broad spectrum of the American biotechnology industry, ABIA members support the development and implementation of equitable, sustainable, mutually beneficial access and benefit sharing (ABS) policies relating to genetic resources.

ActionAid

Hamlyn House
Macdonald Road
London
N19 5PG
UK
Tel: +44 20 7561 7561
Fax: +44 20 7272 0899
Website: www.actionaid.org

ActionAid is an international anti-poverty agency whose aim is to fight poverty worldwide including by campaigning on food rights.

Biological Innovation for Open Society (BiOS)

c/o CAMBIA
GPO Box 3200
Canberra, ACT 2601
Australia
Tel: +61 2 6246 4500
Fax: +61 2 6246 4533
Website: www.bios.net

BiOS has evolved as a response to inequities in food security, nutrition, health and natural resource management. Its goal is to democratize problem solving to enable diverse solutions to problems through decentralized innovation.

Bioversity International (formerly IPGRI)

Via dei Tre Denari
472a 00057 Maccarese (Rome)
Italy
Tel: +39 066118.1
Fax: +39 0661979661
Website: www.bioversityinternational.org

Bioversity is the world's largest international research organization dedicated solely to the conservation and use of agricultural biodiversity. It is one of the CGIAR Centres.

CAMBIA

GPO Box 3200
Canberra, ACT 2601
Australia
Tel: +61 2 6246 4500
Fax: +61 2 6246 4533
Website: www.cambia.org

CAMBIA is an international independent non-profit research institute that is intent on creating new tools to foster innovation and a spirit of collaboration in the life sciences.

Convention on Biological Diversity (CBD)

413, Saint Jacques Street, suite 800
Montreal QC H2Y 1N9
Canada
Tel: +1 514 288 2220
Fax: +1 514 288 6588
Website: www.cbd.int/default.shtml

The United Nations Convention on the Promotion, Protection and Preservation of Global Biological Diversity.

Consultative Group on International Agricultural Research (CGIAR)

MSN G6-601
1818 H Street NW
Washington, DC 20433
USA
Tel: +1 202 473 8951
Fax: +1 202 473 8110
Website: www.cgiar.org

The CGIAR is a strategic alliance of members, partners and international agricultural centres that mobilizes science to benefit the poor.

The Center for Environmental Law (CIEL)

15 rue des Savoises
1205 Geneva
Switzerland
Tel: +41 22 789 0500
Fax: +41 22 789 0739
Website: www.ciel.org

CIEL is working to use international law and institutions to protect the environment, promote human health, and ensure a just and sustainable society.

International Maize and Wheat Improvement Centre (CIMMYT)

Km. 45, Carretera Mexico-Veracruz
El Batan
Texcoco
Edo. de México CP 56130
México
Tel: +52 595 952 1900
Fax: +52 595 952 1983
Website: www.cimmyt.org

CIMMYT is a non-profit CGIAR research and training centre that is committed to improving livelihoods in developing countries by creating, sharing, and using knowledge and technology to increase food security, improve the productivity and profitability of farming systems, and sustain natural resources.

International Potato Centre (CIP)

Av. La Molina 1895
La Molina
Lima
Peru
Postal address: Apartado 1558
Lima 12
Peru
Tel: +51 1 349 6017
Fax: +51 1 317 5326
Website: www.cipotato.org

The International Potato Center seeks to reduce poverty and achieve food security on a sustained basis in developing countries through scientific research and related activities on potatoes, sweet potatoes, and other root and tuber crops, and on the improved management of natural resources in the Andes and other mountain areas.

Eldis Resource Guide

Eldis Programme
Institute of Development Studies
University of Sussex
Brighton BN1 9RE
UK
Tel: +44 1273 877330
Fax: +44 1273 621202
Website: www.eldis.org

Eldis shares the best in development policy, practice and research with over 22,000 summarized documents from over 4500 development organizations for free download.

The Earth Negotiations Bulletin (ENB)

212 East 47th Street, #21F
New York, NY 10017
USA
Tel: +1 646 536 7556
Fax: +1 646 219 0955
Website: www.iisd.ca/

The Earth Negotiations Bulletin is a balanced, timely and independent reporting service that provides daily information in print and electronic formats from multilateral negotiations on environment and development. It is published by the International Institute for Sustainable Development (IISD), a non-profit organization based in Winnipeg, Manitoba, Canada. The office of the Earth Negotiations Bulletin is based in New York City, two blocks from the United Nations.

ETC Group (Erosion, Technology and Concentration Group)

431 Gilmour St, Second Floor
Ottawa, ON K2P 0R5
Canada
Tel: +1 613 241 2267
Fax: +1 613 241 2506
Website: www.etcgroup.org/en

The ETC Group is dedicated to the conservation and sustainable advancement of cultural and ecological diversity and human rights.

Food and Agricultural Organization (FAO)

Viale delle Terme di Caracalla
00100 Rome
Italy
Tel: +39 06 57051
Fax: +39 06 570 53152
Website: www.fao.org/index_en.htm

This United Nations organization leads international efforts to defeat hunger. Serving both developed and developing countries, the FAO acts as a neutral forum where all nations meet as equals to negotiate agreements and debate policy.

Food Ethics Council (FEC)

39–41 Surrey Street
Brighton BN1 3PB
UK
Tel: +44 1273 766 654
Fax: +44 1273 766 653
Website: www.foodethicscouncil.org

The Food Ethics Council challenges government, business and society to make wise choices that lead to better food and farming. It champions decisions that are principled, informed and inclusive.

Global Forum on Agricultural Research (GFAR)

c/o FAO (SDR)
viale delle Terme di Caracalla
00153 Rome
Italy
Tel: +39 06 5705 3413
Fax: +39 06 5705 3898
Website: www.egfar.org

The GFAR is a multi-stakeholder initiative that contributes to eradicating poverty, achieving food security, and conserving and managing natural resources. It enhances national capacities to generate, adapt and transfer knowledge.

GRAIN (formerly Genetic Resources Action International)

Girona 25, pral., E-08010
Barcelona
Spain
Tel: +34 933 011 381
Fax: +34 933 011 627
Website: www.grain.org/front

GRAIN is an international non-governmental organization (NGO) which promotes the sustainable management and use of agricultural biodiversity based on people's control over genetic resources and local knowledge.

Institute for Agriculture and Trade Policy (IATP)

2105 First Avenue South
Minneapolis, MN 55404
USA
Tel: +1 612 870 0453
Fax: +1 612 870 4846
Website: www.iatp.org

The IATP works with organizations around the world to analyse how global trade agreements impact domestic farm and food policies.

International Centre for Trade and Sustainable Development (ICTSD)

International Environmental House 2
7 Chemin de Balexert,
1219 Châtelaine, Geneva
Switzerland
Tel: +41 22 917 8492
Fax: +41 22 917 8093
Website: www.ictsd.org

ICTSD was established to contribute to a better understanding of development and environment concerns in the context of international trade. It produces weekly and monthly newsletters and manages web-portals such as IPRsonline.org, providing resources that link IPRs, environment and agriculture.

International Development Research Centre (IDRC)

PO Box 8500
Ottawa, ON K1G 3H9
Tel: +1 613 236 6163
Fax: +1 613 238 7230
Website: www.idrc.ca

The International Development Research Centre is a Crown corporation created by the Parliament of Canada in 1970 to help developing countries use science and technology to find practical, long-term solutions to the social, economic, and environmental problems they face. Their support is directed towards creating a local research community whose work will build healthier, more equitable and more prosperous societies.

International Fund for Agricultural Development (IFAD)

Via del Serafico, 107
00142 Rome
Italy
Tel: +39 06 54591
Fax: +39 06 5043463
Website: www.ifad.org

IFAD is dedicated to eradicating rural poverty in developing countries, with a focus on country-specific solutions, which can involve increasing rural poor peoples' access to financial services, markets, technology, and land and other natural resources.

International Food Policy Research Institute (IFPRI)

2033 K Street, NW
Washington, DC 20006-1002
USA
Tel: +1 202 862 5600
Fax: +1 202 467 4439
Website: www.ifpri.org

IFPRI's mission is to provide policy solutions that cut hunger and malnutrition.

International Institute for Sustainable Development (IISD)

161 Portage Avenue East, 6th Floor
Winnipeg, MB
Canada
R3B 0Y4
Tel: +1 204 958 7700
Fax: +1 204 958 7710
Website: www.iisd.org

The IISD is in the business of promoting change towards sustainable development. As a policy research institute dedicated to effective communication of its findings, it engages decision makers in government, business, NGOs and other sectors in the development and implementation of policies that are simultaneously beneficial to the global economy, the global environment and social wellbeing.

International Plant Protection Convention (IPPC)

AGPP–FAO
Viale delle Terme di Caracalla
00153 Rome
Italy
Tel: +39 06 5705 4812
Fax: +39 06 5705 4819
Website: www.ippc.int

The IPPC is an international treaty to secure action to prevent the spread and introduction of pests of plants and plant products and to promote appropriate measures for their control.

IP Watch

PO Box 2100
1–5 Route des Morillons
1211 Geneva 2
Switzerland
Tel: +41 22 791 67 16
Fax: +41 22 791 66 35
Website: www.ip-watch.org

Intellectual Property Watch, a non-profit independent news service, reports on the interests and behind-the-scenes dynamics that influence the design and implementation of international IP policies.

International Seed Federation (ISF)

Hemin du Reposoir 7
1260 Nyon
Switzerland
Tel: +41 22 365 44 20
Fax: +41 22 365 44 21
Website: www.worldseed.org

The ISF represents the mainstream of the world seed trade and plant breeders community and serves as an international forum where issues of interest to the world seed industry are discussed.

The World Conservation Union (IUCN)

Rue Mauverney 28
Gland 1196
Switzerland
Tel: +41 22 999 0000
Fax: +41 22 999 0002
Website: www.iucn.org

The Union's mission is to influence, encourage and assist societies throughout the world to conserve the integrity and diversity of nature and to ensure that any use of natural resources is equitable and ecologically sustainable.

Knowledge Ecology International (KEI) (formerly CPTech)

1621 Connecticut Ave., NW, #500
Washington, DC 20009
USA
Tel: +1 202 332 2670
Fax +1 202 332 2673
Website: www.keionline.org; www.cptech.org

The KEI focuses on issues concerning the production of and access to knowledge, including medical inventions, information and cultural goods, and other knowledge goods.

Médecin Sans Frontières (MSF)

Rue de Lausanne 78 CP 116 – 1211
Geneva 21
Switzerland
Tel: +41 22 849 84 00
Fax: +41 22 849 84 04
Website: www.msf.org; www.accessmed-msf.org

The MSF is an international humanitarian aid organization that provides emergency medical assistance to populations in danger. It also has a long-running access to medicines campaign.

Oxfam International

Suite 20, 266 Banbury Road
Oxford OX2 7DL
UK
Tel: +44 1865 339 100
Fax: +44 1865 339 101
Website: www.oxfam.org/en

Oxfam International seeks increased worldwide public understanding that economic reform and social justice are crucial to sustainable development.

Public Interest Intellectual Property Advisors (PIIPA)

1200 Pennsylvania Avenue NW
PO Box 548
Washington, DC 20044-0548
USA
Tel: +1 202 633 0811
Website: www.piipa.org

PIIPA makes intellectual property advice available for developing countries and public interest organizations seeking to promote health, agriculture, biodiversity, science, culture and the environment.

Public Intellectual Property Resource for Agriculture (PIPRA)

University of California
One Shields Avenue
Dept. Plant Sciences
Plant Reproductive Biology Building-Mail Stop 5
Davis, CA 95616
USA
Tel: +1 530 754 2162
Website: www.pipra.org

PIPRA aims to make agricultural technologies more easily available for development and distribution of subsistence crops for humanitarian purposes in the developing world and specialty crops in the developed world.

Quaker International Affairs Programme (QIAP)

574 Somerset St. W. Suite 3
Ottawa, ON
Canada
K1R 5K2
Tel: +1 613 231 7311
Fax: +1 613 231 7290
Website: www.qiap.ca

QIAP works to support the peace and justice concerns of Canadian Quakers in the international arena by using Quaker United Nations Office methodology.

Quaker United National Office (QUNO)

13 Avenue du Mervelet
1209 Geneva
Switzerland
Tel: +41 22 748 4800
Fax: +41 22 748 4819
Website: www.quno.org

QUNO, located in Geneva and New York, represents Quakers through the Friends World Committee for Consultation (FWCC). Since the founding of the United Nations in 1945, Quakers have shared that organization's aims and supported its efforts to abolish war and promote peaceful resolution of conflicts, human rights, economic justice and good governance.

Southeast Asia Regional Initiatives for Community Empowerment (SEARICE)

29 Magiting Street
Teachers Village
Diliman
Quezon City
Philippines
Tel: :+63 2 433 7182 / 433 2067
Fax: +63 2 922 6710
Website: www.searice.org.ph

SEARICE has been primarily working to strengthen farmers' seed systems and to advocate for farmers' rights to plant genetic resources as essential components of sustainable agricultural systems in Southeast Asia.

The South Centre

17–19 Chemin du Champ d'Anier
1209 Petit Saconnex
1211 Geneva 19
Switzerland
Tel: +41 22 791 80 50
Fax: +41 22 798 85 31
Website: www.southcentre.org

The Centre works to assist in developing points of view of the South on major policy issues and to generate ideas and action-oriented proposals for consideration by the collective of South governments, institutions of South–South cooperation, inter-governmental organizations of the South, and non-governmental organizations and the community at large.

Third World Network (TWN)

131, Jalan Macalister
10400, Penang
Malaysia
Tel: +60 4 226 6728/226 6159
Fax: +60 4 226 4505
Website: www.twnside.org.sg

The Third World Network is an independent non-profit international network of organizations and individuals involved in issues relating to development, the third world and North–South issues.

The International Union for the Protection of New Varieties of Plants (UPOV)

34 Chemin des Colombettes
CH-1211
Geneva 20
Switzerland
Tel. +41 22 338 91 11
Fax: +41 22 733 03 36
Website: www.upov.int

The objective of the Convention is the protection of new varieties of plants by an intellectual property right.

USC Canada

56 Sparks Street, Suite 705
Ottawa, ON Canada
K1P 5B1
Tel: +1 613 234 6827
Fax: +1 613 234 6842
Website: www.usc-canada.org

USC Canada is a voluntary organization working to promote strong, healthy and just communities in developing countries. Along with its partners, it works to strengthen community livelihoods, promote food security, and support peoples' actions for social justice and equality.

La Via Campesina

Jl. Mampang Prapatan XIV
No 5 Jakarta Selatan DKI
Jakarta
Indonesia 12790
Tel: +62 21 799 1890
Fax: +62 21 799 3426
Website: http://viacampesina.org

La Via Campesina is an international movement which coordinates peasant organizations of small and medium-sized producers, agricultural workers, rural women and indigenous communities from Asia, America and Europe. It is an autonomous, pluralistic movement, independent from all political, economic or other type of affiliation.

World Intellectual Property Organization (WIPO)

34 Chemin des Colombettes
CH-1211 Geneva 20
Switzerland
Tel: +41 22 338 9111
Fax: +41 22 733 5428
Website: www.wipo.int

WIPO is a specialized agency of the United Nations that is dedicated to developing a balanced and accessible international IP system which rewards creativity, stimulates innovation and contributes to economic development.

World Trade Organization (WTO)

Rue de Lausanne 154
CH-1211 Geneva 21
Switzerland
Tel: +41 22 739 5111
Fax: +41 22 731 4206
Website: www.wto.org

The WTO is the only global international organization dealing with the rules of trade between nations. At its heart are the WTO agreements, negotiated and signed by the bulk of the world's trading nations and ratified in their parliaments.

Appendix 2

23 International Treaties Administered by WIPO

The following list is taken from Musungu and Dutfield (2003), which also provides a short summary of what each treaty does. The list is correct as at 23 May 2007.

Intellectual Property Protection Treaties

Berne Convention for the Protection of Literary and Artistic Works (1886)	163 Contracting Parties.
Brussels Convention Relating to the Distribution of Programme-Carrying Signals Transmitted by Satellite (1974)	30 Contracting Parties.
Convention for the Protection of Producers of Phonograms against Unauthorised Duplication of Their Phonograms (1971)	76 Contacting Parties.
Madrid Agreement for the Repression of False or Deceptive Indications of Source on Goods (1891)	35 Contracting Parties.
Nairobi Treaty on the Protection of the Olympic Symbol (1981)	46 Contracting Parties.
Paris Convention for the Protection of Industrial Property (1883)	171 Contracting Parties.
Patent Law Treaty (PLT) (2000 – not yet in force)	14 Contracting Parties (45 countries and the European Patent Organisation have signed the treaty but are yet to ratify it).
Rome Convention for the Protection of Performers, Producers of Phonograms and Broadcasting Organizations (1961)	86 Contracting Parties.
Trademark Law Treaty (TLT) (1994)	38 Contracting Parties.
WIPO Copyright Treaty (WCT) (1996)	64 Contracting Parties.
WIPO Performances and Phonograms Treaty (WPPT) (1996)	62 Contracting Parties.

Global Protection System Treaties

Budapest Treaty on the International Recognition of the
Deposit of Micro-organisms for the Purposes of Patent
Procedure (1977)

67 Contracting Parties.

Hague Agreement Concerning the International Deposit of
Industrial Designs (1925)

47 Contracting Parties.

Lisbon Agreement for the Protection of Appellations of Origin
and their International Registration (1958)

26 Contracting Parties.

Madrid Agreement Concerning the International Registration
of Marks (1891)

57 Contracting Parties.

Patent Cooperation Treaty (PCT) (1970)

137 Contracting Parties.

Classification Treaties

Locarno Agreement Establishing an International Classification
for Industrial Designs (1968)

49 Contracting Parties.

Nice Agreement Concerning the International Classification of
Goods and Services for the Purposes of the Registration of
Marks (1957)

80 Contracting Parties.

Strasbourg Agreement Concerning the International Patent
Classification (1971)

57 Contracting Parties.

Vienna Agreement Establishing an International Classification of
the Figurative Elements of Marks (1973)

23 Contracting Parties.

Appendix 3

A Short History of the Annex I List

Lim Engsiang and Michael Halewood

1993–1994

Resolution 7/93 of the FAO Conference requested the Director General of the FAO to 'provide a forum for negotiations among governments' for the adaptation of the IU in harmony with the CBD, and for 'consideration of the issue of access on mutually agreed terms to plant genetic resources, including *ex-situ* collection not addressed by the Convention'. At that point, the potential scope of coverage of what would later be called 'the multilateral system of access and benefit sharing' was open; it could have applied to all PGRFA without reference to, or reliance on, explicitly listed genera or species. Nor was there explicit discussion of such a list during the two first international meetings addressing the adaptation of the IU (the Ninth Session of the Working Group, and the First Extraordinary Session of the CPGR). A Secretariat paper submitted to the First Extraordinary Session highlighted the need for delegates to consider whether access arrangements under the revised IU should apply to: a) all PGR in a country, b) all PGRFA in a country, or c) specific genera, species or accessions decided upon by each country. But that paper was not actually considered until later meetings.

1995

In May 1995, during the Tenth Session of the Working Group, the option for a list of crops was proposed 'to add a list of mutually agreed species to which specific provisions of the IU would apply, particularly in relation to access to and the distribution of benefits'. There was also discussion about the criteria for selecting species or gene pools being based on their relevance to food security and strong interdependency between countries. In June 1995, at the Sixth Regular Session of the CGRFA, the EU proposed a list including 231 genera, including major grain crops and grasses.

1996

In December 1996, at the Third Extraordinary Session of the CGRFA, the US submitted a list of 25 crops (at the level of genus) and forages selected according to the criteria of being essential to global food security. Brazil submitted a list of 25 crops selected on the basis of their basic importance for human world food consumption. The African Group proposed that the list should be comprised of whatever species individual state members decided should be included. France suggested that for each species there should be a differentiation between: a) designated material with unrestricted access through an international network of collections and b) non-designated material with negotiated access on a case-by-case basis. No decision was made about which concept was most appropriate: all of these options were included in the negotiating text.

1997

The options remained in the text throughout the negotiations of the Seventh Regular Session of the CGRFA in May 2007. In December, during the Fourth Extraordinary Session of the CGRFA, there was a breakthrough, with everyone agreeing to combine the lists into one tentative list for further negotiation. This list included 37 crops (41 genera), grass forages (28 genera) and legume forages (33 genera).

1998

The content of the list was not altered in 1998, during the Fifth Extraordinary Session of the CGRFA, though two information documents concerning taxonomy (including exploration of the 'gene pool concept') and relevant characteristics of the crops and genera in the tentative list of crops were drawn up.

In January 1999, at the Informal Meeting of Experts of PGRFA in Montreux, Switzerland, there was agreement that the two principal criteria for inclusion in the list of crops should be: a) their importance for food security at local or global levels and b) countries' interdependence with respect to PGR. In April, the Eighth Session of the CGRFA confirmed these criteria.

1999

The Second Intersessional Meeting of the Contact Group, in April 1999, included a statement from the EU that it would have preferred the MLS to include all PGRFA. Brazil made a statement linking the size of the 'window' they were opening 'on the bilateral benefit sharing arrangements of the CBD' through the creation of the MLS to 'meaningful finance and benefit sharing'. Nonetheless, the tentative list annexed to the composite draft text of the revised IU was unchanged.

2000

In August 2000, at the Third Intersessional Meeting of the Contact Group, regions were invited to submit a list of materials that they would like to see included in the MLS. The Africa Group submitted a list of 10 crops; Asia a list of 20 crop genera, two forage genera, and 298 crops including fruits, vegeta-

bles, nuts, herbs, spices and forages; and Latin America and the Caribbean 29 crops. North America and Korea were supportive of the tentative list already agreed to and included in Annex I of the consolidated draft text. The Secretariat compiled a list from the preferences of the different regions and submitted it as an information paper.

2001

In April 2001, at the Sixth Intersessional meeting of the Contact Group in Spoleto, Italy, there were protracted negotiations concerning the list by a working group. The working group used the criteria of food security and interdependence to select the crops for the list, which they drew from the compilation of regional submissions put together in 2000. The working group first identified those crops that were commonly identified by all regions. Then it compiled a second list – of crops under discussion – where one or more regions had reservations. The group agreed that the working basis should be crops, with genera as indicative of crops, and species designation in cases where required. Following this method, the working group achieved consensus on 30 food crops. A further group of widely consumed food crops, for which there was considerable support from most regions, remained under discussion. The group recommended that considerable further work had to be done to identify forages.

The final negotiation session concerning the text of the Treaty, including the list, was the Sixth Extraordinary Session of the CRGFA. Not surprisingly, the meeting was dramatic, with a number of bargaining twists and turns. As far as the list was concerned, two genera 'under discussion' in Spoleto were added to the list (the grass pea *Lathyrus* and the eggplant *Solanum melangena*, Brassica complex), but the following were not: onion, garlic et al (*Allium*); groundnut/Peanut (*Arachis*); oil palm (*Elaeis*); soya bean (*Glycine*); tomato (*Lycopersicon*); sugarcane (*Saccharum*); minor millets (various); olive (*Olea*); pear (*Pyrus*); vine/grapes (*Vitis*); fruit trees (*Prunus*); melon, cucumber (*Cucumis*); pumpkins, squashes (*Cucurbita*); flax (*Linum*).

The full list of what was finally included in Annex I of the Treaty is given below.

Annex 1 of the International Treaty: List of crops covered under the MLS

FOOD CROPS (listed by crop, genus plus any observations)

Breadfruit *Artocarpus*. Breadfruit only.

Asparagus *Asparagus*

Oat *Avena*

Beet *Beta*

Brassica complex *Brassica* et al. Genera included are: *Brassica, Armoracia, Barbarea, Camelina, Crambe, Diplotaxis, Eruca, Isatis, Lepidium, Raphanobrassica, Raphanus, Rorippa,* and *Sinapis*. This comprises oilseed and vegetable crops such as cabbage, rapeseed, mustard, cress, rocket, radish and turnip. The species *Lepidium meyenii* (maca) is excluded.

Pigeon pea *Cajanus*

Chickpea *Cicer*

Citrus *Citrus*. Genera *Poncirus* and *Fortunella* are included as root stock.

Coconut *Cocos*

Major aroids *Colocasia, Xanthosoma*. Major aroids include taro, cocoyam, dasheen and tannia.

Carrot *Daucus*

Yams *Dioscorea*

Finger millet *Eleusine*

Strawberry *Fragaria*

Sunflower *Helianthus*

Barley *Hordeum*

Sweet potato *Ipomoea*

Grass pea *Lathyrus*

Lentil *Lens*

Apple *Malus*

Cassava *Manihot. Manihot esculenta* only.

Banana/plantain *Musa*. Except *Musa textilis*.

Rice *Oryza*

Pearl millet *Pennisetum*

Beans *Phaseolus*. Except *Phaseolus polyanthus*.

Pea *Pisum*

Rye *Secale*

Potato *Solanum*. Section tuberosa included, except *Solanum phureja*.

Eggplant *Solanum*. Section melongena included.

Sorghum *Sorghum*

Triticale *Triticosecale*

Wheat *Triticum* et al. Including *Agropyron, Elymus*, and *Secale*.

Faba bean/vetch *Vicia*

Cowpea et al *Vigna*

Maize *Zea*. Excluding *Zea perennis, Zea diploperennis* and *Zea luxurians*.

FORAGES (listed by genera – and species)

LEGUME FORAGES

Astragalus – chinensis, cicer, arenarius

Canavalia – ensiformis

Coronilla – varia

Hedysarum – coronarium

Lathyrus – cicera, ciliolatus, hirsutus, ochrus, odoratus, sativus

Lespedeza – cuneata, striata, stipulacea

Lotus – corniculatus, subbiflorus, uliginosus

Lupinus – albus, angustifolius, luteus

Medicago – arborea, falcata, sativa, scutellata, rigidula, truncatula

Melilotus – albus, officinalis

Onobrychis – viciifolia

Ornithopus – sativus

Prosopis – affinis, alba, chilensis, nigra, pallida

Pueraria – phaseoloides

Trifolium – alexandrinum, alpestre, ambiguum, angustifolium, arvense, agrocicerum, hybridum, incarnatum, pratense, repens, resupinatum, rueppellianum, semipilosum, subterraneum, vesiculosum

GRASS FORAGES

Andropogon – gayanus

Agropyron – cristatum, desertorum

Agrostis – stolonifera, tenuis Alopecurus pratensis

Arrhenatherum – elatius

Dactylis – *glomerata*

Festuca – *arundinacea, gigantea, heterophylla, ovina, pratensis, rubra*

Lolium – *hybridum, multiflorum, perenne, rigidum, temulentum*

Phalaris – *aquatica, arundinacea*

Phleum – *pratense*

Poa – *alpina, annua, pratensis*

Tripsacum – *laxum*

OTHER FORAGES

Atriplex – *halimus, nummularia*

Salsola – *vermiculata*

Glossary

Different sources give a variety of definitions for many of the terms given below. Some terms are specifically defined in the language of the agreements discussed in this book, such as in the CBD and the ITPGRFA, while other agreements, such as TRIPS, offer no definition of terms. Deciding what terms mean or whether to define them at all is itself part of the negotiating process. In many of the negotiations described in this book there was considerable debate over definitions, and the need to compromise influenced the often ambiguous wording of definitions such as 'plant genetic resources for food and agriculture' in the ITPGRFA (Bragdon, 2004). Not defining terms in an agreement offers greater flexibility – and uncertainty – in implementing it, as the terms may be defined differently in different jurisdictions. Definitions and their interpretation can be very important in determining whether intellectual property (IP) protection can apply or not.

Agricultural biodiversity or agrobiodiversity: 'the variety and variability of animals, plants and micro-organisms used directly or indirectly for food and agriculture (crops, livestock, forestry and fisheries). It comprises the diversity of genetic resources (varieties, breeds, etc) and species used for food, fuel, fodder, fibre and pharmaceuticals.'[a] It also includes the diversity of non-harvested species that support production (for example soil micro-organisms, predators and pollinators) and those in the wider environment that support agro-ecosystems (agricultural, pastoral, forest and aquatic), as well as the diversity of the agro-ecosystems themselves.

Another definition is that agricultural biodiversity encompasses the variety and variability of animals, plants and micro-organisms which are necessary to sustain key functions of the agroecosystem, its structure and processes for, and in support of, food production and food security.[b]

Biological diversity or biodiversity: 'the variability among living organisms from all sources including, inter alia, terrestrial, marine and other aquatic ecosystems and the ecological complexes of which they are part; this includes diversity within species, between species and of ecosystems' (CBD, Article 2).

Diversity within and between species and ecosystems permits them 'to adapt to new pests and diseases and changes in the environment, climate and agricultural methods.'[c]

Biological resources: 'genetic resources, organisms or parts thereof, populations, or any other biotic component of ecosystems with actual or potential use or value for humanity' (CBD, Article 2).

Biopiracy: see Chapter 7, pp146–149).

Biotechnology: biotechnology has been defined by many, in particular by the major proponents of modern biotechnology, as a process encompassing any technique that harnesses and uses living organisms, living or dead cells, and cell components to undertake processes for specific applications.[d] With this broad definition, biotechnology can technically go back 10,000 years or earlier, to the origins of the domestication processes of plants and animals, and include things such as the selective breeding of crops and animals and the fermentation process involved in the production of bread. The CBD also adopted a broad definition: 'any technological application that uses biological systems, living organisms, or derivatives thereof, to make or modify products or processes for specific use' (Article 2). In this book, 'biotechnology' refers to modern biotechnology involving the specific use and application of recent novel technologies in the manipulation of living organisms, such as recombinant DNA technology and cell culture, tissue culture and embryonic transfer.

Cell line: 'cells removed from humans, or other organisms, that are manipulated to sustain continuous, long-term growth in an artificial culture. ... Cell lines provide an inexhaustible supply of the DNA of the organism they are taken from.'[c]

Centre of origin: 'a geographical area where a plant species, either domesticated or wild, first developed its distinctive properties' (ITPGRFA, Article 2).

Centre of crop diversity: In the ITPGRFA this means 'a geographic area containing a high level of genetic diversity for crop species in *in-situ* conditions' (Article 2).

Compulsory licence: 'a licence to exploit a patented invention granted by the state upon request to a third party, for instance in order to remedy an abuse of rights by the patentee'.[e]

Copyright: 'exclusive rights of the creators of original literary, scientific and artistic works, which are created, without formalities, with the creation of the work and last (as a general rule) for the life of the creator plus 50 years (70 years in the US and EU). It prevents unauthorized reproduction, public performance, recording, broadcasting, translation or adaptation and allows for the collection of royalties for authorized use'.[e]

Cross-licensing: 'mutual exchange of licences between patent holders'.[e]

Disclosure of origin/source/legal provenance: see Chapter 7, pp159–160.

Ex-situ conservation: literally means conservation 'off-site' or outside an organism's natural habitat, such as in gene banks or botanical gardens.[a,c] In the CBD it means 'the conservation of components of biological diversity outside their natural habitats' (Article 2), and in the ITPGRFA it means 'the conservation of plant genetic resources for food and agriculture outside their natural habitat' (Article 2).

Ex-situ collection: 'a collection of plant genetic resource for food and agriculture maintained outside their natural habitat' (ITPGRFA, Article 2).

Farmers' rights: see Chapter 6, pp128–131.

Gene: the functional unit of heredity consisting of a sequence of DNA (deoxyribonucleic acid) that codes for a specific biochemical function in a living organism.[c,f]

Gene bank: 'a form of *ex-situ* conservation for plant, seed, and animal germplasm. Gene banks are usually humidity- and temperature-controlled facilities where seeds and other reproductive materials are stored for future use in research and breeding programmes.'[c]

Genera: 'a subdivision of a family that included one or more closely related species'.[f]

Genetic engineering: experimental or industrial technologies used to manipulate and alter the genome (all the genes carried by a given organism) of a living cell so that it can produce more or different molecules than it is already programmed to make; also the manipulation of genes to bypass natural reproductive processes (normal or asexual reproduction).

Genetic erosion: 'the loss of genetic diversity within a population of the same species, the reduction of the genetic base of a species or the loss of an entire species over time'.[a]

Genetic material: 'any material of plant origin, including reproductive and vegetative propagating material, containing functional units of heredity' (ITPGRFA, Article 2).

Genetic resources: 'genetic material of actual or potential value' (CBD, Article 2).

Genomics: 'the scientific discipline of mapping, sequencing and analysing genomes' ('all of the genes carried by a given organism').[e,f]

Germplasm: 'the total genetic variability, represented by germ cells or seeds, available to a particular population'.[c]

Hybrid varieties: see Chapter 2, pp29–30.

Intellectual property rights (IPRs): 'rights awarded by society to individuals or organizations over inventions, literary and artistic works, and symbols, names, images and designs used in their commerce. They give the titleholder the right to prevent others from making unauthorized use of their property for a limited period'[e] (see also Chapter 1, pp11–17).

In-situ conservation: literally means conservation 'on-site': in the wild or on farmers' fields. In the CBD and ITPGRFA it has the same meaning: 'the conservation of ecosystems and natural habitats and the maintenance and recovery of viable populations of species in their natural surroundings and, in the case of domesticated or cultivated species, in the surroundings where they have developed their distinctive properties' (Article 2 in both agreements).

Landraces, folk varieties or farmers' varieties: 'a crop cultivar or animal breed that evolved with and has been genetically improved by traditional agriculturalists, but has not been influenced by modern breeding practices'.[e]

Living modified organisms (LMOs): see Chapter 5, p106–110.

Micro-organism: in practice, there is no common scientific definition. The defining property is the microscopic size of the organisms. It is used as a term that frequently includes bacteria and cyanobacteria, archaea-bacteria, algae, protozoa, slime moulds, fungi, bacteriophages, plasmids and viruses.[g] Given the 'very flexible interpretation given to the concept of patentable subject matter in some developed countries'[h] for patent protection, the term micro-organism is often applied to other types of biological material, including cell lines of plants and animals and human genetic materials.[c]

Open-pollinating variety: 'a variety multiplied through random fertilization; as opposed to a hybrid variety'.[a]

Open source: 'products such as software, publications or genetic material in which the source is made publicly available'[e] (see also Chapter 8, p193).

Patent: 'an exclusive right awarded to an inventor to prevent others from making, selling, distributing, importing or using their invention, without licence or authorization, for a fixed period of time. In return, society requires that the patentee discloses the invention to the public. There are usually three requirements for patentability: novelty (new characteristics which are not prior art), inventive step or non-obviousness (knowledge not obvious to one skilled in the field), and industrial applicability or utility (US)'[e] (see also Chapter 1, pp20–23 and Chapter 3, p54–64).

Plant breeders' rights (PBRs): 'rights granted to breeders of new distinct, uniform and stable plant varieties. These normally offer protection for at least twenty years. Most countries have exceptions for farmers to save and replant seeds on their holdings, and for further research and breeding'[e] (see Chapter 2, pp27–37).

Plant genetic resources for food and agriculture (PGRFA): 'any genetic material of plant origin of actual or potential value for food and agriculture' (ITPGRFA, Article 2).

Plant variety or cultivar: 'in classical botany, a variety is a subdivision of a species. An agricultural variety is a group of similar plants that by structural features and performance can be identified from other varieties within the same species'.[a] In the ITPGRFA it means 'a plant grouping, within a single botanical taxon of the lowest known rank, defined by the reproductive expression of its distinguishing and other genetic characteristics' (Article 2). In UPOV the definition has been revised to contain a more detailed definition (see Chapter 2, page 37) to distinguish 'plant varieties' which cannot be patented but to which PBRs can be applied from a 'plant' which can be patented in some jurisdictions.

Prior art: 'publications or other public disclosures made before the filing (or priority) date of a patent application and against which the novelty and inventiveness of the invention in the patent application is judged'.[e] In some jurisdictions only prior art within that jurisdiction is recognized, or only prior art in certain forms (for example written but not oral).

Prior informed consent (PIC): 'the consent given by any party to an activity after being fully informed of all material facts relating to that activity. The CBD requires that access to genetic resources shall be subject to PIC of the country providing the resources.'[e]

Search: 'a search of the prior art by a patent examiner, which brings to the patent applicant's attention documents which are thought by the patent examiner to establish whether the invention in the patent application is novel and inventive. Primary search material is the disclosure in other patent applications, but all forms of prior art, in principle, should be covered.'[e]

Species: 'a group of closely related individuals, usually interbreeding freely; the unit of classification (taxon) below genus'.[h]

Sui generis: 'Latin expression meaning "of its own kind". A *sui generis* system of protection, for example for traditional knowledge, would be a system of protection separate from the existing IP system.'[e]

Sustainable use: 'the use of components of biological diversity in a way and at a rate that does not lead to the long-term decline of biological diversity, thereby maintaining its potential to meet the needs and aspirations of present and future generations' (CBD, Article 2).

Trade secret: see Chapter 1, pp19–20. 'Commercially valuable information about production methods, business plans, clientele and so on. They are protected as long as they remain secret by laws which prevent acquisition by commercially unfair means and unauthorized disclosure.'[e]

Trademark: 'exclusive rights to use distinctive signs, such as symbols, colours, letters, shapes or names, to identify the producer of a product and protect its associated reputation. The period of protection varies, but a trademark can be renewed indefinitely.'[e] (See also Chapter 1, p12 and Chapter 8, p173.)

Traditional knowledge (TK): 'whilst there is no generally acceptable definition, TK includes, for example, tradition-based creations, innovations, literary, artistic or scientific works, performances, and designs. Such knowledge is often transmitted from generation to generation and is often associated with a particular people or territory.'[e]

Transgenic organism: 'any organism that has been genetically engineered to contain a gene from another organism, usually a different species'.[c]

TRIPS-plus: in principle, this refers to commitments that go beyond those already included or consolidated in the TRIPS Agreement[i] (see also Chapter 7, pp142–146).

Sources: [a] Vernooy (2003);
[b] FAO (1999); see also the UKabc website: www.ukabc.org;
[c] RAFI and CBDCP (1996);
[d] Mannion (1995);
[e] IPRs Commission (2002);
[f] Lappé and Bailey (1998);
[g] Adcock and Llewelyn (2000);
[h] Jensen and Salisbury (1984);
[i] Vivas-Eugui (2003).

Index